TSUYOSHI WATANABE

DRAGONS RIOTING

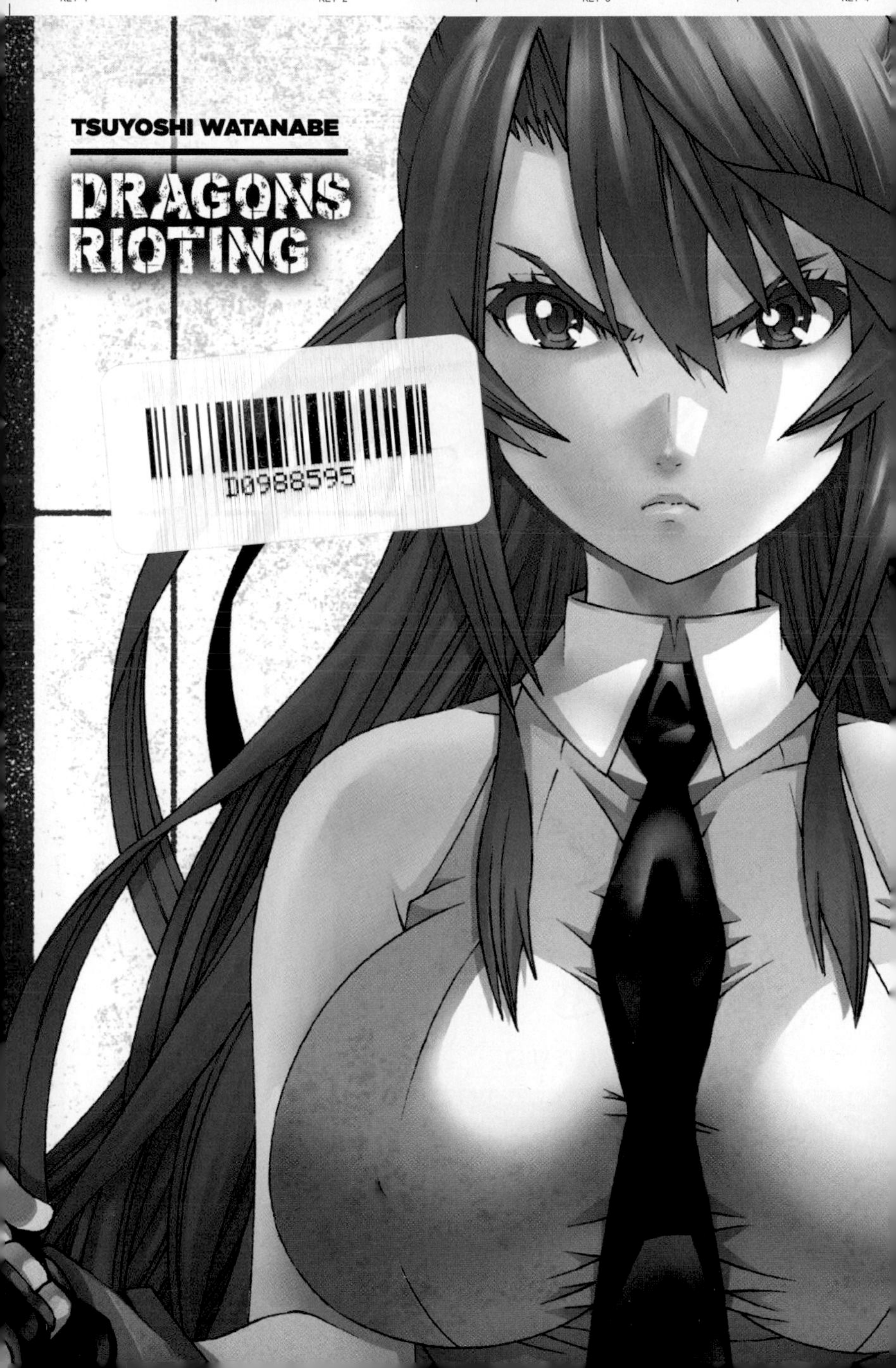

男獄煉

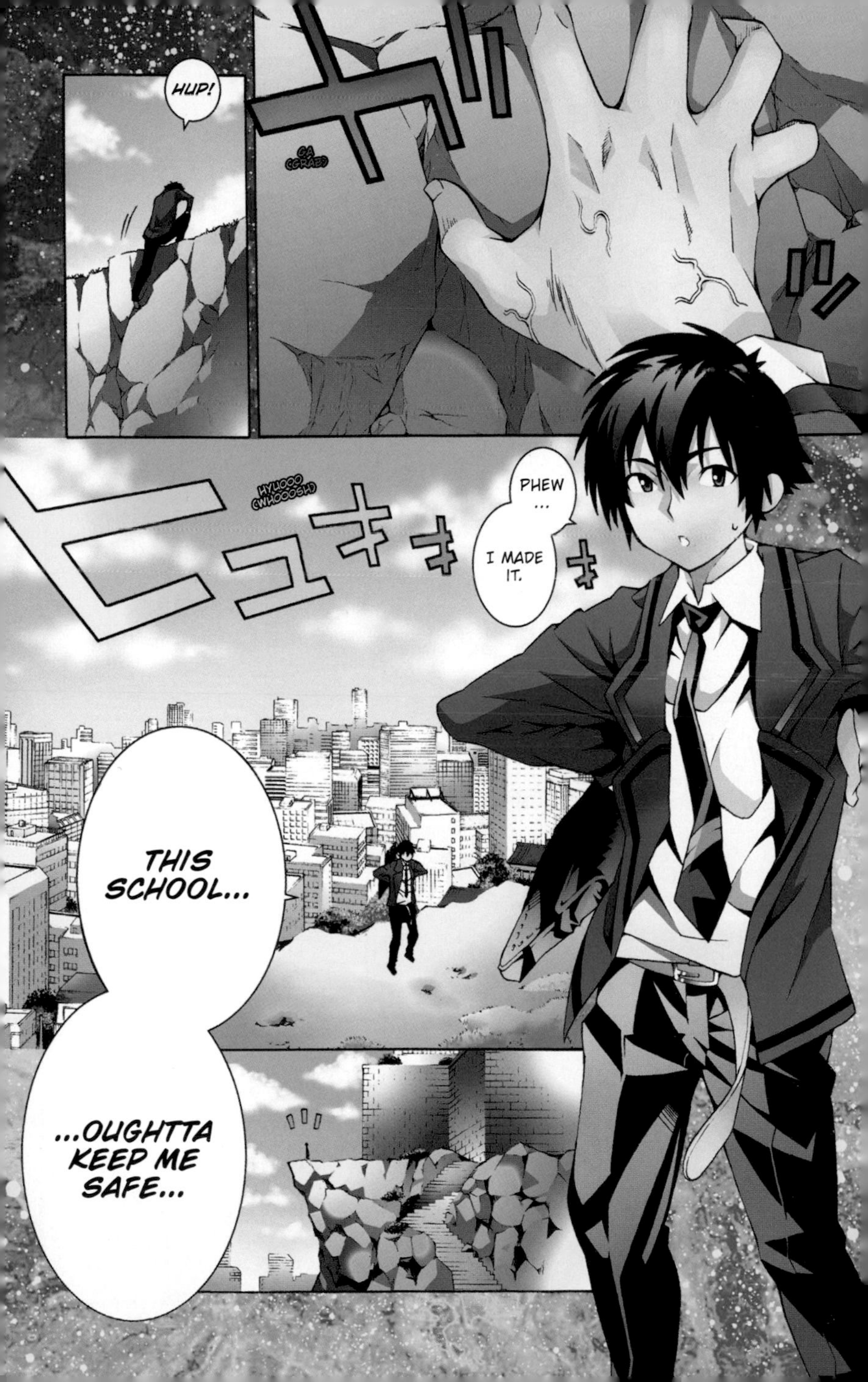
GA (GRAB)
HUP!
HYUOOO (WHOOOSH)
PHEW ... I MADE IT.
THIS SCHOOL...
...OUGHTTA KEEP ME SAFE...

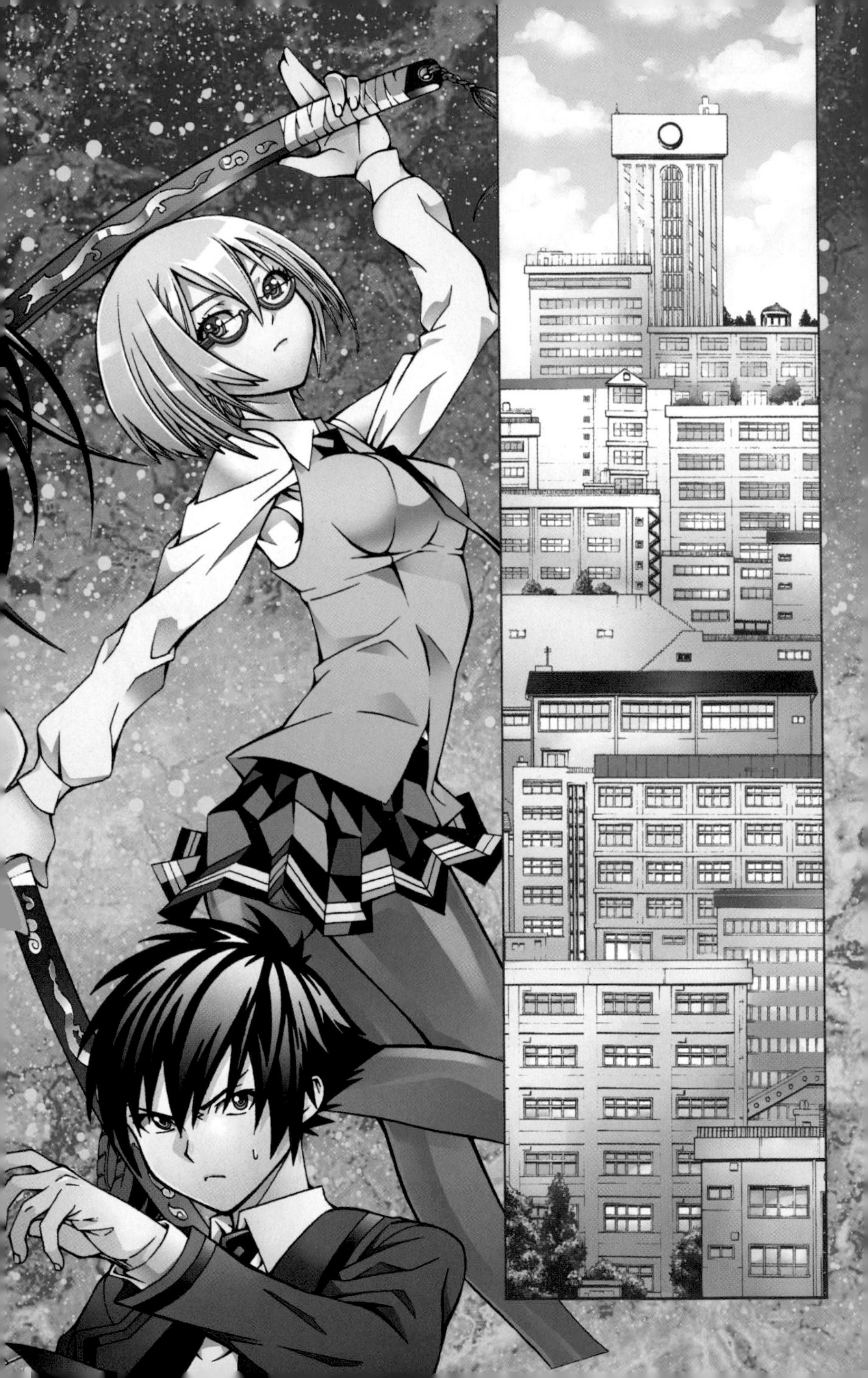

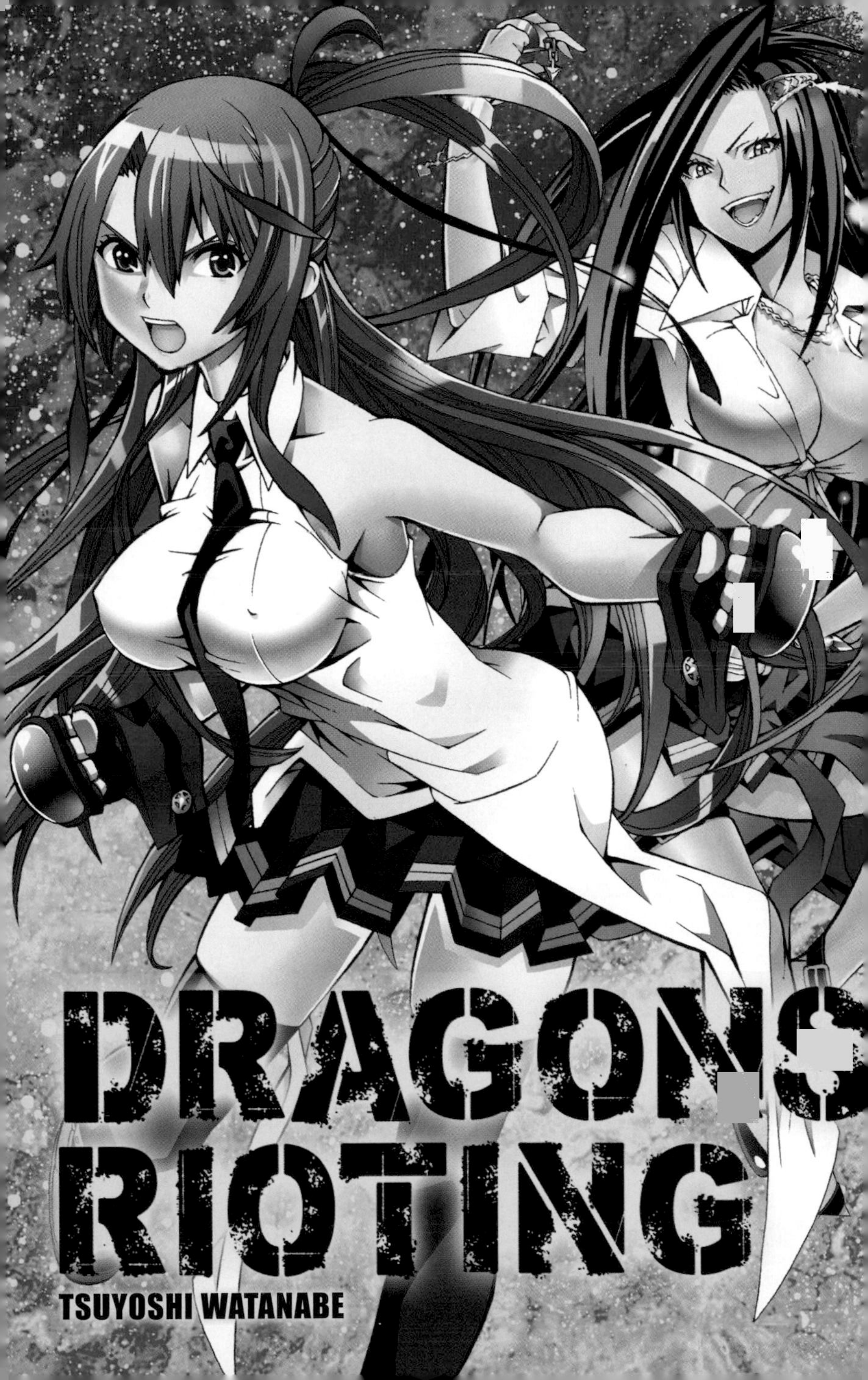
DRAGONS
RIOTING
TSUYOSHI WATANABE

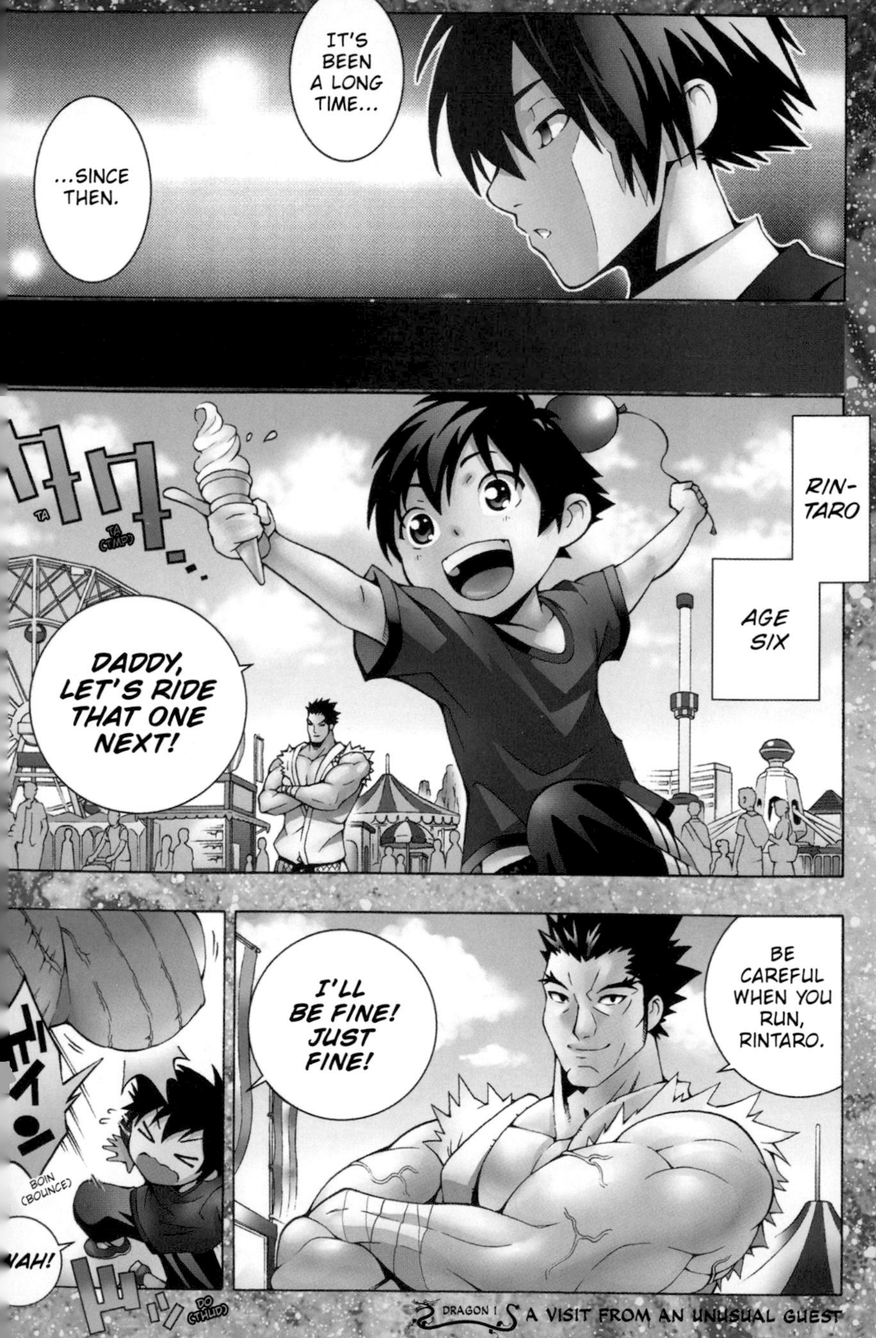
IT'S BEEN A LONG TIME...
...SINCE THEN.
RIN-TARO
AGE SIX
TA
TA (STOMP)
DADDY, LET'S RIDE THAT ONE NEXT!
BE CAREFUL WHEN YOU RUN, RINTARO.
I'LL BE FINE! JUST FINE!
BOIN (BOUNCE)
AH!
DO (THUD)

DRAGON 1 A VISIT FROM AN UNUSUAL GUEST

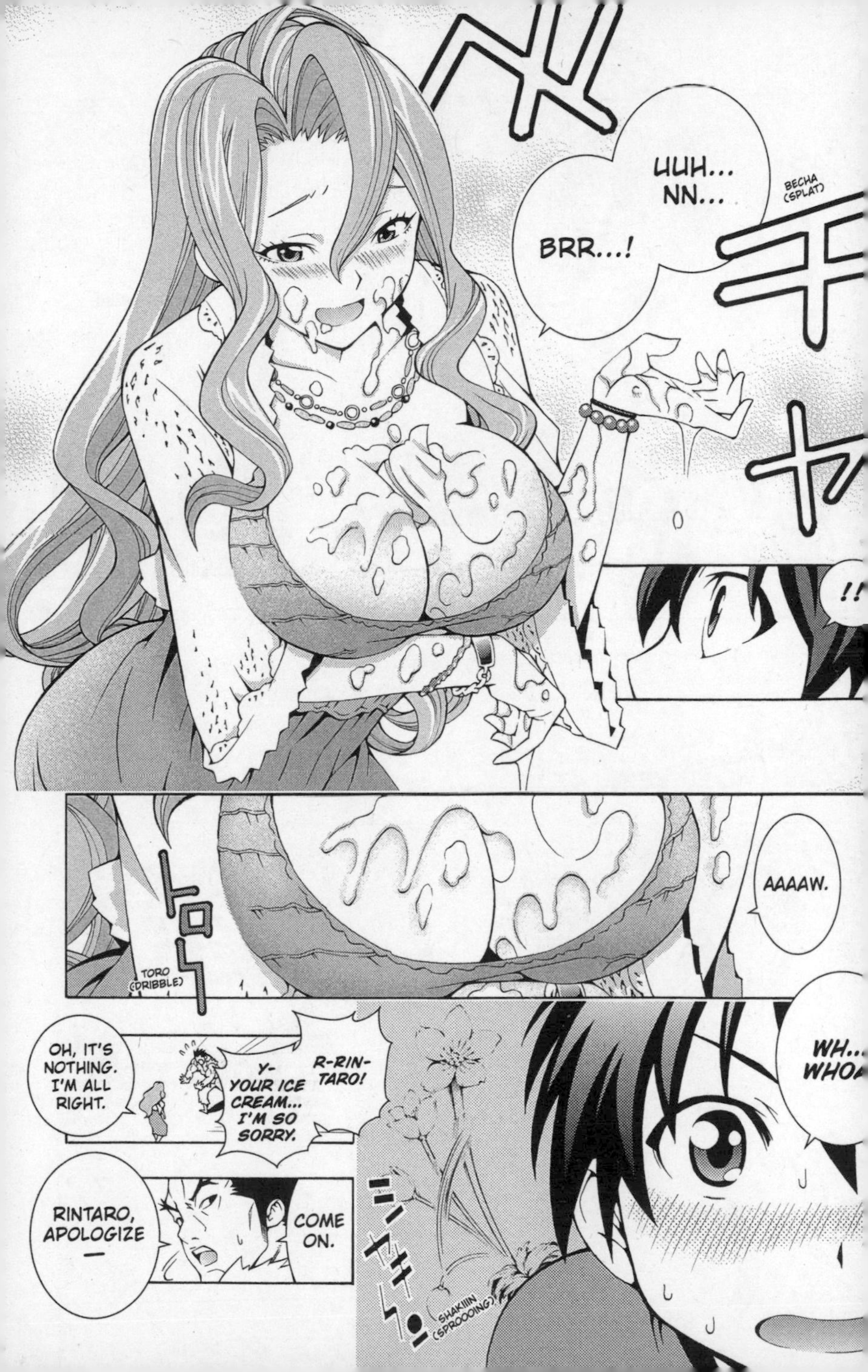
UUH... NN...
BRR...!
BECHA (SPLAT)
!!
AAAAW.
TORO (DRIBBLE)
WH... WHOA
SHAKIIIN (SPROOOING)
R-RINTARO!
Y-YOUR ICE CREAM... I'M SO SORRY.
OH, IT'S NOTHING. I'M ALL RIGHT.
COME ON.
RINTARO, APOLOGIZE—

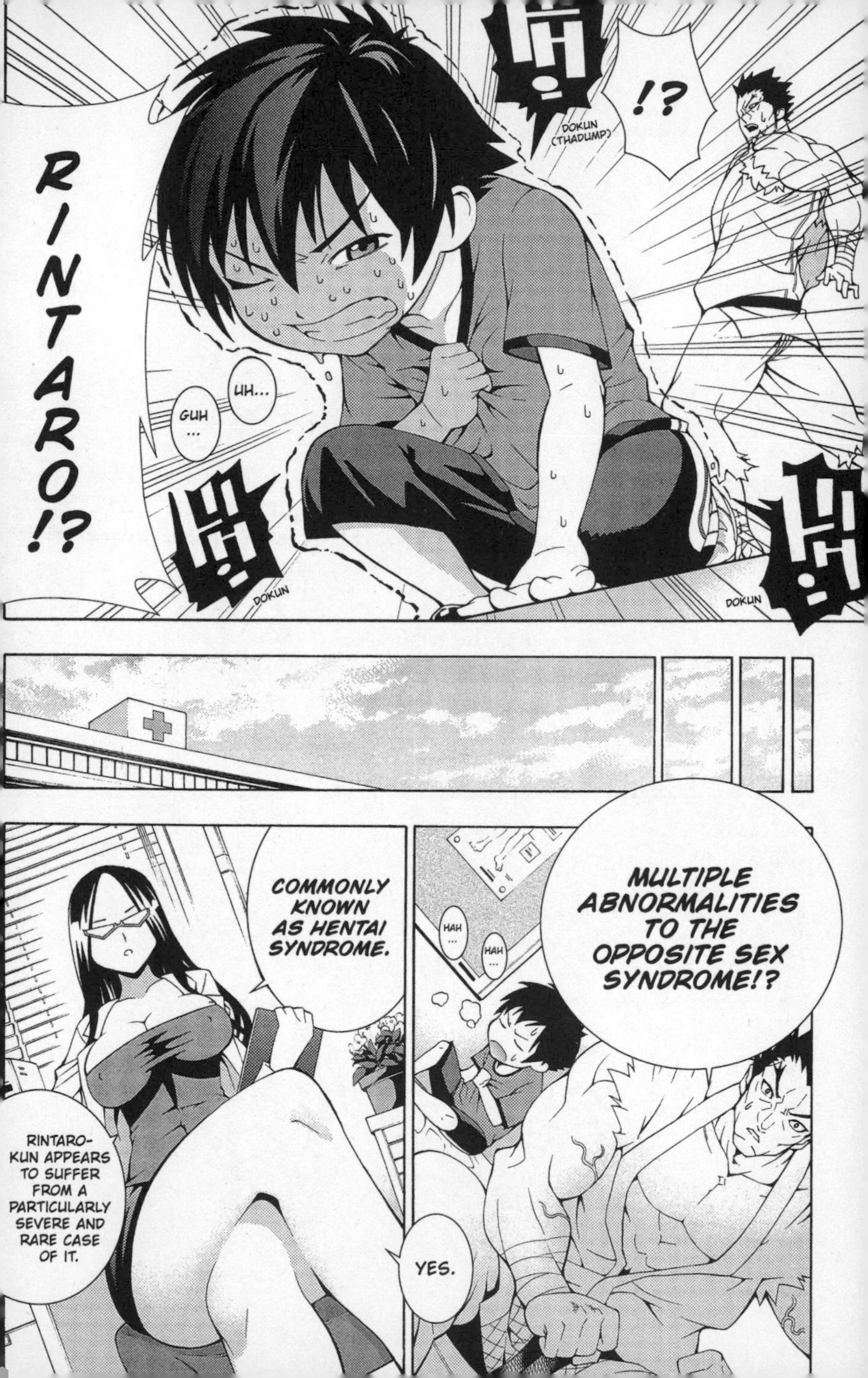
!?
DOKUN (THADUMP)
DOKUN
UH...
GUH ...
DOKUN
RINTARO!?
MULTIPLE ABNORMALITIES TO THE OPPOSITE SEX SYNDROME!?
HAH ...
HAH ...
YES.
COMMONLY KNOWN AS HENTAI SYNDROME.
RINTARO-KUN APPEARS TO SUFFER FROM A PARTICULARLY SEVERE AND RARE CASE OF IT.

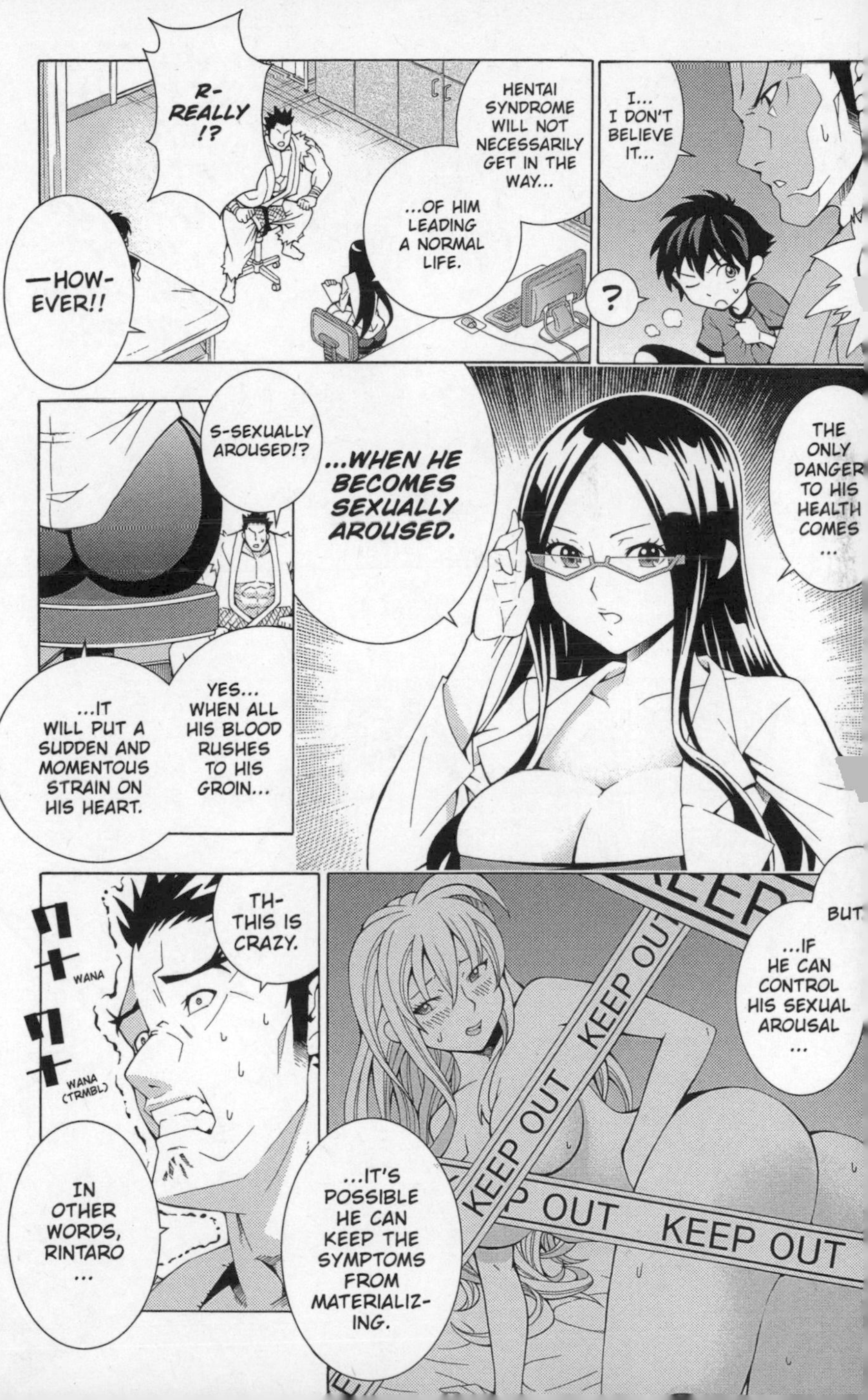
I... I DON'T BELIEVE IT...
?
HENTAI SYNDROME WILL NOT NECESSARILY GET IN THE WAY...
R-REALLY!?
...OF HIM LEADING A NORMAL LIFE.
—HOW-EVER!!
THE ONLY DANGER TO HIS HEALTH COMES ...
...WHEN HE BECOMES SEXUALLY AROUSED.
S-SEXUALLY AROUSED!?
YES... WHEN ALL HIS BLOOD RUSHES TO HIS GROIN...
...IT WILL PUT A SUDDEN AND MOMENTOUS STRAIN ON HIS HEART.
BUT
...IF HE CAN CONTROL HIS SEXUAL AROUSAL ...
KEEP OUT
KEEP OUT
KEEP OUT
KEEP OUT
...IT'S POSSIBLE HE CAN KEEP THE SYMPTOMS FROM MATERIALIZ-ING.
TH-THIS IS CRAZY.
WANA
WANA (TRMBL)
IN OTHER WORDS, RINTARO ...

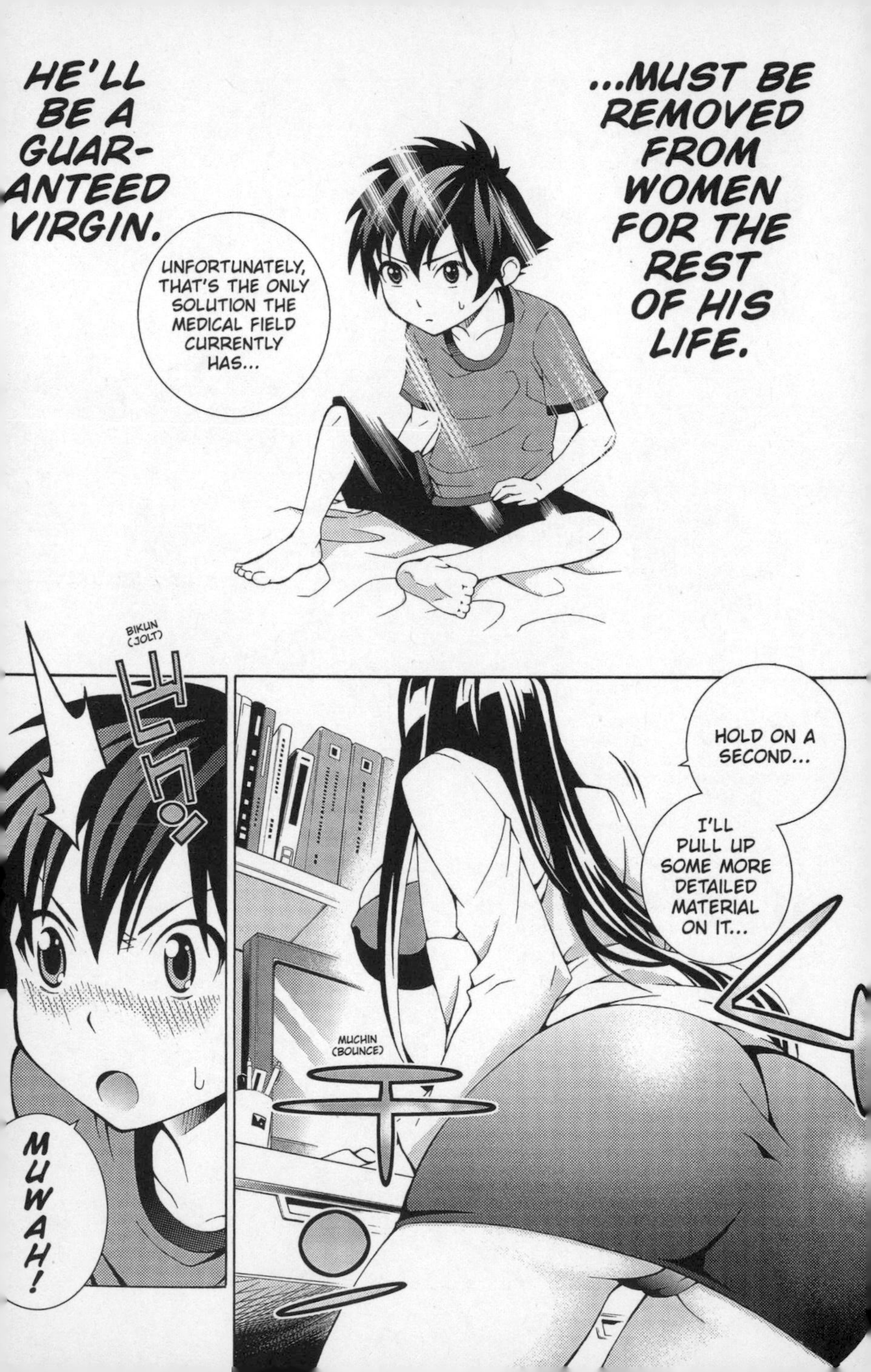
...MUST BE REMOVED FROM WOMEN FOR THE REST OF HIS LIFE.
HE'LL BE A GUARANTEED VIRGIN.
UNFORTUNATELY, THAT'S THE ONLY SOLUTION THE MEDICAL FIELD CURRENTLY HAS...
HOLD ON A SECOND...
I'LL PULL UP SOME MORE DETAILED MATERIAL ON IT...
MUCHIN (BOUNCE)
BIKUN (JOLT)
MUWAH!

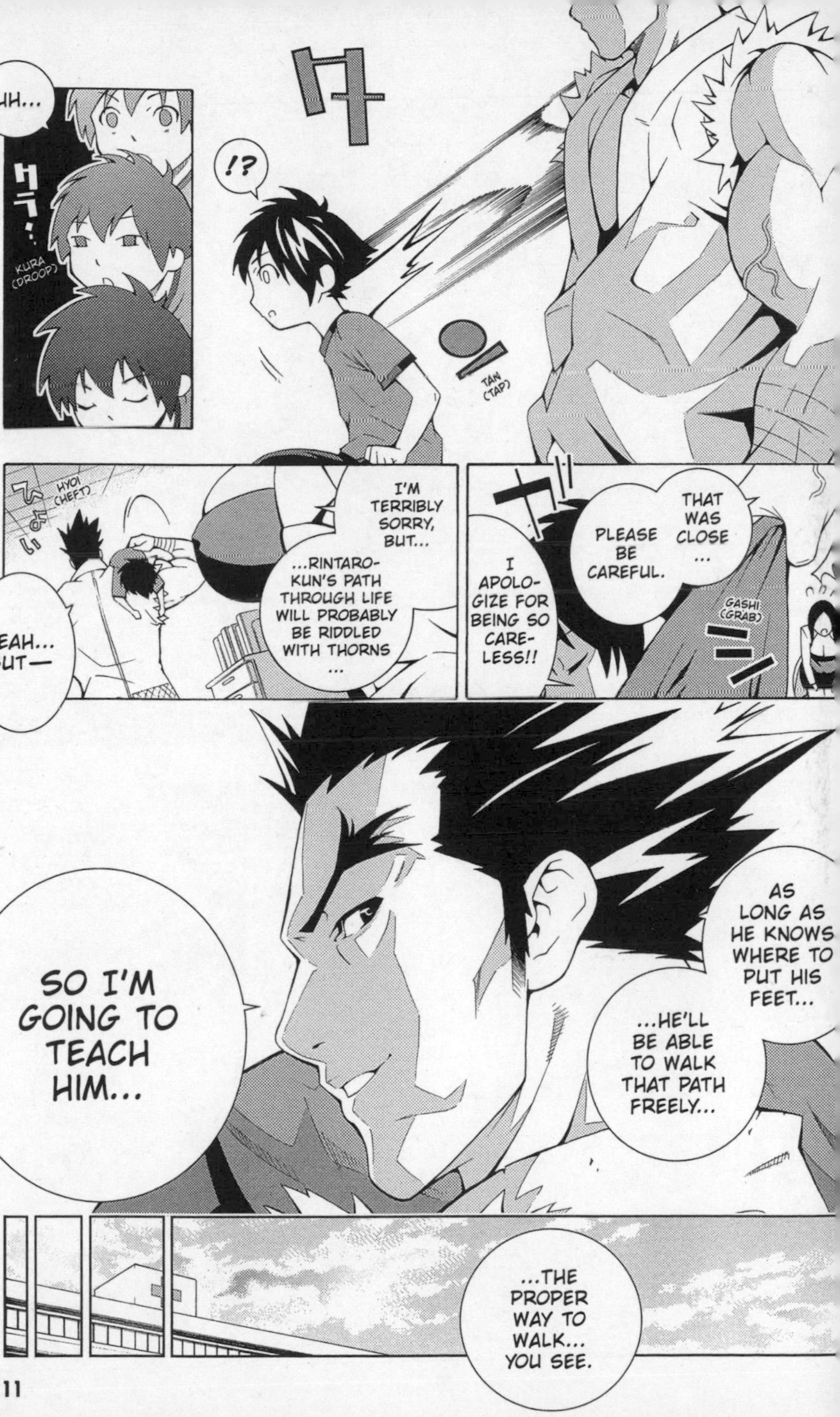
!?
TAN (TAP)
UH...
KURA (DROOP)
THAT WAS CLOSE...
PLEASE BE CAREFUL.
GASHI (GRAB)
I APOLOGIZE FOR BEING SO CARELESS!!
I'M TERRIBLY SORRY, BUT...
...RINTARO-KUN'S PATH THROUGH LIFE WILL PROBABLY BE RIDDLED WITH THORNS...
HYOI (HEFT)
YEAH... BUT—
AS LONG AS HE KNOWS WHERE TO PUT HIS FEET...
...HE'LL BE ABLE TO WALK THAT PATH FREELY...
SO I'M GOING TO TEACH HIM...
...THE PROPER WAY TO WALK... YOU SEE.

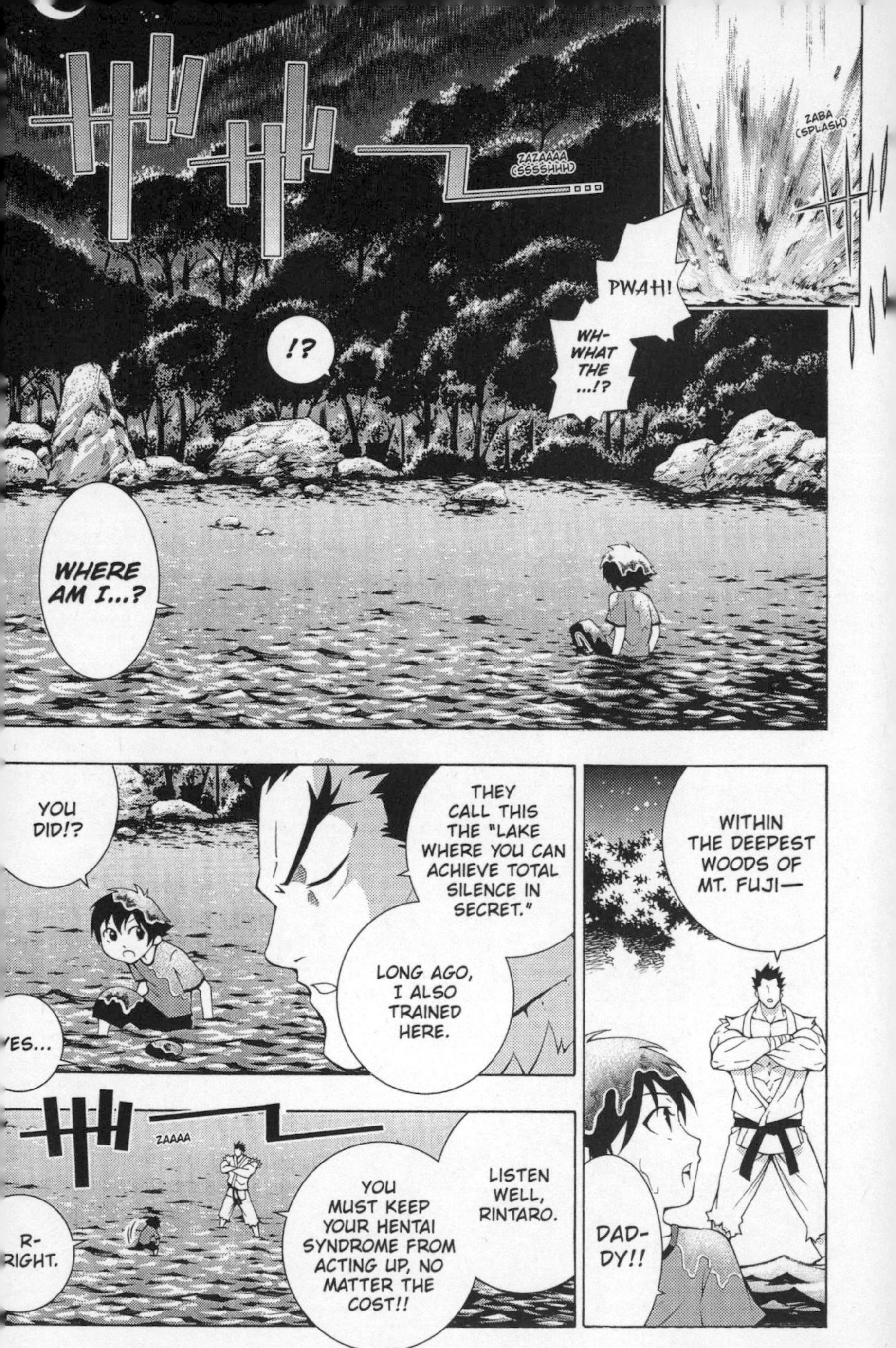
ZABA (SPLASH)
PWAH!
WH- WHAT THE ...!?
ZAZAAAA (SSSSHHH)
!?
WHERE AM I...?
WITHIN THE DEEPEST WOODS OF MT. FUJI—
DADDY!!
THEY CALL THIS THE "LAKE WHERE YOU CAN ACHIEVE TOTAL SILENCE IN SECRET."
LONG AGO, I ALSO TRAINED HERE.
YOU DID!?
YES...
LISTEN WELL, RINTARO.
YOU MUST KEEP YOUR HENTAI SYNDROME FROM ACTING UP, NO MATTER THE COST!!
ZAAAA
R-RIGHT.

LABELS (RIGHT TO LEFT): SOUL, BODY, SKILL

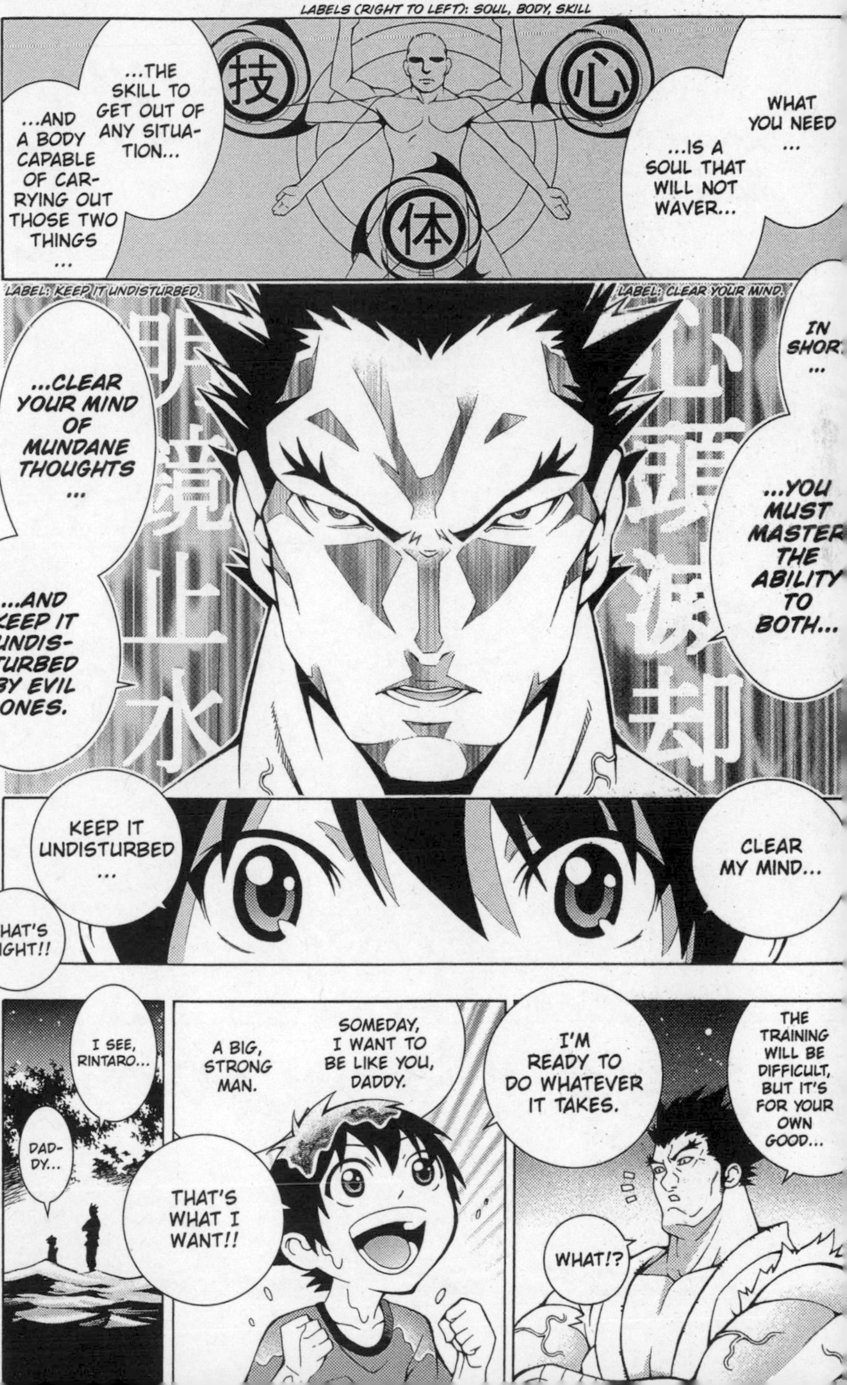
WHAT YOU NEED...
...IS A SOUL THAT WILL NOT WAVER...
...THE SKILL TO GET OUT OF ANY SITUATION...
...AND A BODY CAPABLE OF CARRYING OUT THOSE TWO THINGS...
LABEL: CLEAR YOUR MIND.
IN SHORT...
...YOU MUST MASTER THE ABILITY TO BOTH...
LABEL: KEEP IT UNDISTURBED.
...CLEAR YOUR MIND OF MUNDANE THOUGHTS...
...AND KEEP IT UNDISTURBED BY EVIL ONES.
CLEAR MY MIND...
KEEP IT UNDISTURBED...
THAT'S RIGHT!!
THE TRAINING WILL BE DIFFICULT, BUT IT'S FOR YOUR OWN GOOD...
I'M READY TO DO WHATEVER IT TAKES.
WHAT!?
SOMEDAY, I WANT TO BE LIKE YOU, DADDY.
A BIG, STRONG MAN.
THAT'S WHAT I WANT!!
I SEE, RINTARO...
DADDY...

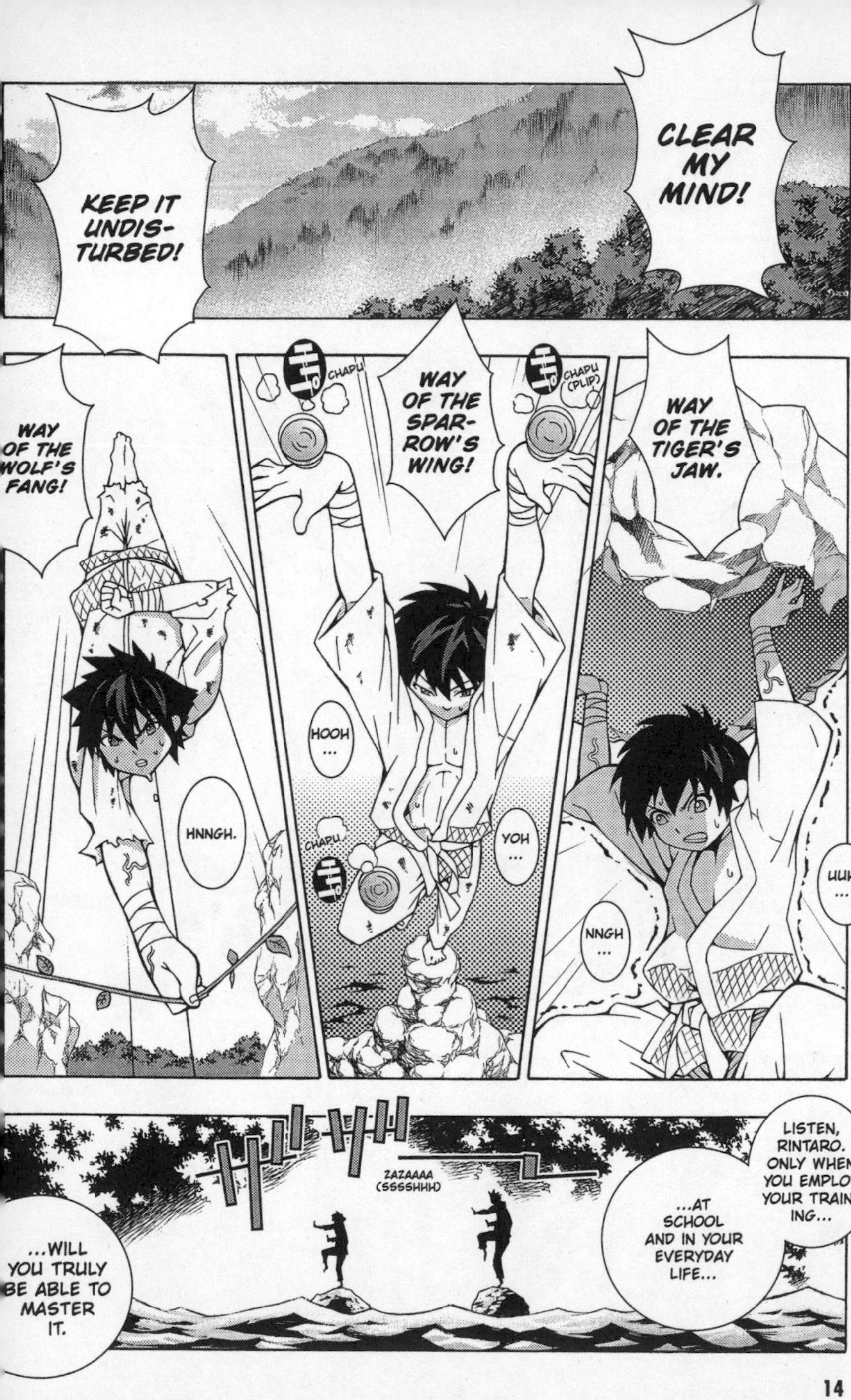

CLEAR MY MIND!
KEEP IT UNDIS-TURBED!
WAY OF THE TIGER'S JAW.
UUH ...
NNGH ...
CHAPU (PLIP)
WAY OF THE SPAR-ROW'S WING!
CHAPU
HOOH ...
YOH ...
CHAPU
WAY OF THE WOLF'S FANG!
HNNGH.
LISTEN, RINTARO. ONLY WHEN YOU EMPLOY YOUR TRAIN-ING...
...AT SCHOOL AND IN YOUR EVERYDAY LIFE...
ZAZAAAA (SSSSHHH)
...WILL YOU TRULY BE ABLE TO MASTER IT.

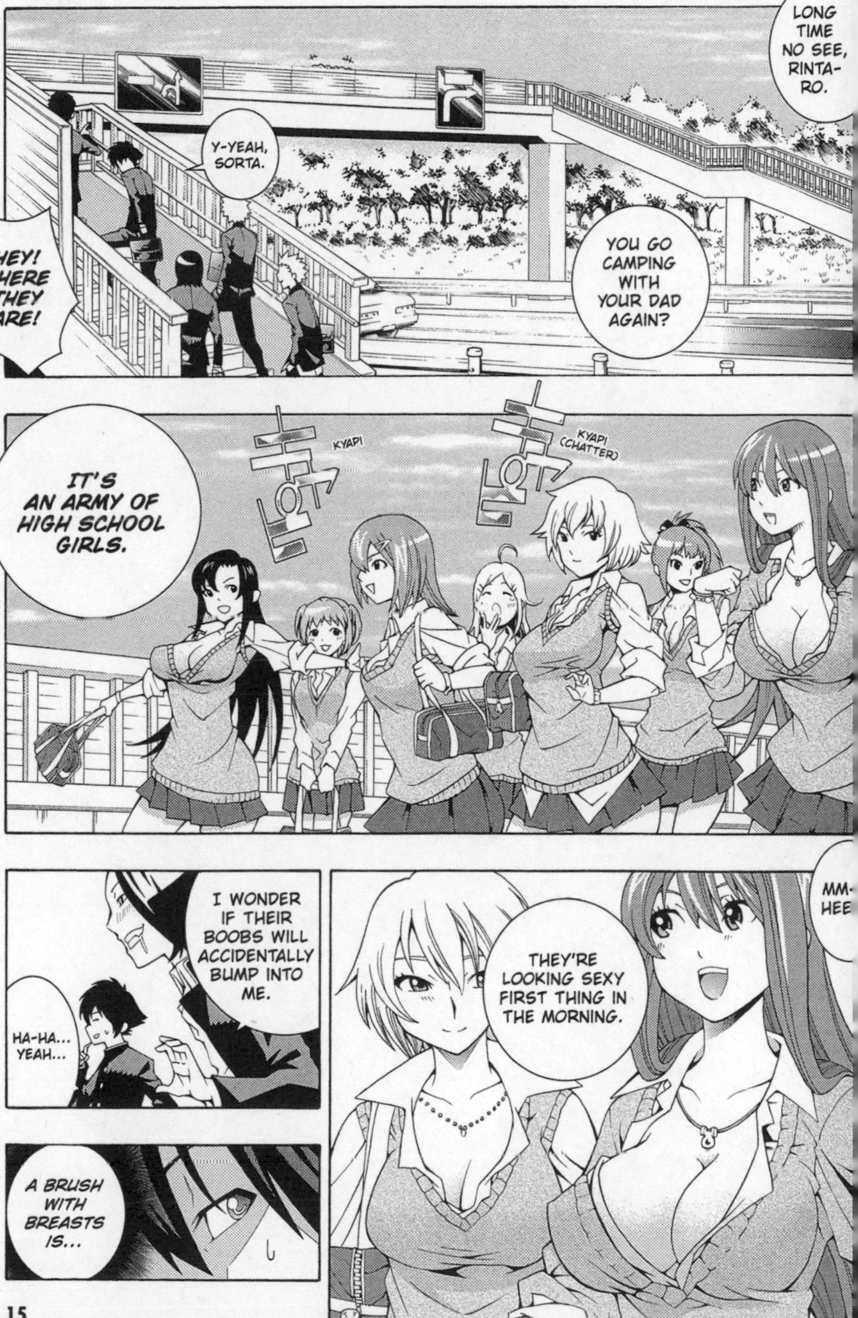
LONG TIME NO SEE, RINTA-RO.
YOU GO CAMPING WITH YOUR DAD AGAIN?
Y-YEAH, SORTA.
HEY! THERE THEY ARE!
KYAPI (CHATTER)
KYAPI
IT'S AN ARMY OF HIGH SCHOOL GIRLS.
MM-HEE
THEY'RE LOOKING SEXY FIRST THING IN THE MORNING.
I WONDER IF THEIR BOOBS WILL ACCIDENTALLY BUMP INTO ME.
HA-HA... YEAH...
A BRUSH WITH BREASTS IS...

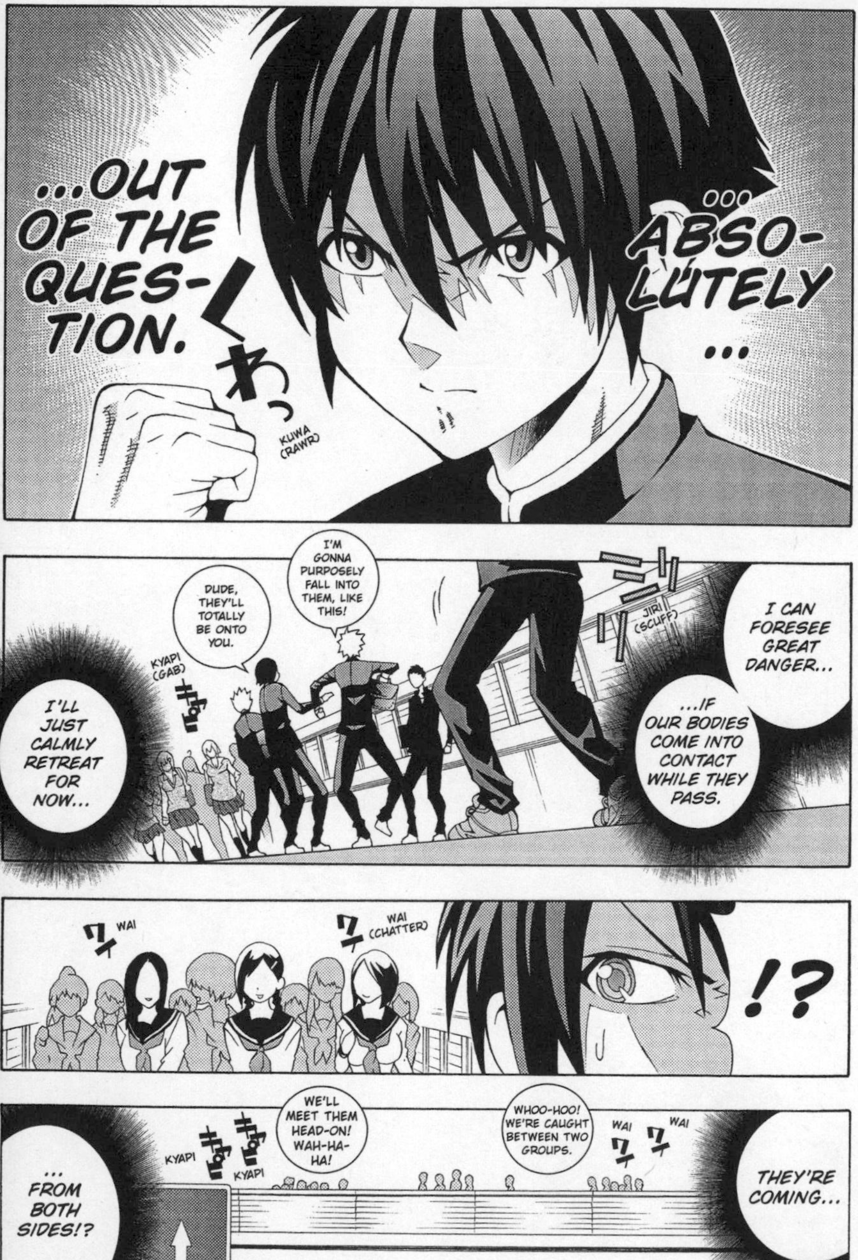
...ABSO-LUTELY...
...OUT OF THE QUES-TION.
くわっ
KUWA (RAWR)
I CAN FORESEE GREAT DANGER...
...IF OUR BODIES COME INTO CONTACT WHILE THEY PASS.
JIRI (SCUFF)
I'M GONNA PURPOSELY FALL INTO THEM, LIKE THIS!
DUDE, THEY'LL TOTALLY BE ONTO YOU.
KYAPI (GAB)
I'LL JUST CALMLY RETREAT FOR NOW...
!?
WAI (CHATTER)
WAI
THEY'RE COMING...
WAI
WAI
WHOO-HOO! WE'RE CAUGHT BETWEEN TWO GROUPS.
WE'LL MEET THEM HEAD-ON! WAH-HA-HA!
KYAPI
KYAPI
...FROM BOTH SIDES!?

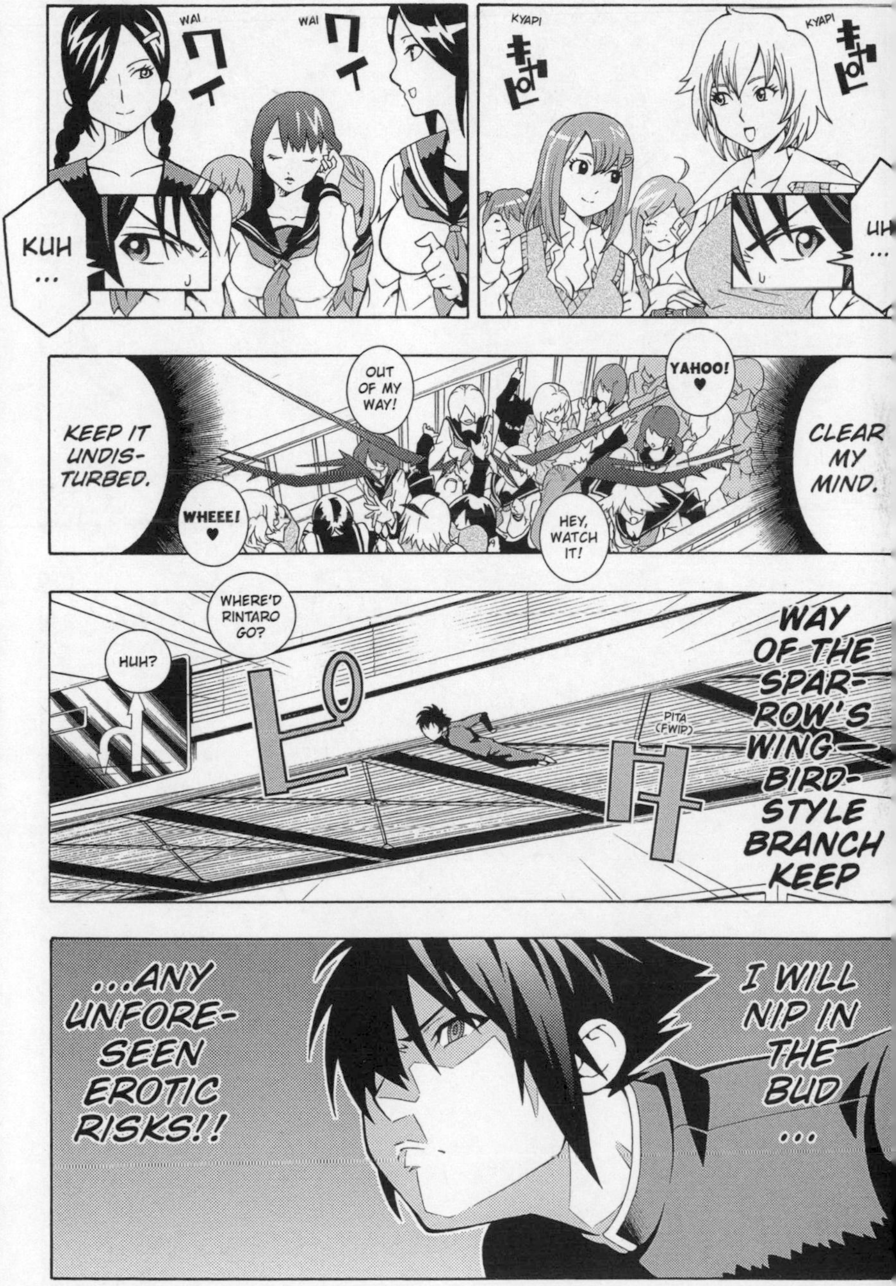
KYAPI
KYAPI
UH ...
WAI
WAI
KUH ...
CLEAR MY MIND.
YAHOO! ♥
OUT OF MY WAY!
HEY, WATCH IT!
KEEP IT UNDIS-TURBED.
WHEEE! ♥
WAY OF THE SPAR-ROW'S WING— BIRD-STYLE BRANCH KEEP
PITA (FWIP)
WHERE'D RINTARO GO?
HUH?
I WILL NIP IN THE BUD ...
...ANY UNFORE-SEEN EROTIC RISKS!!

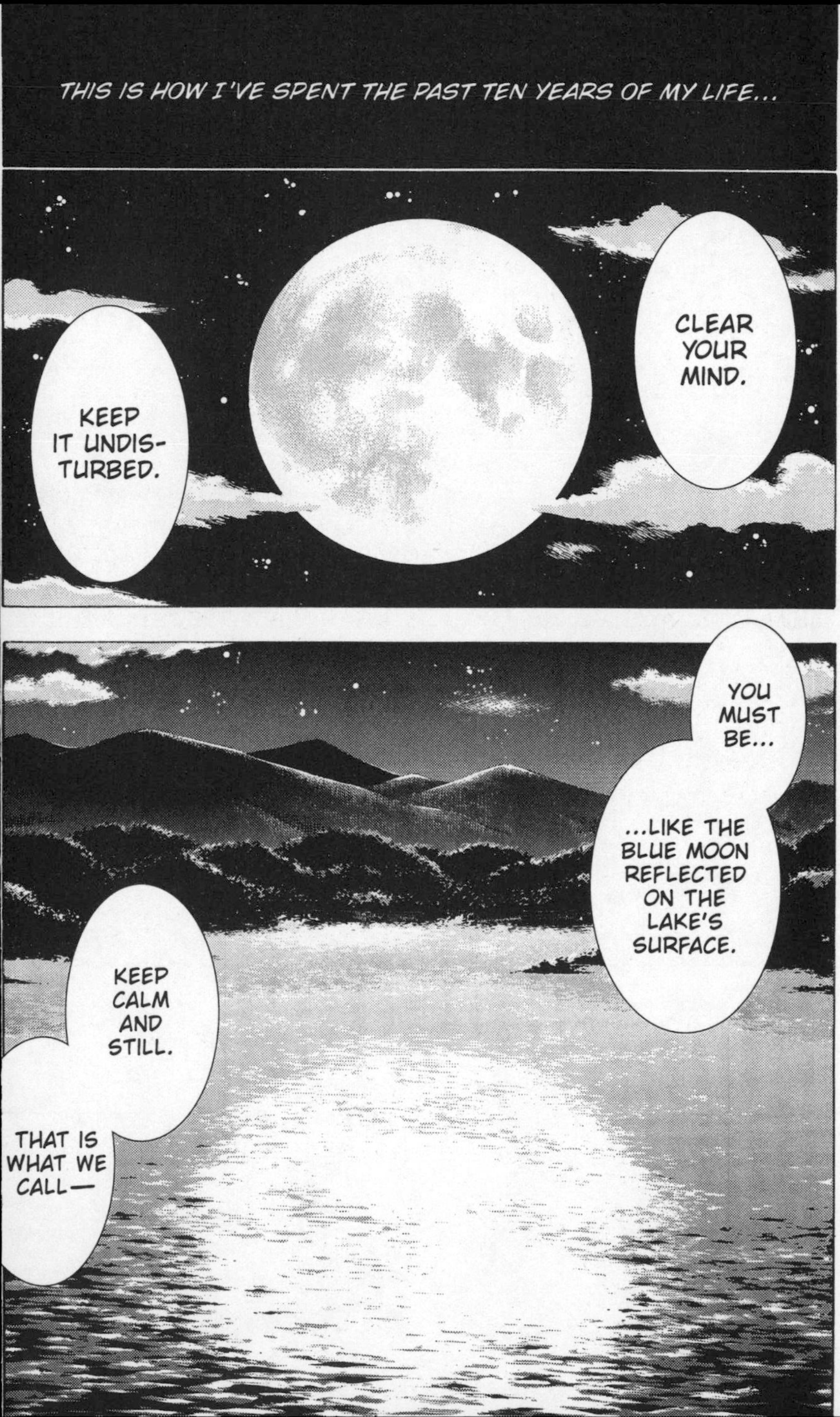
THIS IS HOW I'VE SPENT THE PAST TEN YEARS OF MY LIFE...
CLEAR YOUR MIND.
KEEP IT UNDIS-TURBED.
YOU MUST BE...
...LIKE THE BLUE MOON REFLECTED ON THE LAKE'S SURFACE.
KEEP CALM AND STILL.
THAT IS WHAT WE CALL—

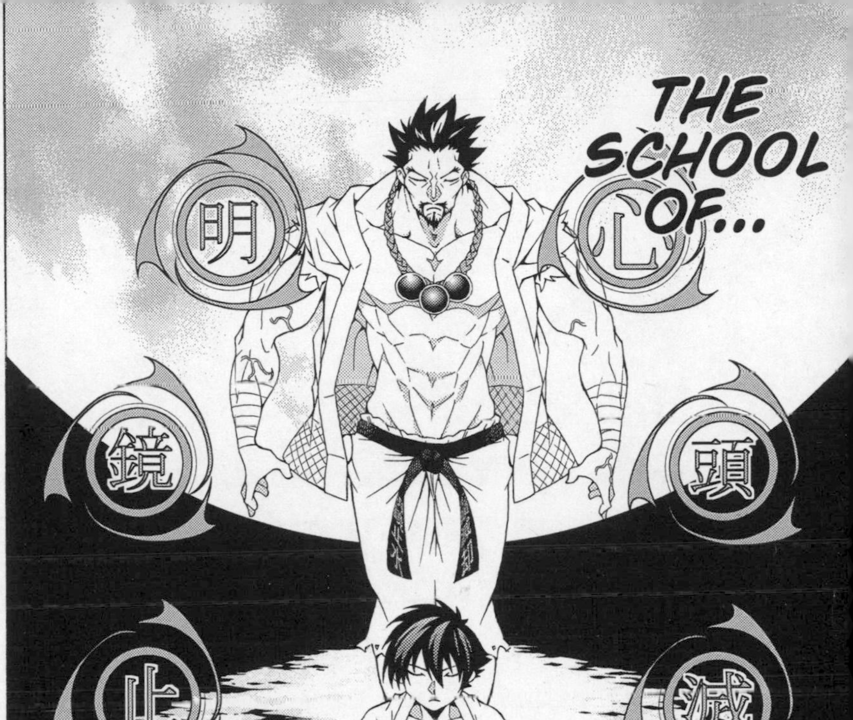
THE SCHOOL OF...
心
頭
滅
却
明
鏡
止
水
...THE BLUE MOON RE-FLECTED ON A LAKE

LABELS: KEEP THE MIND CLEAR, UNDISTURBED BY EVIL THOUGHTS.

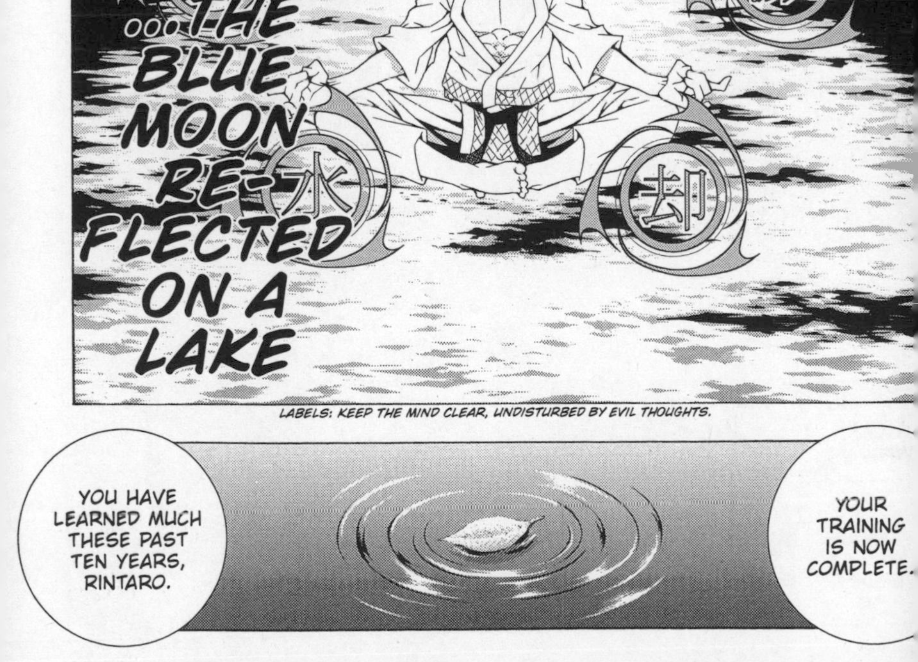
YOUR TRAINING IS NOW COMPLETE.
YOU HAVE LEARNED MUCH THESE PAST TEN YEARS, RINTARO.

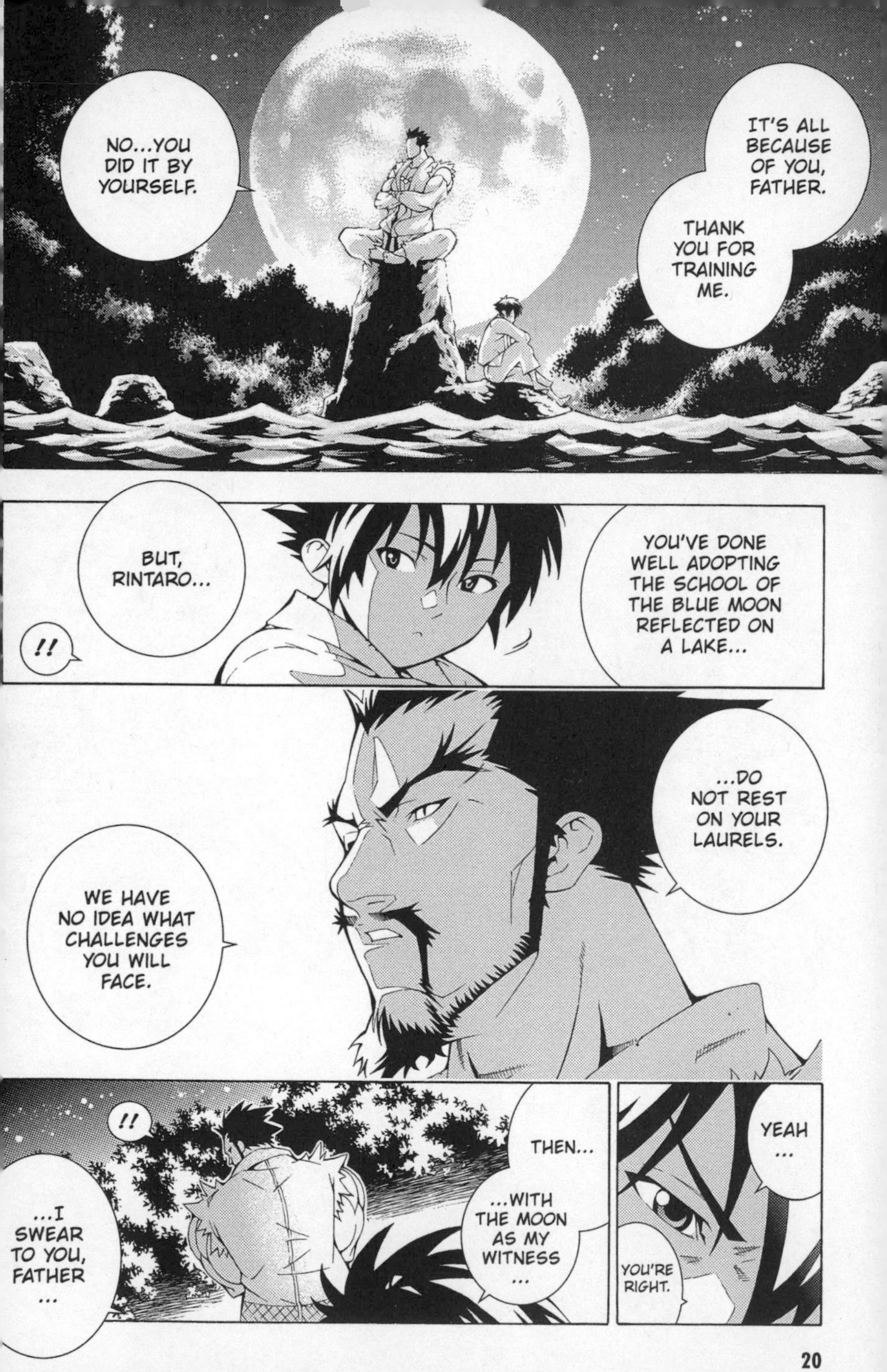
IT'S ALL BECAUSE OF YOU, FATHER.
THANK YOU FOR TRAINING ME.
NO...YOU DID IT BY YOURSELF.
YOU'VE DONE WELL ADOPTING THE SCHOOL OF THE BLUE MOON REFLECTED ON A LAKE...
BUT, RINTARO...
!!
...DO NOT REST ON YOUR LAURELS.
WE HAVE NO IDEA WHAT CHALLENGES YOU WILL FACE.
YEAH ...
YOU'RE RIGHT.
THEN...
...WITH THE MOON AS MY WITNESS ...
!!
...I SWEAR TO YOU, FATHER ...

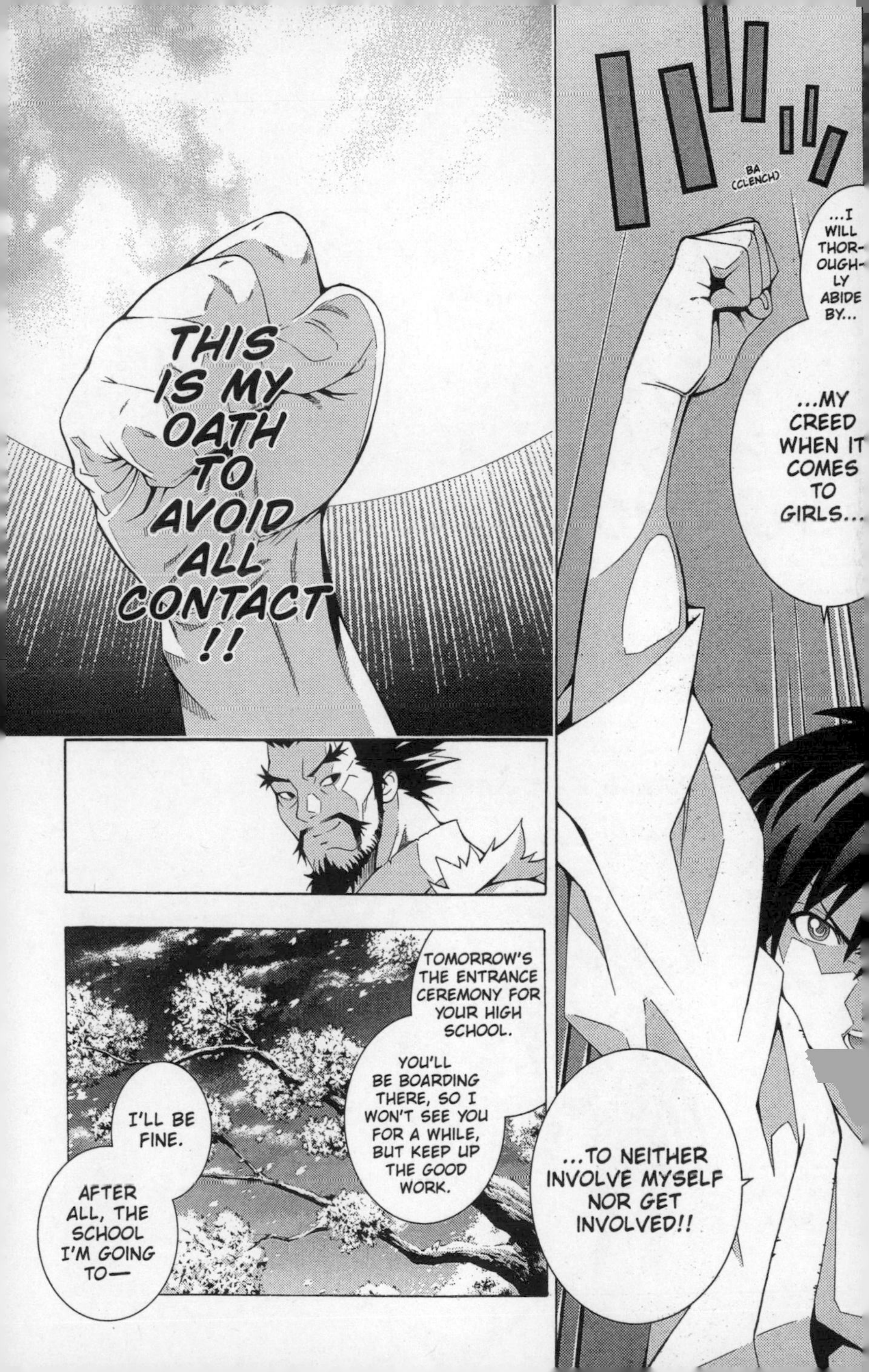
BA (CLENCH)
...I WILL THOROUGHLY ABIDE BY...
...MY CREED WHEN IT COMES TO GIRLS...
...TO NEITHER INVOLVE MYSELF NOR GET INVOLVED!!
THIS IS MY OATH TO AVOID ALL CONTACT!!
TOMORROW'S THE ENTRANCE CEREMONY FOR YOUR HIGH SCHOOL.
YOU'LL BE BOARDING THERE, SO I WON'T SEE YOU FOR A WHILE, BUT KEEP UP THE GOOD WORK.
I'LL BE FINE.
AFTER ALL, THE SCHOOL I'M GOING TO—

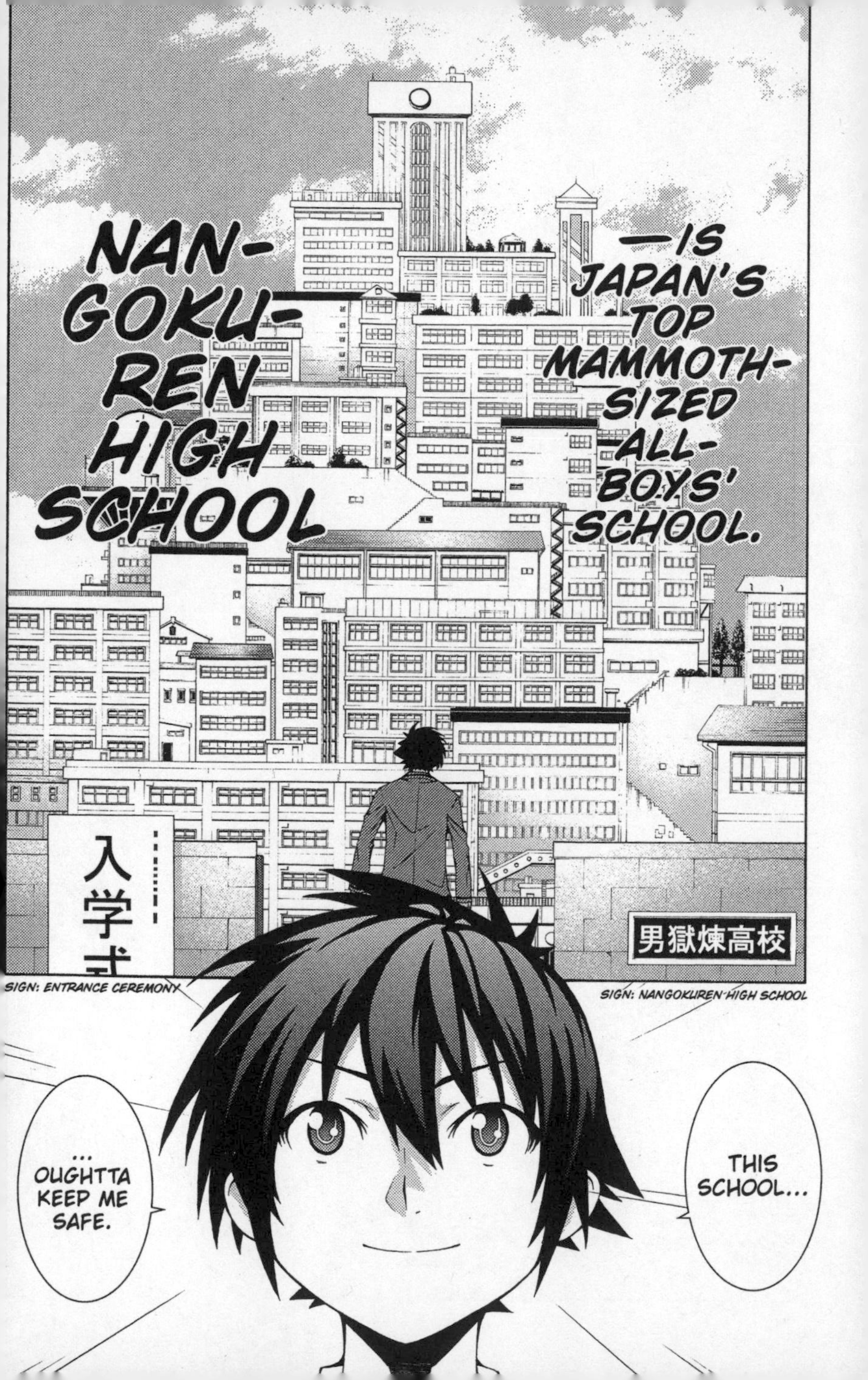

NAN-GOKU-REN HIGH SCHOOL
—IS JAPAN'S TOP MAMMOTH-SIZED ALL-BOYS' SCHOOL.
男獄煉高校
入学式
SIGN: NANGOKUREN HIGH SCHOOL
SIGN: ENTRANCE CEREMONY
THIS SCHOOL...
...OUGHTTA KEEP ME SAFE.

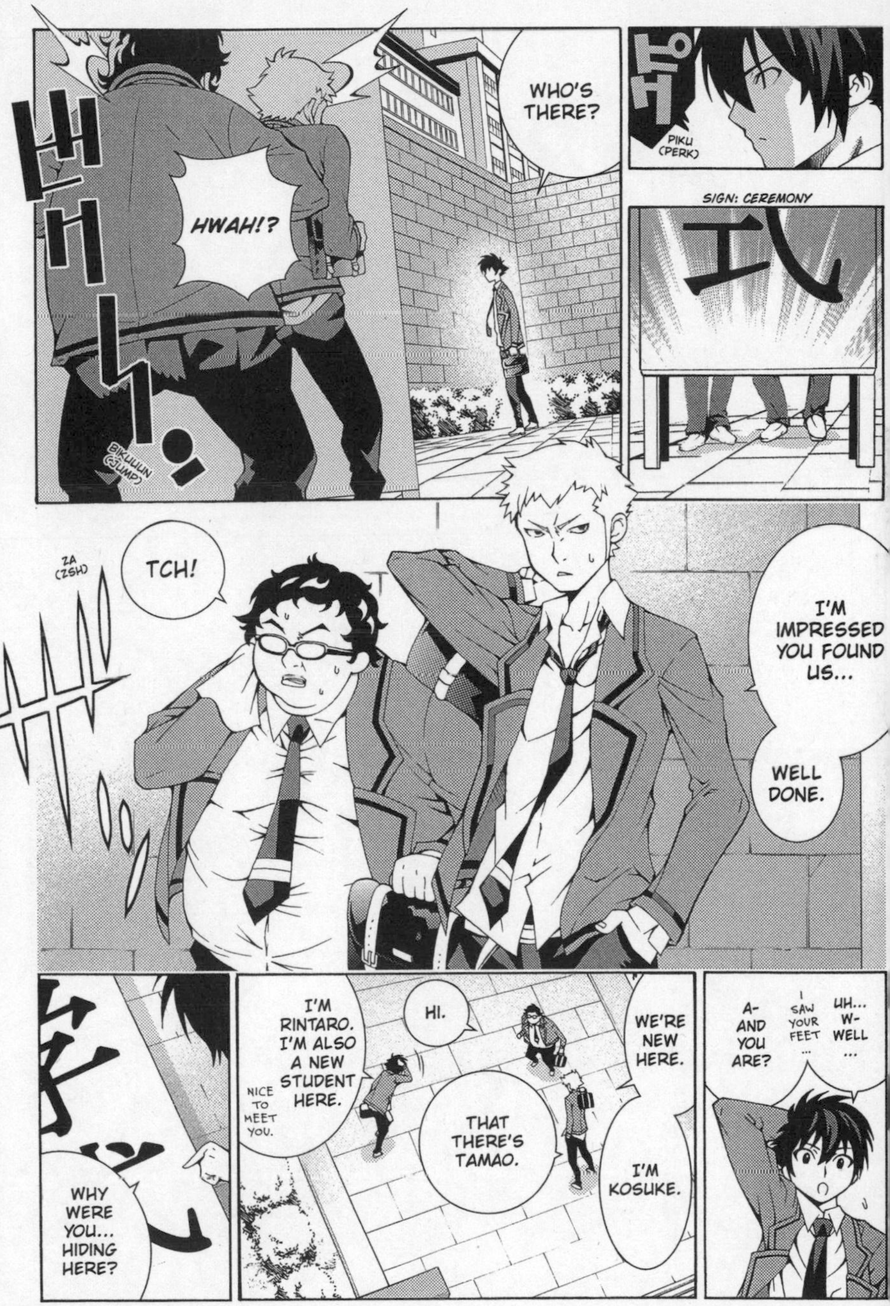
PIKU (PERK)
SIGN: CEREMONY
WHO'S THERE?
HWAH!?
BIKUUUN (JUMP)
I'M IMPRESSED YOU FOUND US...
WELL DONE.
TCH!
ZA (ZSH)
UH... W-WELL...
I SAW YOUR FEET...
A- AND YOU ARE?
WE'RE NEW HERE.
I'M KOSUKE.
THAT THERE'S TAMAO.
HI.
I'M RINTARO. I'M ALSO A NEW STUDENT HERE.
NICE TO MEET YOU.
WHY WERE YOU... HIDING HERE?

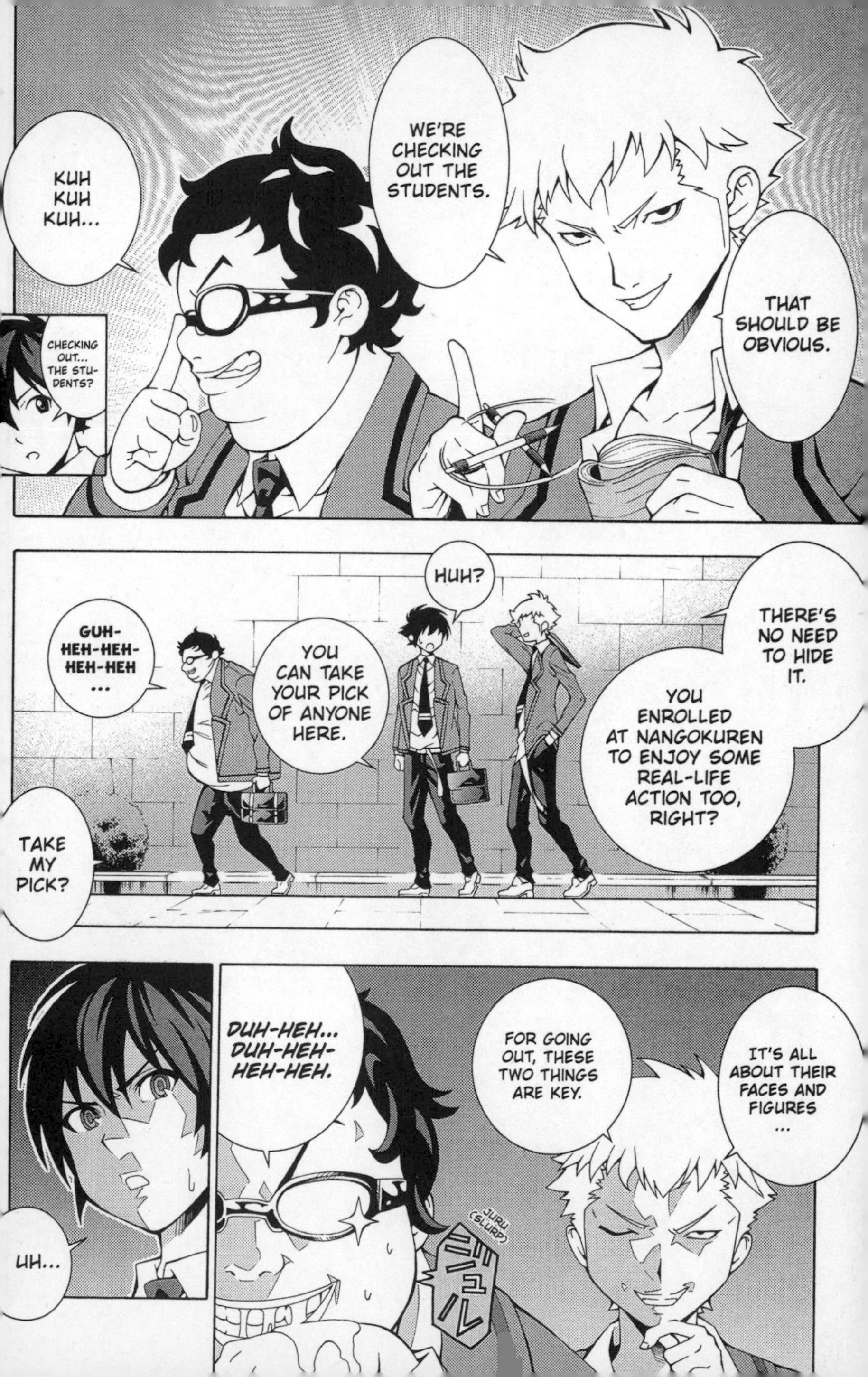
WE'RE CHECKING OUT THE STUDENTS.
THAT SHOULD BE OBVIOUS.
KUH KUH KUH...
CHECKING OUT... THE STU-DENTS?
HUH?
THERE'S NO NEED TO HIDE IT.
YOU ENROLLED AT NANGOKUREN TO ENJOY SOME REAL-LIFE ACTION TOO, RIGHT?
YOU CAN TAKE YOUR PICK OF ANYONE HERE.
GUH-HEH-HEH-HEH-HEH...
TAKE MY PICK?
IT'S ALL ABOUT THEIR FACES AND FIGURES...
FOR GOING OUT, THESE TWO THINGS ARE KEY.
DUH-HEH... DUH-HEH-HEH-HEH.
JURU (SLURP)
UH...

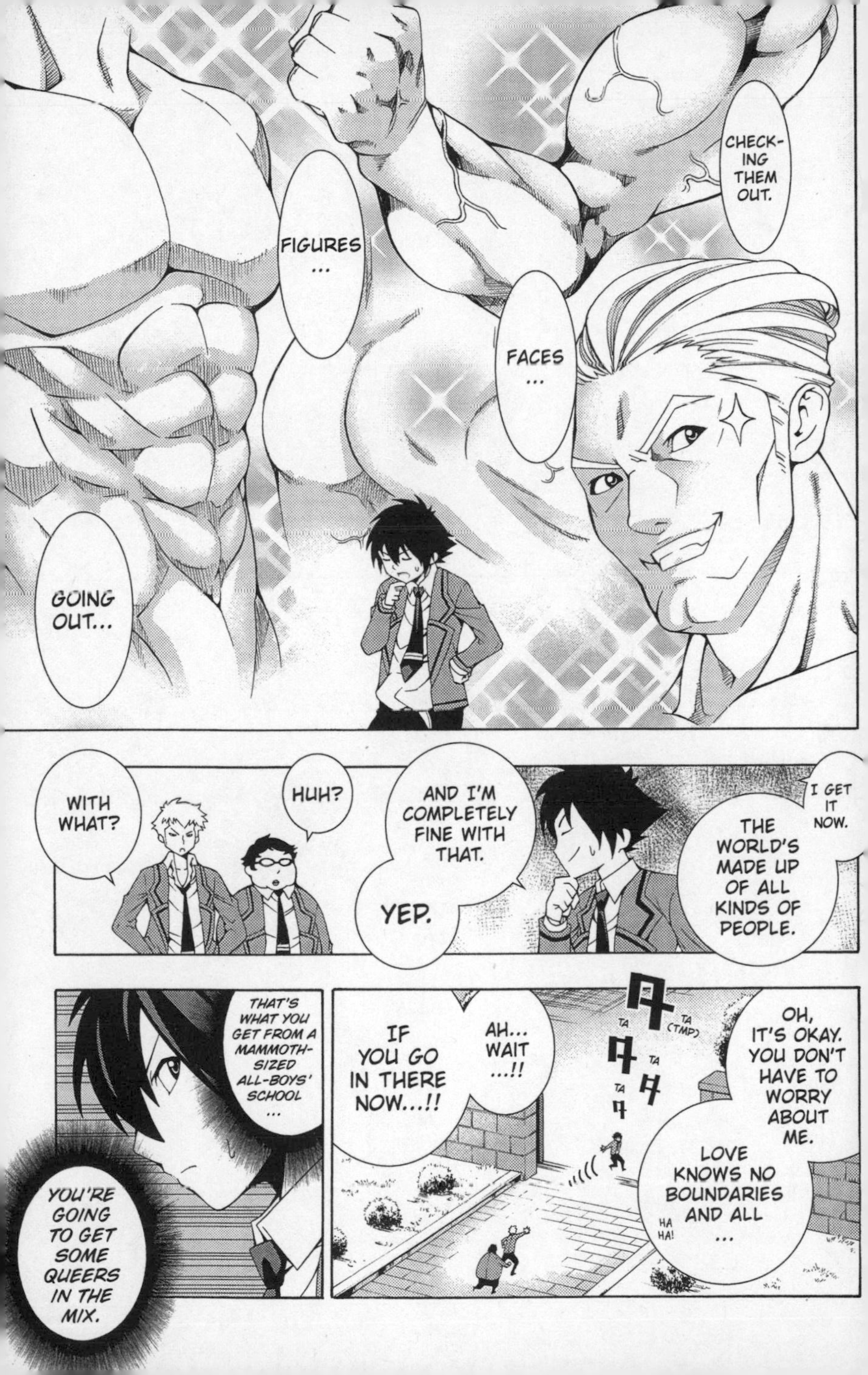
CHECKING THEM OUT.
FACES ...
FIGURES ...
GOING OUT...
I GET IT NOW.
THE WORLD'S MADE UP OF ALL KINDS OF PEOPLE.
YEP.
AND I'M COMPLETELY FINE WITH THAT.
HUH?
WITH WHAT?
OH, IT'S OKAY. YOU DON'T HAVE TO WORRY ABOUT ME.
LOVE KNOWS NO BOUNDARIES AND ALL ...
HA HA!
TA TA (TMP) TA TA TA
AH... WAIT ...!!
IF YOU GO IN THERE NOW...!!
THAT'S WHAT YOU GET FROM A MAMMOTH-SIZED ALL-BOYS' SCHOOL ...
YOU'RE GOING TO GET SOME QUEERS IN THE MIX.

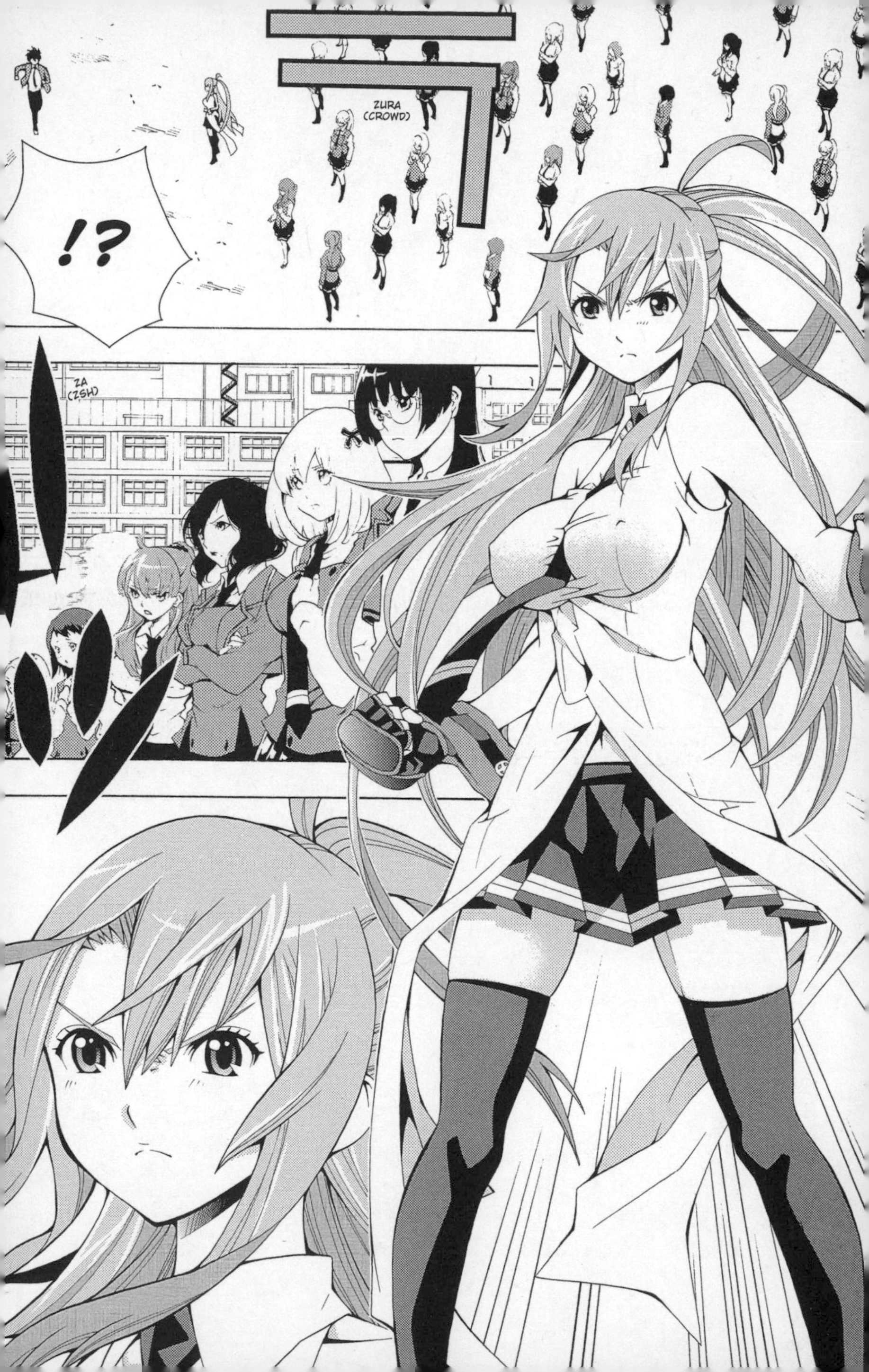
ZURA
(CROWD)
!?
ZA
(ZSH)

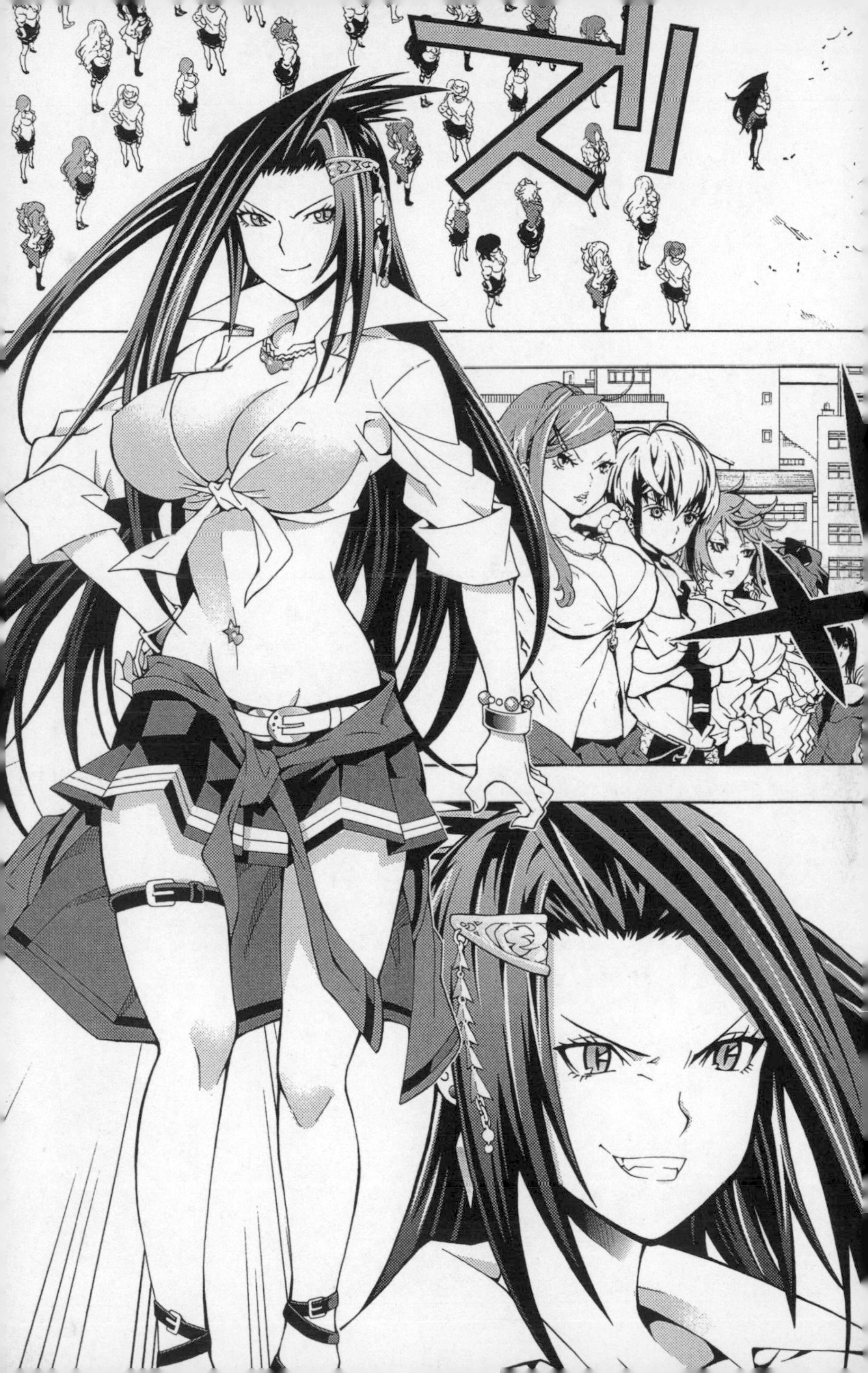

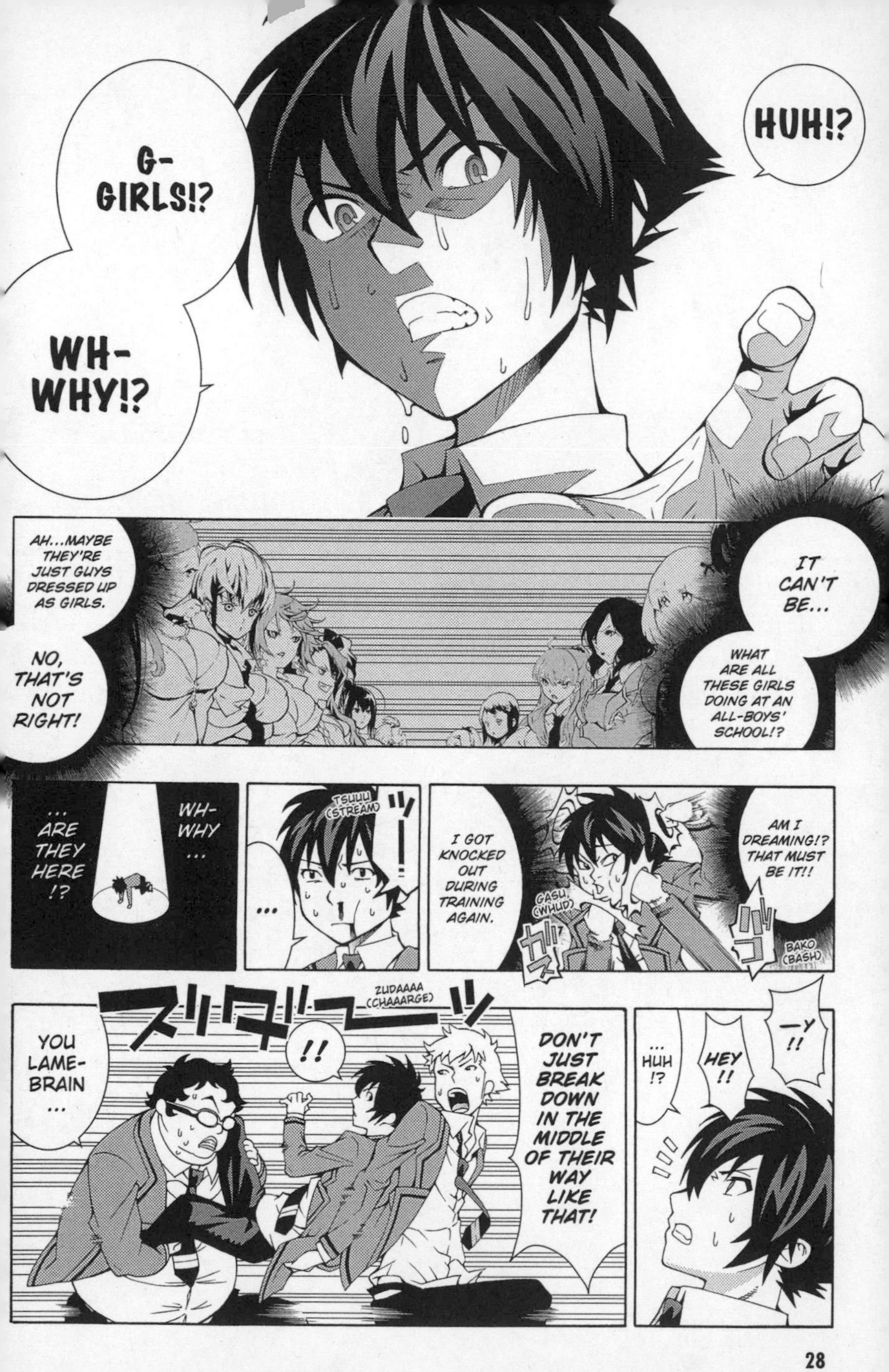
HUH!?
G-GIRLS!?
WH-WHY!?
IT CAN'T BE...
WHAT ARE ALL THESE GIRLS DOING AT AN ALL-BOYS' SCHOOL!?
AH...MAYBE THEY'RE JUST GUYS DRESSED UP AS GIRLS.
NO, THAT'S NOT RIGHT!
AM I DREAMING!? THAT MUST BE IT!!
I GOT KNOCKED OUT DURING TRAINING AGAIN.
BAKO (BASH)
GASU (WHUD)
TSUUU (STREAM)
...
WH-WHY...
...ARE THEY HERE!?
—Y!!
HEY!!
...HUH!?
ZUDAAAA (CHAAARGE)
DON'T JUST BREAK DOWN IN THE MIDDLE OF THEIR WAY LIKE THAT!
!!
YOU LAME-BRAIN...

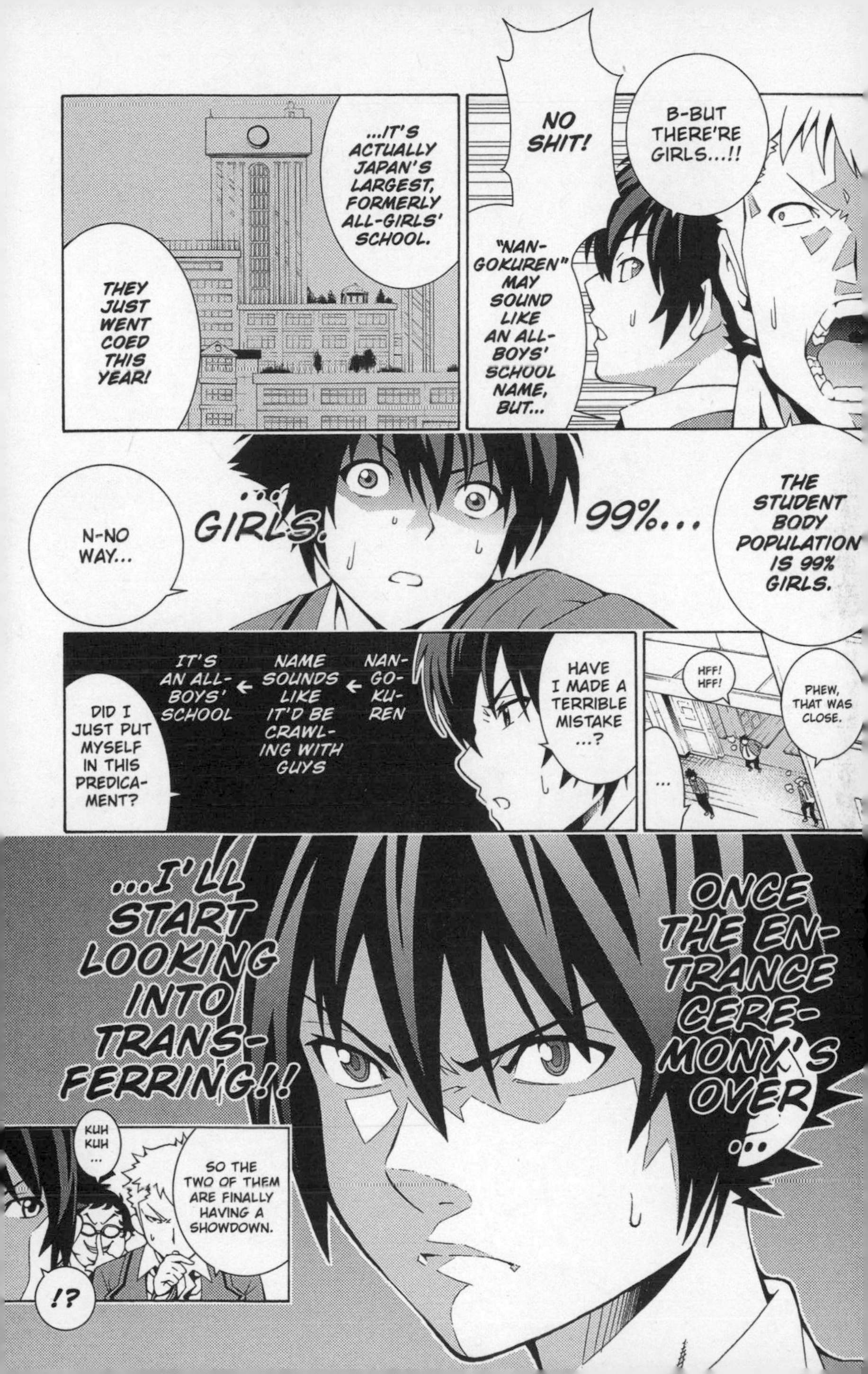
B-BUT THERE'RE GIRLS...!!
NO SHIT!
"NAN-GOKUREN" MAY SOUND LIKE AN ALL-BOYS' SCHOOL NAME, BUT...
...IT'S ACTUALLY JAPAN'S LARGEST, FORMERLY ALL-GIRLS' SCHOOL.
THEY JUST WENT COED THIS YEAR!
THE STUDENT BODY POPULATION IS 99% GIRLS.
99%...
...GIRLS.
N-NO WAY...
PHEW, THAT WAS CLOSE.
HFF! HFF!
...
HAVE I MADE A TERRIBLE MISTAKE ...?
IT'S AN ALL-BOYS' SCHOOL ← NAME SOUNDS LIKE IT'D BE CRAWLING WITH GUYS ← NAN-GO-KU-REN
DID I JUST PUT MYSELF IN THIS PREDICAMENT?
ONCE THE ENTRANCE CEREMONY'S OVER...
...I'LL START LOOKING INTO TRANSFERRING!!
SO THE TWO OF THEM ARE FINALLY HAVING A SHOWDOWN.
KUH KUH ...
!?

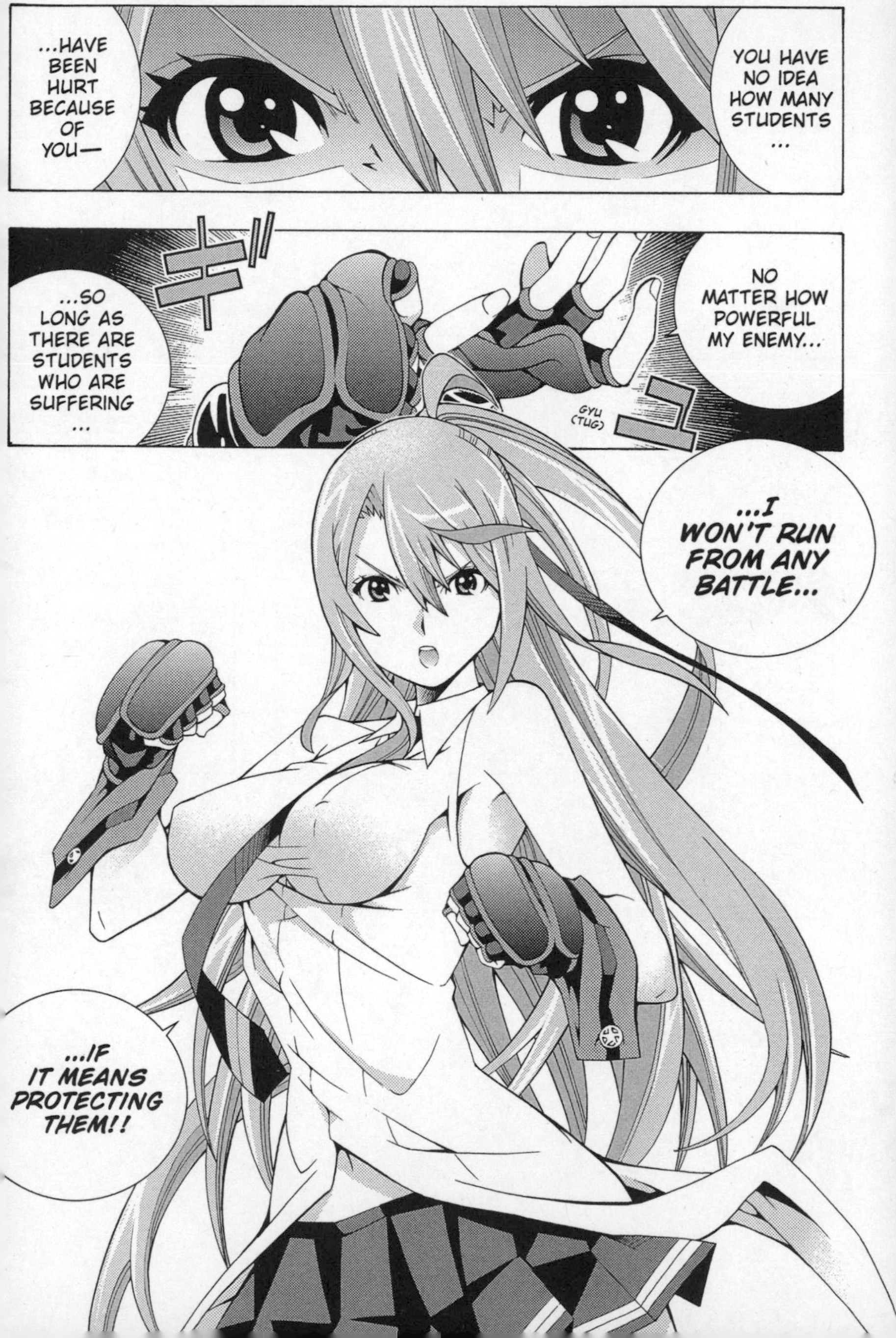
YOU HAVE NO IDEA HOW MANY STUDENTS ...
...HAVE BEEN HURT BECAUSE OF YOU—
NO MATTER HOW POWERFUL MY ENEMY...
GYU (TUG)
...SO LONG AS THERE ARE STUDENTS WHO ARE SUFFERING ...
...I WON'T RUN FROM ANY BATTLE...
...IF IT MEANS PROTECTING THEM!!

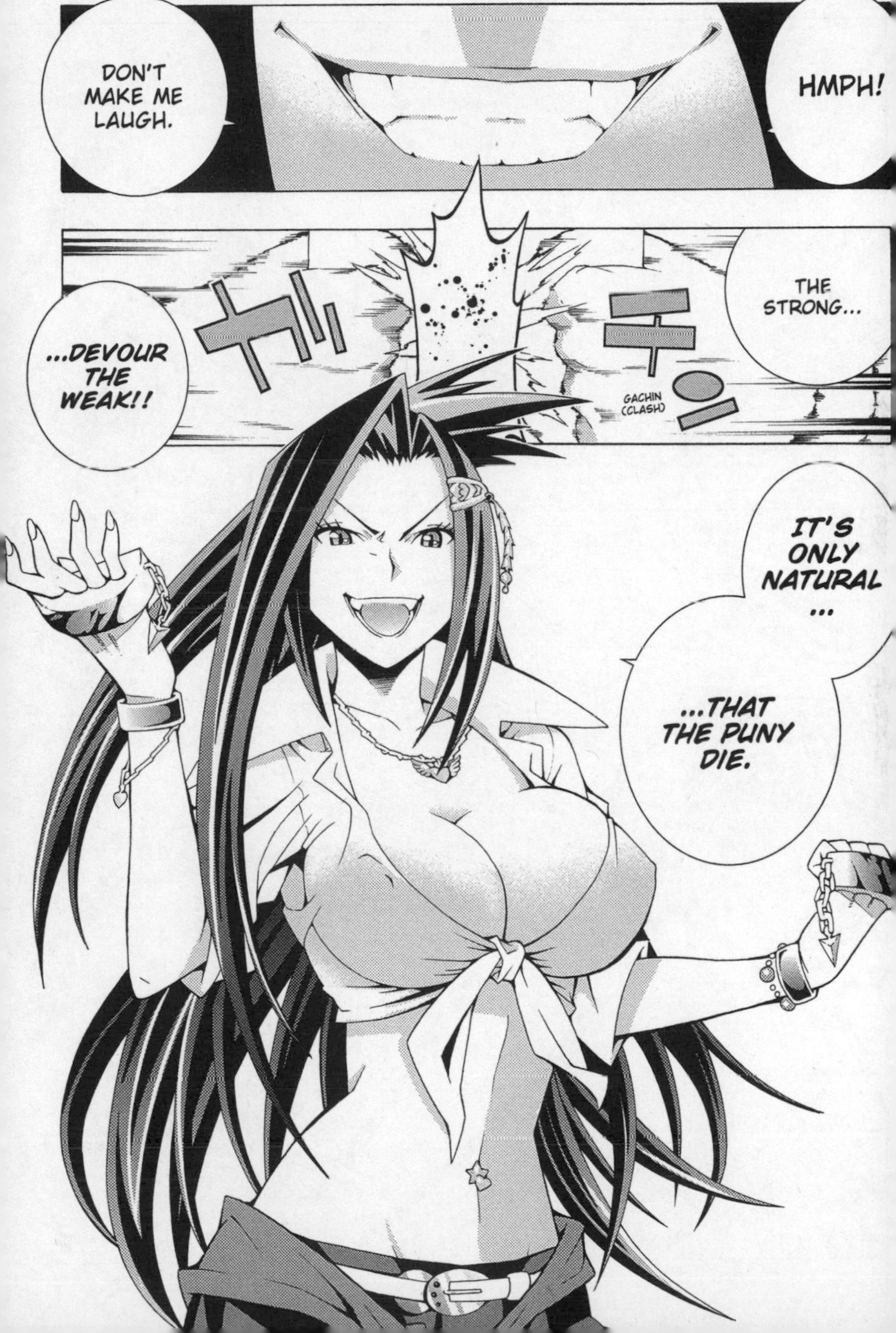
HMPH!
DON'T MAKE ME LAUGH.
THE STRONG...
GACHIN (CLASH)
...DEVOUR THE WEAK!!
IT'S ONLY NATURAL...
...THAT THE PUNY DIE.

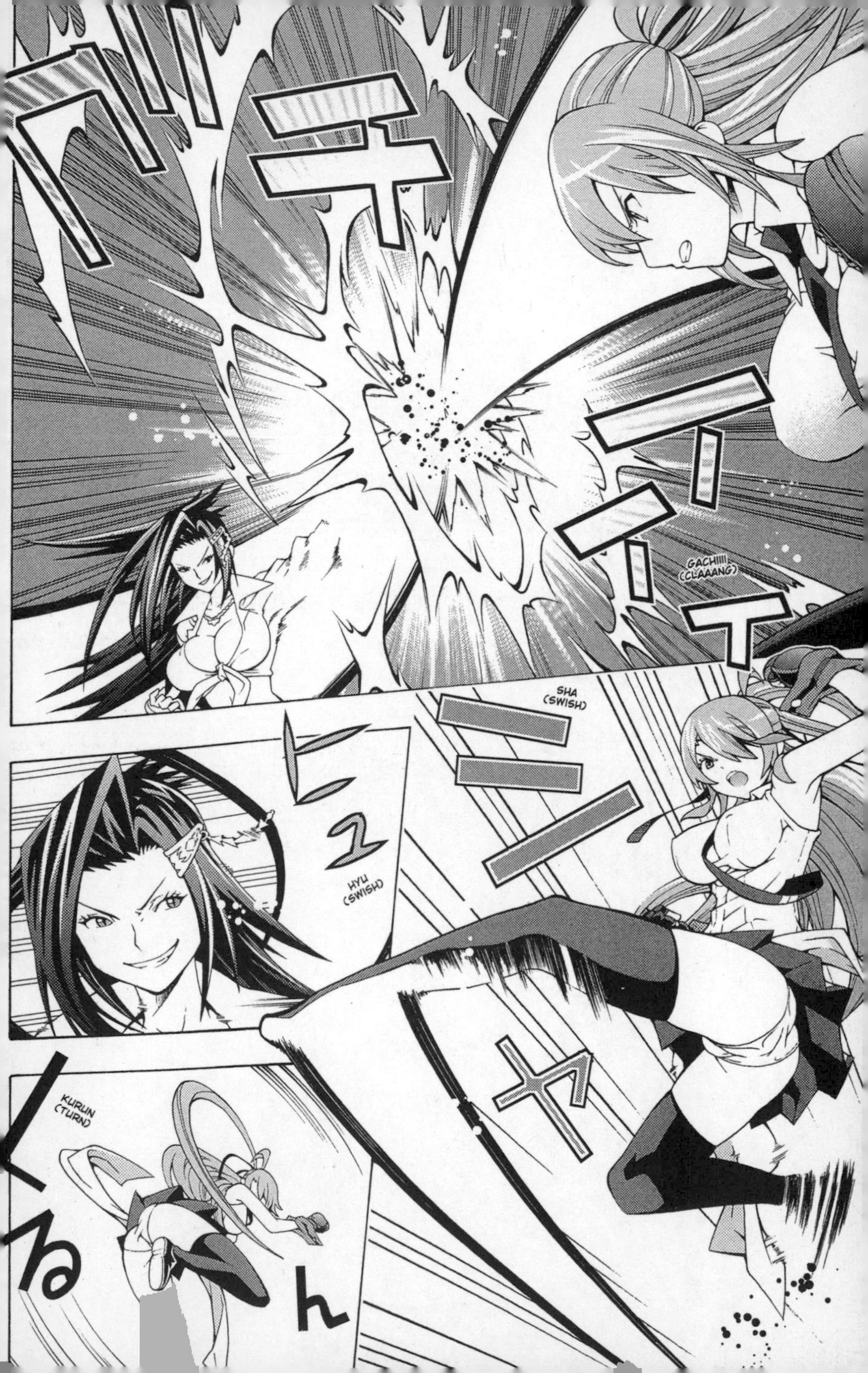
GACHIIIII
(CLAAANG)
SHA
(SWISH)
HYU
(SWISH)
KURUN
(TURN)

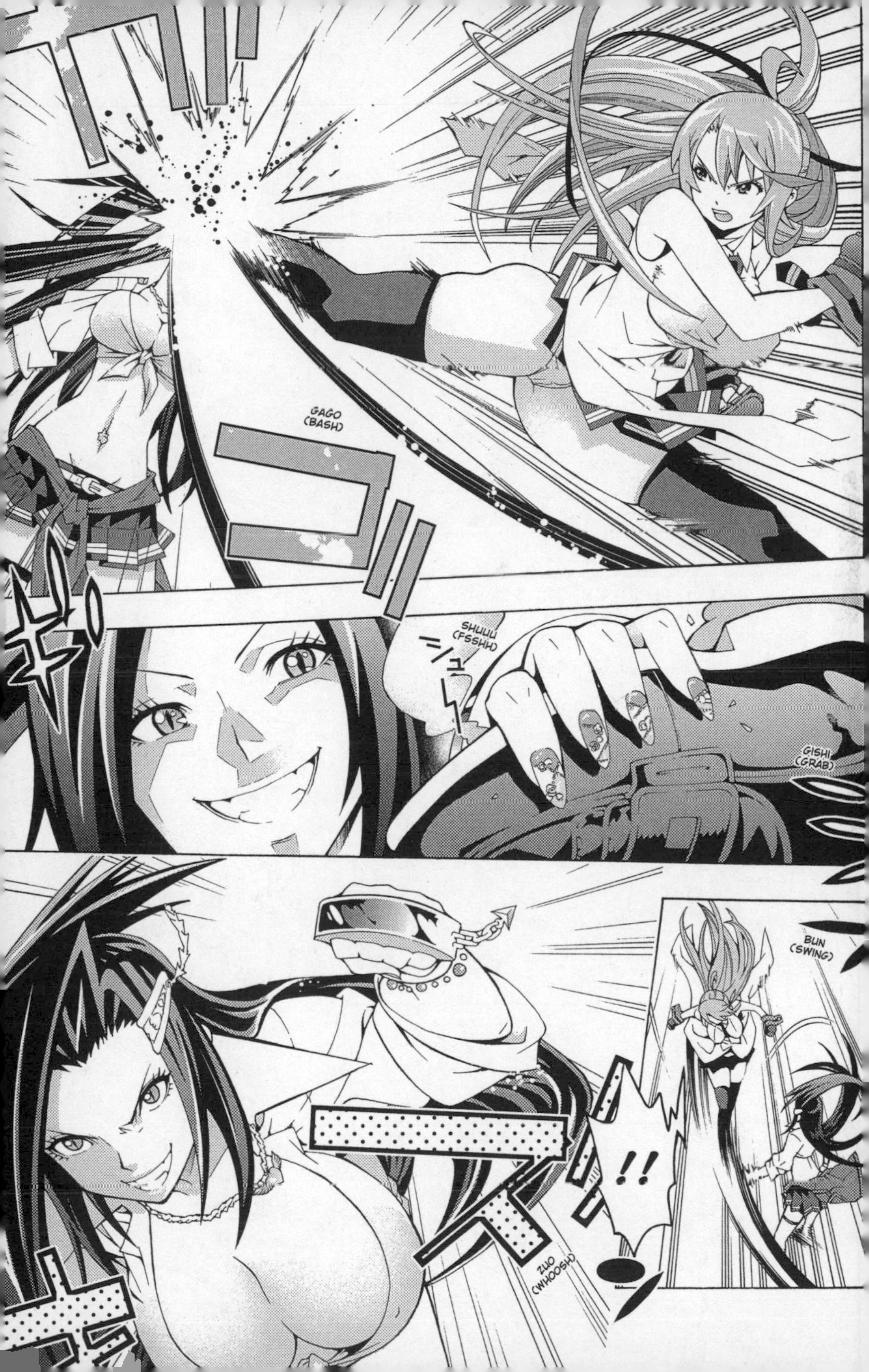
GAGO
(BASH)
SHUUU
(FSSHH)
GISHI
(GRAB)
BUN
(SWING)
!!
ZUO
(WHOOSH)

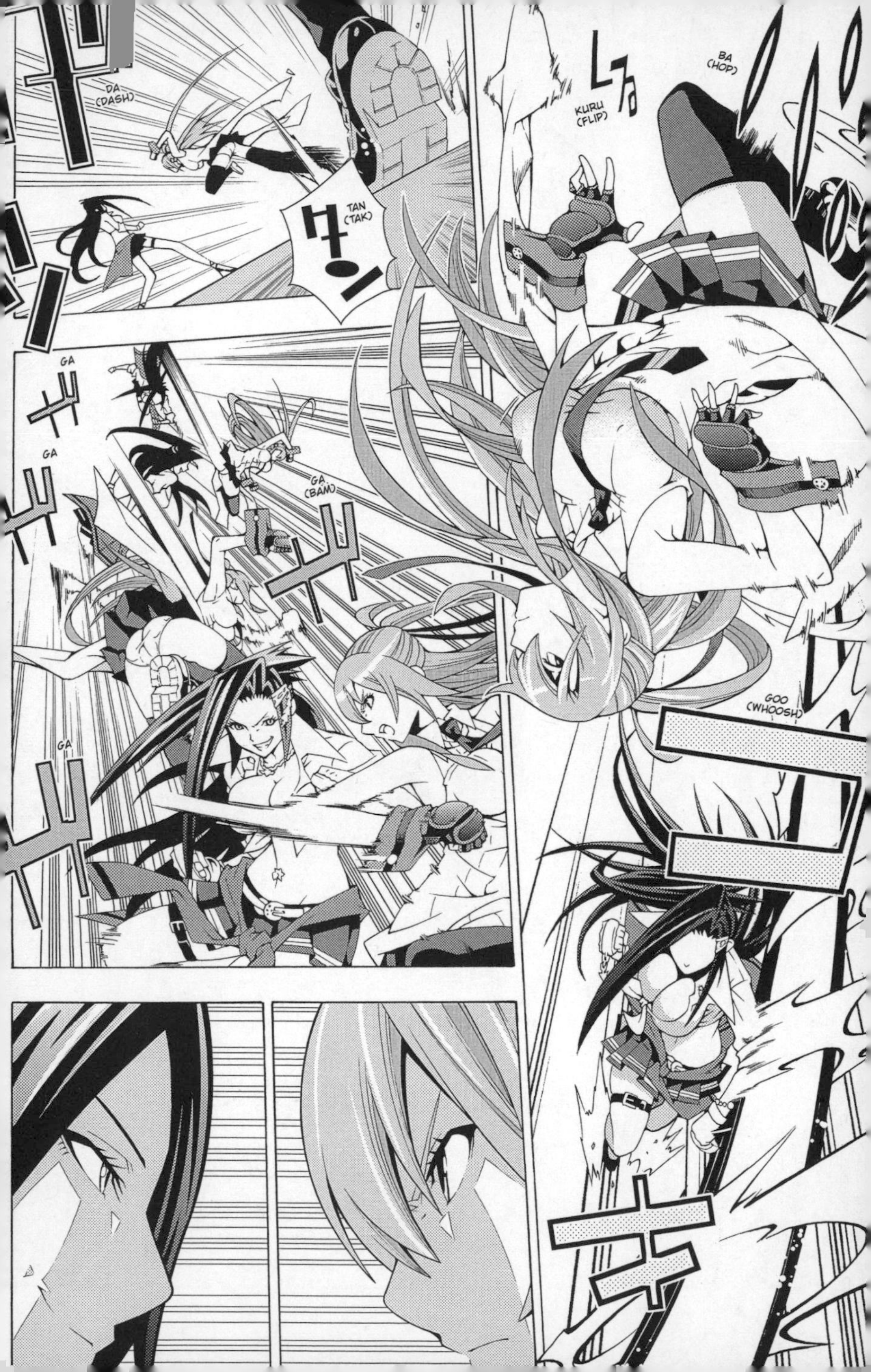

BA (HOP)
KURU (FLIP)
GOO (WHOOSH)
TAN (TAK)
DA (DASH)
GA (BAM)
GA
GA
GA

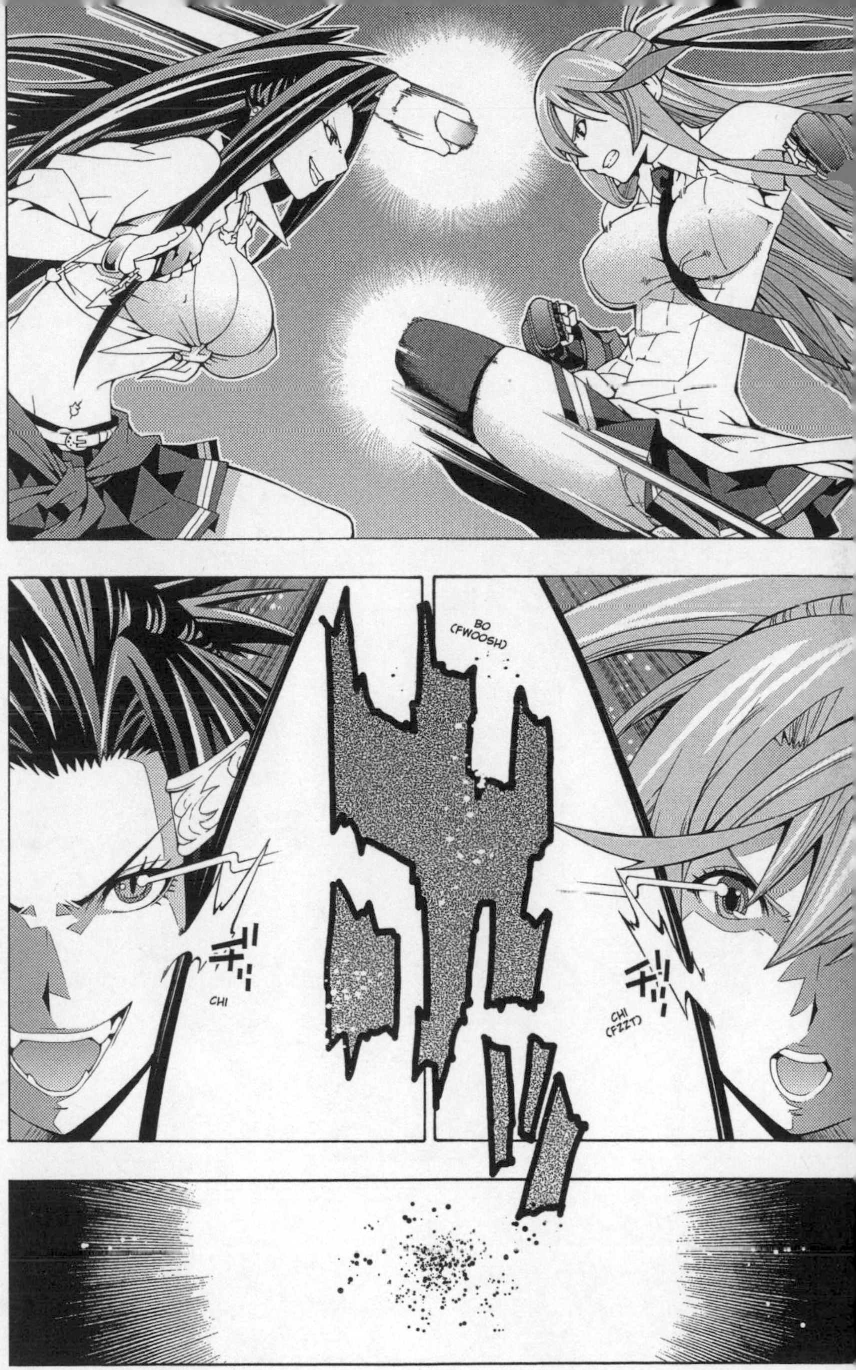
BO
(FWOOSH)
CHI
(FZZT)
CHI

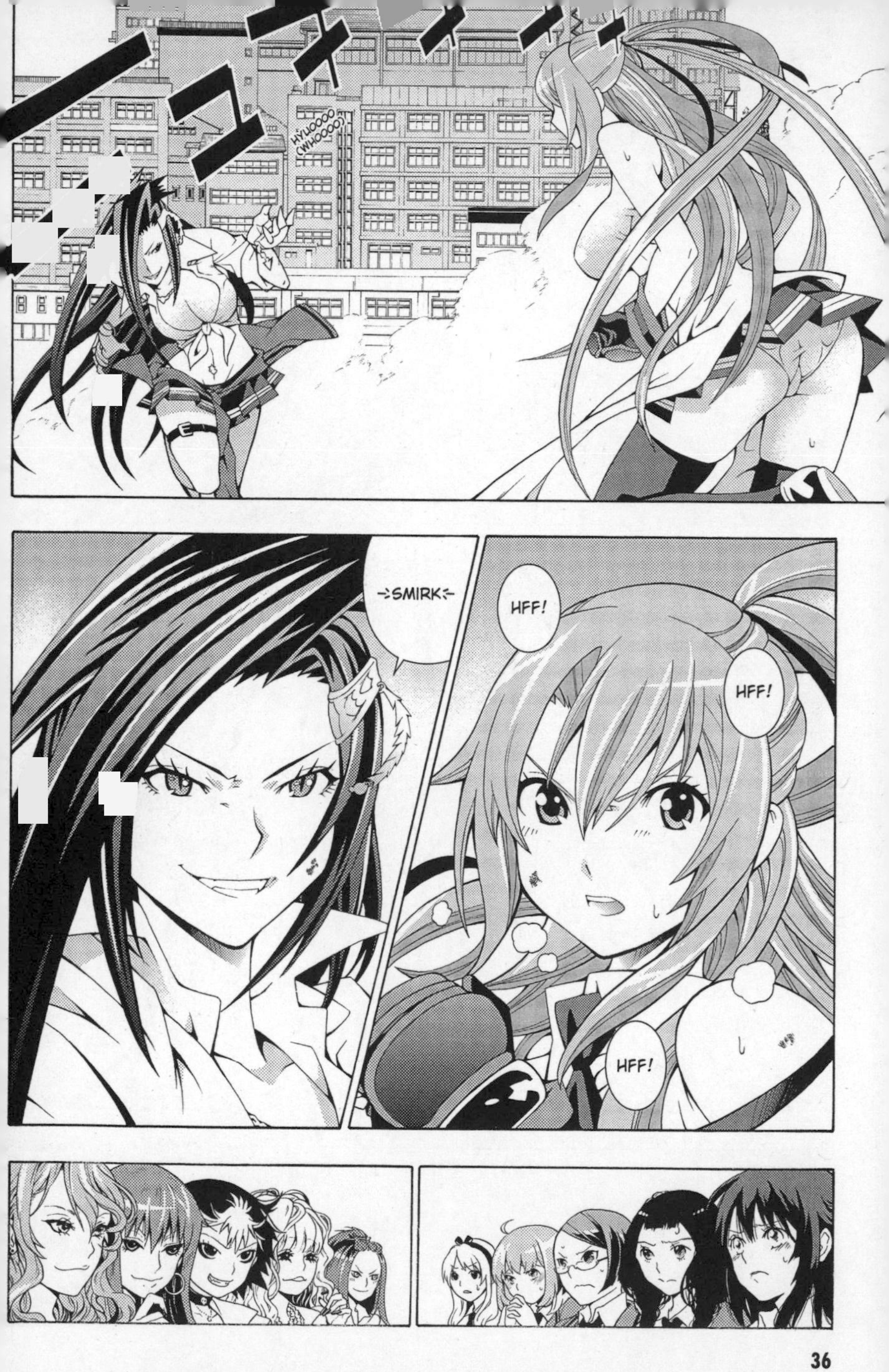
HYUOOOO
(WHOOOO)
HFF!
HFF!
HFF!
-SMIRK-

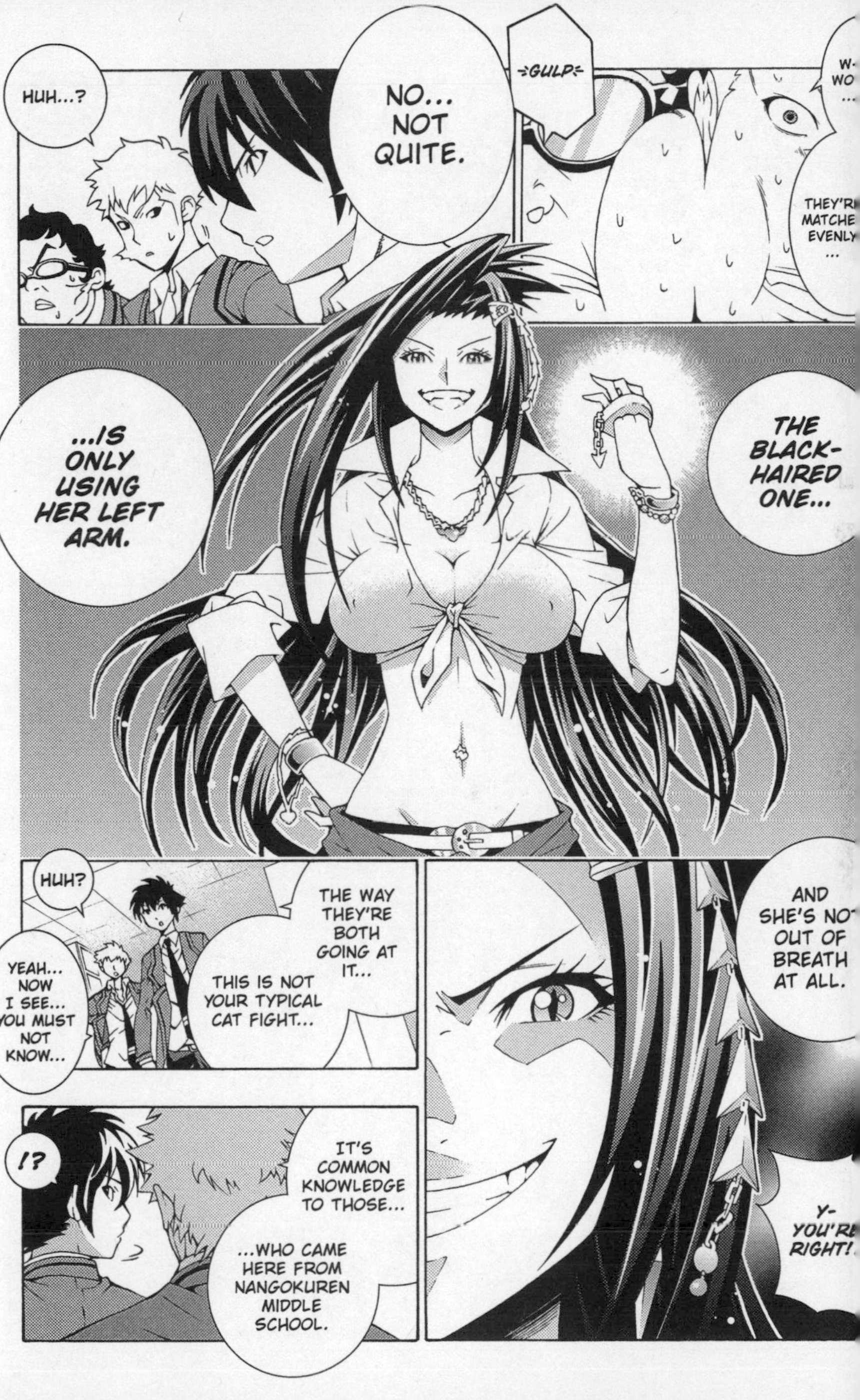

W-
WO
...
GULP
THEY'R MATCHE EVENLY ...
NO... NOT QUITE.
HUH...?
THE BLACK-HAIRED ONE...
...IS ONLY USING HER LEFT ARM.
AND SHE'S NO OUT OF BREATH AT ALL.
Y- YOU'R RIGHT!
THE WAY THEY'RE BOTH GOING AT IT...
THIS IS NOT YOUR TYPICAL CAT FIGHT...
HUH?
YEAH... NOW I SEE... YOU MUST NOT KNOW...
IT'S COMMON KNOWLEDGE TO THOSE...
...WHO CAME HERE FROM NANGOKUREN MIDDLE SCHOOL.
!?

LABEL: NANGOKUREN

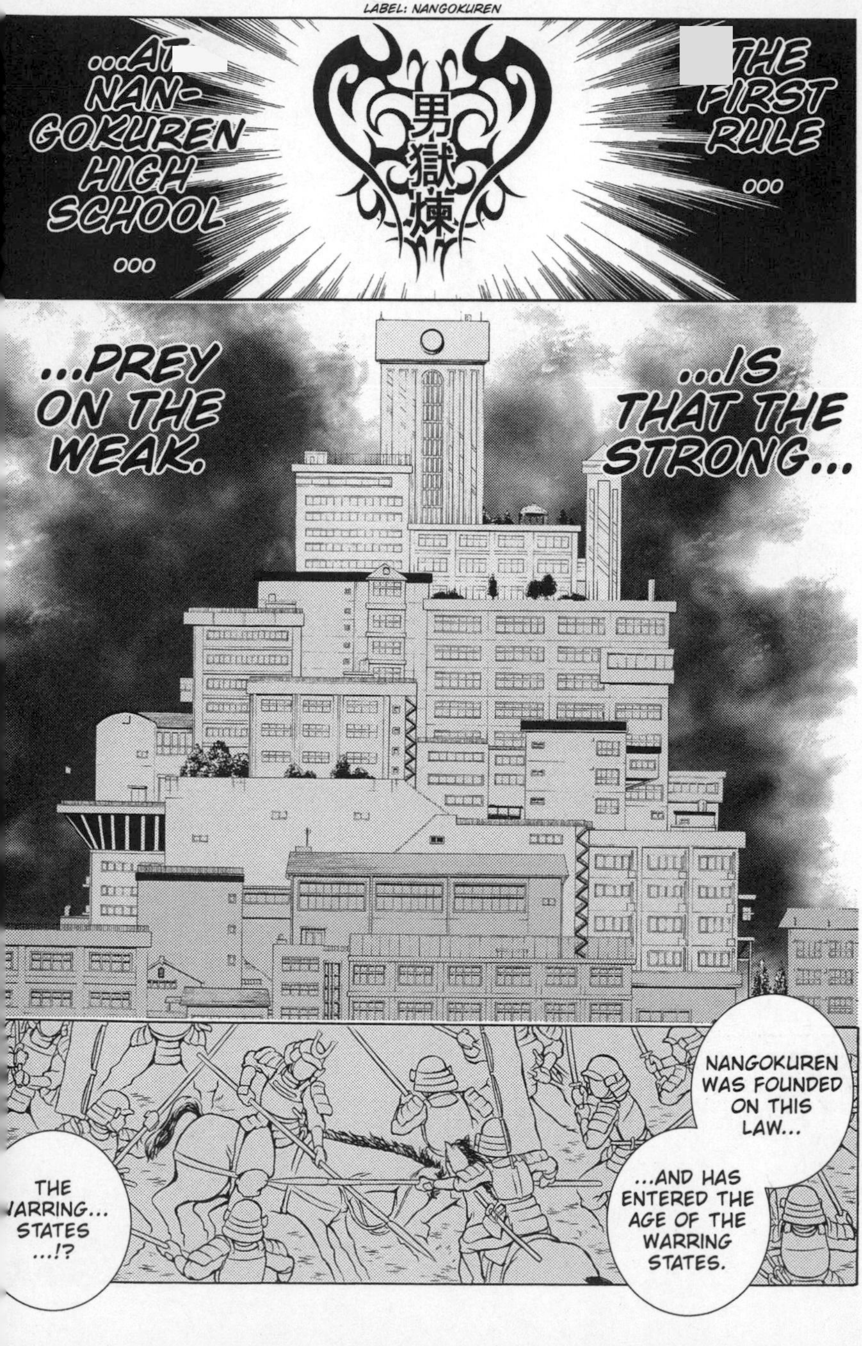
THE FIRST RULE...
...AT NANGOKUREN HIGH SCHOOL...
男獄煉
...IS THAT THE STRONG...
...PREY ON THE WEAK.
NANGOKUREN WAS FOUNDED ON THIS LAW...
...AND HAS ENTERED THE AGE OF THE WARRING STATES.
THE WARRING... STATES ...!?

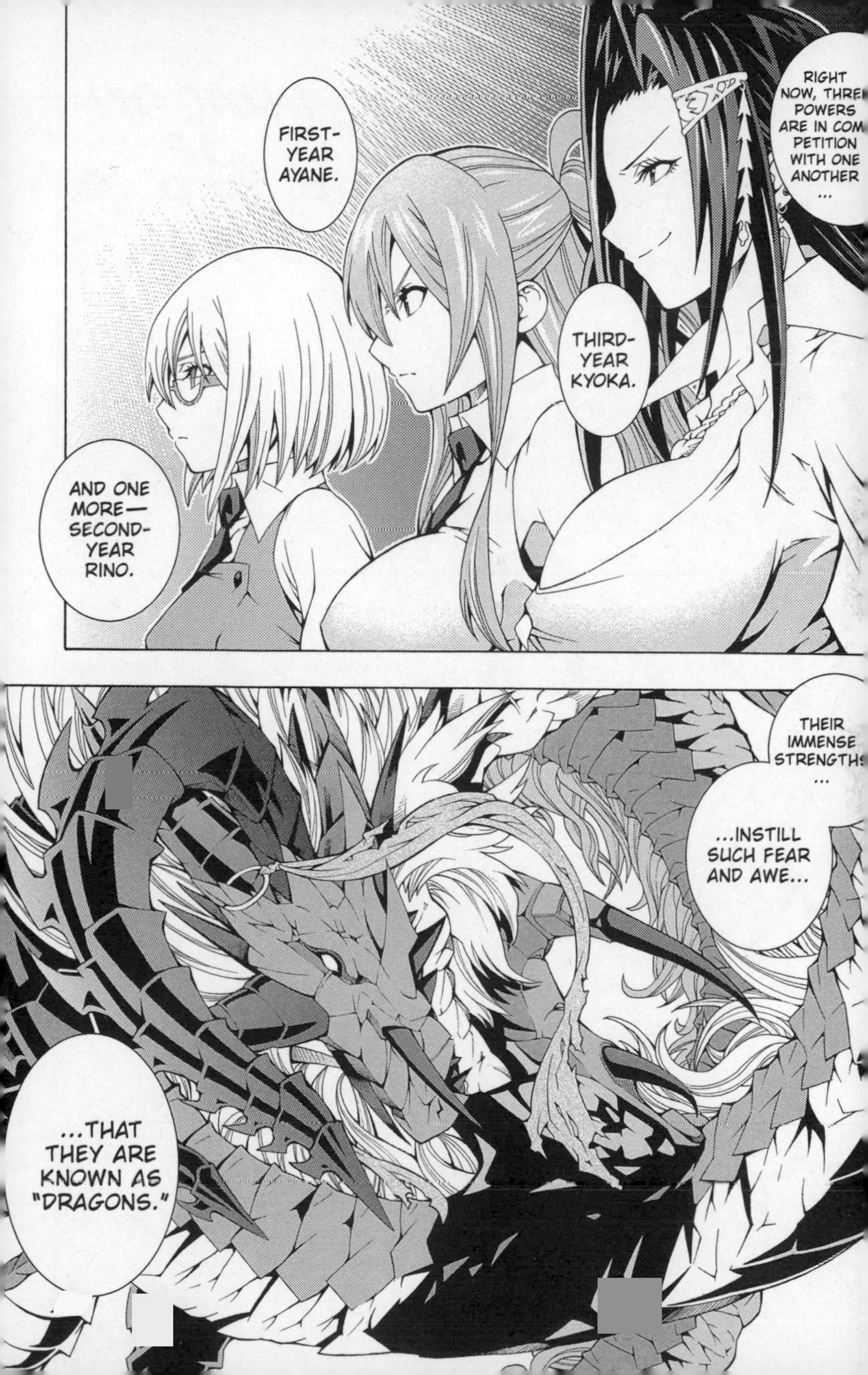
RIGHT NOW, THRE POWERS ARE IN COM PETITION WITH ONE ANOTHER ...
FIRST-YEAR AYANE.
THIRD-YEAR KYOKA.
AND ONE MORE—SECOND-YEAR RINO.
THEIR IMMENSE STRENGTHS ...
...INSTILL SUCH FEAR AND AWE...
...THAT THEY ARE KNOWN AS "DRAGONS."

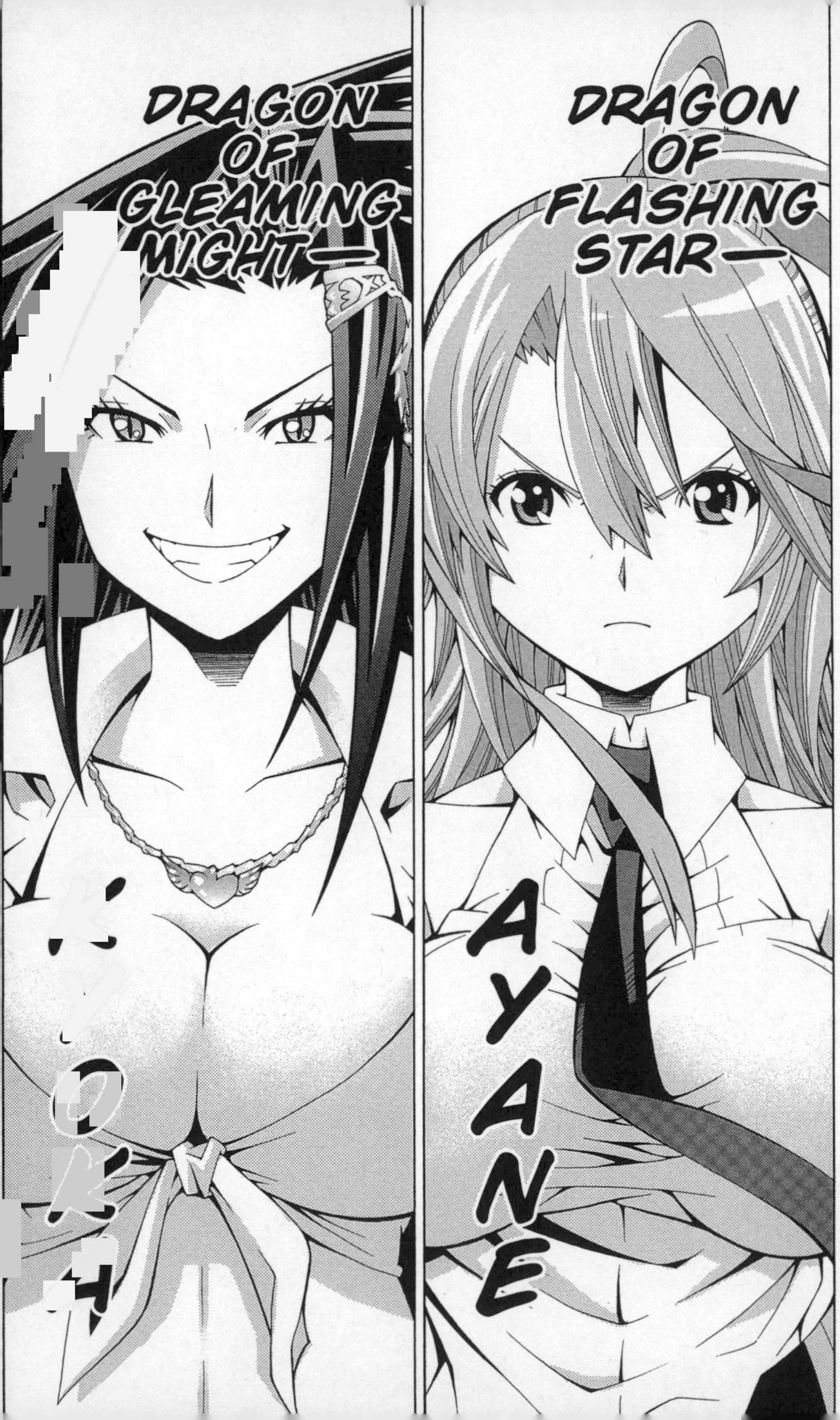
DRAGON OF FLASHING STAR—
AYANE
DRAGON OF GLEAMING MIGHT—

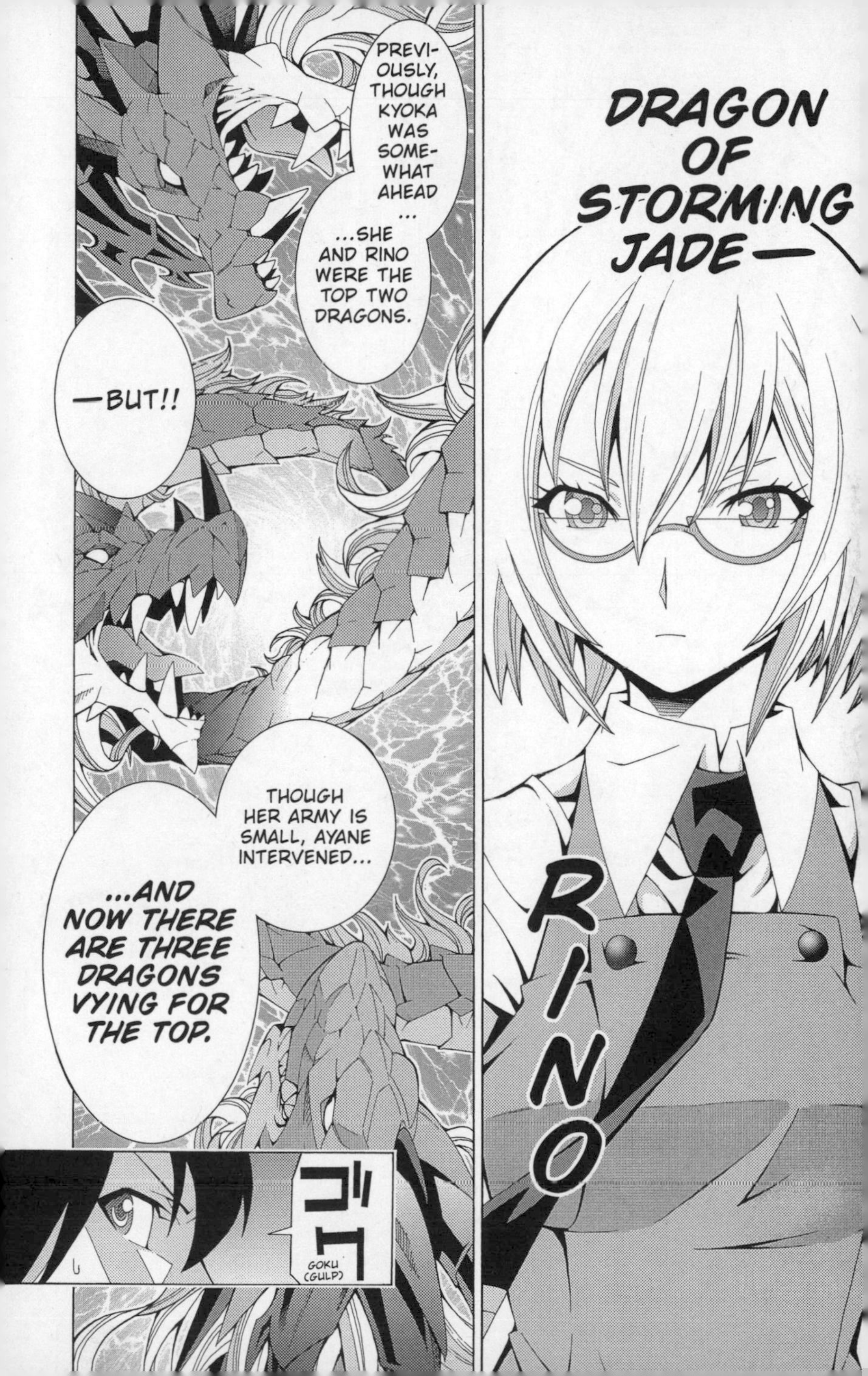
DRAGON OF STORMING JADE—
RINO
PREVIOUSLY, THOUGH KYOKA WAS SOMEWHAT AHEAD ...
...SHE AND RINO WERE THE TOP TWO DRAGONS.
—BUT!!
THOUGH HER ARMY IS SMALL, AYANE INTERVENED...
...AND NOW THERE ARE THREE DRAGONS VYING FOR THE TOP.
ゴク
GOKU (GULP)

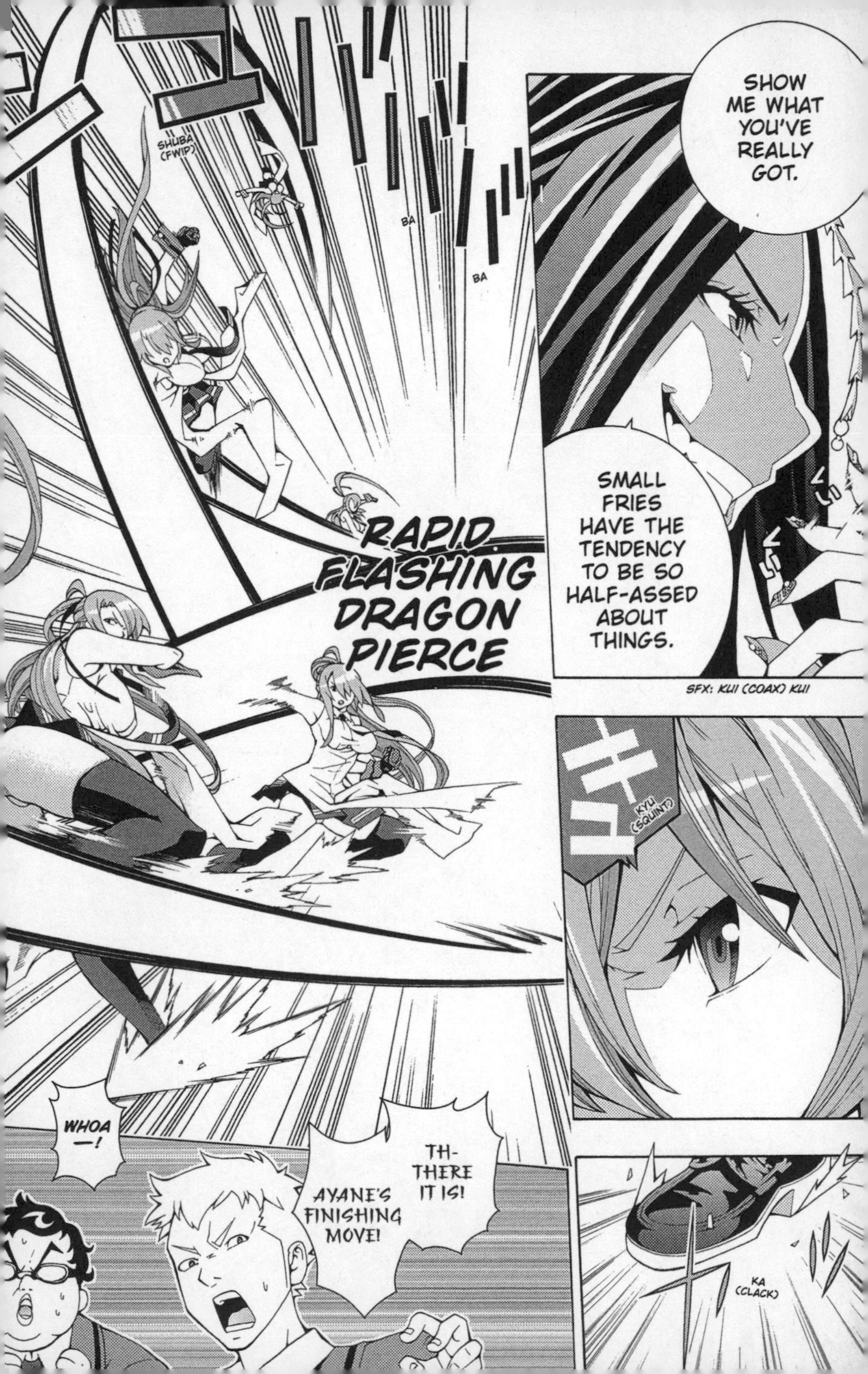
SHOW ME WHAT YOU'VE REALLY GOT.
SMALL FRIES HAVE THE TENDENCY TO BE SO HALF-ASSED ABOUT THINGS.
SFX: KUI (COAX) KUI
KYU (SQUINT)
KA (CLACK)
SHUBA (FWIP)
BA
BA
RAPID FLASHING DRAGON PIERCE
TH-THERE IT IS!
AYANE'S FINISHING MOVE!
WHOA—!

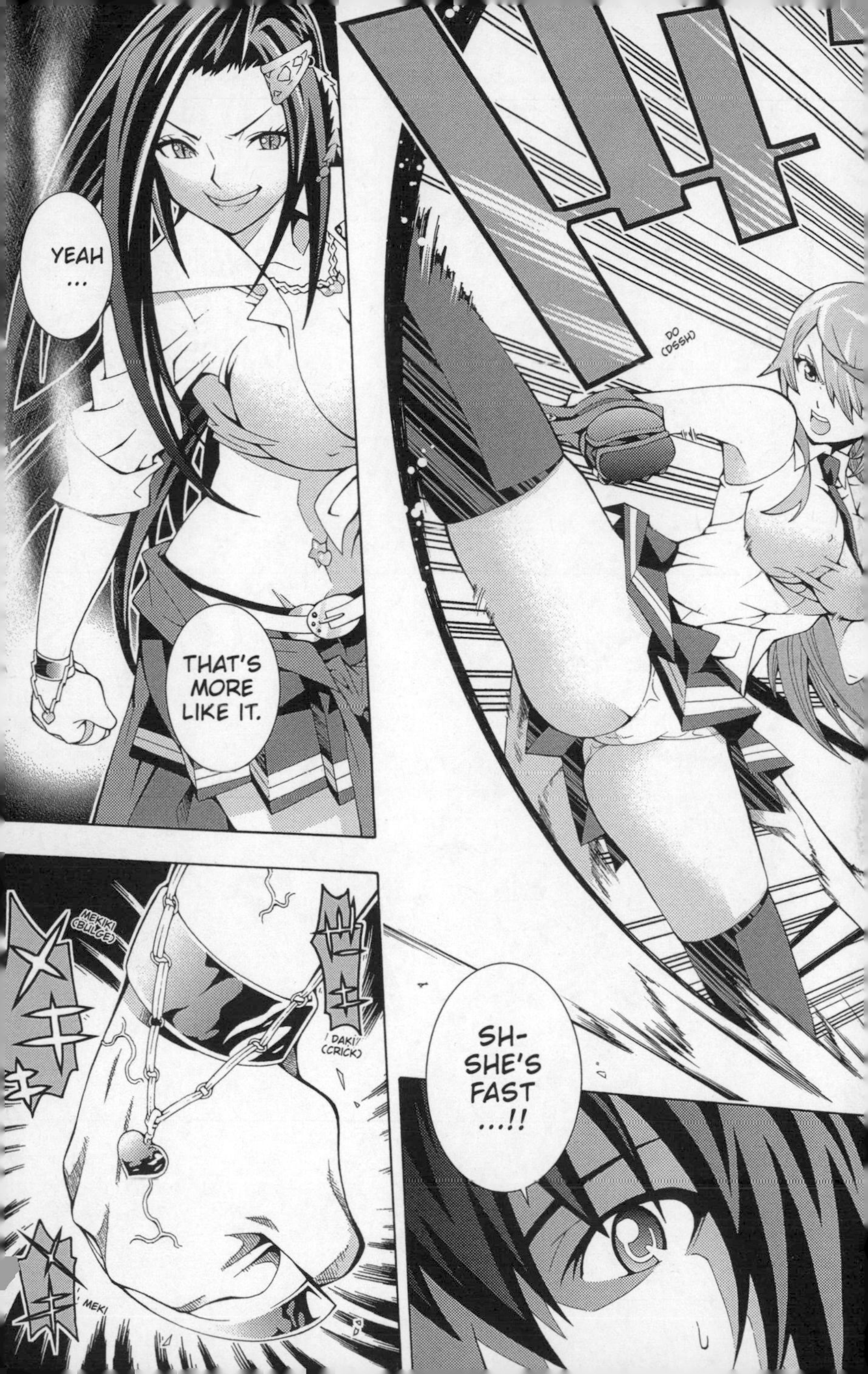
DO (DSSH)
YEAH ...
THAT'S MORE LIKE IT.
SH-SHE'S FAST ...!!
MEKIKI (BULGE)
DAKI (CRICK)
MEKI

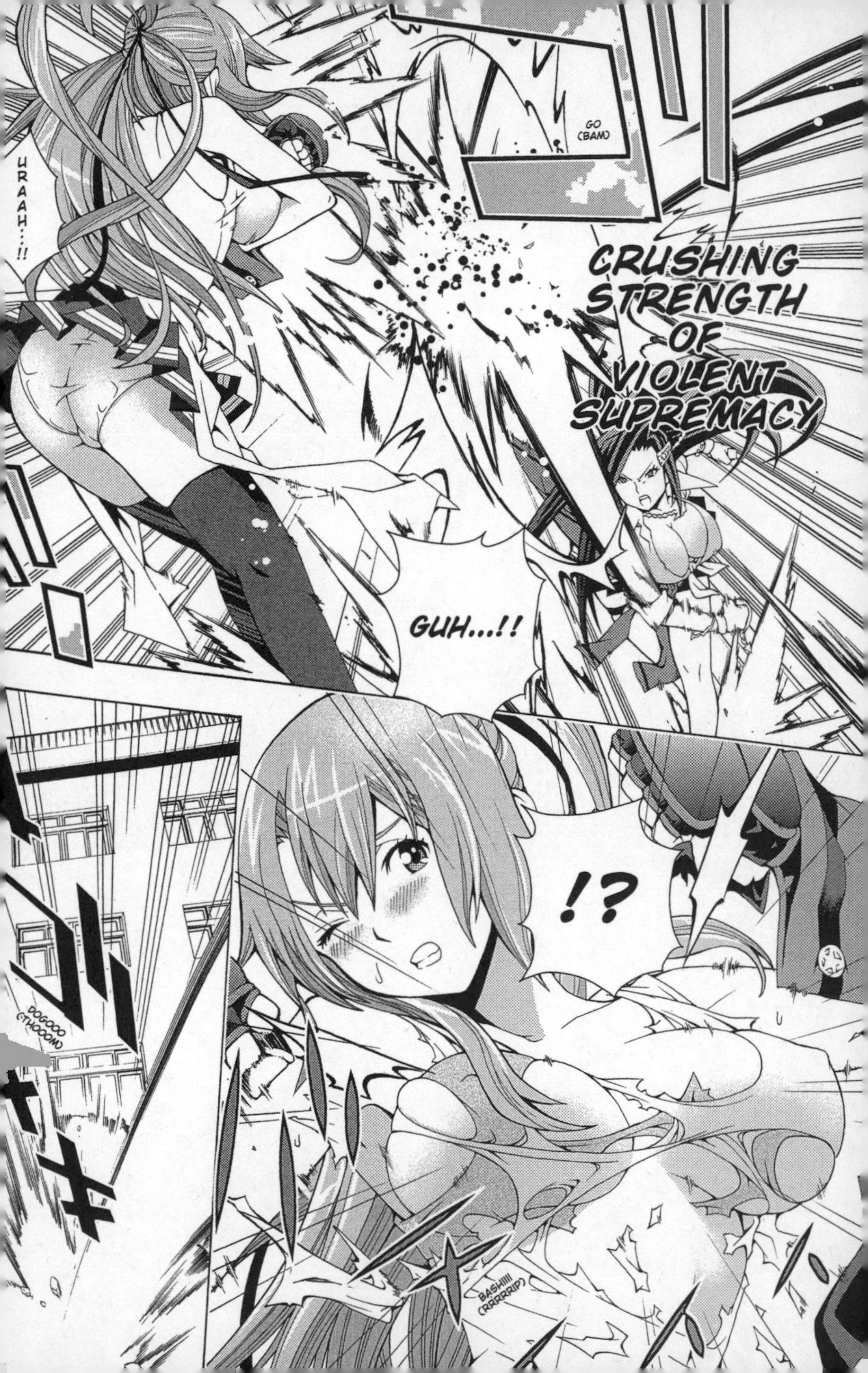
GO (BAM)
CRUSHING STRENGTH OF VIOLENT SUPREMACY
URAAAH...!!
GUH...!!
!?
DOGOOO (THOOOM)
BASHIIII (RRRRRIP)

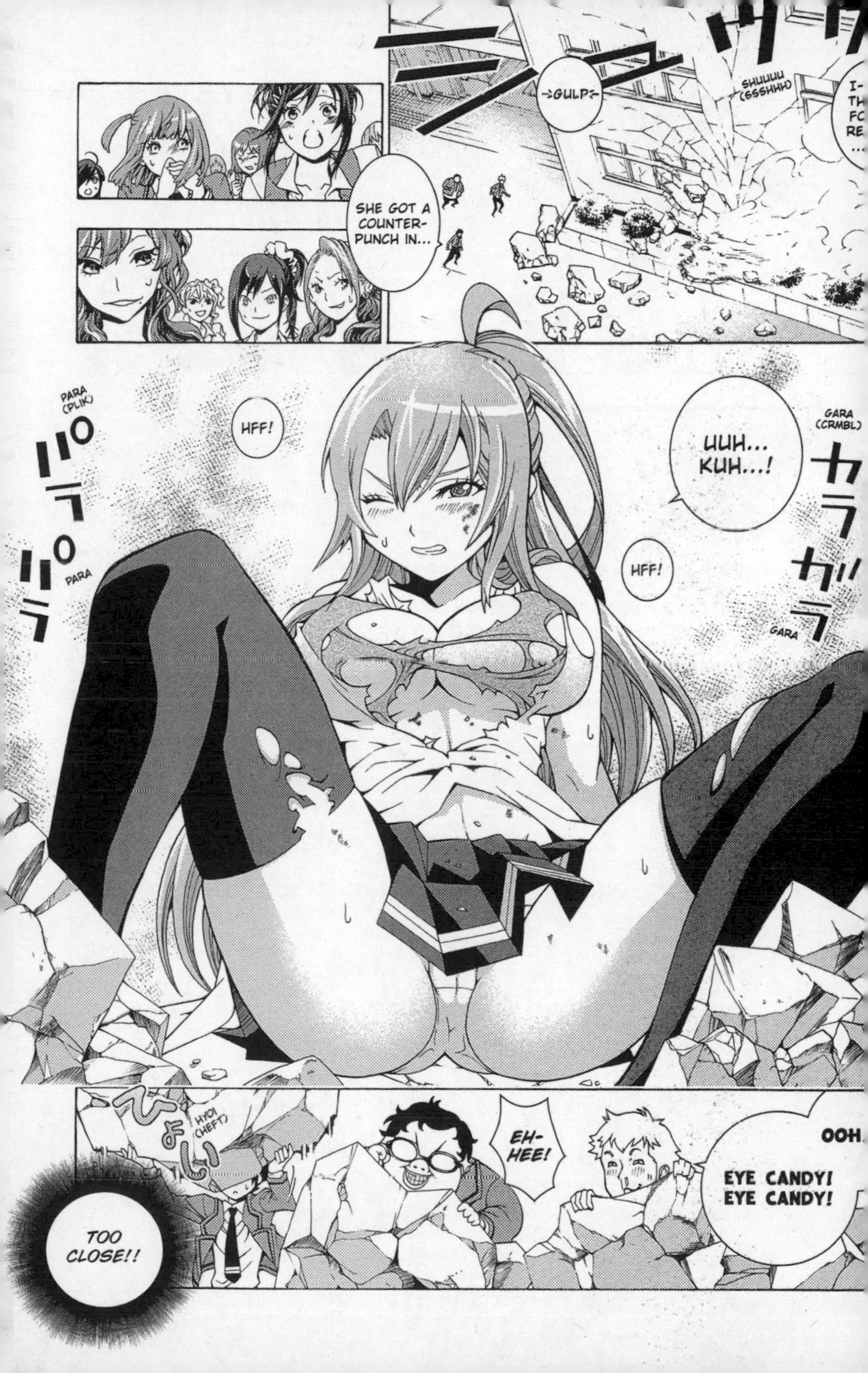
SHUUUU (SSSHHH)
GULP
SHE GOT A COUNTER-PUNCH IN...
GARA (CRMBL)
UUH... KUH...!
GARA
HFF!
HFF!
PARA (PLIK)
PARA
OOH.
EYE CANDY! EYE CANDY!
EH-HEE!
HYOI (HEFT)
TOO CLOSE!!

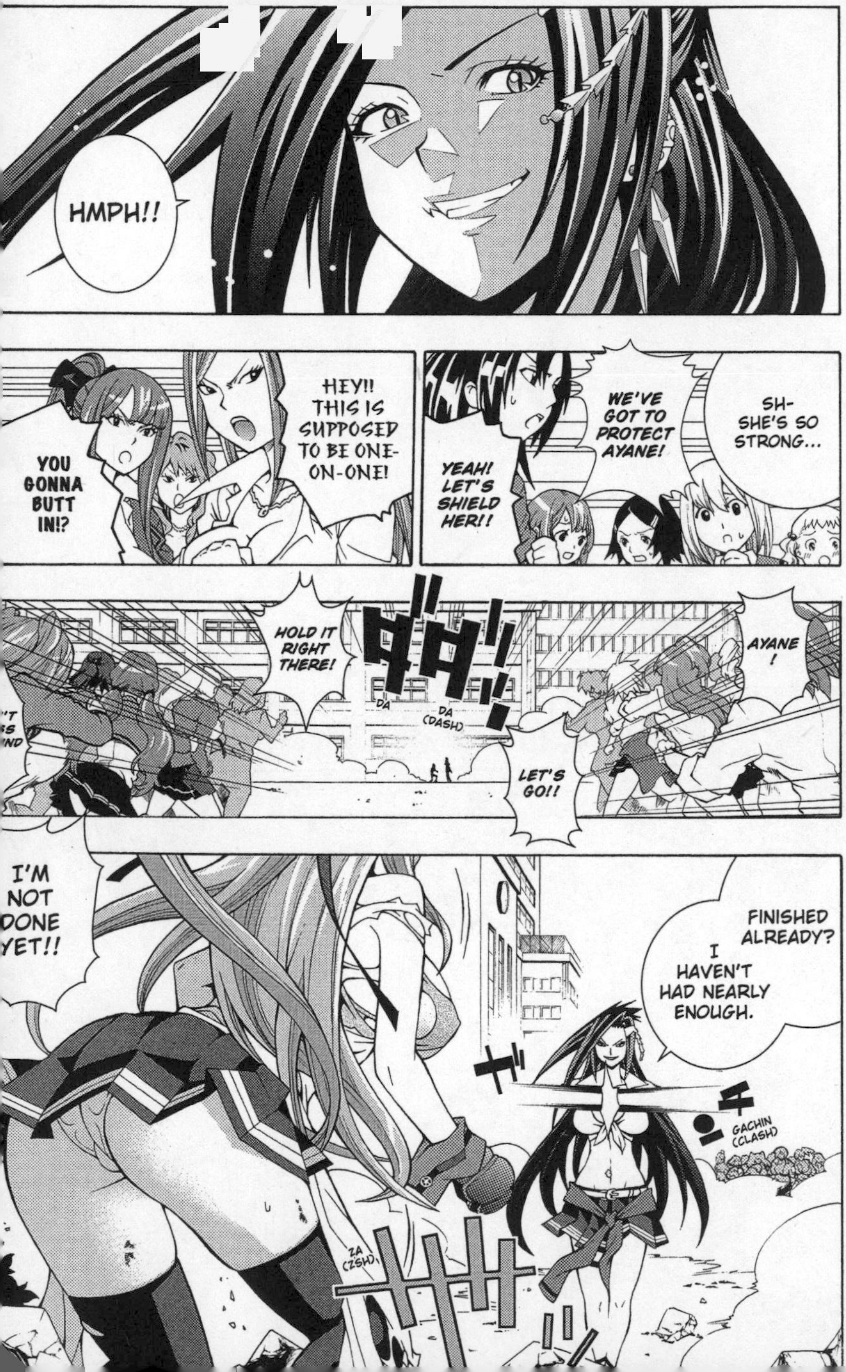
HMPH!!
SH- SHE'S SO STRONG...
WE'VE GOT TO PROTECT AYANE!
YEAH! LET'S SHIELD HER!!
HEY!! THIS IS SUPPOSED TO BE ONE-ON-ONE!
YOU GONNA BUTT IN!?
AYANE!
LET'S GO!!
DA DA (DASH)
HOLD IT RIGHT THERE!
FINISHED ALREADY? I HAVEN'T HAD NEARLY ENOUGH.
GACHIN (CLASH)
ZA (ZSH)
I'M NOT DONE YET!!

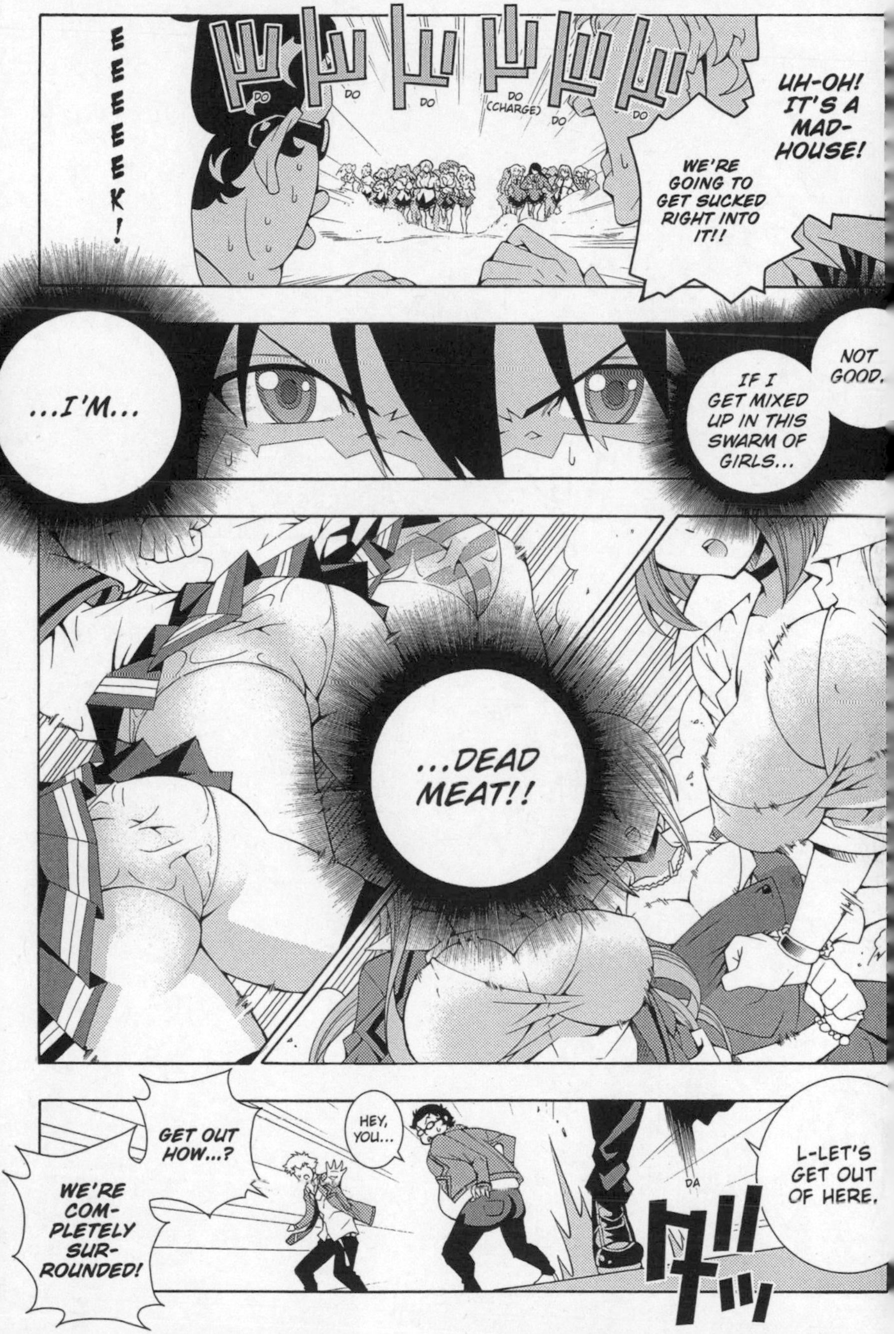
UH-OH! IT'S A MAD-HOUSE!
WE'RE GOING TO GET SUCKED RIGHT INTO IT!!
DO DO DO (CHARGE) DO DO DO
EEEEEEK!
NOT GOOD.
IF I GET MIXED UP IN THIS SWARM OF GIRLS...
...I'M...
...DEAD MEAT!!
L-LET'S GET OUT OF HERE.
DA
HEY, YOU...
GET OUT HOW...?
WE'RE COM-PLETELY SUR-ROUNDED!

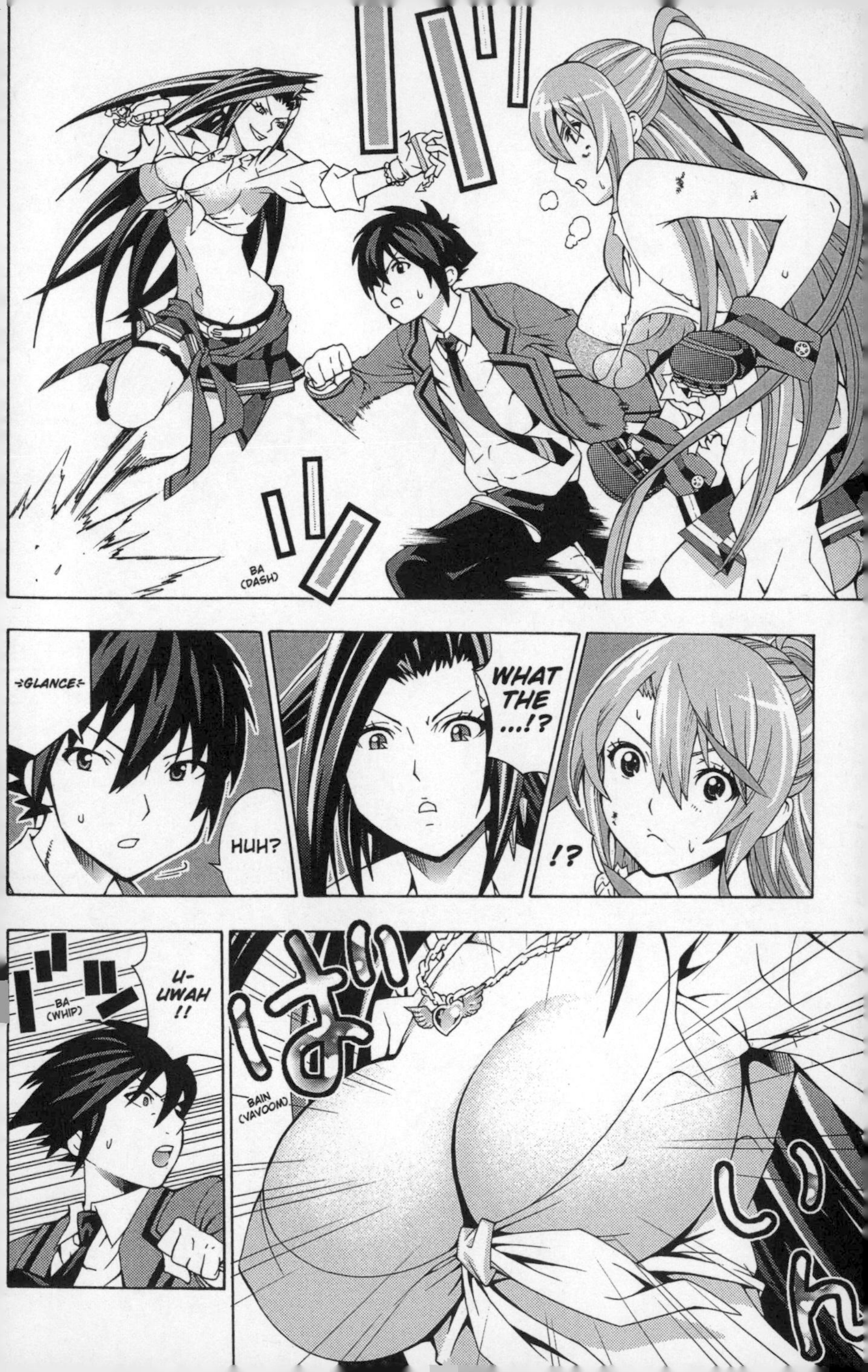
BA
(DASH)
!?
WHAT THE ...!?
≈GLANCE≈
HUH?
BAIN
(VAVOOM)
BA
(WHIP)
U-UWAH !!

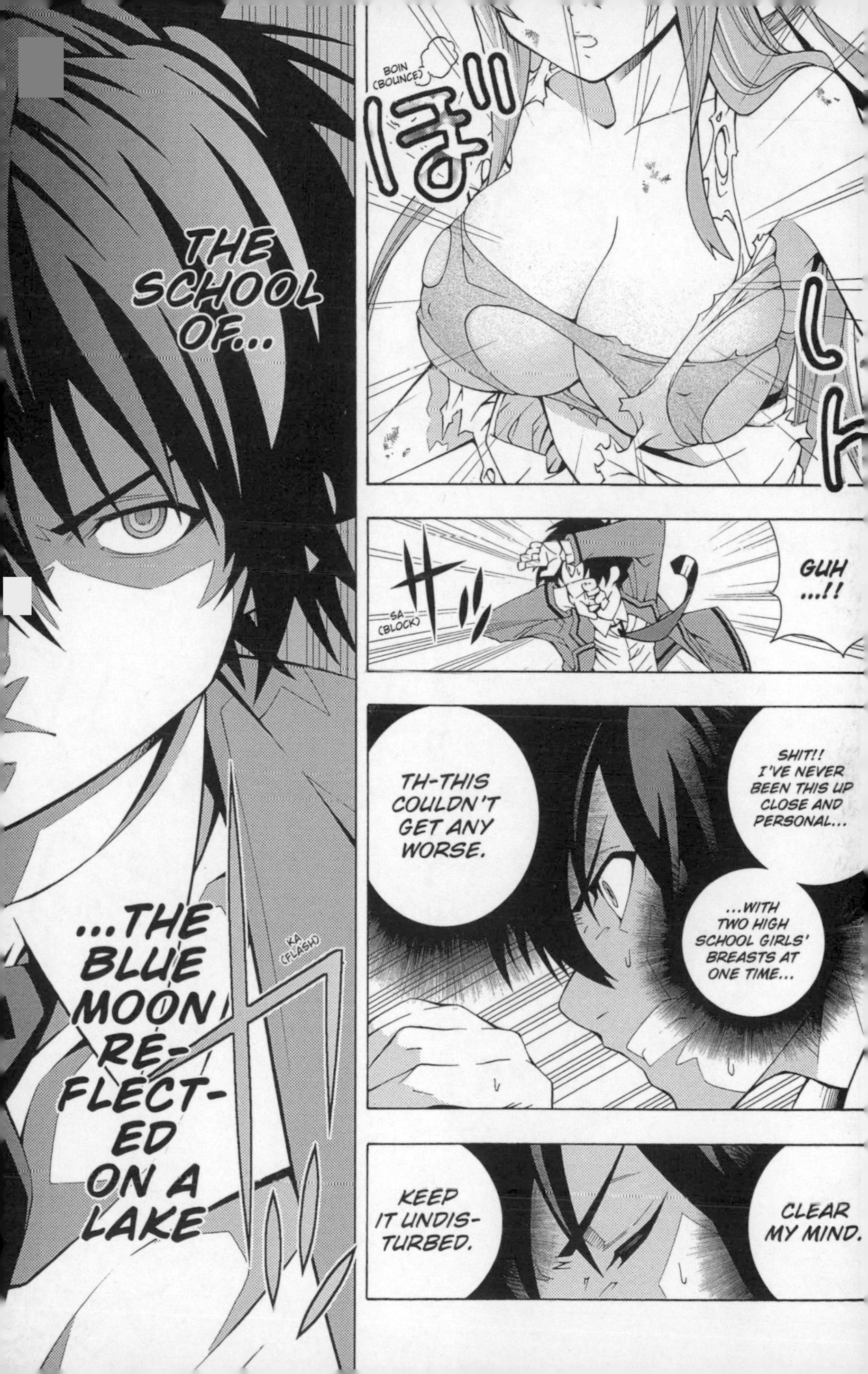
BOIN (BOUNCE)
SA (BLOCK)
GUH ...!!
SHIT!! I'VE NEVER BEEN THIS UP CLOSE AND PERSONAL...
...WITH TWO HIGH SCHOOL GIRLS' BREASTS AT ONE TIME...
TH-THIS COULDN'T GET ANY WORSE.
CLEAR MY MIND.
KEEP IT UNDIS-TURBED.
THE SCHOOL OF...
...THE BLUE MOON RE-FLECTED ON A LAKE
KA (FLASH)

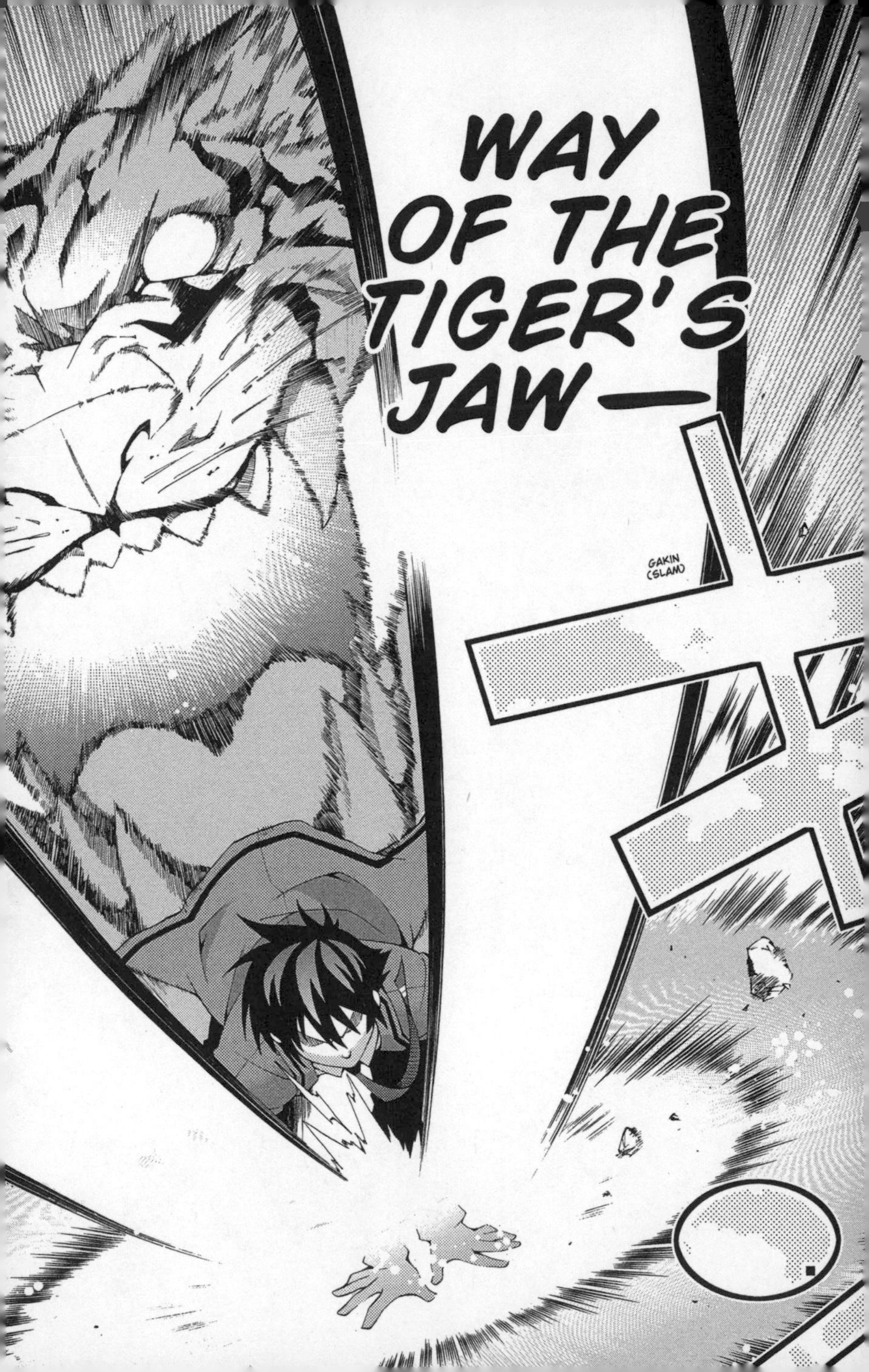
WAY OF THE TIGER'S JAW—
GAKIN (SLAM)

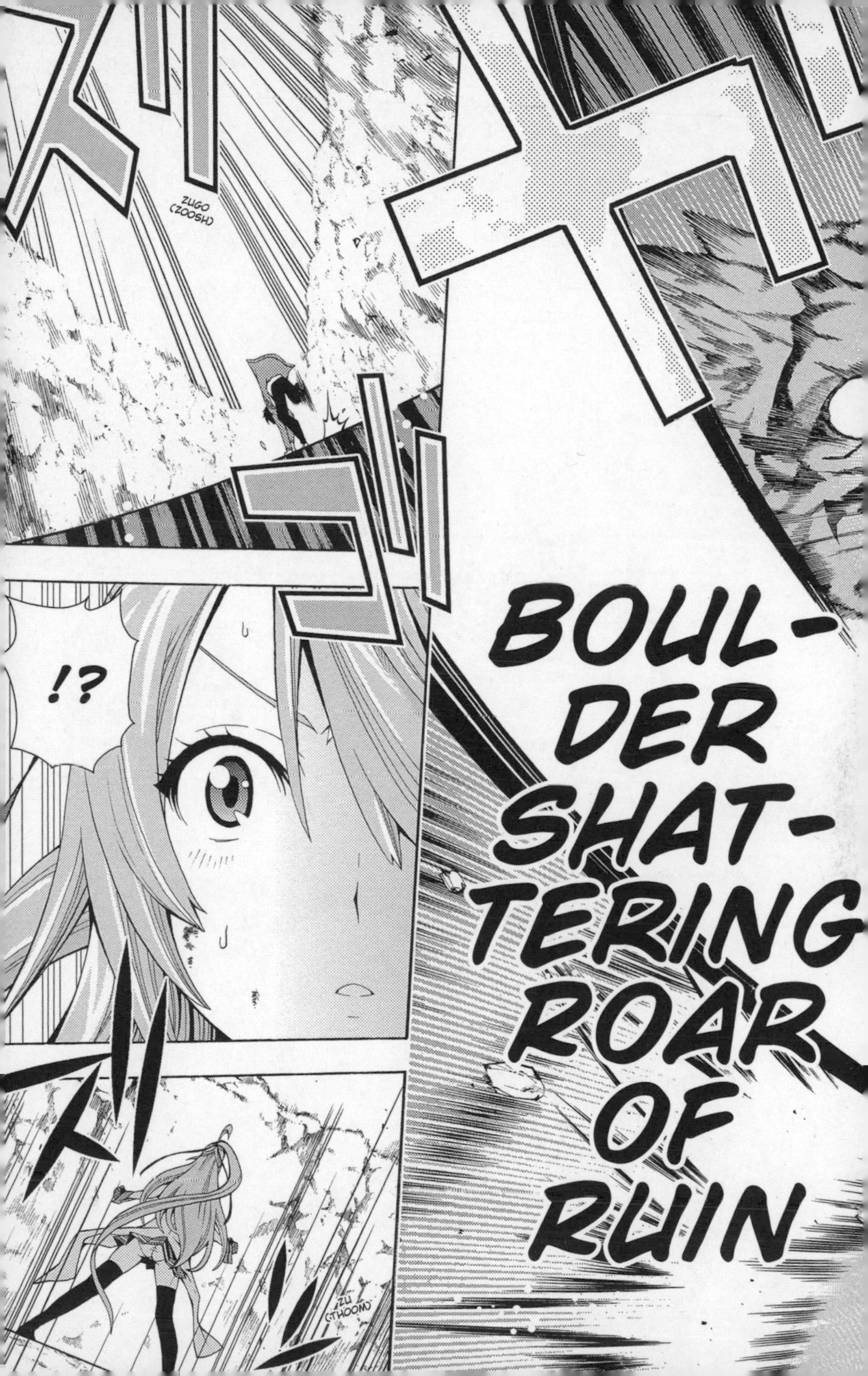
BOUL-
DER
SHAT-
TERING
ROAR
OF
RUIN
ZUGO (ZOOSH)
!?
ZU (THOOM)

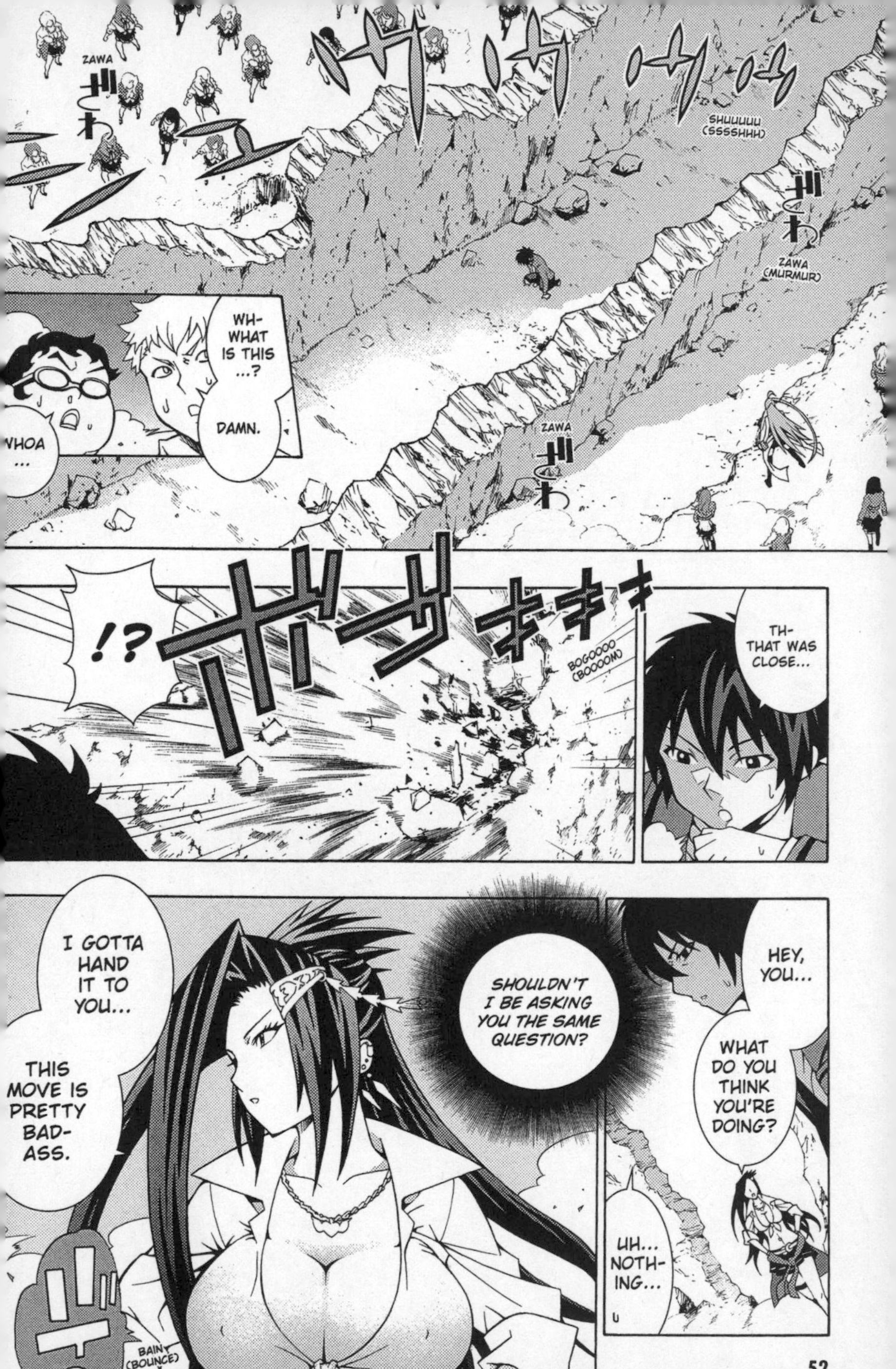
ZAWA
SHUUUUU (SSSSHHH)
ZAWA (MURMUR)
ZAWA
WH- WHAT IS THIS ...?
DAMN.
WHOA ...
TH- THAT WAS CLOSE...
!?
BOGOOOO (BOOOOM)
HEY, YOU...
WHAT DO YOU THINK YOU'RE DOING?
UH... NOTHING...
SHOULDN'T I BE ASKING YOU THE SAME QUESTION?
I GOTTA HAND IT TO YOU...
THIS MOVE IS PRETTY BAD-ASS.
BAIN (BOUNCE)

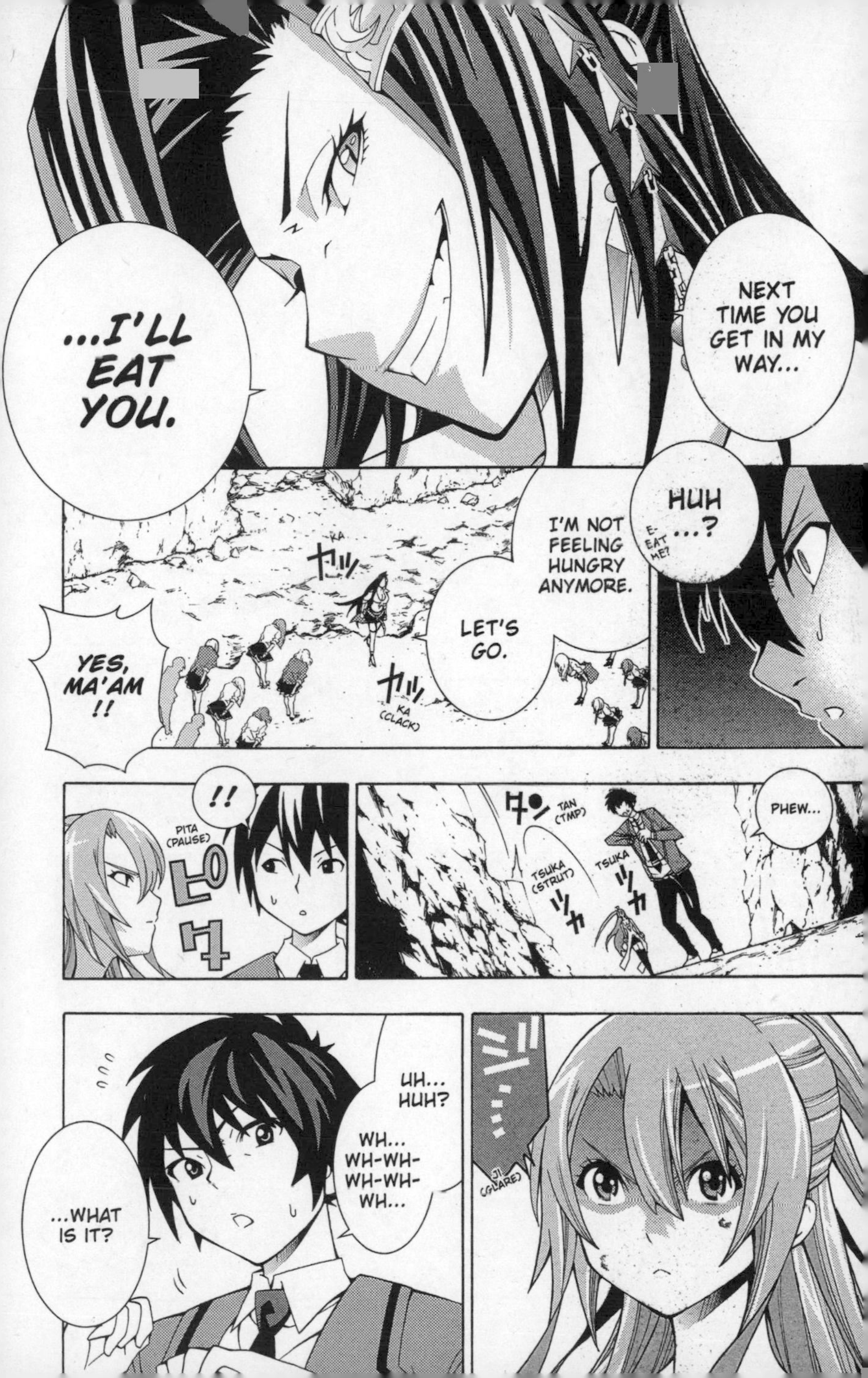
NEXT TIME YOU GET IN MY WAY...
...I'LL EAT YOU.
HUH ...?
E-EAT ME?
I'M NOT FEELING HUNGRY ANYMORE.
LET'S GO.
KA
KA (CLACK)
YES, MA'AM !!
PHEW...
TAN (TMP)
TSUKA
TSUKA (STRUT)
!!
PITA (PAUSE)
JI (GLARE)
UH... HUH?
WH... WH-WH-WH-WH-WH...
...WHAT IS IT?

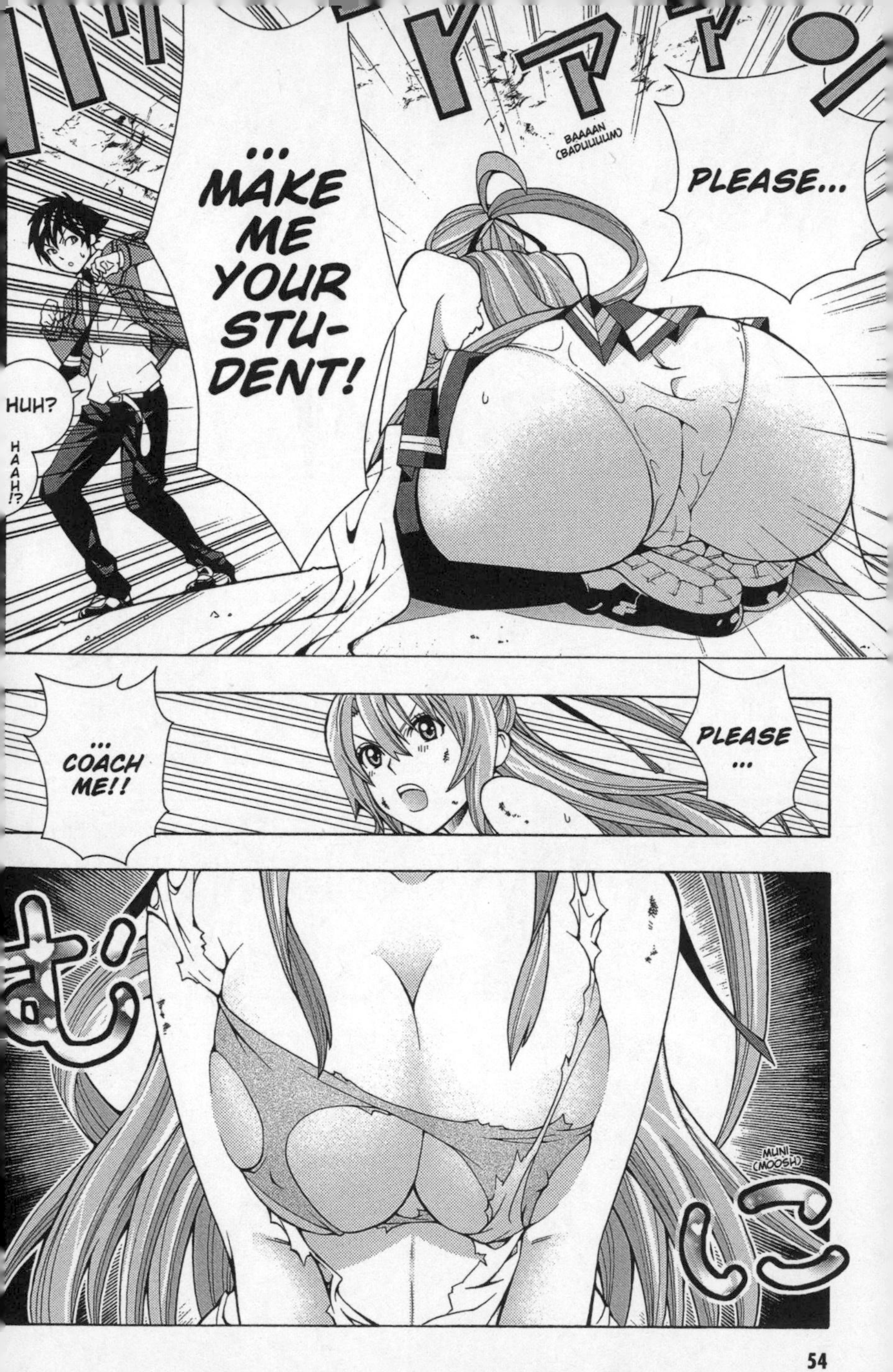

PLEASE...
BAAAAN (BADUUUUUM)
...MAKE ME YOUR STU-DENT!
HUH?
HAAAH!?
PLEASE...
...COACH ME!!
MUNI (MOOSH)

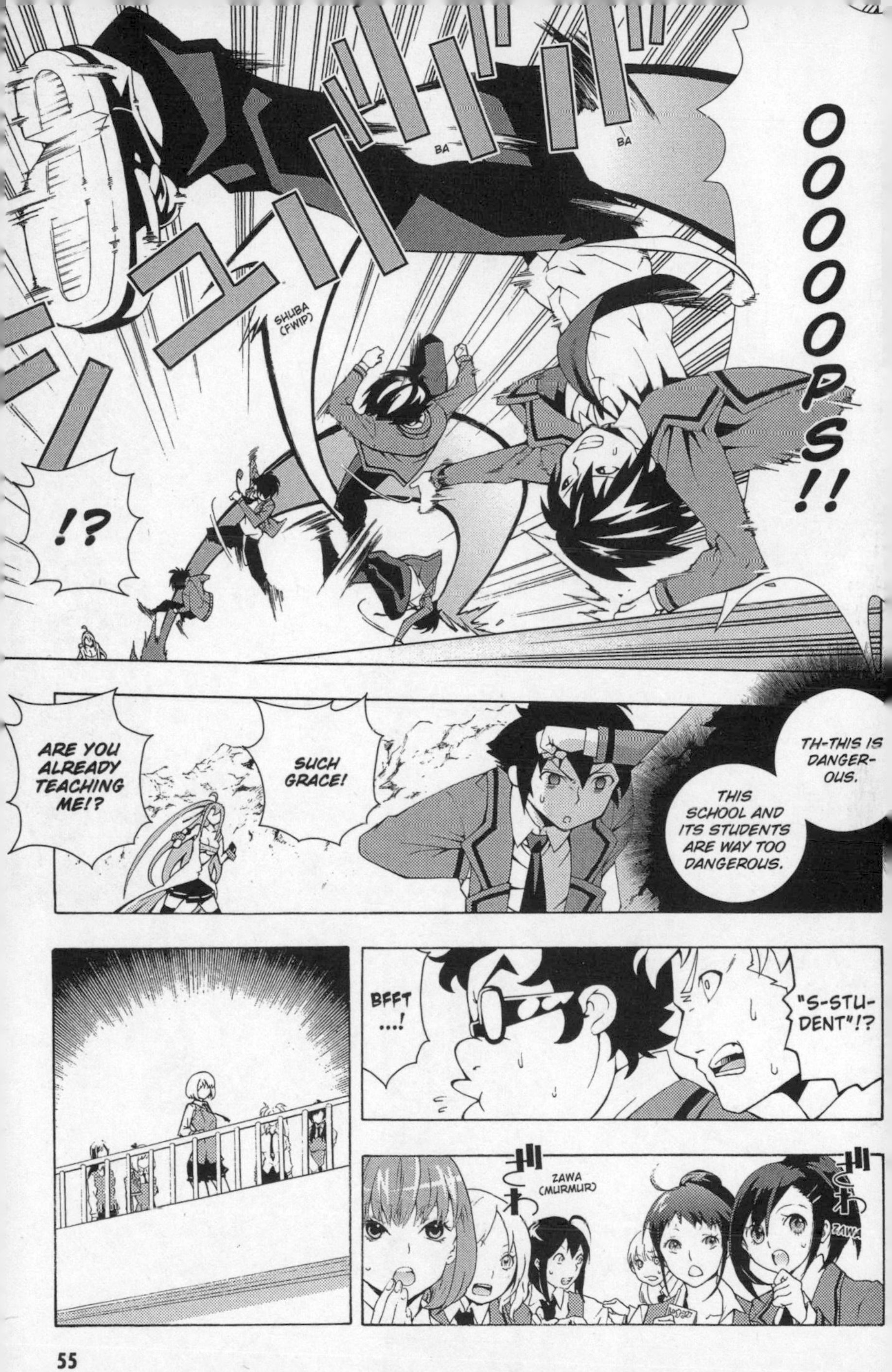
OOOOOOPS!!
BA
BA
SHUBA (FWIP)
!?
TH-THIS IS DANGER-OUS.
THIS SCHOOL AND ITS STUDENTS ARE WAY TOO DANGEROUS.
SUCH GRACE!
ARE YOU ALREADY TEACHING ME!?
"S-STU-DENT"!?
BFFT ...!
ZAWA
ZAWA (MURMUR)

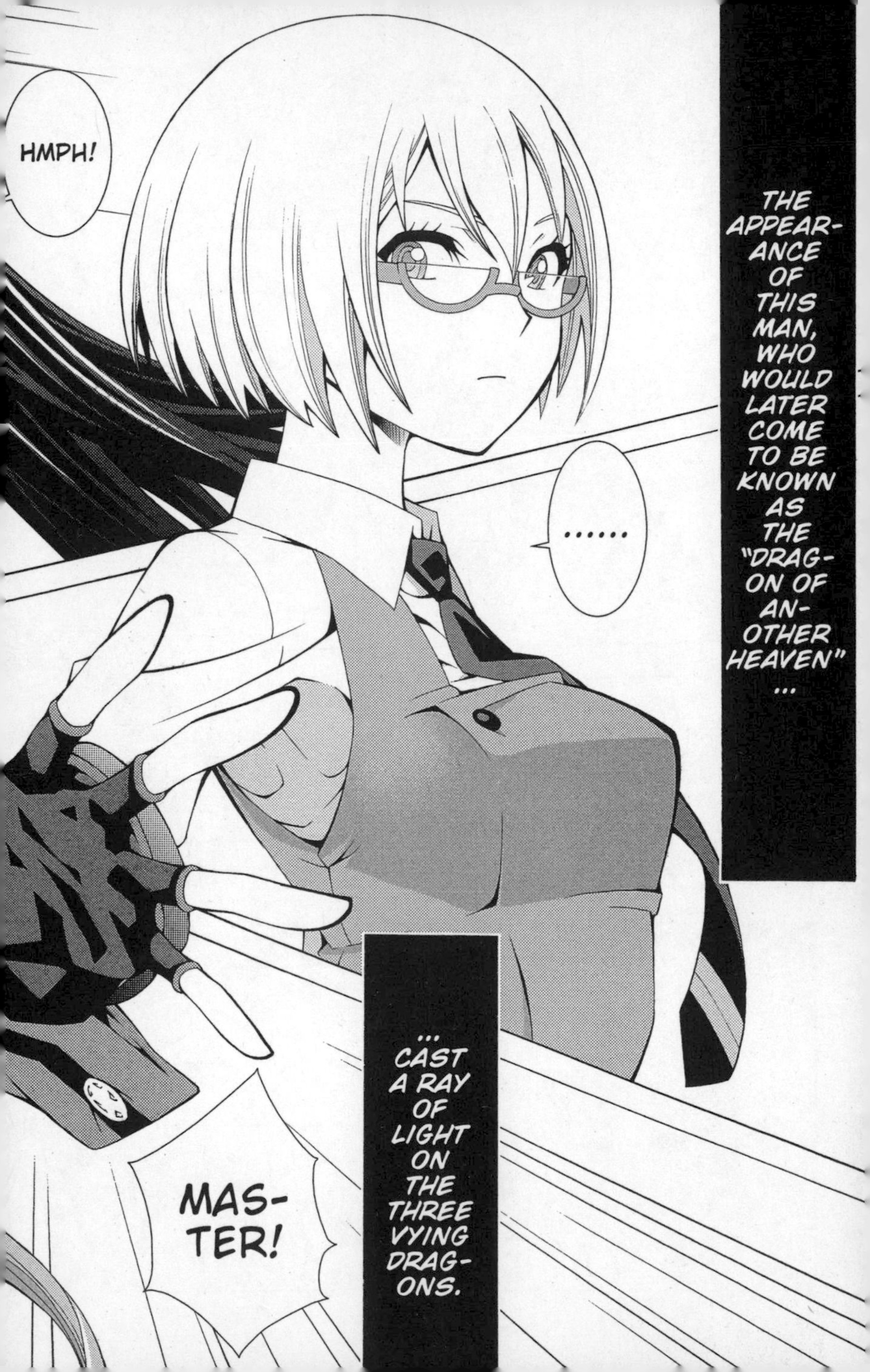
THE APPEARANCE OF THIS MAN, WHO WOULD LATER COME TO BE KNOWN AS THE "DRAGON OF ANOTHER HEAVEN"...
HMPH!
......
...CAST A RAY OF LIGHT ON THE THREE VYING DRAGONS.
MASTER!

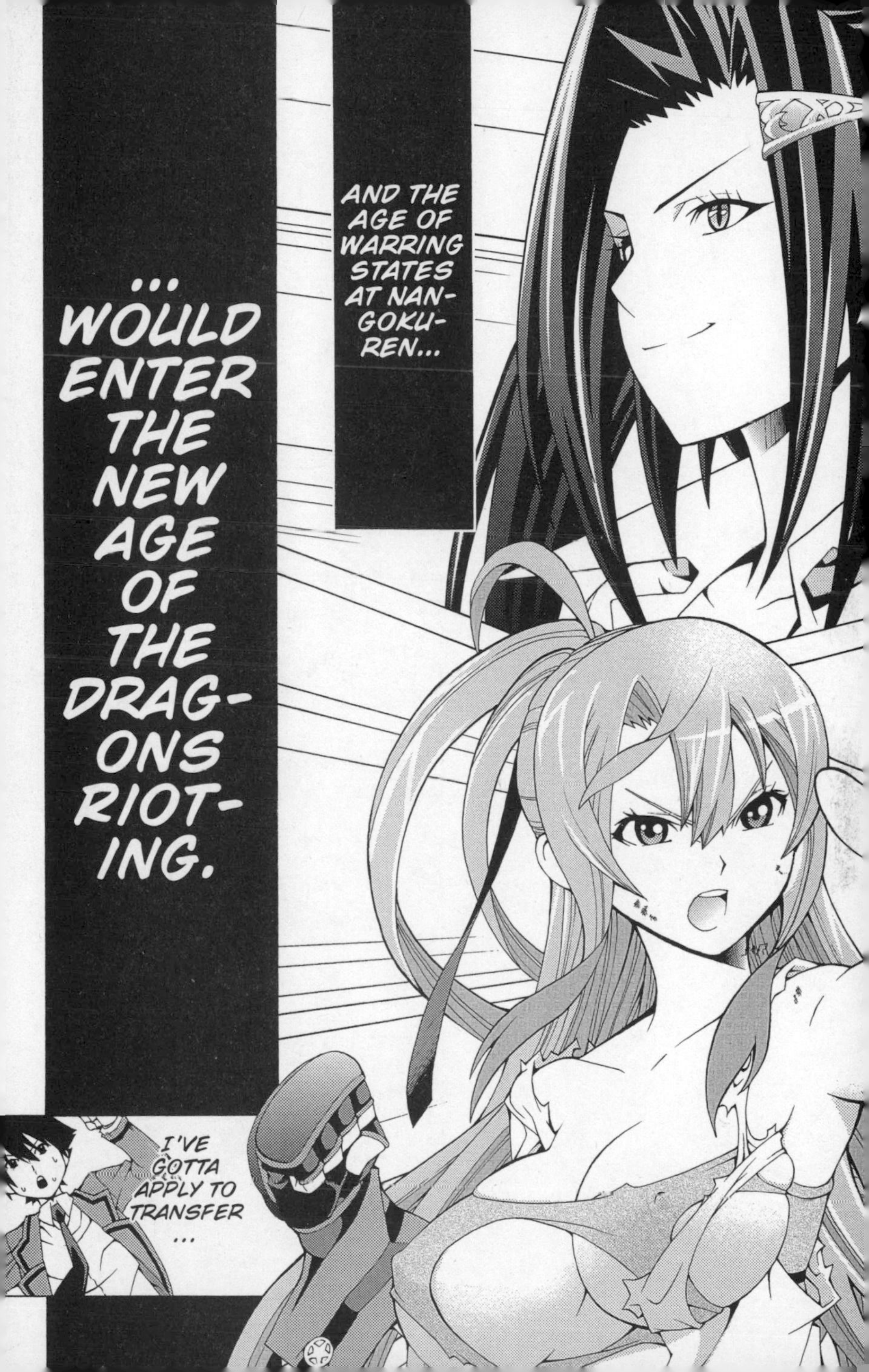
AND THE AGE OF WARRING STATES AT NAN-GOKU-REN...
... WOULD ENTER THE NEW AGE OF THE DRAG-ONS RIOT-ING.
I'VE GOTTA APPLY TO TRANSFER ...

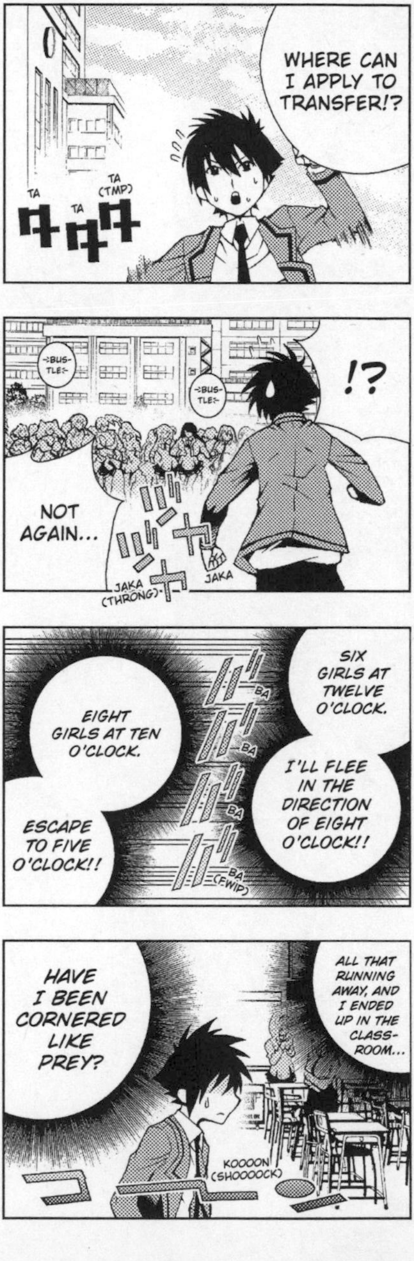
WHERE CAN I APPLY TO TRANSFER!?
TA (TMP)
TA
TA
!?
-BUSTLE-
-BUSTLE-
NOT AGAIN...
JAKA
JAKA (THRONG)
SIX GIRLS AT TWELVE O'CLOCK.
I'LL FLEE IN THE DIRECTION OF EIGHT O'CLOCK!!
EIGHT GIRLS AT TEN O'CLOCK.
ESCAPE TO FIVE O'CLOCK!!
BA
BA
BA
BA (FWIP)
ALL THAT RUNNING AWAY, AND I ENDED UP IN THE CLASS-ROOM...
HAVE I BEEN CORNERED LIKE PREY?
KOOOON (SHOOOOCK)

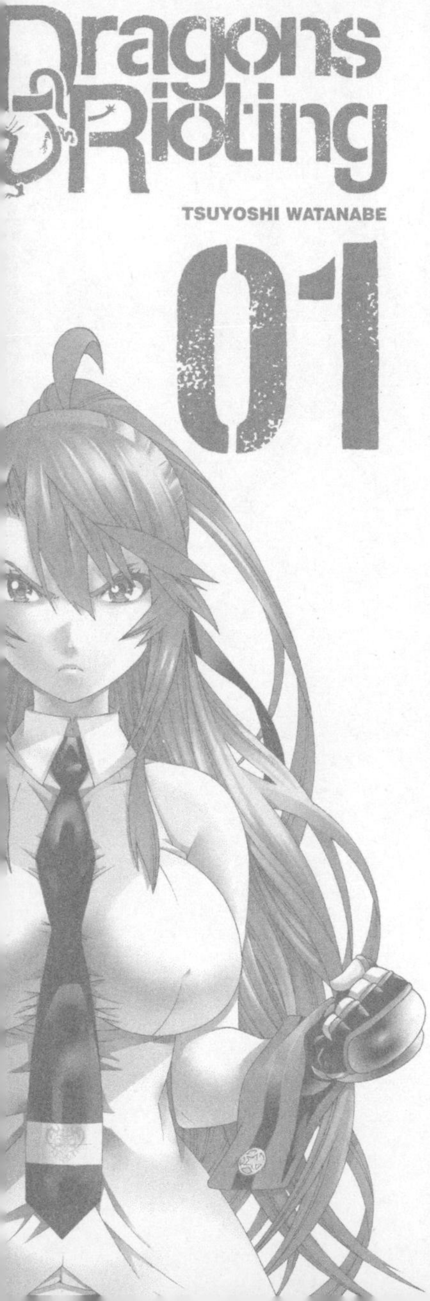
Dragons Rioting
TSUYOSHI WATANABE
01

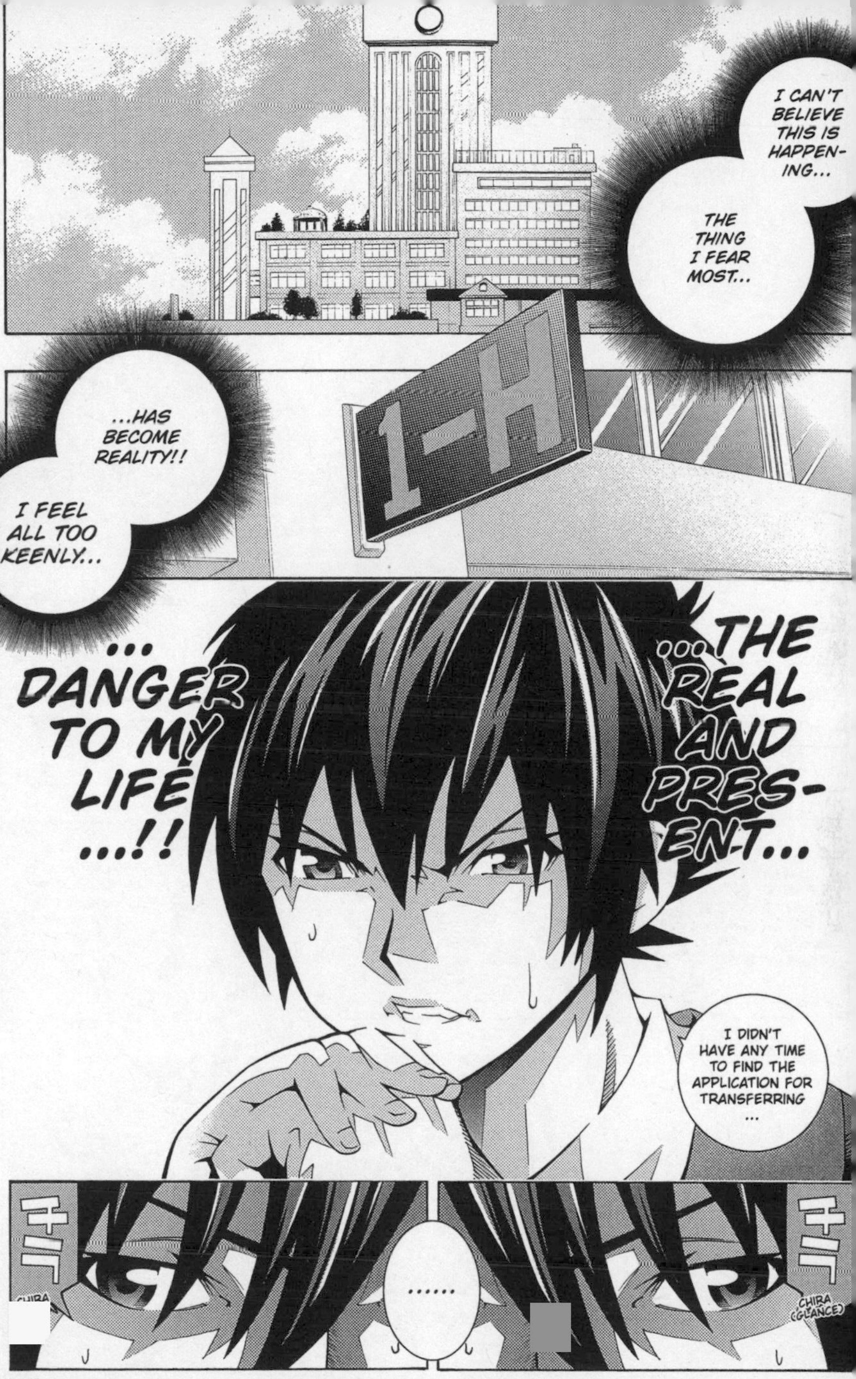
I CAN'T BELIEVE THIS IS HAPPENING...
THE THING I FEAR MOST...
1-H
...HAS BECOME REALITY!!
I FEEL ALL TOO KEENLY...
...THE REAL AND PRESENT...
...DANGER TO MY LIFE ...!!
I DIDN'T HAVE ANY TIME TO FIND THE APPLICATION FOR TRANSFERRING ...
チラ
CHIRA (GLANCE)
......
チラ
CHIRA

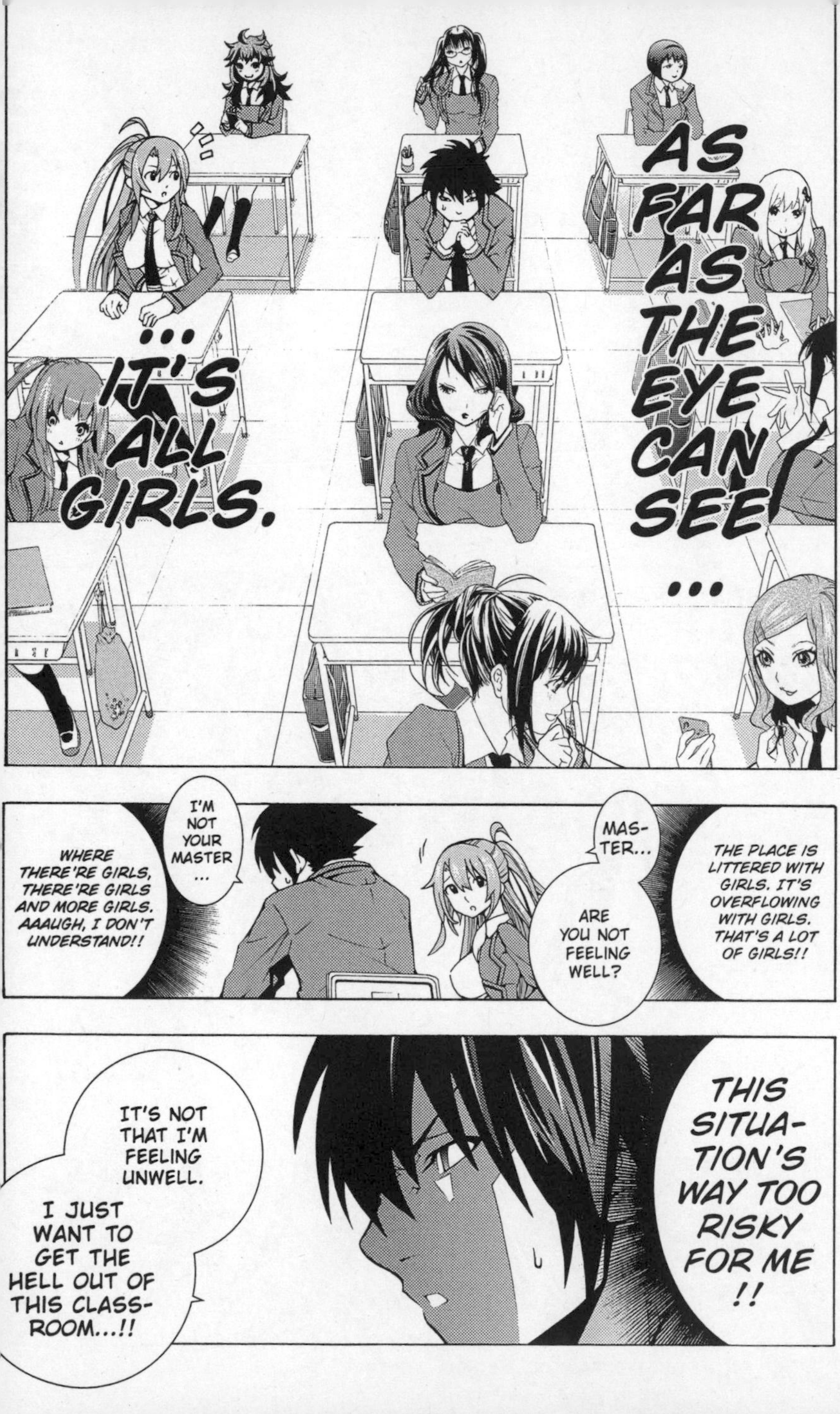
AS FAR AS THE EYE CAN SEE...
...IT'S ALL GIRLS.
THE PLACE IS LITTERED WITH GIRLS. IT'S OVERFLOWING WITH GIRLS. THAT'S A LOT OF GIRLS!!
MASTER...
ARE YOU NOT FEELING WELL?
I'M NOT YOUR MASTER...
WHERE THERE'RE GIRLS, THERE'RE GIRLS AND MORE GIRLS. AAAUGH, I DON'T UNDERSTAND!!
THIS SITUATION'S WAY TOO RISKY FOR ME!!
IT'S NOT THAT I'M FEELING UNWELL.
I JUST WANT TO GET THE HELL OUT OF THIS CLASSROOM...!!

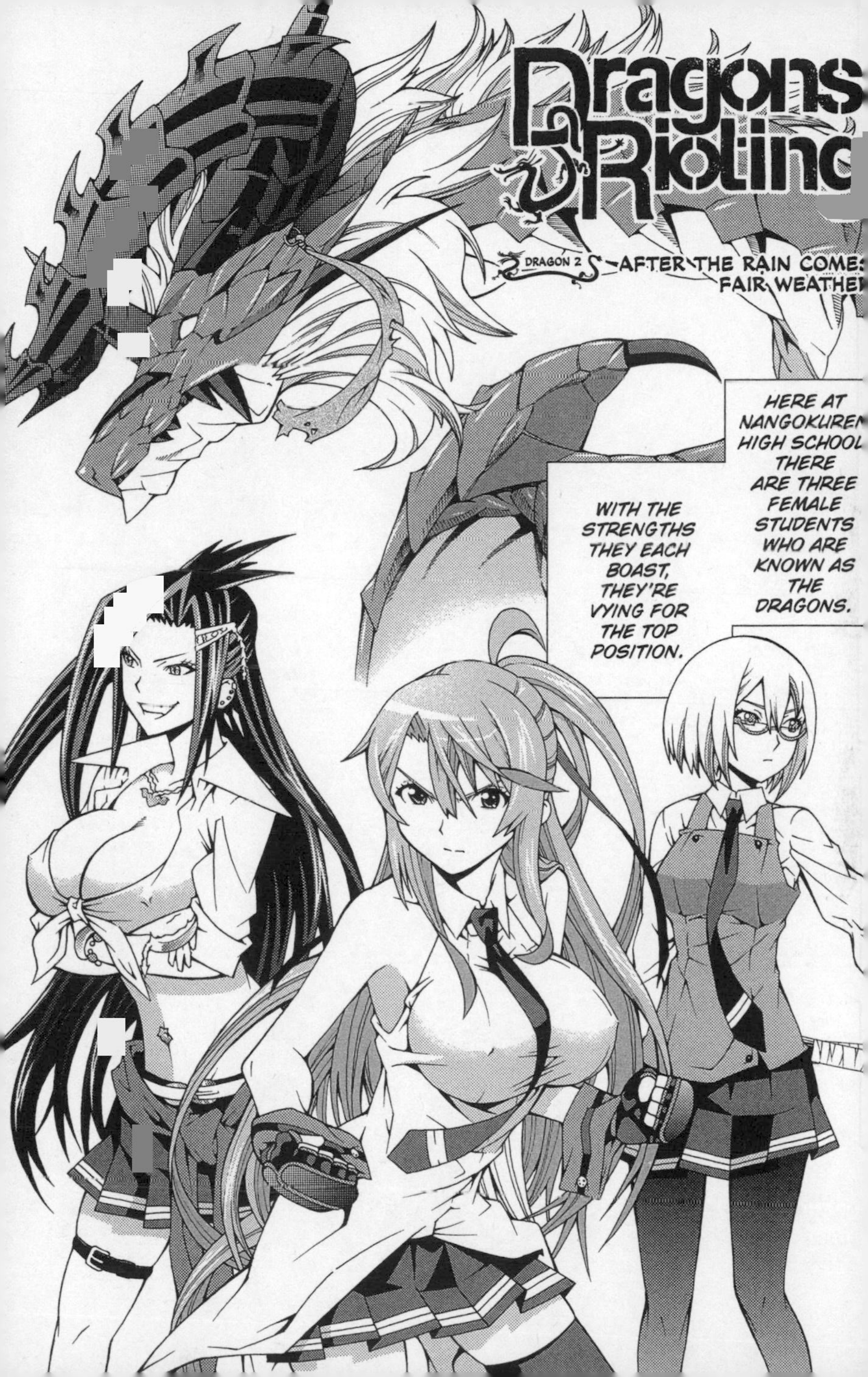
Dragons Rioting
DRAGON 2
AFTER THE RAIN COMES FAIR WEATHER
HERE AT NANGOKUREN HIGH SCHOOL THERE ARE THREE FEMALE STUDENTS WHO ARE KNOWN AS THE DRAGONS.
WITH THE STRENGTHS THEY EACH BOAST, THEY'RE VYING FOR THE TOP POSITION.

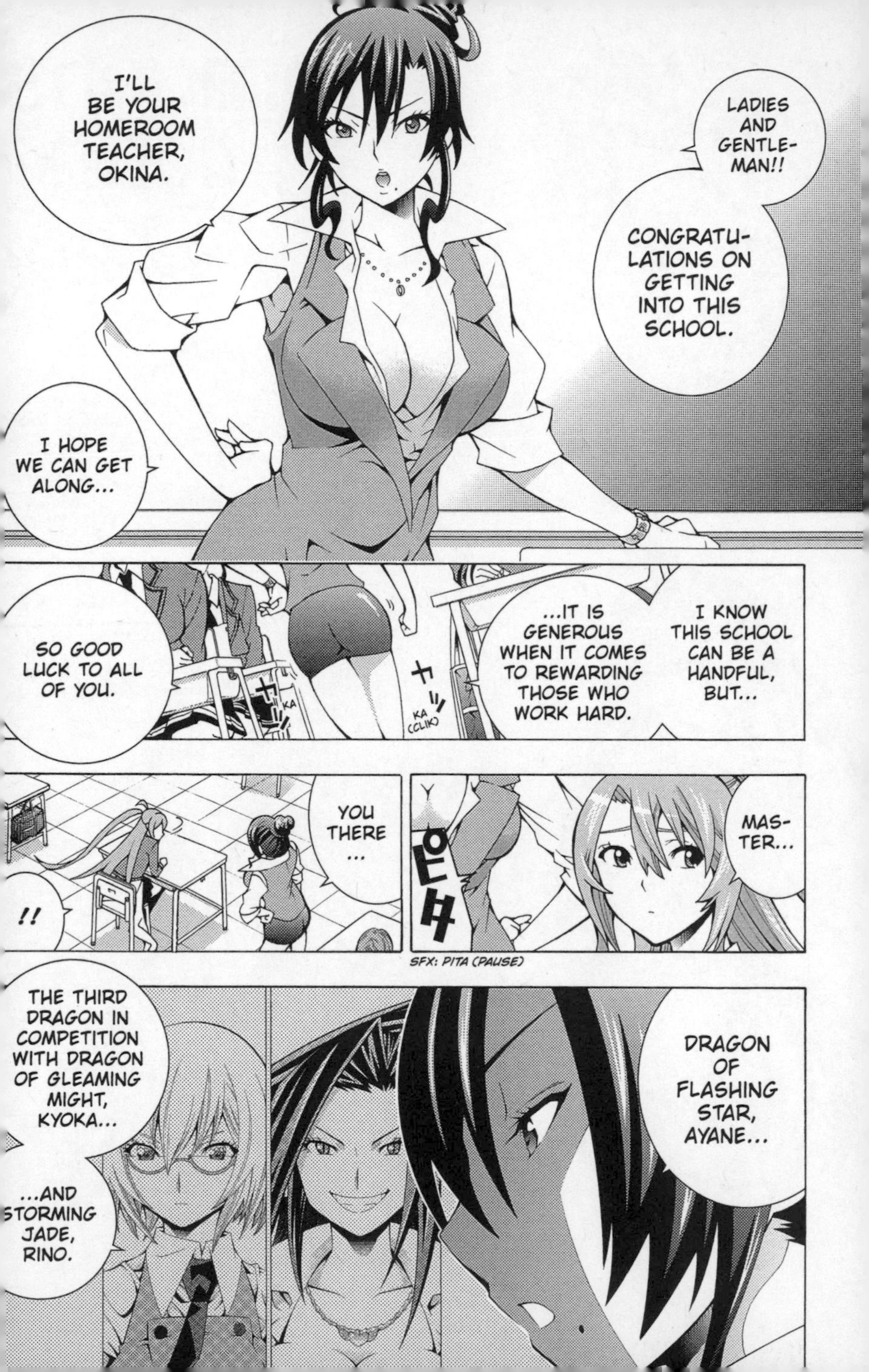
LADIES AND GENTLE-MAN!!
CONGRATU-LATIONS ON GETTING INTO THIS SCHOOL.
I'LL BE YOUR HOMEROOM TEACHER, OKINA.
I HOPE WE CAN GET ALONG...
I KNOW THIS SCHOOL CAN BE A HANDFUL, BUT...
...IT IS GENEROUS WHEN IT COMES TO REWARDING THOSE WHO WORK HARD.
KA (CLIK)
KA
SO GOOD LUCK TO ALL OF YOU.
MAS-TER...
SFX: PITA (PAUSE)
YOU THERE ...
!!
DRAGON OF FLASHING STAR, AYANE...
THE THIRD DRAGON IN COMPETITION WITH DRAGON OF GLEAMING MIGHT, KYOKA...
...AND STORMING JADE, RINO.

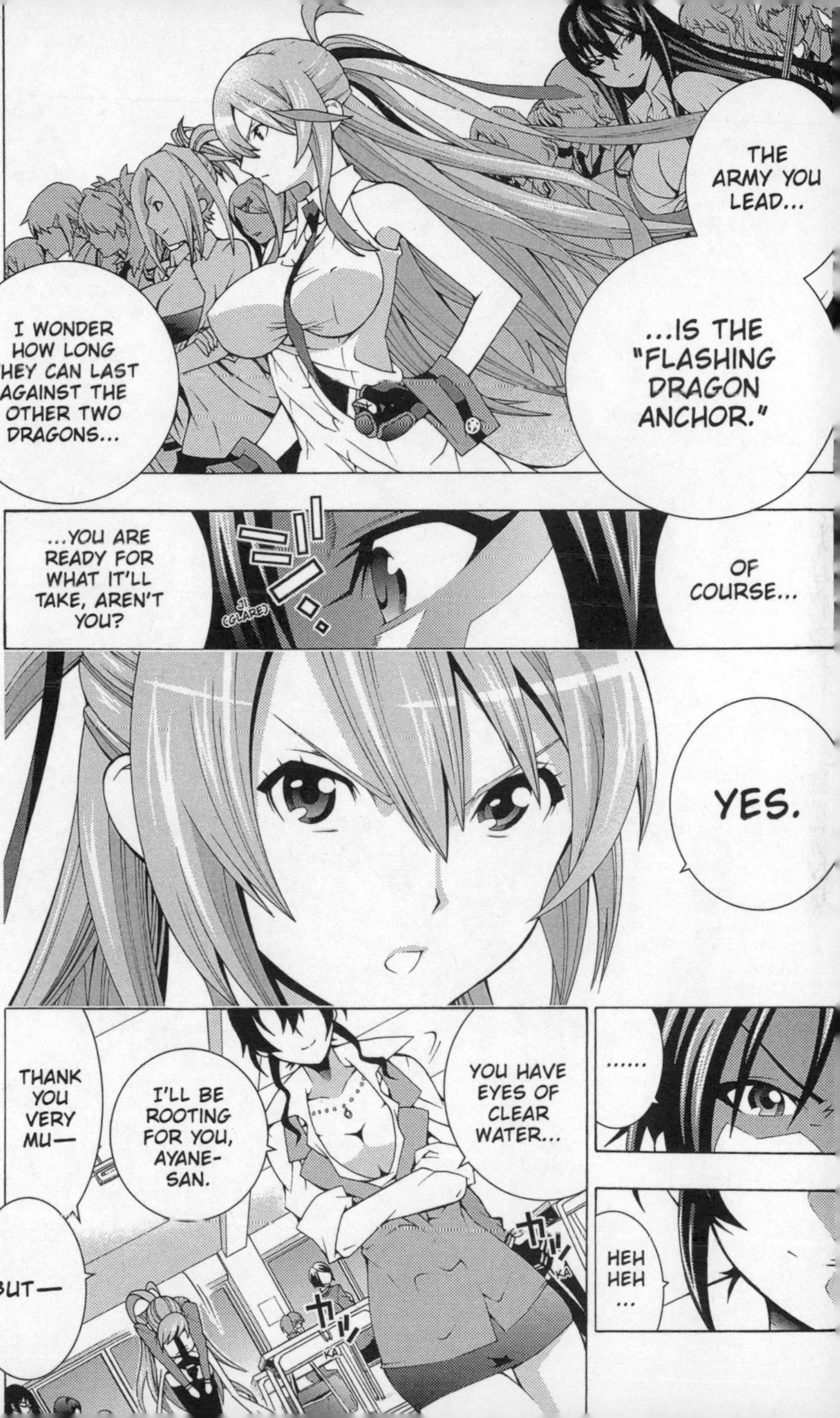
THE ARMY YOU LEAD...
...IS THE "FLASHING DRAGON ANCHOR."
I WONDER HOW LONG THEY CAN LAST AGAINST THE OTHER TWO DRAGONS...
OF COURSE...
JI (GLARE)
...YOU ARE READY FOR WHAT IT'LL TAKE, AREN'T YOU?
YES.
......
HEH HEH ...
YOU HAVE EYES OF CLEAR WATER...
I'LL BE ROOTING FOR YOU, AYANE-SAN.
THANK YOU VERY MU—
BUT—
KA
KA

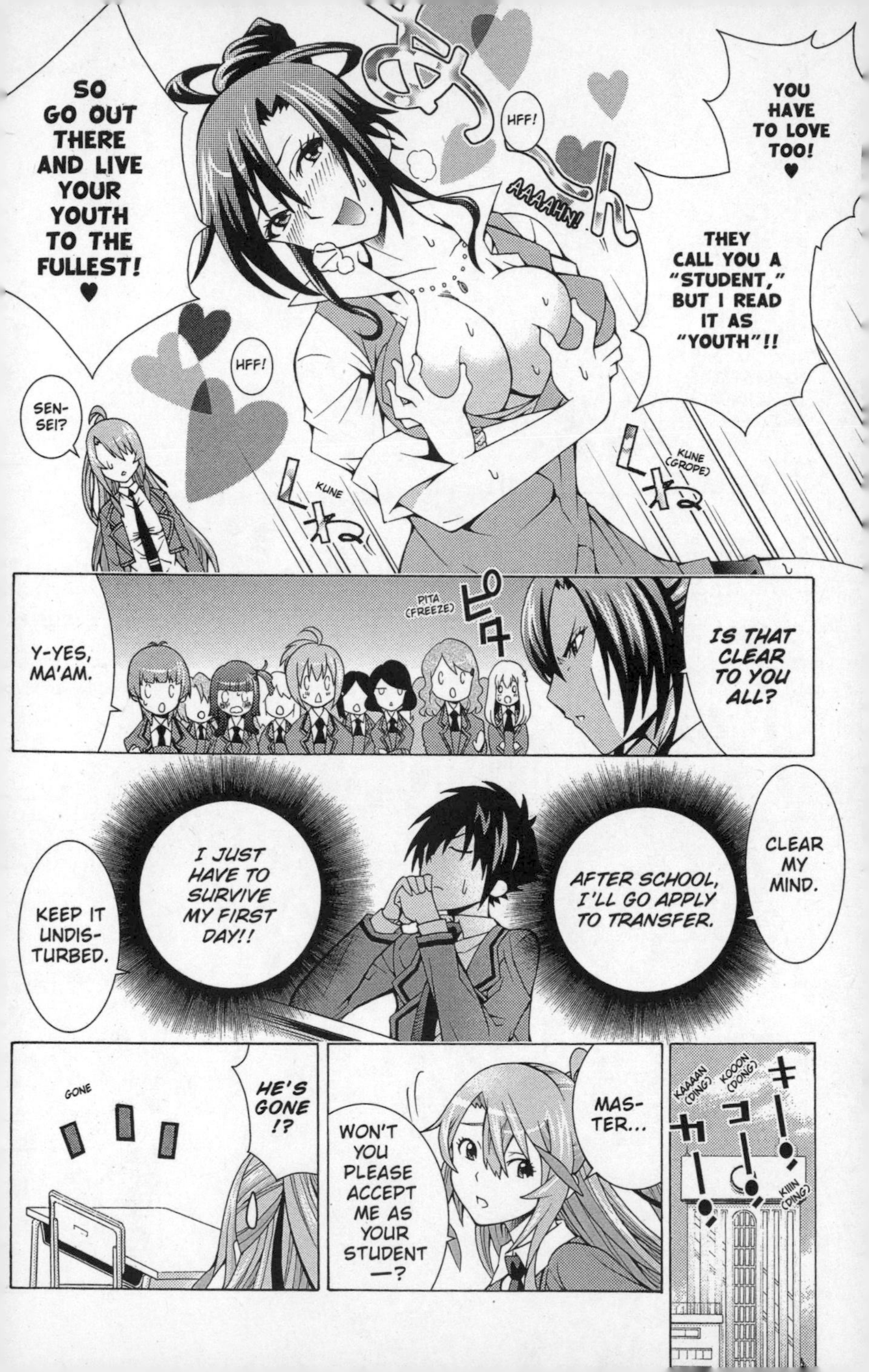

YOU HAVE TO LOVE TOO! ♥
THEY CALL YOU A "STUDENT," BUT I READ IT AS "YOUTH"!!
HFF!
AAAAHN!
KUNE (GROPE)
SO GO OUT THERE AND LIVE YOUR YOUTH TO THE FULLEST! ♥
HFF!
KUNE
SEN-SEI?
IS THAT CLEAR TO YOU ALL?
PITA (FREEZE)
Y-YES, MA'AM.
CLEAR MY MIND.
AFTER SCHOOL, I'LL GO APPLY TO TRANSFER.
I JUST HAVE TO SURVIVE MY FIRST DAY!!
KEEP IT UNDIS-TURBED.
KOOON (DONG)
KAAAAN (DING)
KIIIN (DING)
MAS-TER...
WON'T YOU PLEASE ACCEPT ME AS YOUR STUDENT—?
HE'S GONE!?
GONE

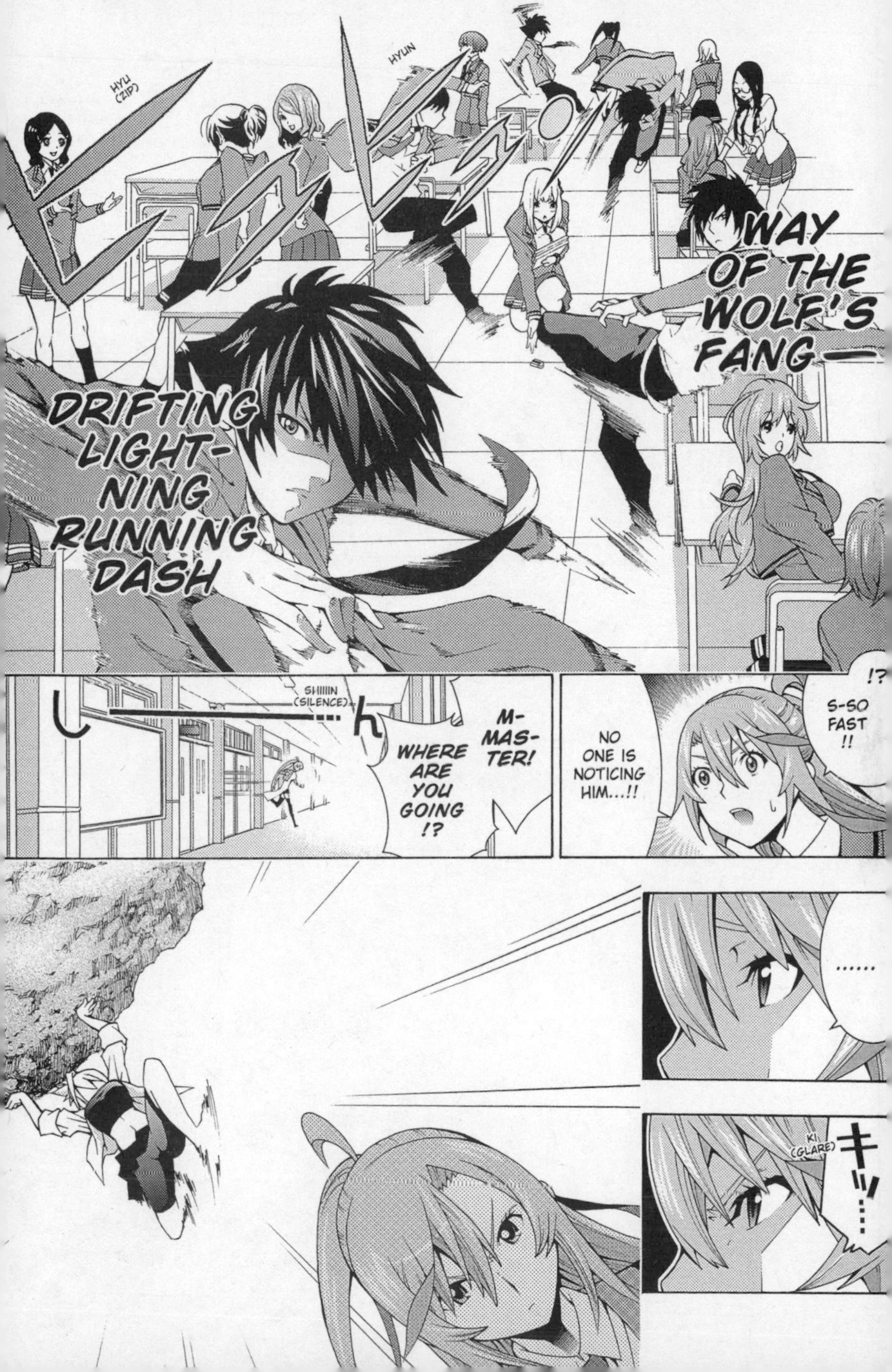
HYUN
HYU (ZIP)
WAY OF THE WOLF'S FANG—
DRIFTING LIGHT-NING RUNNING DASH
!?
S-SO FAST !!
NO ONE IS NOTICING HIM...!!
M-MAS-TER!
WHERE ARE YOU GOING !?
SHIIIIN (SILENCE)
......
KI (GLARE)

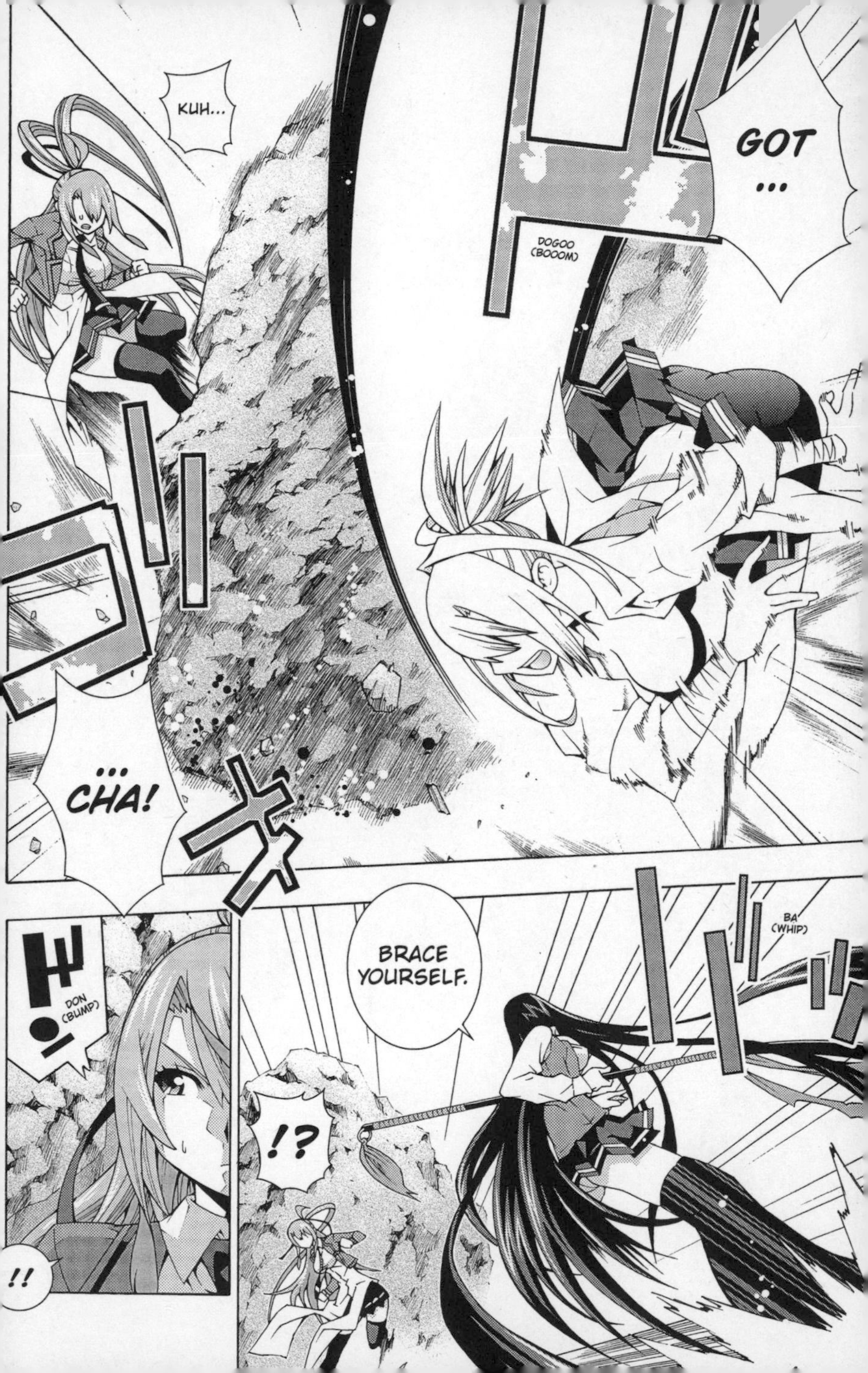
GOT ...
DOGOO (BOOOM)
KUH...
... CHA!
BA (WHIP)
BRACE YOURSELF.
!?
DON (BUMP)
!!

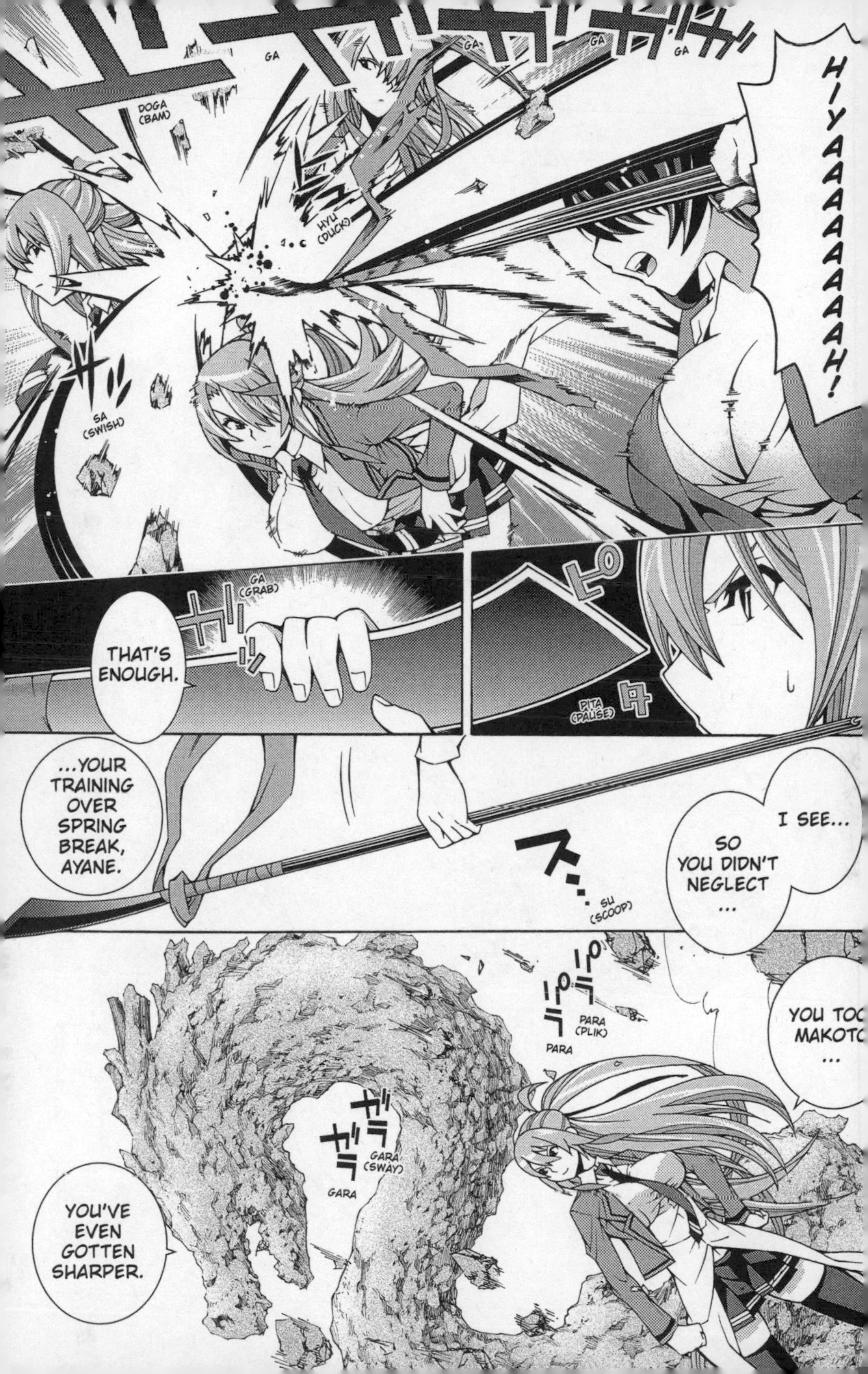
HIYAAAAAAAAAH!
GA
GA
GA
GA
DOGA (BAM)
HYU (DUCK)
SA (SWISH)
PITA (PAUSE)
GA (GRAB)
THAT'S ENOUGH.
I SEE... SO YOU DIDN'T NEGLECT ...
SU (SCOOP)
...YOUR TRAINING OVER SPRING BREAK, AYANE.
YOU TOO MAKOTO ...
PARA (PLIK)
PARA
GARA (SWAY)
GARA
YOU'VE EVEN GOTTEN SHARPER.

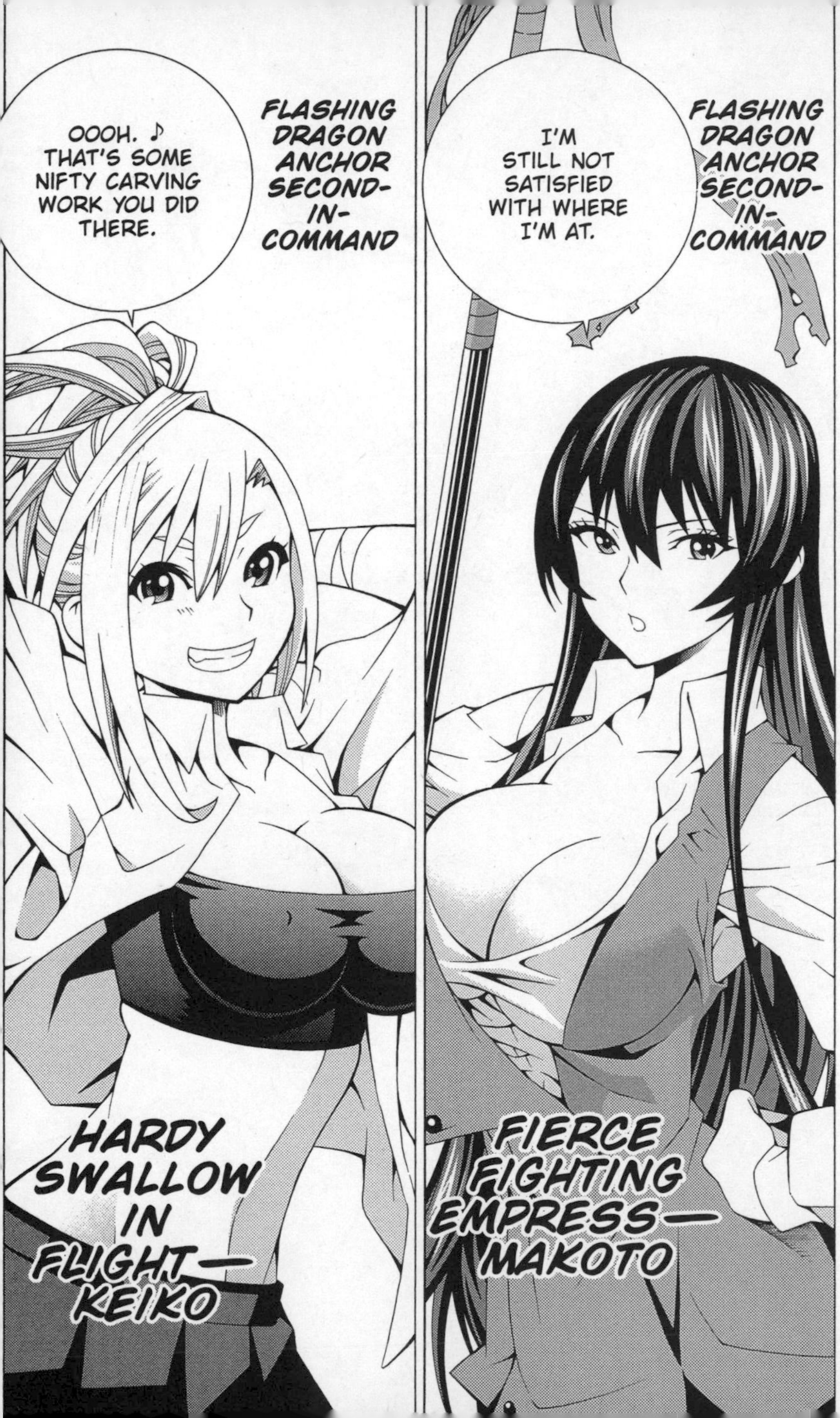
FLASHING DRAGON ANCHOR SECOND-IN-COMMAND
I'M STILL NOT SATISFIED WITH WHERE I'M AT.
FIERCE FIGHTING EMPRESS—MAKOTO
FLASHING DRAGON ANCHOR SECOND-IN-COMMAND
OOOH. ♪ THAT'S SOME NIFTY CARVING WORK YOU DID THERE.
HARDY SWALLOW IN FLIGHT—KEIKO

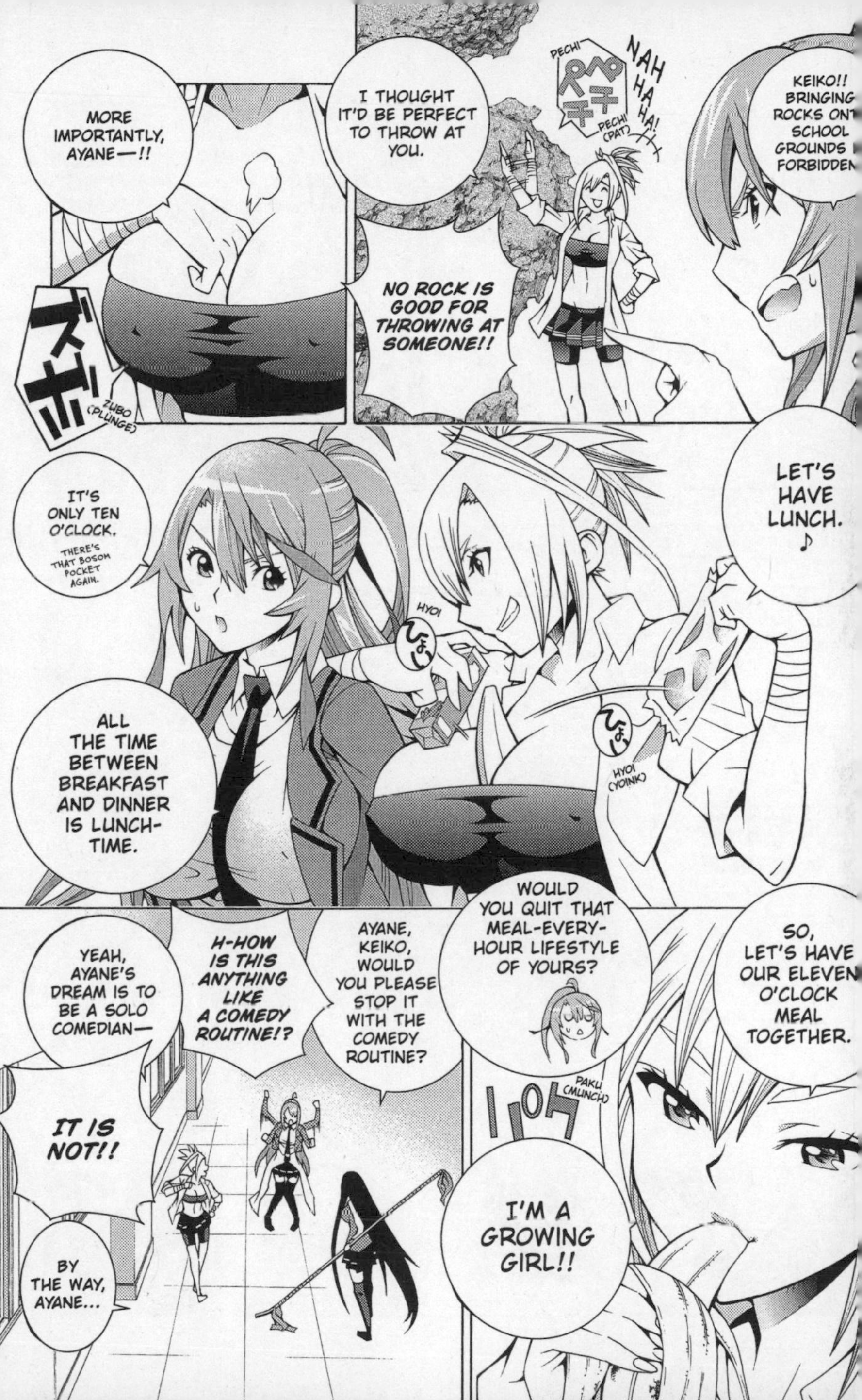
KEIKO!! BRINGING ROCKS ONT SCHOOL GROUNDS I FORBIDDEN
PECHI PECHI (PAT)
NAH HA HA!
I THOUGHT IT'D BE PERFECT TO THROW AT YOU.
NO ROCK IS GOOD FOR THROWING AT SOMEONE!!
MORE IMPORTANTLY, AYANE—!!
ZUBO (PLUNGE)
LET'S HAVE LUNCH. ♪
HYOI (YOINK)
HYOI
IT'S ONLY TEN O'CLOCK.
THERE'S THAT BOSOM POCKET AGAIN.
ALL THE TIME BETWEEN BREAKFAST AND DINNER IS LUNCH-TIME.
SO, LET'S HAVE OUR ELEVEN O'CLOCK MEAL TOGETHER.
WOULD YOU QUIT THAT MEAL-EVERY-HOUR LIFESTYLE OF YOURS?
PAKU (MUNCH)
I'M A GROWING GIRL!!
AYANE, KEIKO, WOULD YOU PLEASE STOP IT WITH THE COMEDY ROUTINE?
H-HOW IS THIS ANYTHING LIKE A COMEDY ROUTINE!?
YEAH, AYANE'S DREAM IS TO BE A SOLO COMEDIAN—
IT IS NOT!!
BY THE WAY, AYANE...

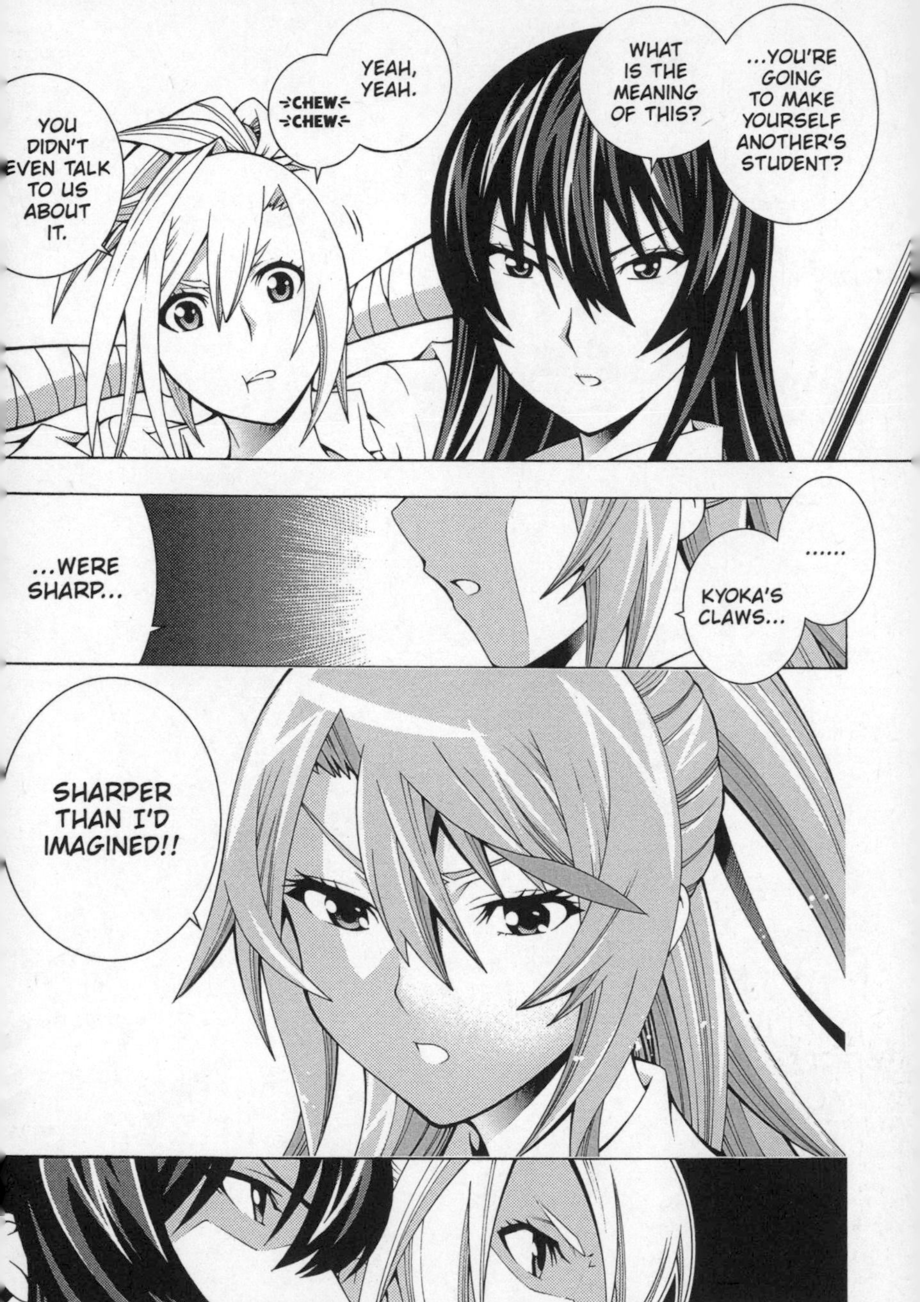
WHAT IS THE MEANING OF THIS?
...YOU'RE GOING TO MAKE YOURSELF ANOTHER'S STUDENT?
YEAH, YEAH.
CHEW CHEW
YOU DIDN'T EVEN TALK TO US ABOUT IT.
......
KYOKA'S CLAWS...
...WERE SHARP...
SHARPER THAN I'D IMAGINED!!

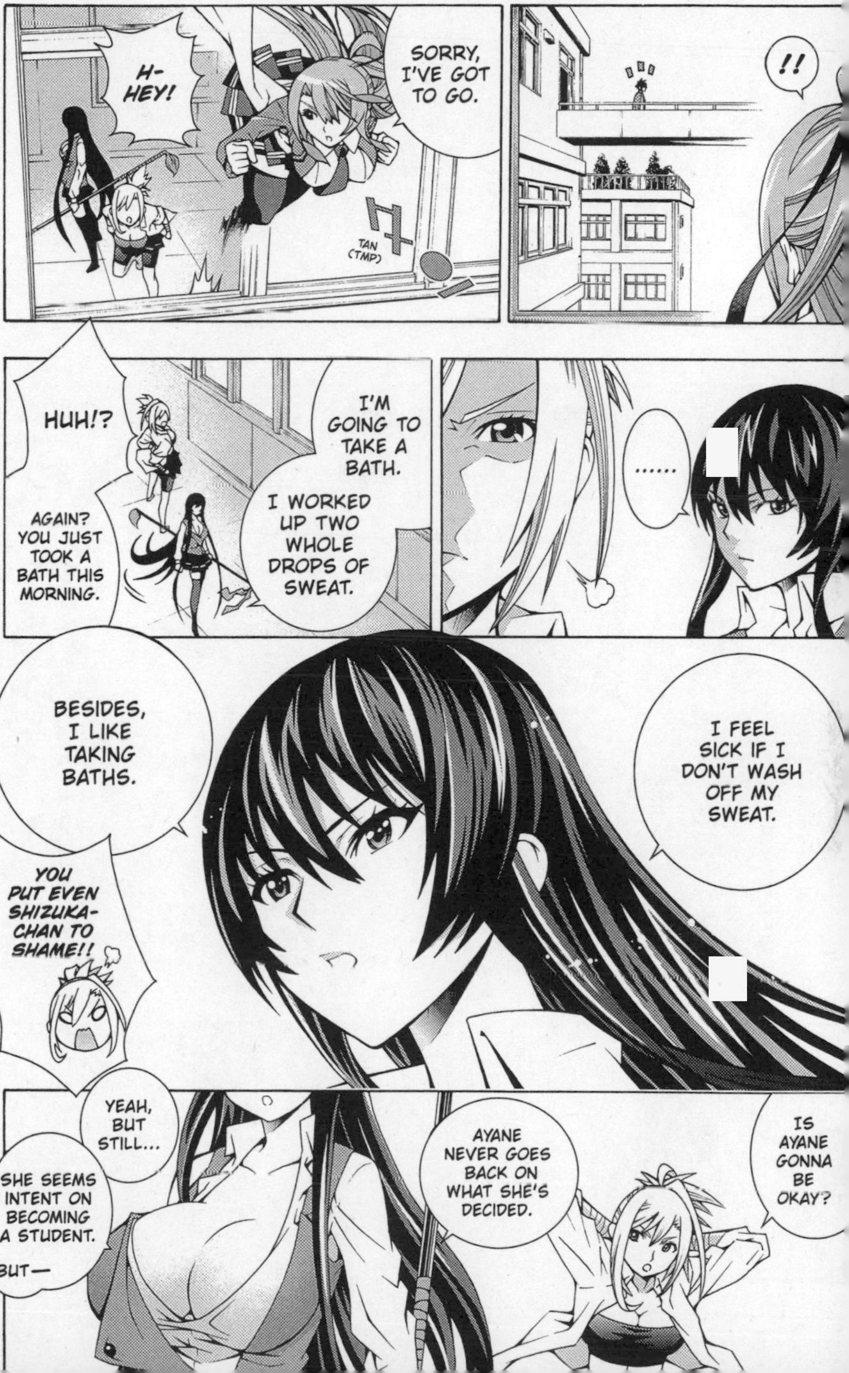
!!
SORRY, I'VE GOT TO GO.
H-HEY!
TAN (TMP)
......
I'M GOING TO TAKE A BATH.
I WORKED UP TWO WHOLE DROPS OF SWEAT.
HUH!?
AGAIN? YOU JUST TOOK A BATH THIS MORNING.
I FEEL SICK IF I DON'T WASH OFF MY SWEAT.
BESIDES, I LIKE TAKING BATHS.
YOU PUT EVEN SHIZUKA-CHAN TO SHAME!!
IS AYANE GONNA BE OKAY?
AYANE NEVER GOES BACK ON WHAT SHE'S DECIDED.
YEAH, BUT STILL...
SHE SEEMS INTENT ON BECOMING A STUDENT.
BUT—

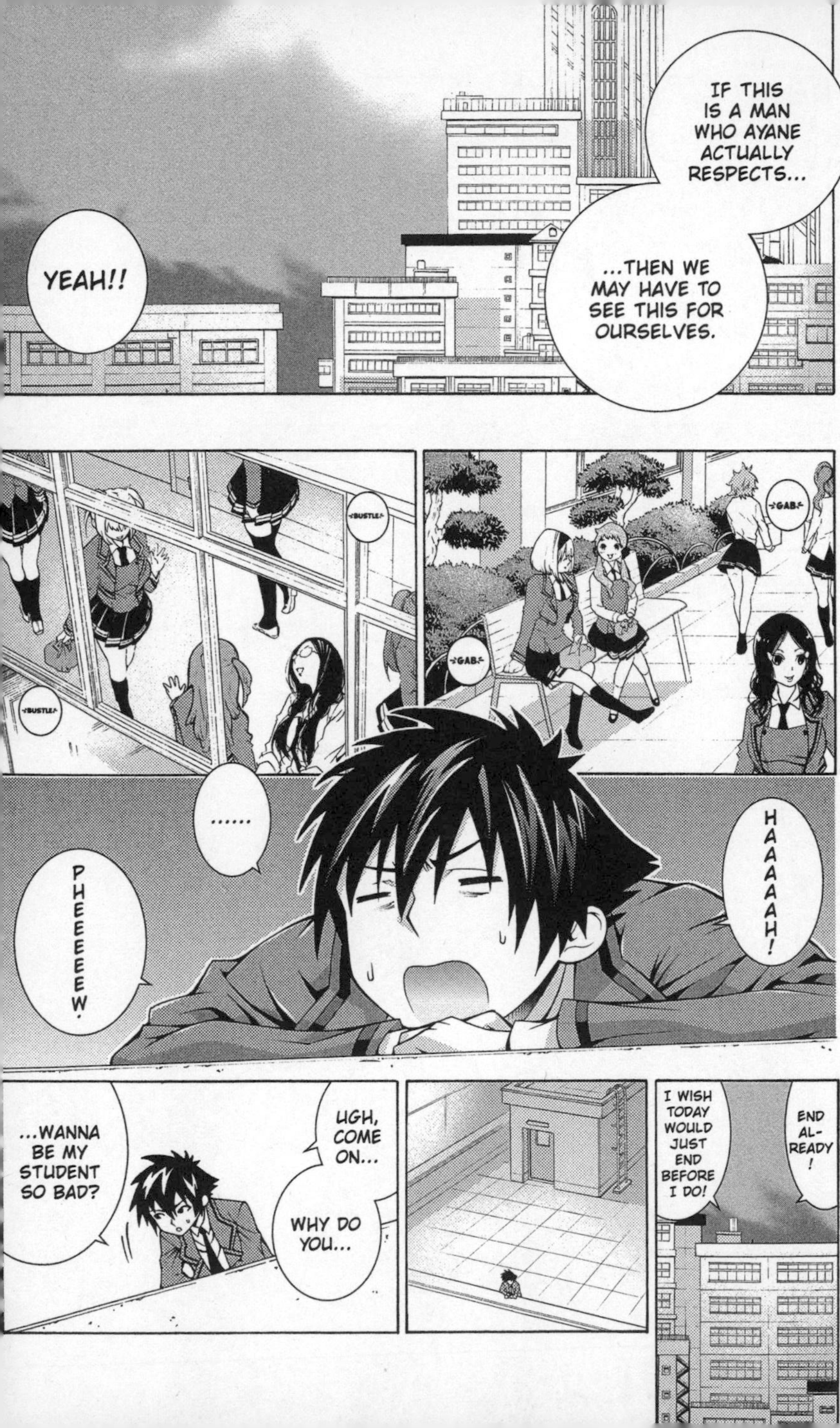
IF THIS IS A MAN WHO AYANE ACTUALLY RESPECTS...
...THEN WE MAY HAVE TO SEE THIS FOR OURSELVES.
YEAH!!
GAB
GAB
BUSTLE
BUSTLE
HAAAAAH!
......
PHEEEEEEW.
END AL-READY!
I WISH TODAY WOULD JUST END BEFORE I DO!
UGH, COME ON...
WHY DO YOU...
...WANNA BE MY STUDENT SO BAD?

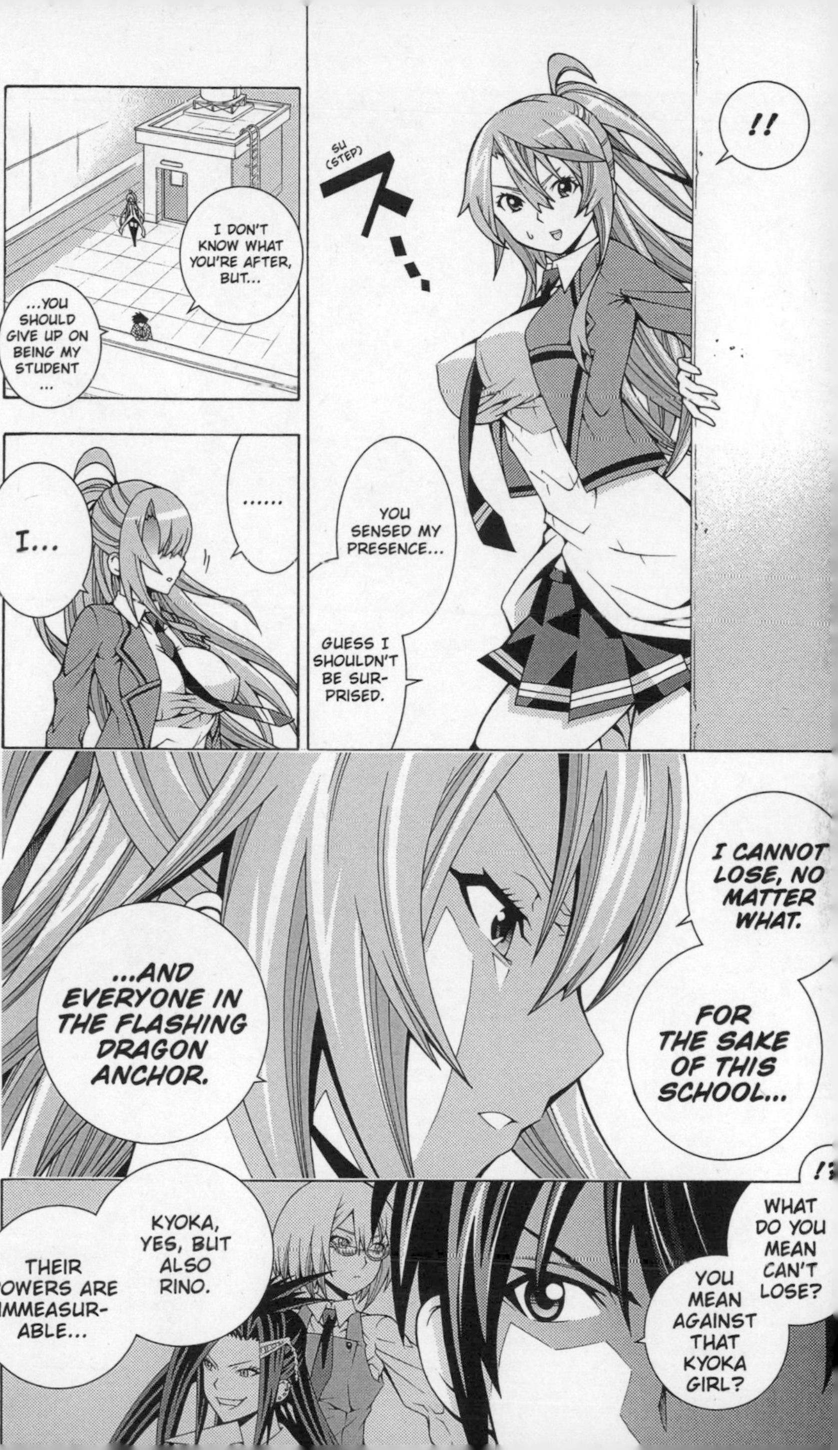
!!
SU (STEP)
YOU SENSED MY PRESENCE...
GUESS I SHOULDN'T BE SUR-PRISED.
I DON'T KNOW WHAT YOU'RE AFTER, BUT...
...YOU SHOULD GIVE UP ON BEING MY STUDENT ...
......
I...
I CANNOT LOSE, NO MATTER WHAT.
FOR THE SAKE OF THIS SCHOOL...
...AND EVERYONE IN THE FLASHING DRAGON ANCHOR.
!?
WHAT DO YOU MEAN CAN'T LOSE?
YOU MEAN AGAINST THAT KYOKA GIRL?
KYOKA, YES, BUT ALSO RINO.
THEIR POWERS ARE IMMEASUR-ABLE...

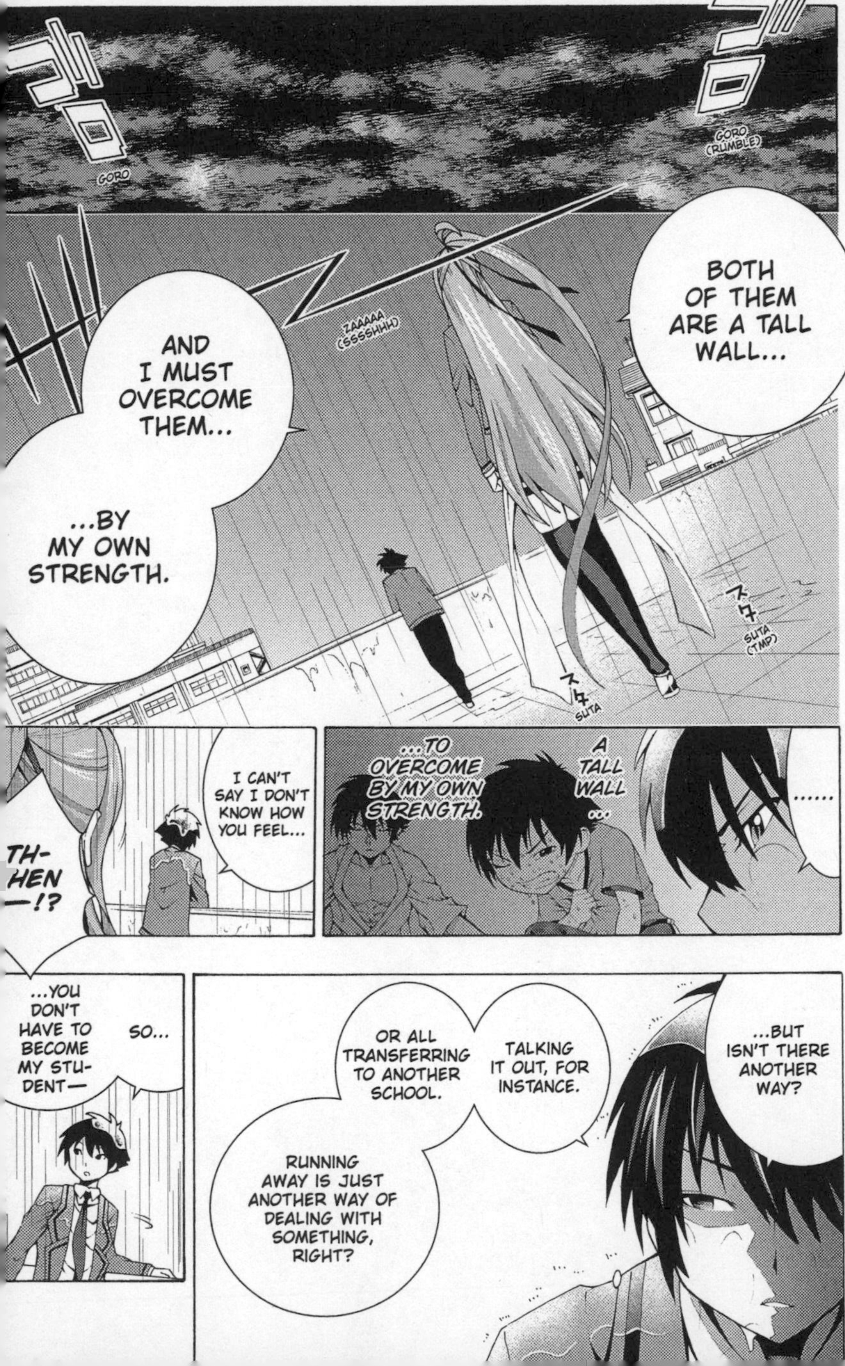
GORO (RUMBLE)
GORO
BOTH OF THEM ARE A TALL WALL...
ZAAAAA (SSSSHHH)
AND I MUST OVERCOME THEM...
...BY MY OWN STRENGTH.
SUTA (TMP)
SUTA
......
A TALL WALL...
...TO OVERCOME BY MY OWN STRENGTH.
I CAN'T SAY I DON'T KNOW HOW YOU FEEL...
TH-HEN—!?
...BUT ISN'T THERE ANOTHER WAY?
TALKING IT OUT, FOR INSTANCE.
OR ALL TRANSFERRING TO ANOTHER SCHOOL.
RUNNING AWAY IS JUST ANOTHER WAY OF DEALING WITH SOMETHING, RIGHT?
SO...
...YOU DON'T HAVE TO BECOME MY STU-DENT—

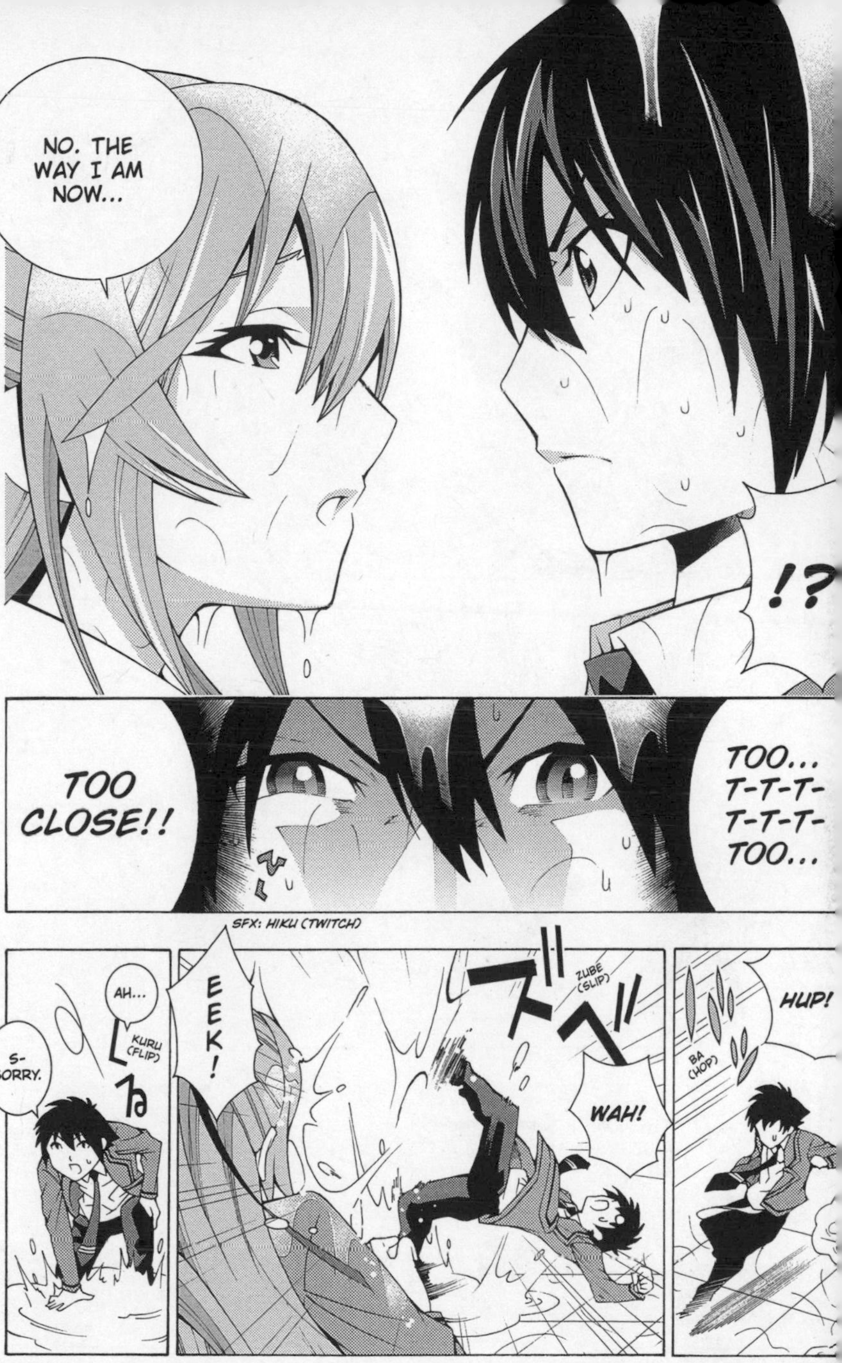

NO. THE WAY I AM NOW...
!?
TOO... T-T-T-T-T-T-TOO...
TOO CLOSE!!
SFX: HIKU (TWITCH)
HUP!
BA (HOP)
ZUBE (SLIP)
WAH!
EEK!
AH...
KURU (FLIP)
S-SORRY.

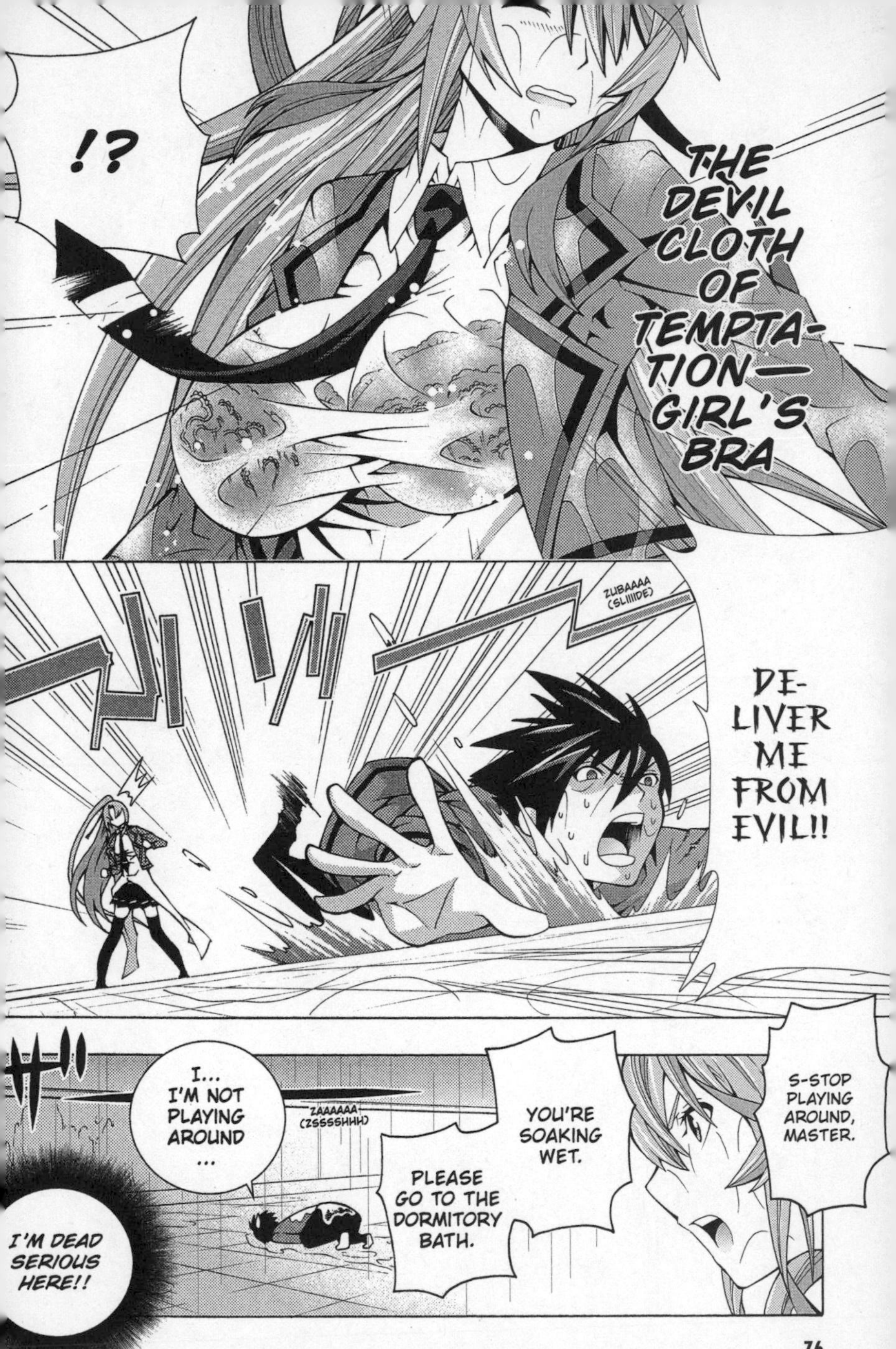
THE DEVIL CLOTH OF TEMPTATION—GIRL'S BRA
!?
ZUBAAAA (SLIIIIDE)
DELIVER ME FROM EVIL!!
S-STOP PLAYING AROUND, MASTER.
YOU'RE SOAKING WET.
PLEASE GO TO THE DORMITORY BATH.
ZAAAAAA (ZSSSSHHH)
I... I'M NOT PLAYING AROUND ...
I'M DEAD SERIOUS HERE!!

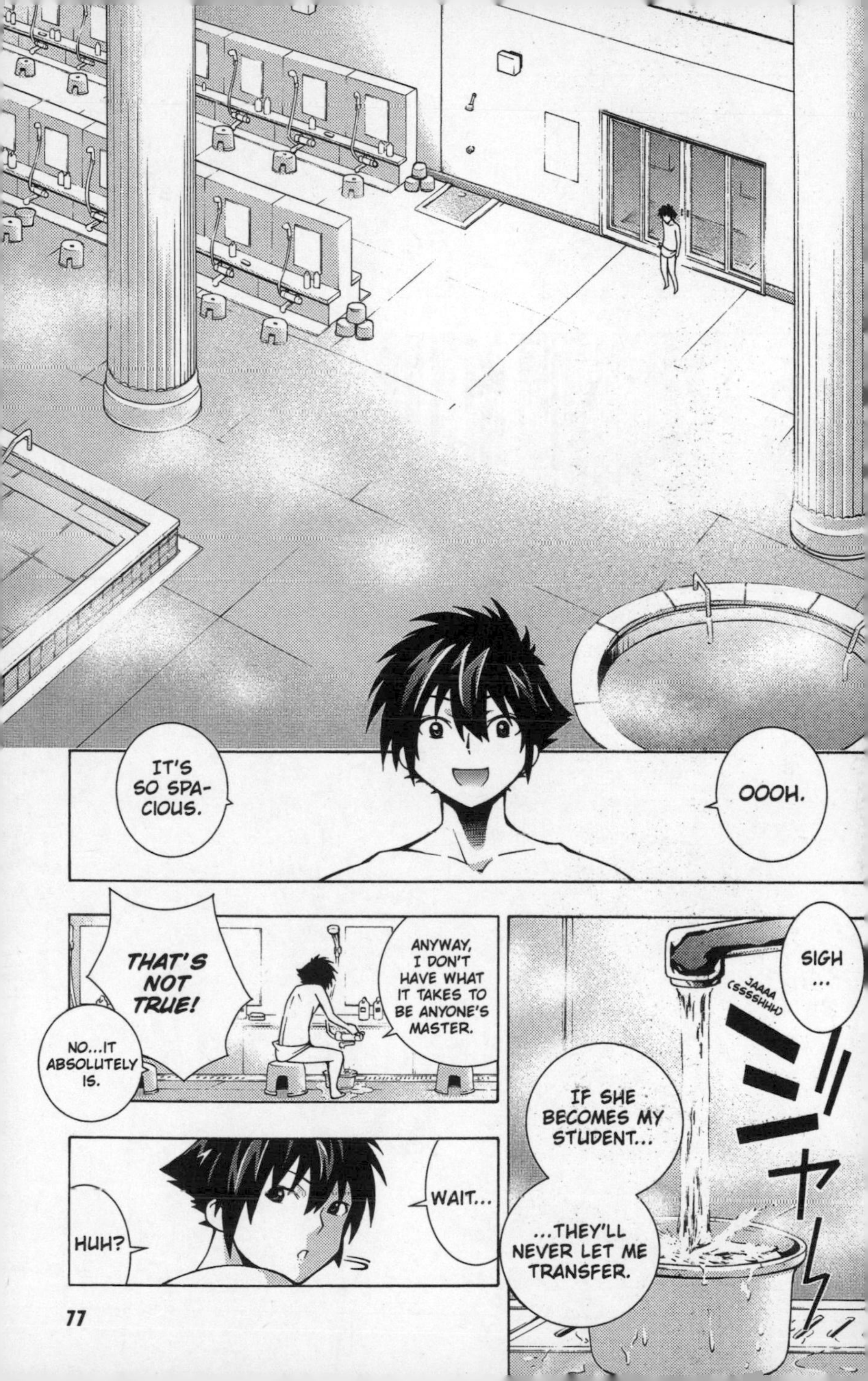
OOOH.
IT'S SO SPA-CIOUS.
SIGH ...
JAAAA (SSSSHHH)
IF SHE BECOMES MY STUDENT...
...THEY'LL NEVER LET ME TRANSFER.
ANYWAY, I DON'T HAVE WHAT IT TAKES TO BE ANYONE'S MASTER.
THAT'S NOT TRUE!
NO...IT ABSOLUTELY IS.
WAIT...
HUH?

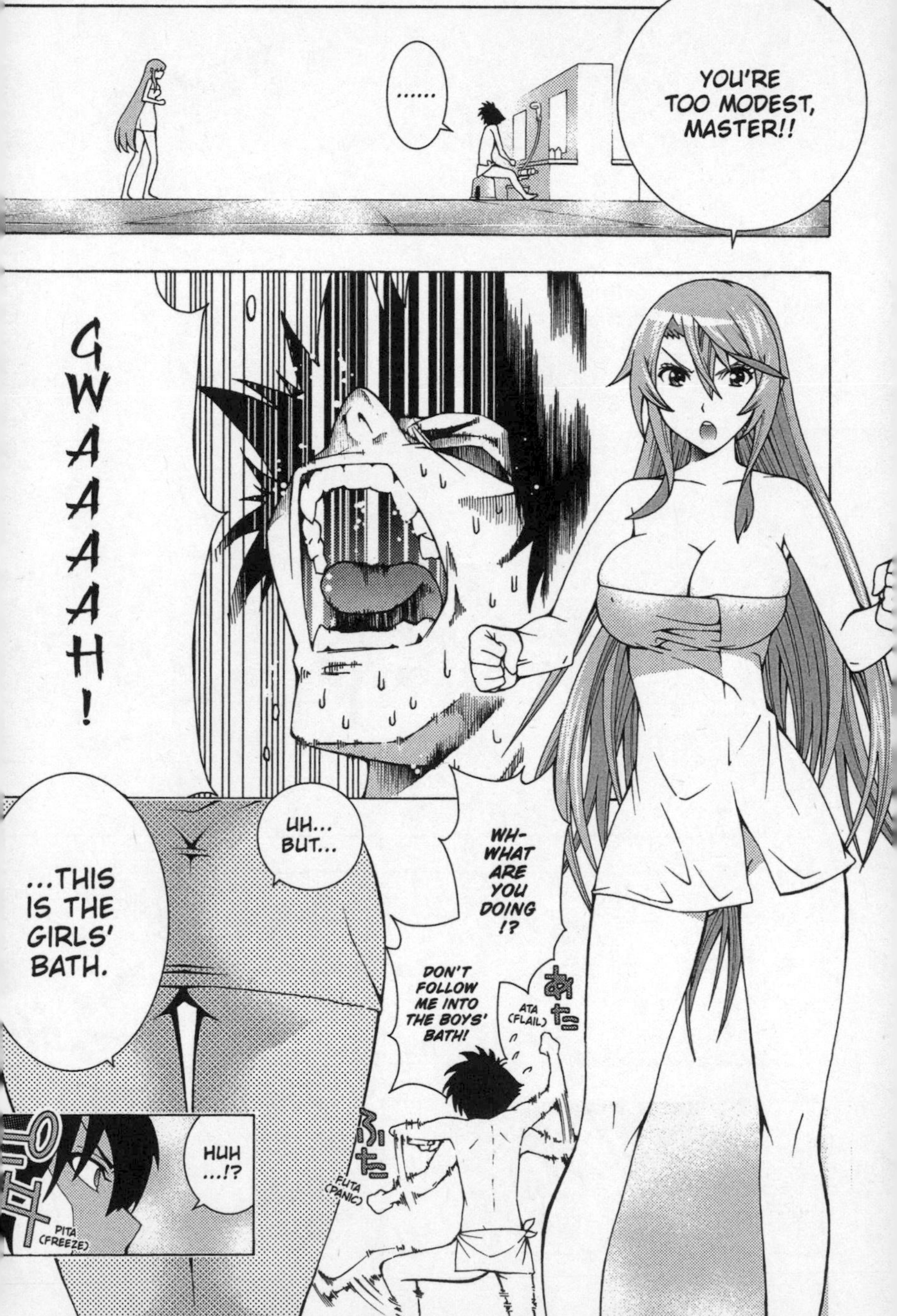
YOU'RE TOO MODEST, MASTER!!
......
GWAAAAAAH!
WH-WHAT ARE YOU DOING!?
DON'T FOLLOW ME INTO THE BOYS' BATH!
ATA (FLAIL)
FUTA (PANIC)
UH... BUT...
...THIS IS THE GIRLS' BATH.
HUH ...!?
PITA (FREEZE)

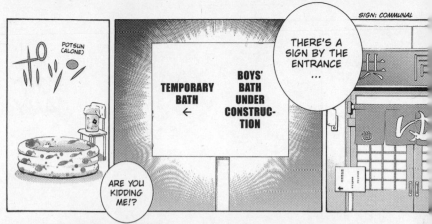

SIGN: COMMUNAL
THERE'S A SIGN BY THE ENTRANCE ...
BOYS' BATH UNDER CONSTRUCTION
TEMPORARY BATH ←
ARE YOU KIDDING ME!?
POTSUN (ALONE)
I... I'M SO SORRY!!
RETREATING IN KOWTOW POSITION
YASA
YASA
YASA (SCUTTLE)
YASA
YASA
YASA
YASA
C... COCK-ROACH ...!?
SIGN: PLEASE CLOSE THE DOOR BEHIND YOU.
NO MATTER HOW MUCH I WANT TO BE YOUR STUDENT...
...I WOULD NEVER FOLLOW YOU INTO THE BATH...
RIGHT...
WHAT'S WRONG WITH ME!!?
YOU CAN ONLY BE SO SUICIDAL.
NOW THAT I THINK ABOUT IT RATIONALLY ...
...THERE'S NO REASON THEY'D HAVE A UNISEX BATH!!
HM...
WAIT.
NO MATTER HOW MUCH I WANT TO BE YOUR STUDENT...
...I WOULD NEVER FOLLOW YOU INTO THE BATH...

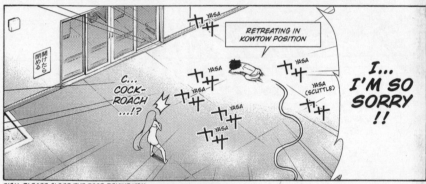

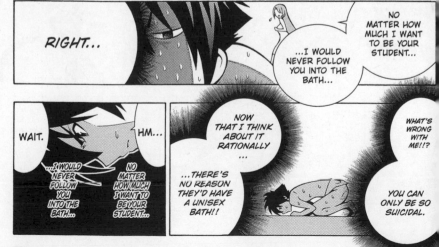

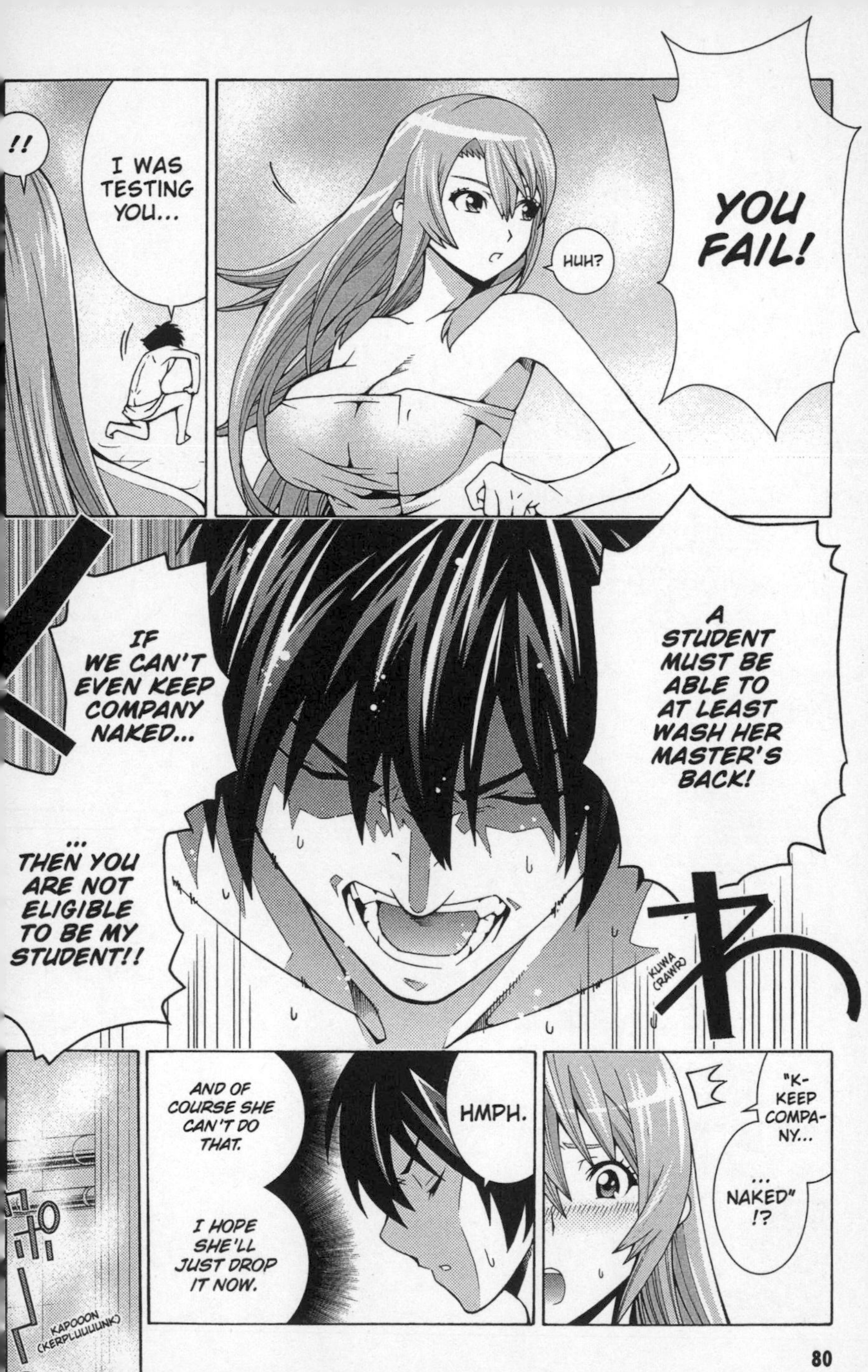
YOU FAIL!
HUH?
I WAS TESTING YOU...
!!
A STUDENT MUST BE ABLE TO AT LEAST WASH HER MASTER'S BACK!
KUWA (RAWR)
IF WE CAN'T EVEN KEEP COMPANY NAKED...
... THEN YOU ARE NOT ELIGIBLE TO BE MY STUDENT!!
"K-KEEP COMPA-NY...
... NAKED" !?
HMPH.
AND OF COURSE SHE CAN'T DO THAT.
I HOPE SHE'LL JUST DROP IT NOW.
KAPOOON (KERPLUUUUNK)

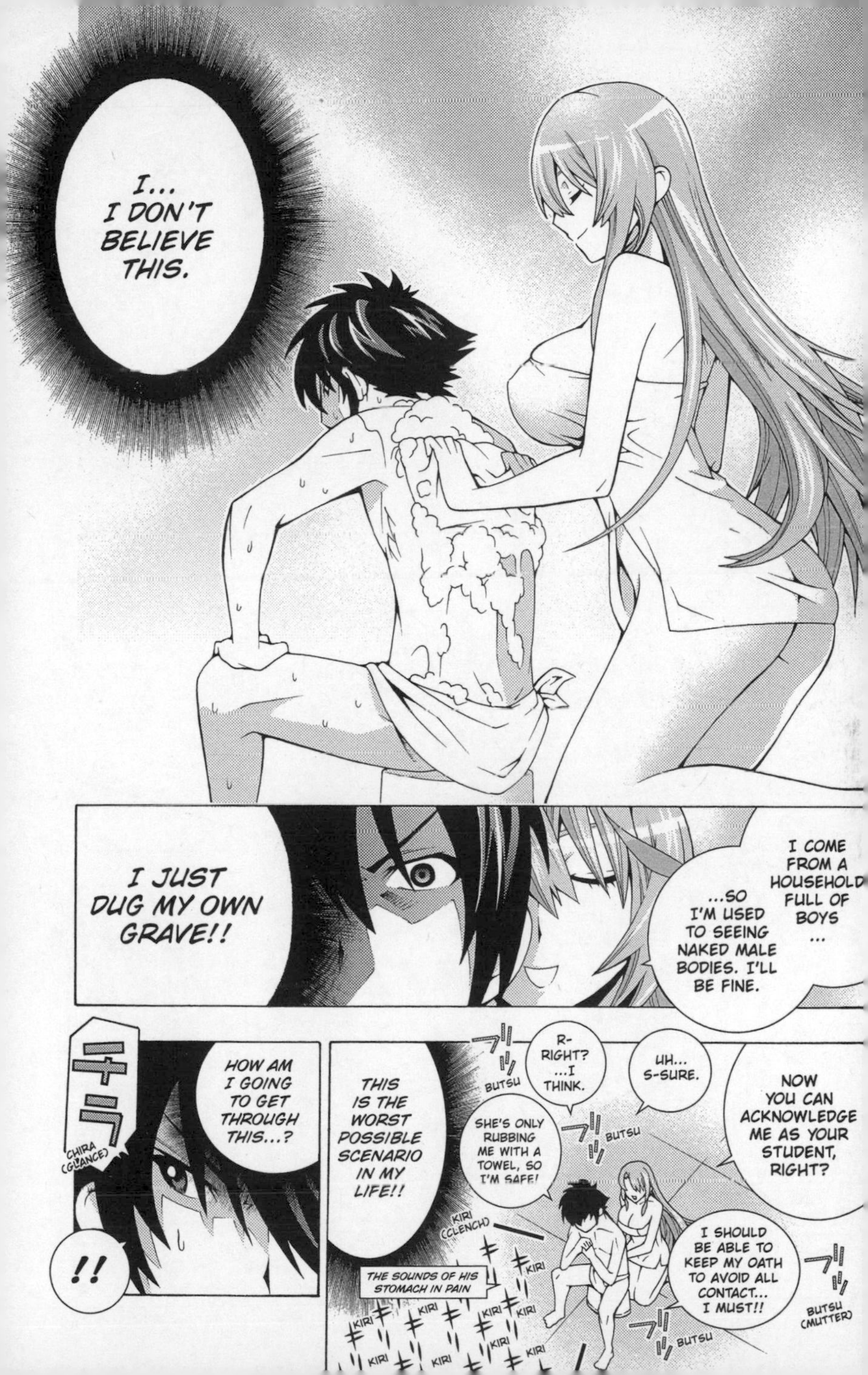
I... I DON'T BELIEVE THIS.
I COME FROM A HOUSEHOLD FULL OF BOYS...
...SO I'M USED TO SEEING NAKED MALE BODIES. I'LL BE FINE.
I JUST DUG MY OWN GRAVE!!
NOW YOU CAN ACKNOWLEDGE ME AS YOUR STUDENT, RIGHT?
UH... S-SURE.
R-RIGHT? ...I THINK.
BUTSU
BUTSU
SHE'S ONLY RUBBING ME WITH A TOWEL, SO I'M SAFE!
THIS IS THE WORST POSSIBLE SCENARIO IN MY LIFE!!
I SHOULD BE ABLE TO KEEP MY OATH TO AVOID ALL CONTACT... I MUST!!
BUTSU (MUTTER)
BUTSU
KIRI (CLENCH)
KIRI
THE SOUNDS OF HIS STOMACH IN PAIN
KIRI
KIRI
KIRI
KIRI
KIRI
KIRI
KIRI
KIRI
HOW AM I GOING TO GET THROUGH THIS...?
CHIRA (GLANCE)
!!

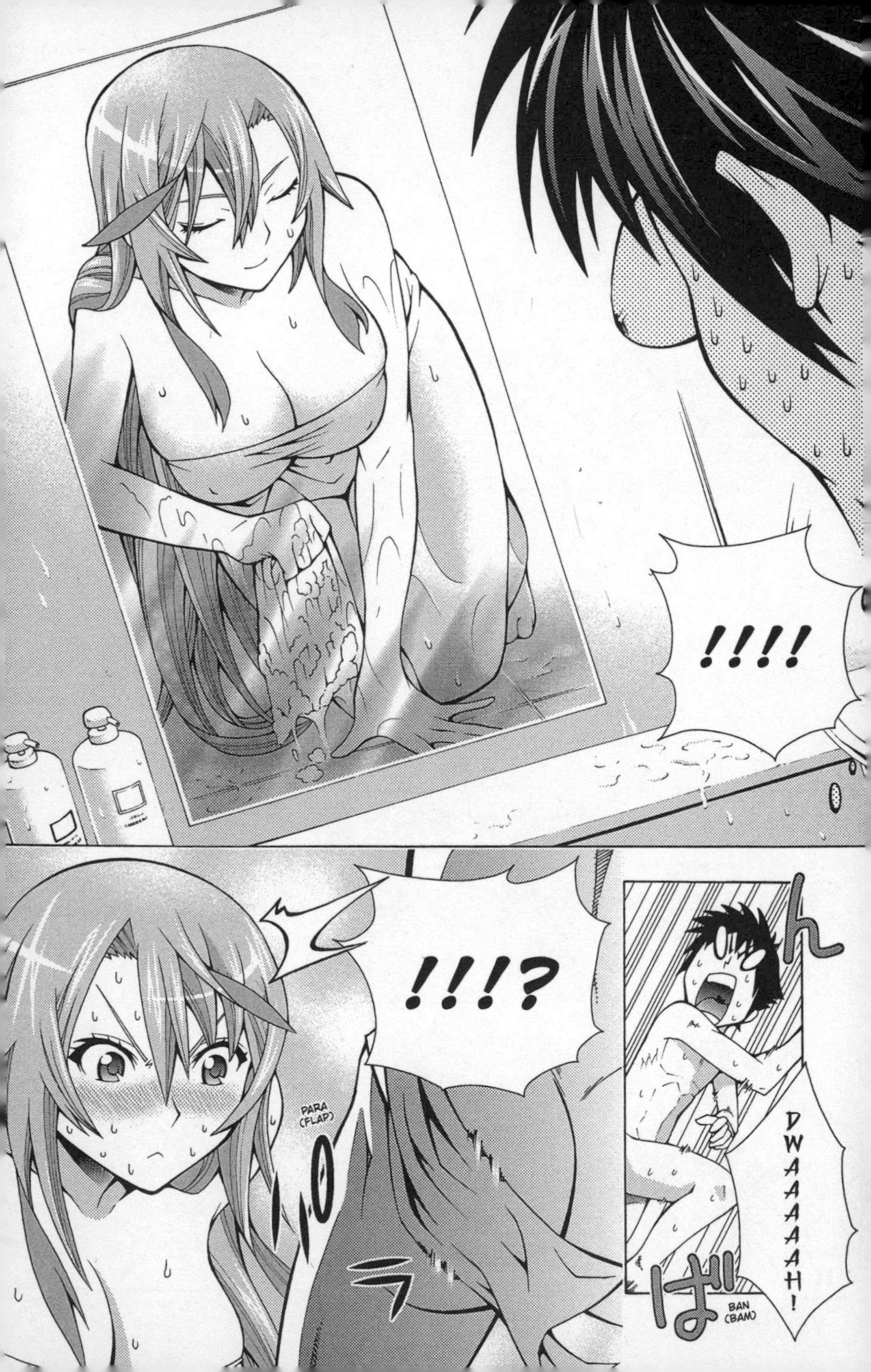
!!!!
DWAAAAAAH!
BAN (BAM)
!!!?
PARA (FLAP)

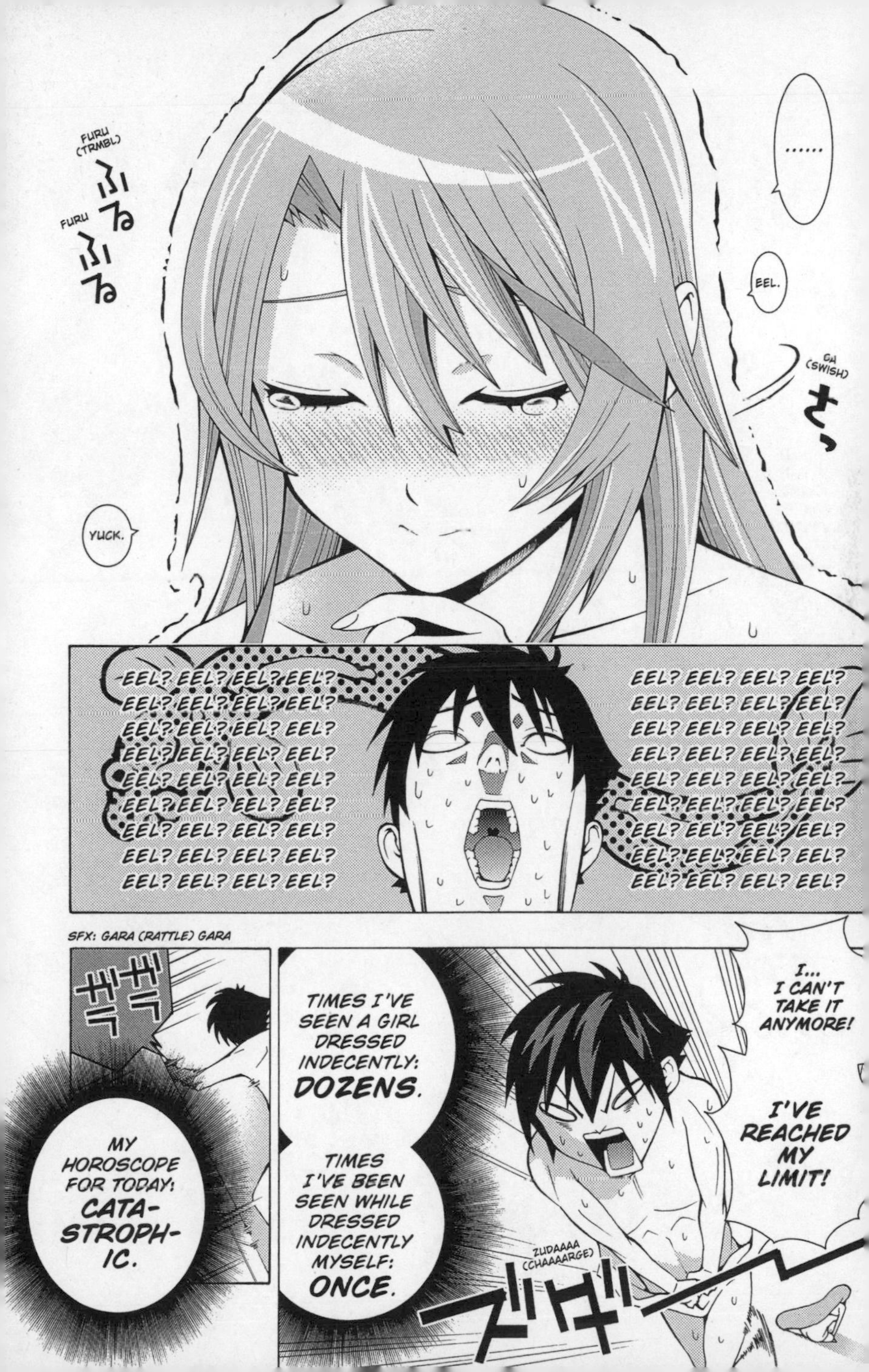
......
EEL.
GA (SWISH)
FURU (TRMBL) FURU
YUCK.
EEL? EEL? EEL? EEL? EEL? EEL? EEL? EEL? EEL? EEL? EEL? EEL? EEL? EEL? EEL? EEL? EEL? EEL? EEL? EEL? EEL? EEL? EEL? EEL? EEL? EEL? EEL? EEL? EEL? EEL? EEL? EEL? EEL? EEL? EEL? EEL?
EEL? EEL? EEL? EEL? EEL? EEL? EEL? EEL? EEL? EEL? EEL? EEL? EEL? EEL? EEL? EEL? EEL? EEL? EEL? EEL? EEL? EEL? EEL? EEL? EEL? EEL? EEL? EEL? EEL? EEL? EEL? EEL? EEL? EEL? EEL? EEL?
SFX: GARA (RATTLE) GARA
I... I CAN'T TAKE IT ANYMORE!
I'VE REACHED MY LIMIT!
ZUDAAAA (CHAAAARGE)
TIMES I'VE SEEN A GIRL DRESSED INDECENTLY: DOZENS.
TIMES I'VE BEEN SEEN WHILE DRESSED INDECENTLY MYSELF: ONCE.
MY HOROSCOPE FOR TODAY: CATA-STROPH-IC.

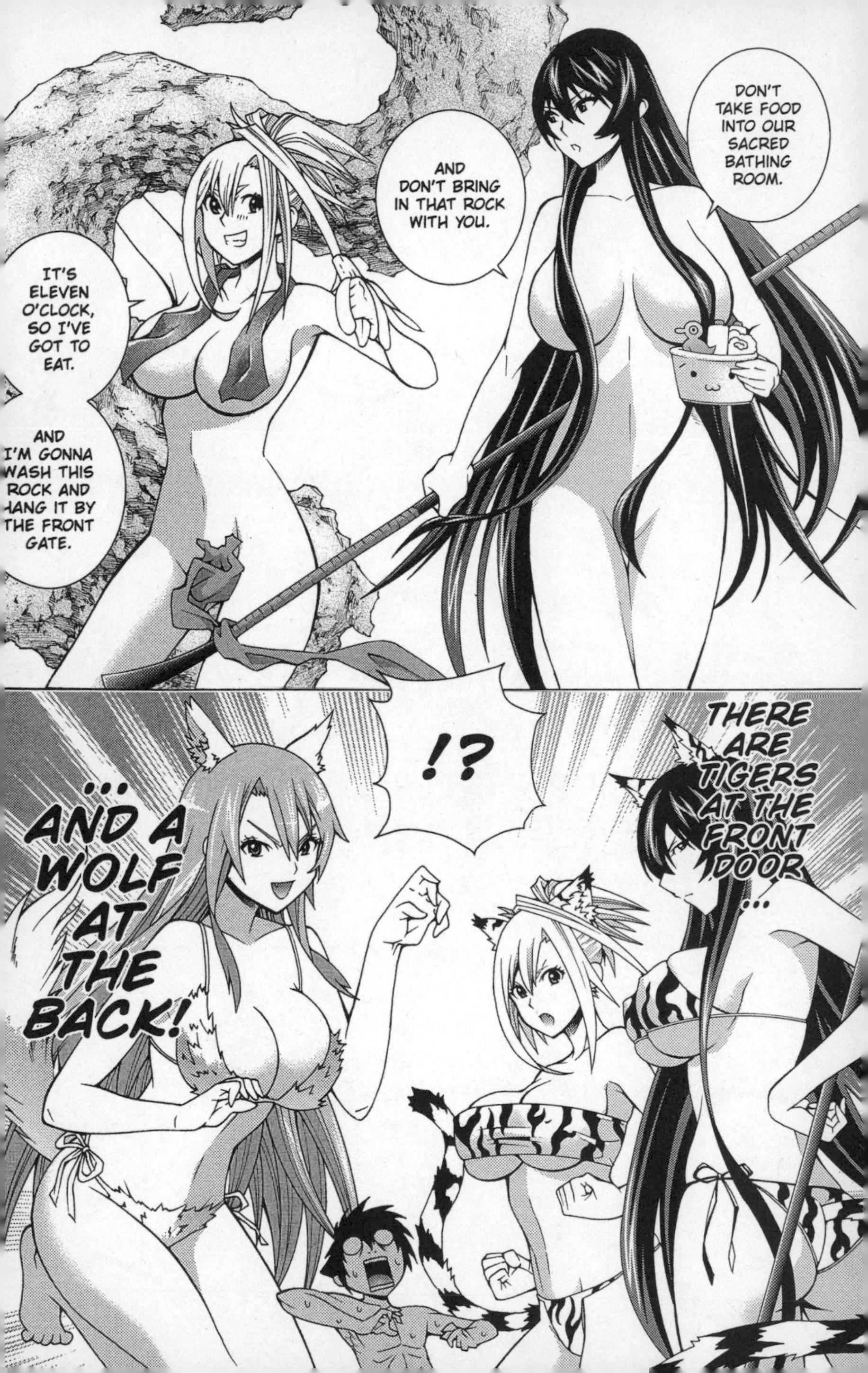
DON'T TAKE FOOD INTO OUR SACRED BATHING ROOM.
AND DON'T BRING IN THAT ROCK WITH YOU.
IT'S ELEVEN O'CLOCK, SO I'VE GOT TO EAT.
AND I'M GONNA WASH THIS ROCK AND HANG IT BY THE FRONT GATE.
THERE ARE TIGERS AT THE FRONT DOOR...
!?
...AND A WOLF AT THE BACK!

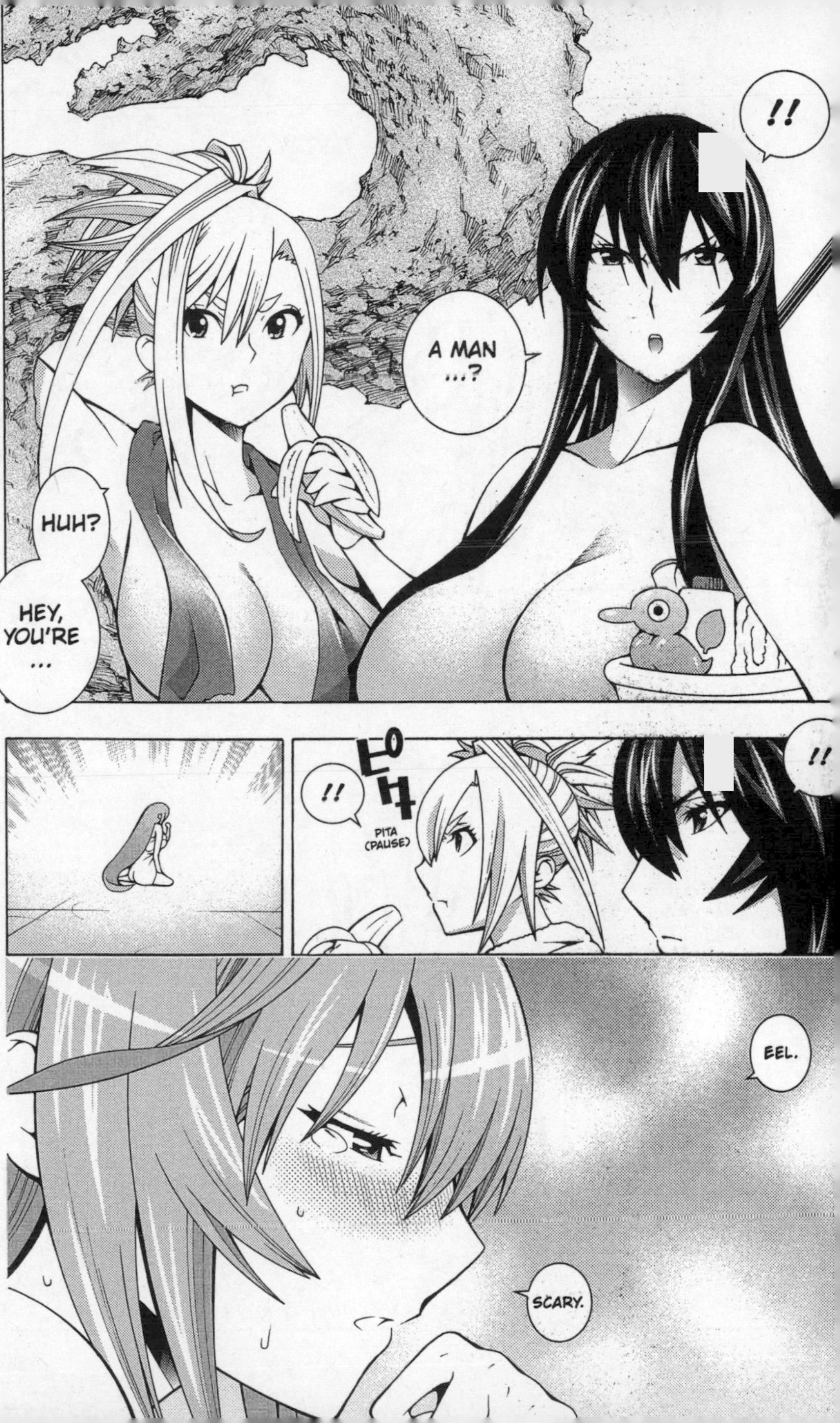
!!
A MAN ...?
HUH?
HEY, YOU'RE ...
!!
!!
ピタ
PITA (PAUSE)
EEL.
SCARY.

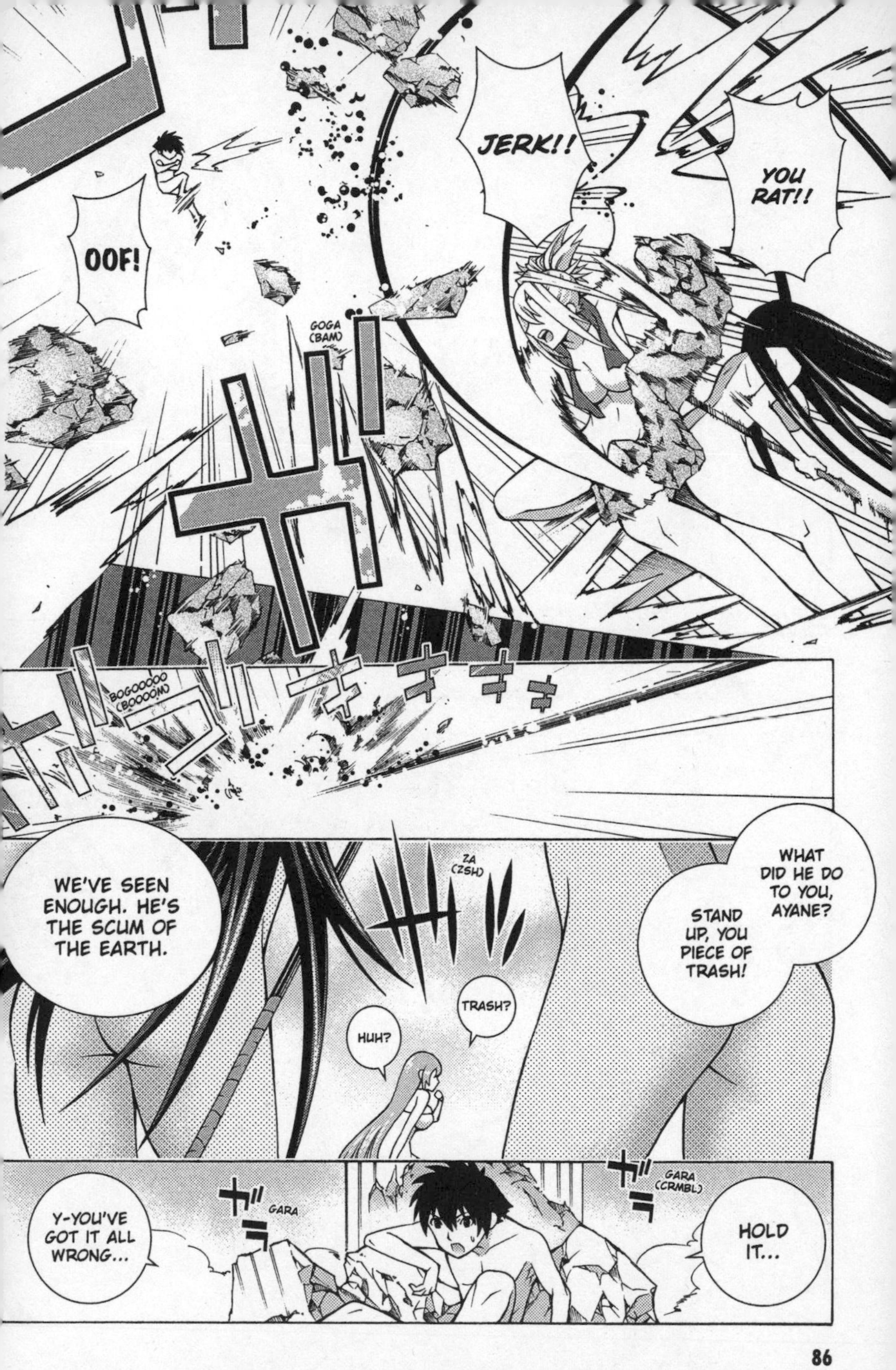
YOU RAT!!
JERK!!
OOF!
GOGA (BAM)
BOGOOOOO (BOOOOM)
WHAT DID HE DO TO YOU, AYANE?
STAND UP, YOU PIECE OF TRASH!
ZA (ZSH)
TRASH?
HUH?
WE'VE SEEN ENOUGH. HE'S THE SCUM OF THE EARTH.
HOLD IT...
GARA (CRMBL)
GARA
Y-YOU'VE GOT IT ALL WRONG...

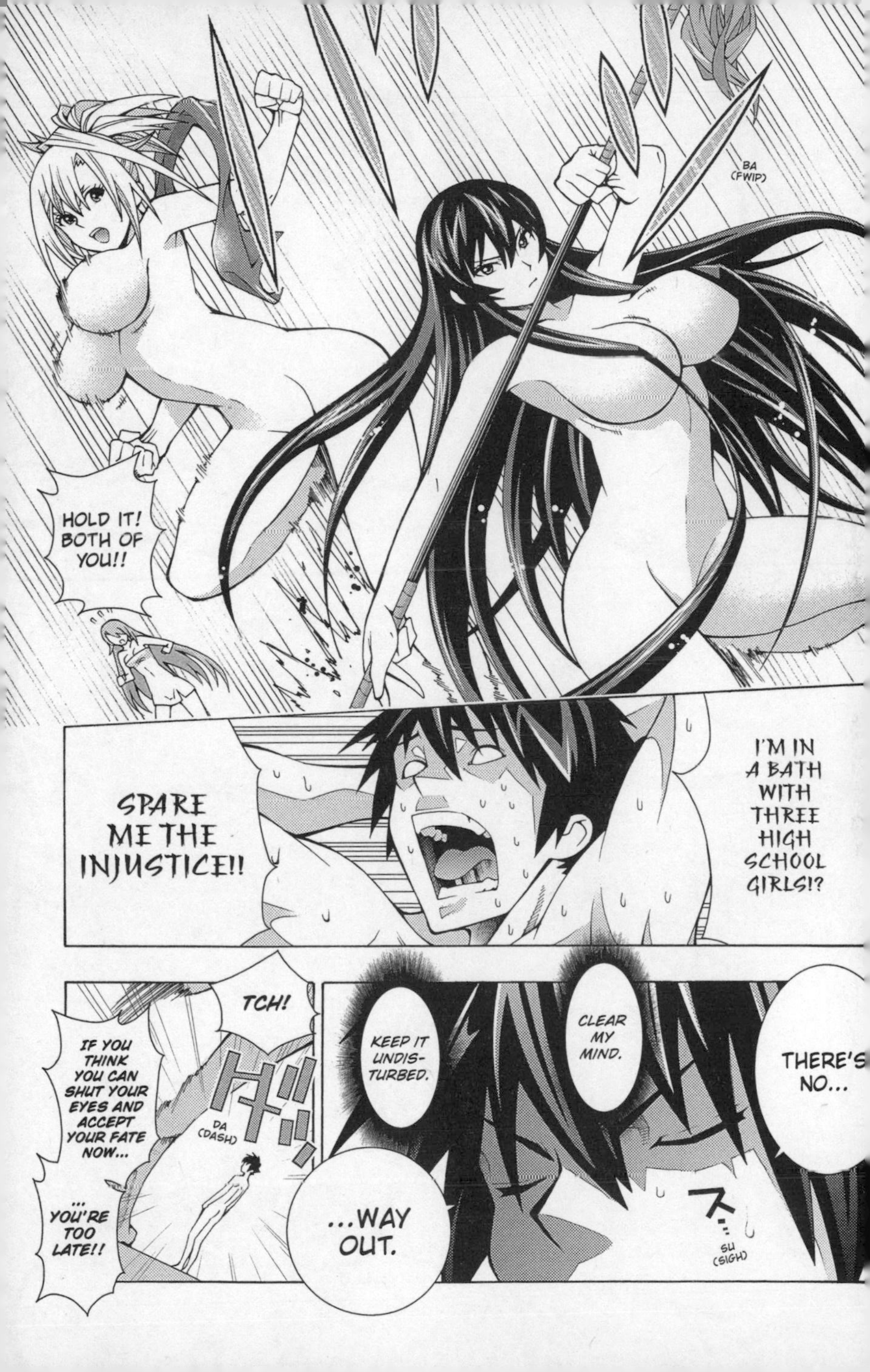
BA
(FWIP)
HOLD IT! BOTH OF YOU!!
I'M IN A BATH WITH THREE HIGH SCHOOL GIRLS!?
SPARE ME THE INJUSTICE!!
THERE'S NO...
CLEAR MY MIND.
KEEP IT UNDIS-TURBED.
SU
(SIGH)
...WAY OUT.
TCH!
DA
(DASH)
IF YOU THINK YOU CAN SHUT YOUR EYES AND ACCEPT YOUR FATE NOW...
...YOU'RE TOO LATE!!

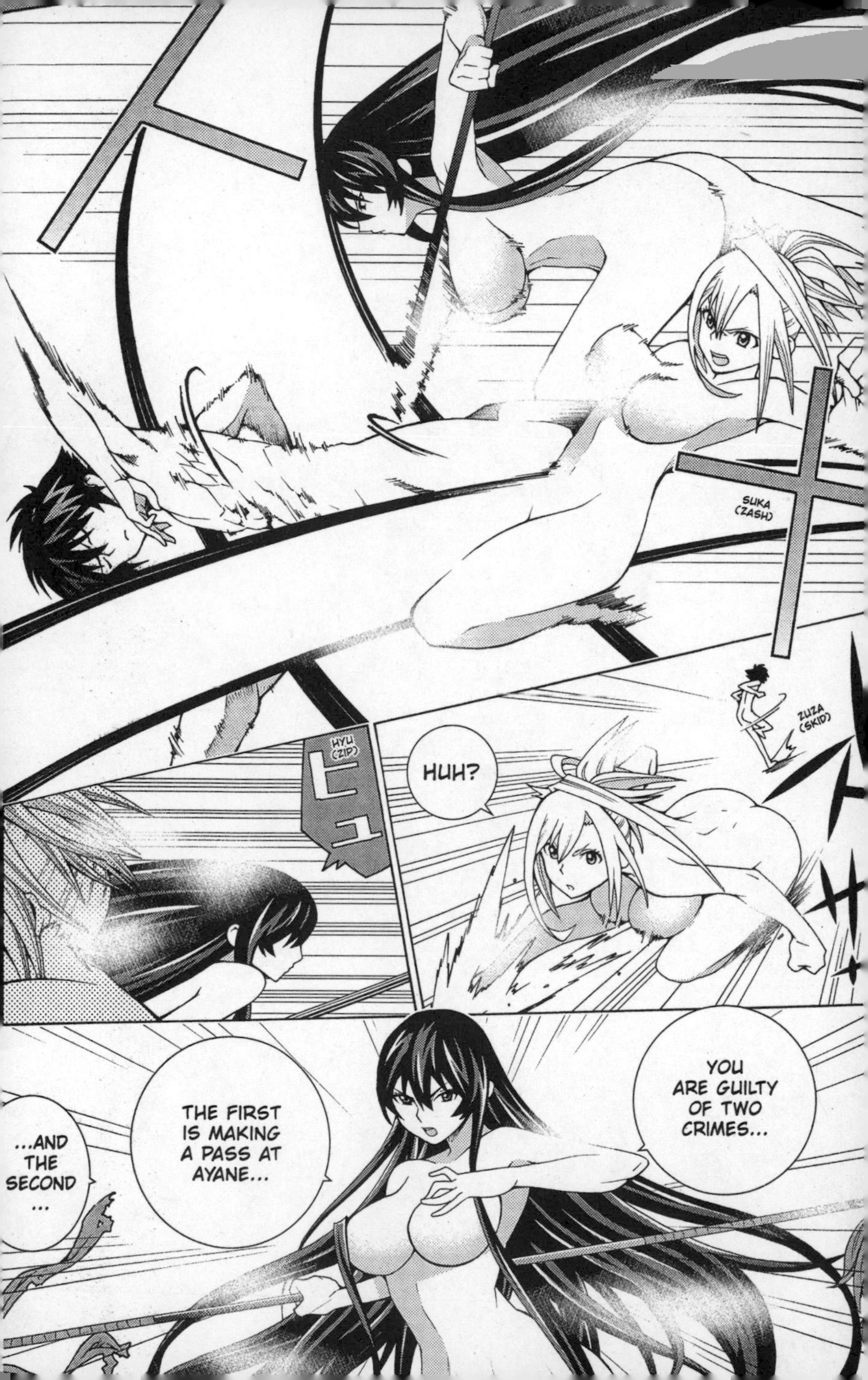
SUKA (ZASH)
ZUZA (SKID)
HUH?
ヒュ HYU (ZIP)
YOU ARE GUILTY OF TWO CRIMES...
THE FIRST IS MAKING A PASS AT AYANE...
...AND THE SECOND ...

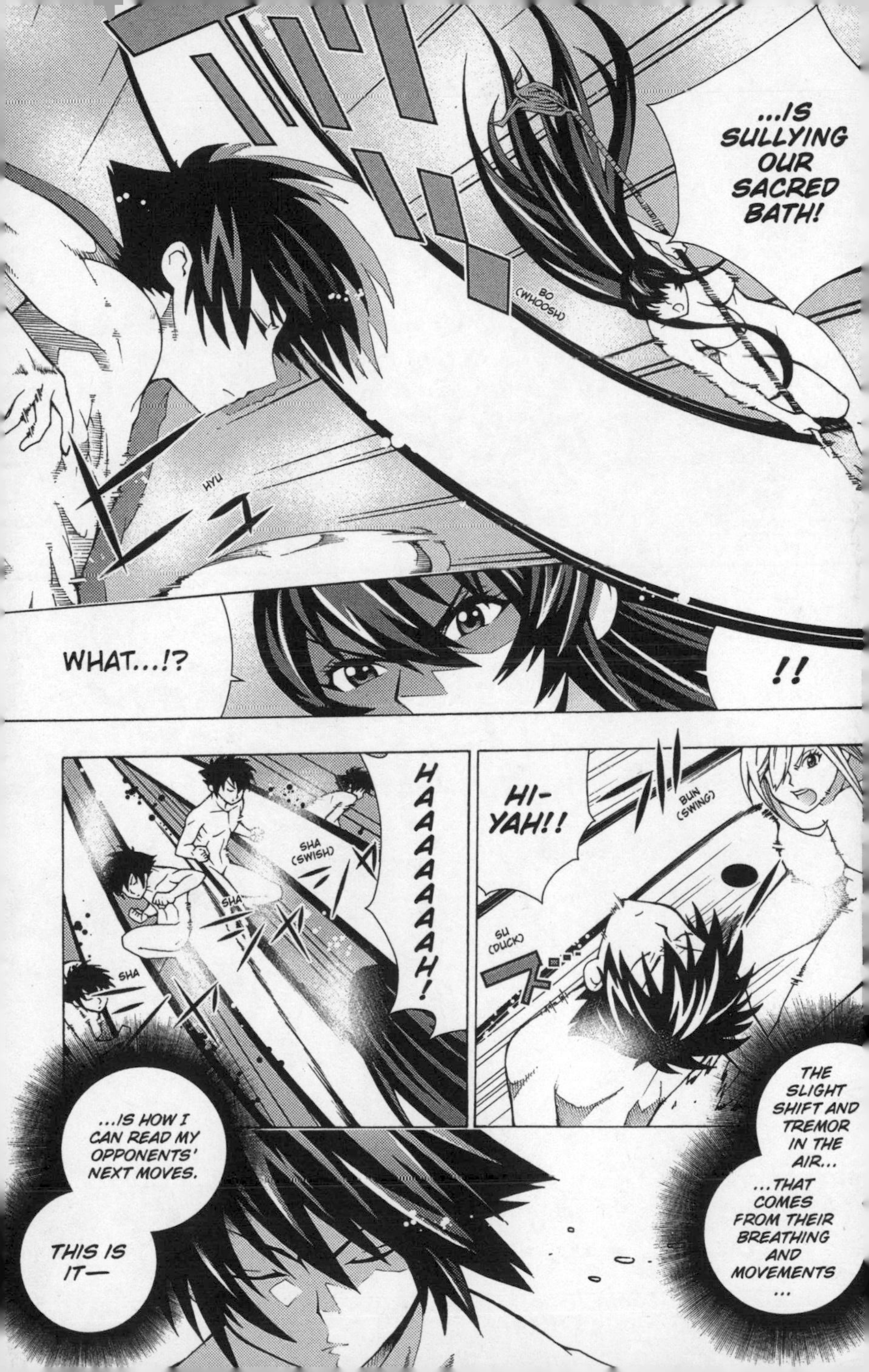
...IS SULLYING OUR SACRED BATH!
BO (WHOOSH)
HYU
!!
WHAT...!?
BUN (SWING)
HI-YAH!!
SU (DUCK)
HAAAAAAAAH!
SHA (SWISH)
SHA
SHA
THE SLIGHT SHIFT AND TREMOR IN THE AIR...
...THAT COMES FROM THEIR BREATHING AND MOVEMENTS...
...IS HOW I CAN READ MY OPPONENTS' NEXT MOVES.
THIS IS IT—

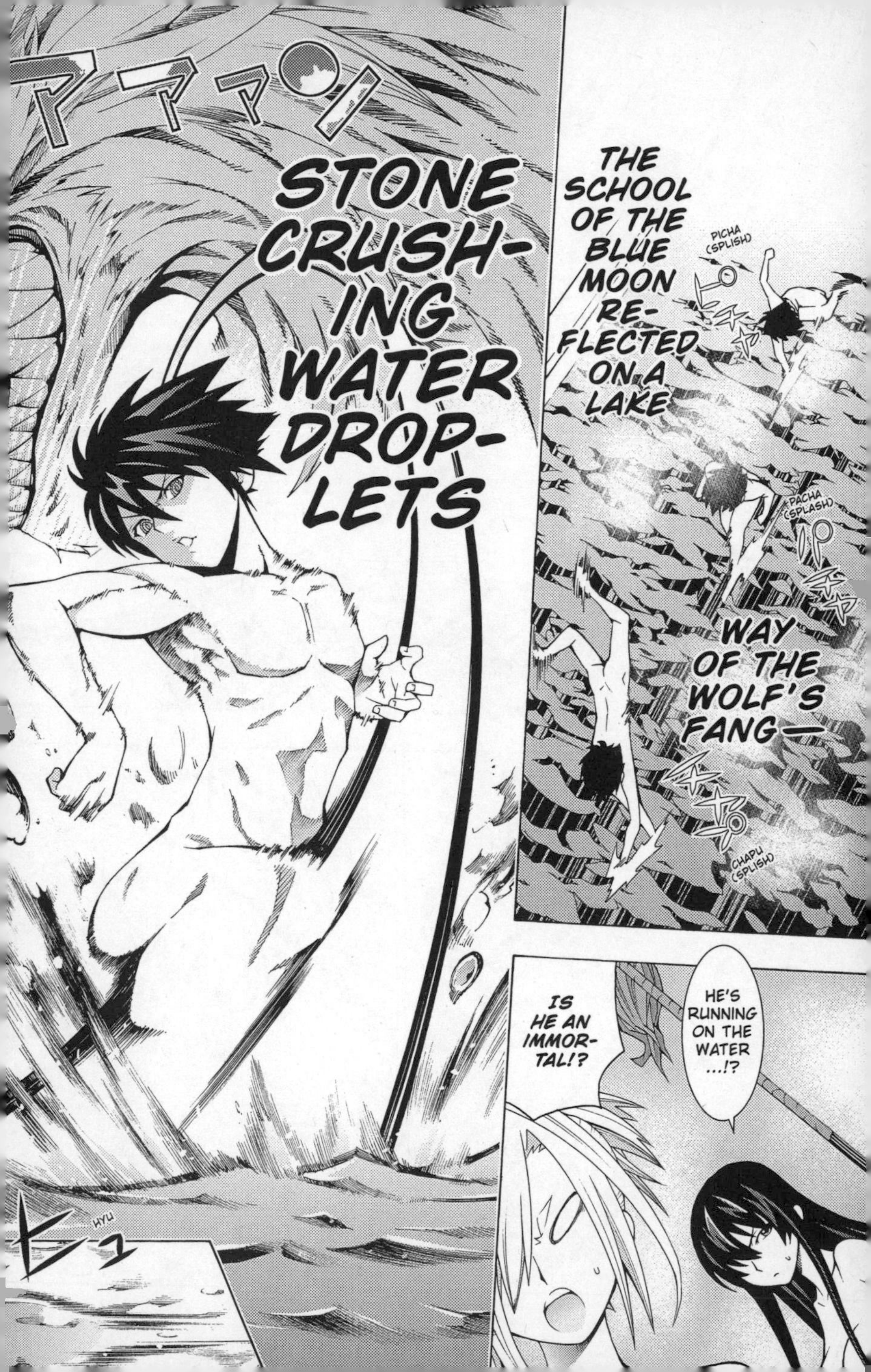

PICHA (SPLISH)
WAY OF THE WOLF'S FANG—
THE SCHOOL OF THE BLUE MOON REFLECTED ON A LAKE
PACHA (SPLASH)
CHAPU (SPLISH)
HE'S RUNNING ON THE WATER ...!?
IS HE AN IMMORTAL!?
STONE CRUSHING WATER DROPLETS
HYU

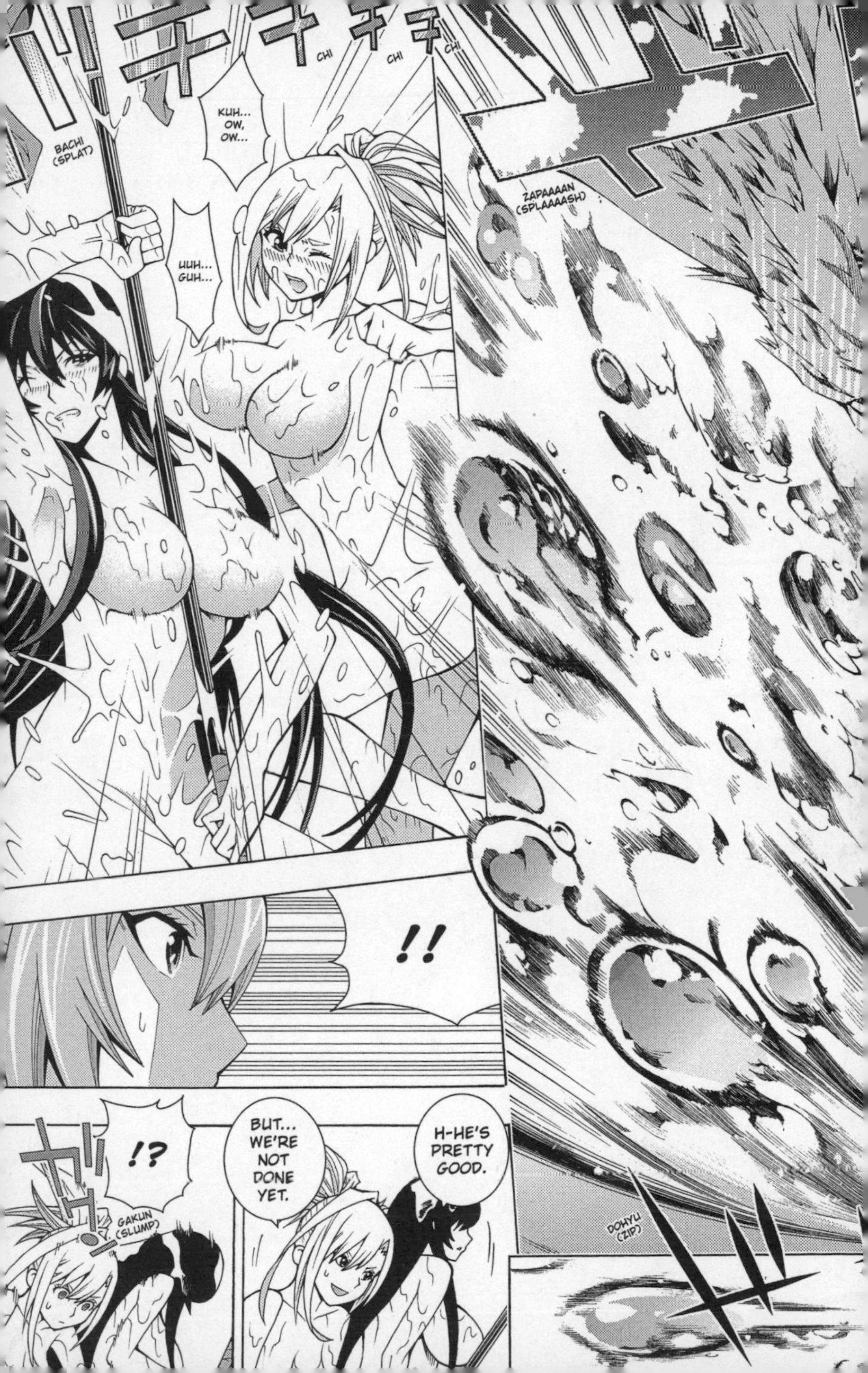
ZAPAAAAN (SPLAAAASH)
DOHYU (ZIP)
CHI
CHI
CHI
KUH... OW, OW...
BACHI (SPLAT)
UUH... GUH...
!!
H-HE'S PRETTY GOOD.
BUT... WE'RE NOT DONE YET.
!?
GAKUN (SLUMP)

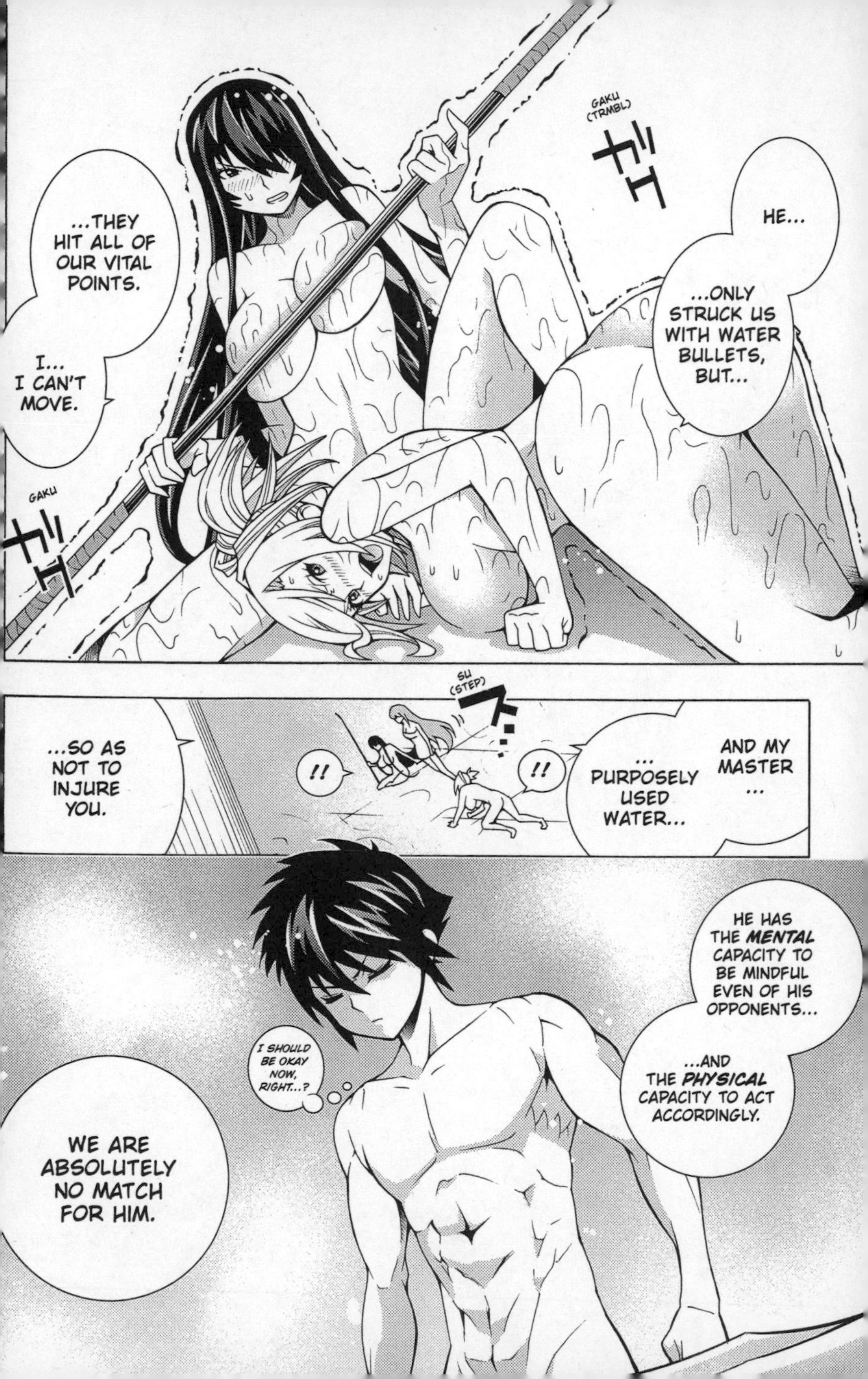
GAKU (TRMBL)
HE...
...ONLY STRUCK US WITH WATER BULLETS, BUT...
...THEY HIT ALL OF OUR VITAL POINTS.
I... I CAN'T MOVE.
GAKU
AND MY MASTER ...
... PURPOSELY USED WATER...
!!
SU (STEP)
!!
...SO AS NOT TO INJURE YOU.
HE HAS THE MENTAL CAPACITY TO BE MINDFUL EVEN OF HIS OPPONENTS...
...AND THE PHYSICAL CAPACITY TO ACT ACCORDINGLY.
I SHOULD BE OKAY NOW, RIGHT...?
WE ARE ABSOLUTELY NO MATCH FOR HIM.

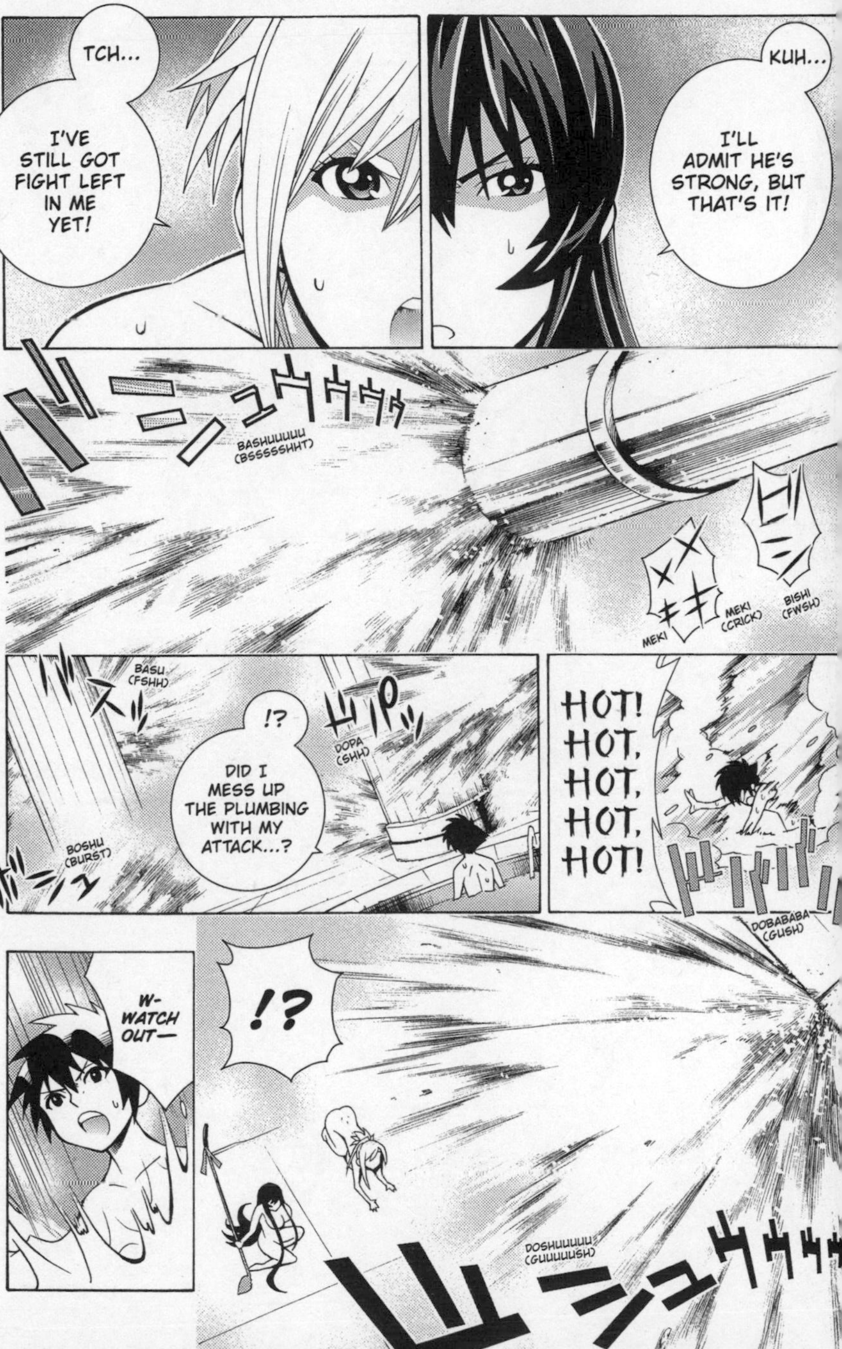
KUH...
I'LL ADMIT HE'S STRONG, BUT THAT'S IT!
TCH...
I'VE STILL GOT FIGHT LEFT IN ME YET!
BISHI (FWSH)
MEKI (CRICK)
MEKI
BASHUUUUU (BSSSSSHHT)
HOT! HOT, HOT, HOT, HOT!
DOBABABA (GUSH)
DOPA (SHH)
!?
DID I MESS UP THE PLUMBING WITH MY ATTACK...?
BASU (FSHH)
BOSHU (BURST)
!?
DOSHUUUUU (GUUUUUSH)
W-WATCH OUT—

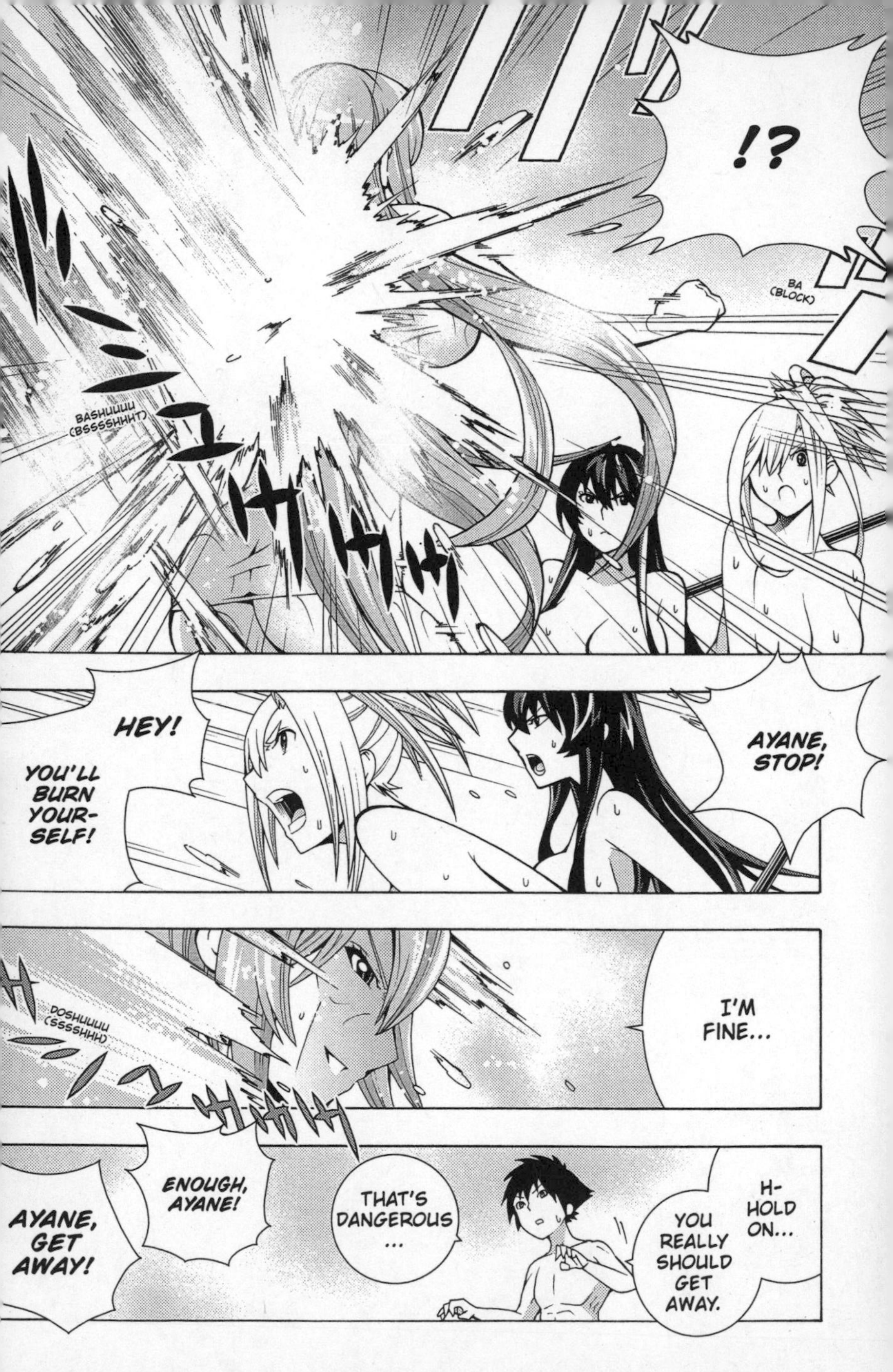
!?
BA
(BLOCK)
BASHUUUU
(BSSSSHHHT)
AYANE, STOP!
HEY!
YOU'LL BURN YOUR-SELF!
I'M FINE...
DOSHUUUU
(SSSSHHH)
H-HOLD ON...
YOU REALLY SHOULD GET AWAY.
THAT'S DANGEROUS...
ENOUGH, AYANE!
AYANE, GET AWAY!

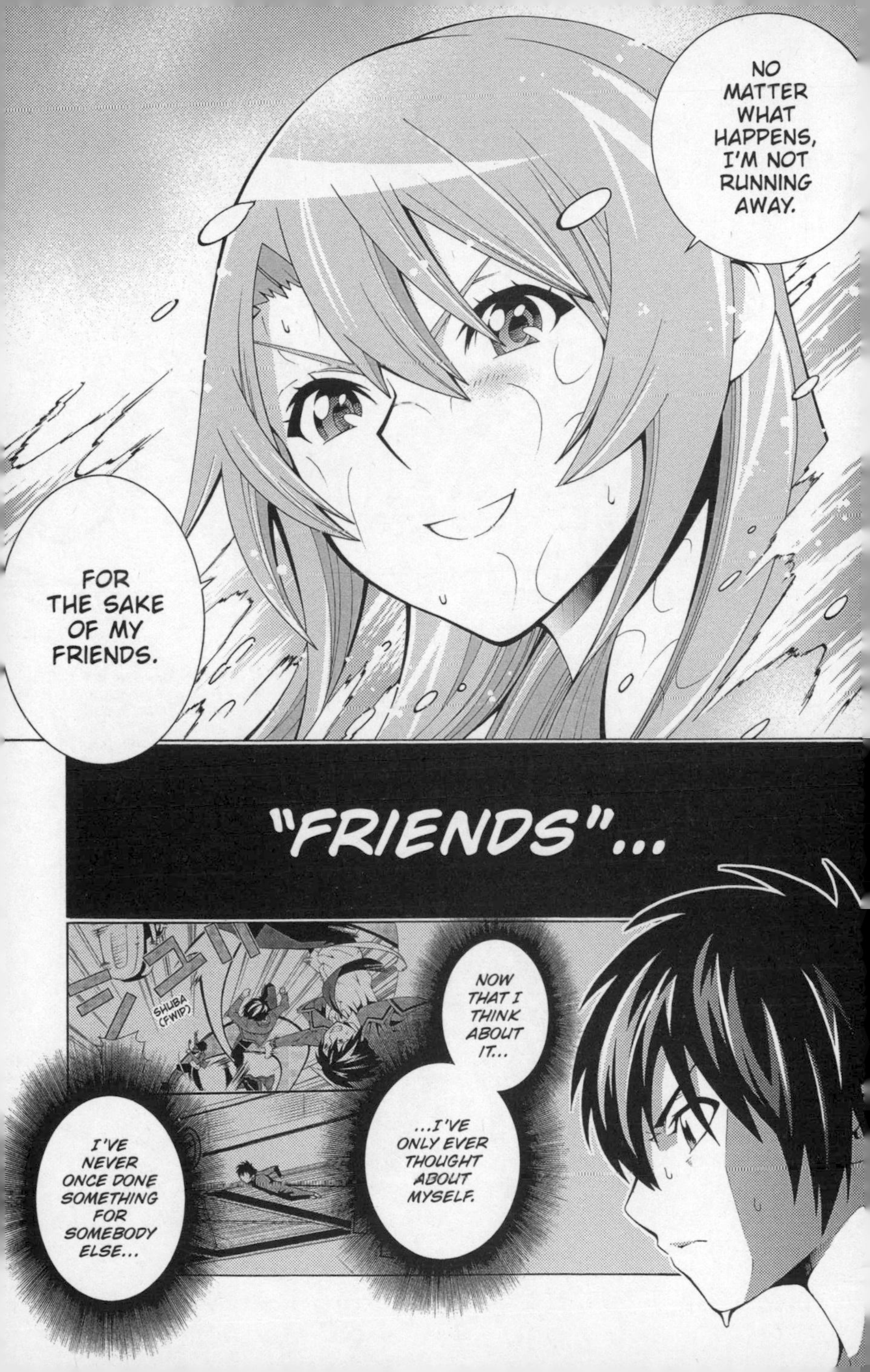
NO MATTER WHAT HAPPENS, I'M NOT RUNNING AWAY.
FOR THE SAKE OF MY FRIENDS.
"FRIENDS"...
NOW THAT I THINK ABOUT IT...
...I'VE ONLY EVER THOUGHT ABOUT MYSELF.
SHUBA (FWIP)
I'VE NEVER ONCE DONE SOMETHING FOR SOMEBODY ELSE...

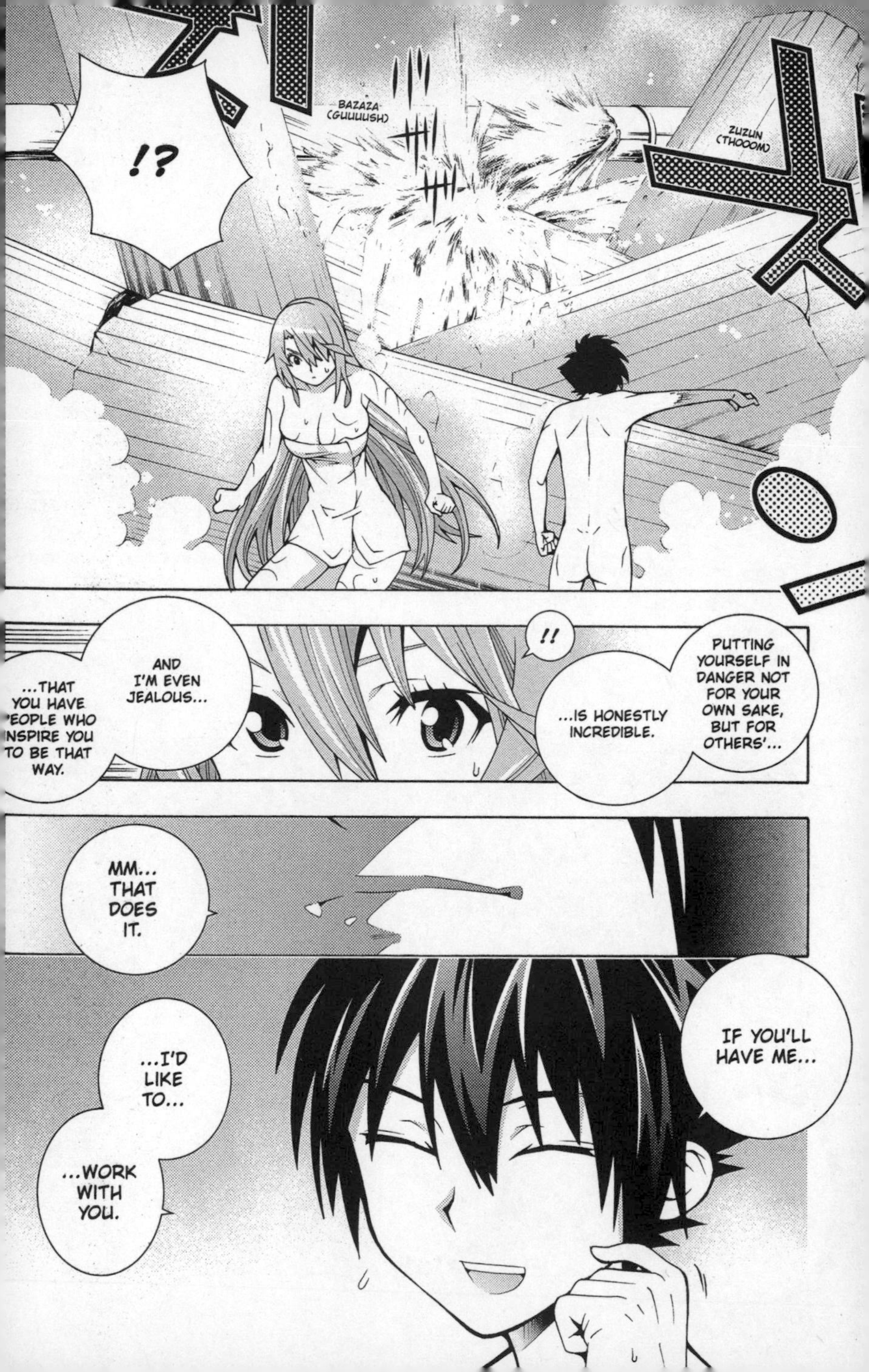
ZUZUN (THOOOM)
BAZAZA (GUUUUSH)
!?
!!
PUTTING YOURSELF IN DANGER NOT FOR YOUR OWN SAKE, BUT FOR OTHERS'...
...IS HONESTLY INCREDIBLE.
AND I'M EVEN JEALOUS...
...THAT YOU HAVE 'EOPLE WHO NSPIRE YOU TO BE THAT WAY.
MM... THAT DOES IT.
IF YOU'LL HAVE ME...
...I'D LIKE TO...
...WORK WITH YOU.

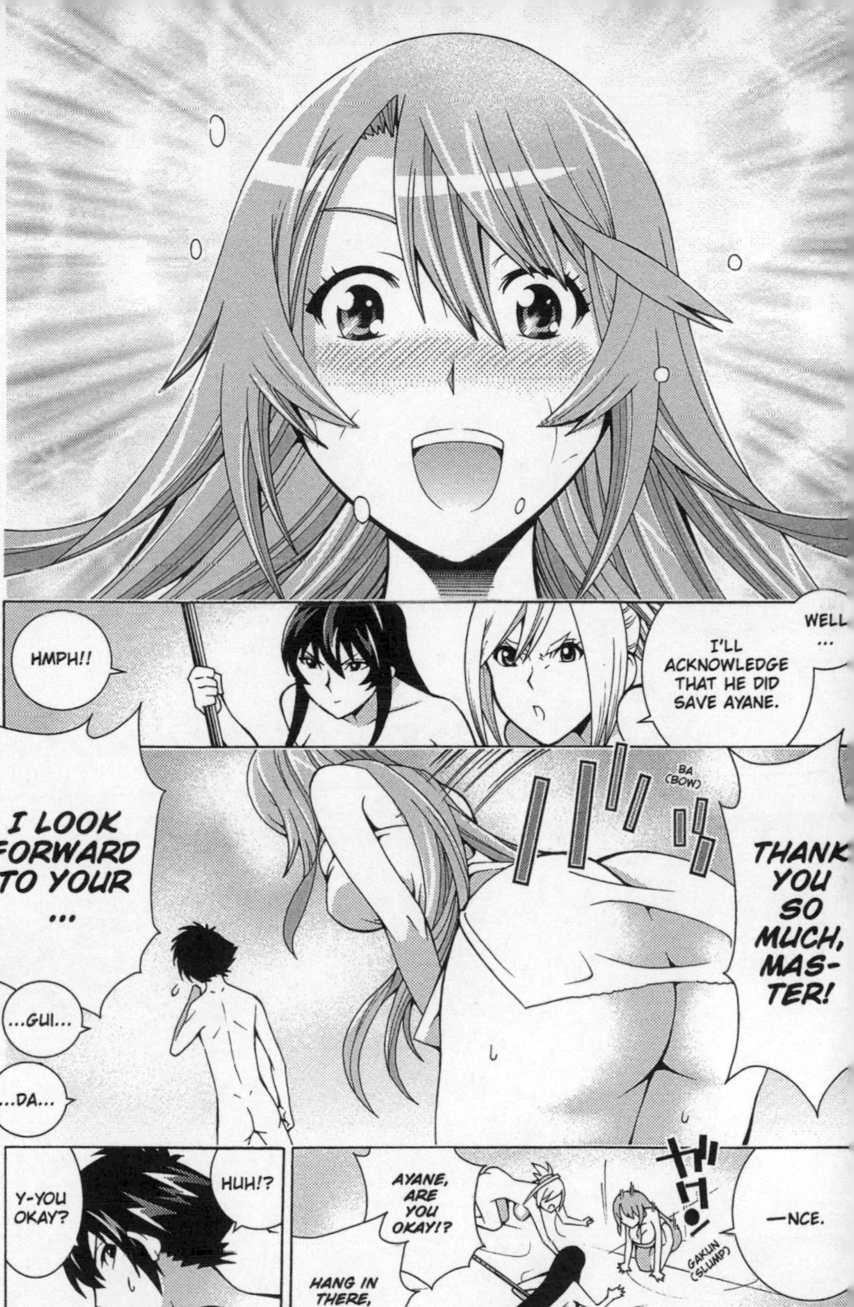
WELL ...
I'LL ACKNOWLEDGE THAT HE DID SAVE AYANE.
HMPH!!
THANK YOU SO MUCH, MASTER!
BA (BOW)
I LOOK FORWARD TO YOUR ...
...GUI...
...DA...
—NCE.
GAKUN (SLUMP)
AYANE, ARE YOU OKAY!?
HANG IN THERE, AYANE!
HUH!?
Y-YOU OKAY?

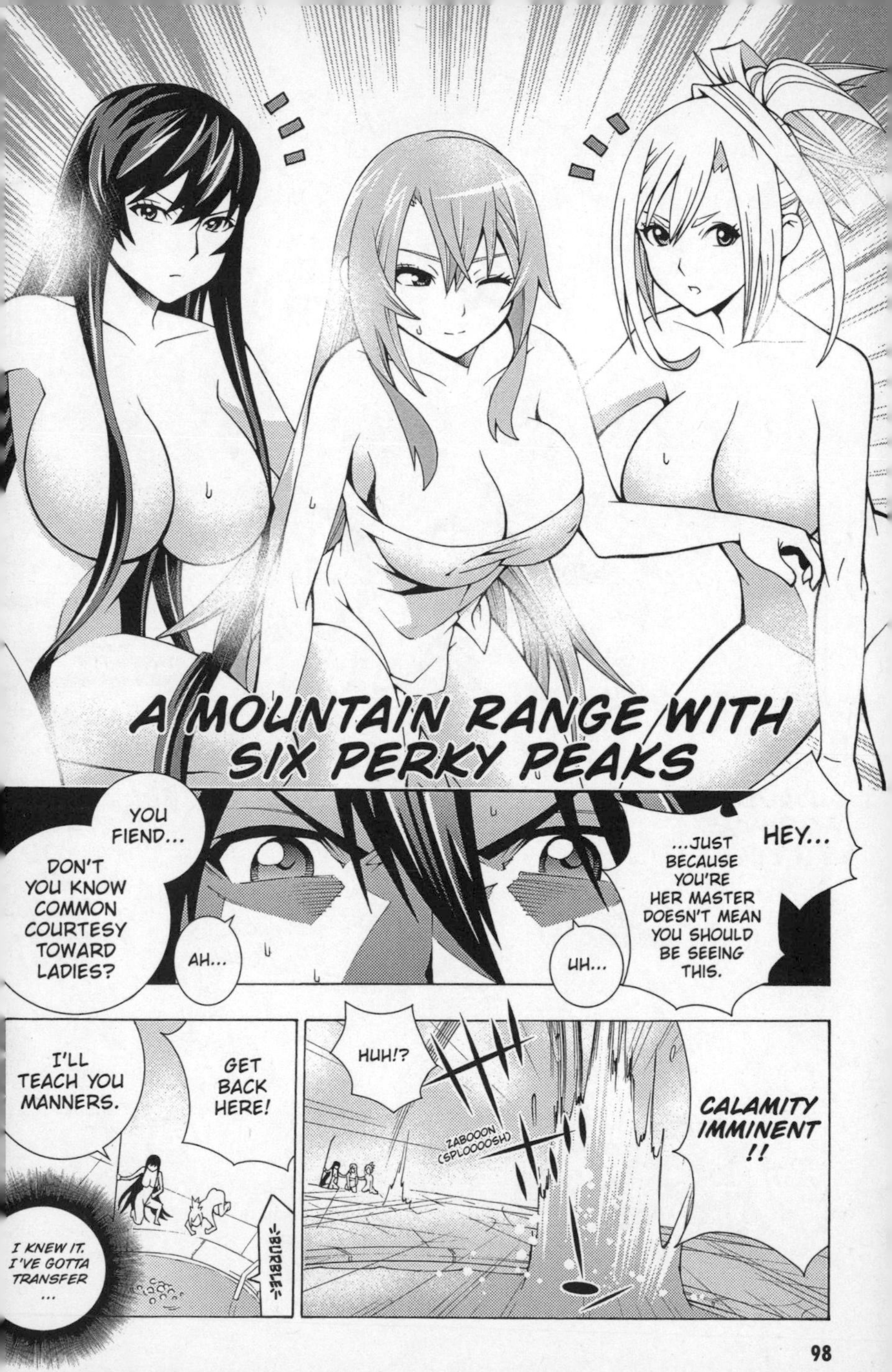
A MOUNTAIN RANGE WITH SIX PERKY PEAKS
HEY...
...JUST BECAUSE YOU'RE HER MASTER DOESN'T MEAN YOU SHOULD BE SEEING THIS.
UH...
AH...
YOU FIEND...
DON'T YOU KNOW COMMON COURTESY TOWARD LADIES?
CALAMITY IMMINENT !!
ZABOOON (SPLOOOOSH)
HUH!?
GET BACK HERE!
I'LL TEACH YOU MANNERS.
BUBBLE
I KNEW IT. I'VE GOTTA TRANSFER ...

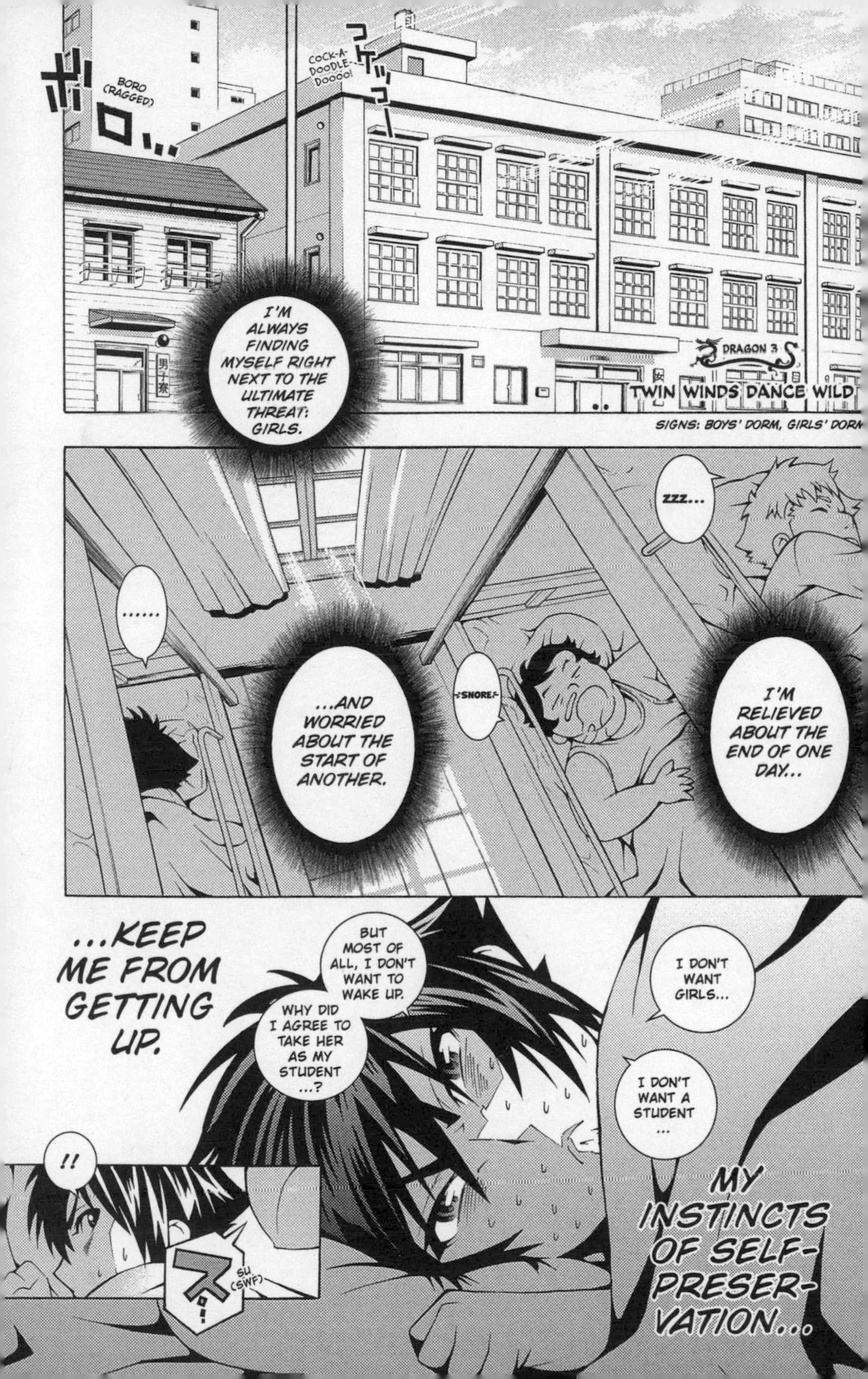
COCK-A-DOODLE-DOOOO!
BORO (RAGGED)
DRAGON 3
TWIN WINDS DANCE WILD
男子寮
I'M ALWAYS FINDING MYSELF RIGHT NEXT TO THE ULTIMATE THREAT: GIRLS.
SIGNS: BOYS' DORM, GIRLS' DORM
ZZZ...
I'M RELIEVED ABOUT THE END OF ONE DAY...
SNORE
...AND WORRIED ABOUT THE START OF ANOTHER.
....
I DON'T WANT GIRLS...
I DON'T WANT A STUDENT...
BUT MOST OF ALL, I DON'T WANT TO WAKE UP.
WHY DID I AGREE TO TAKE HER AS MY STUDENT...?
MY INSTINCTS OF SELF-PRESERVATION...
...KEEP ME FROM GETTING UP.
!!
SU (SWF)

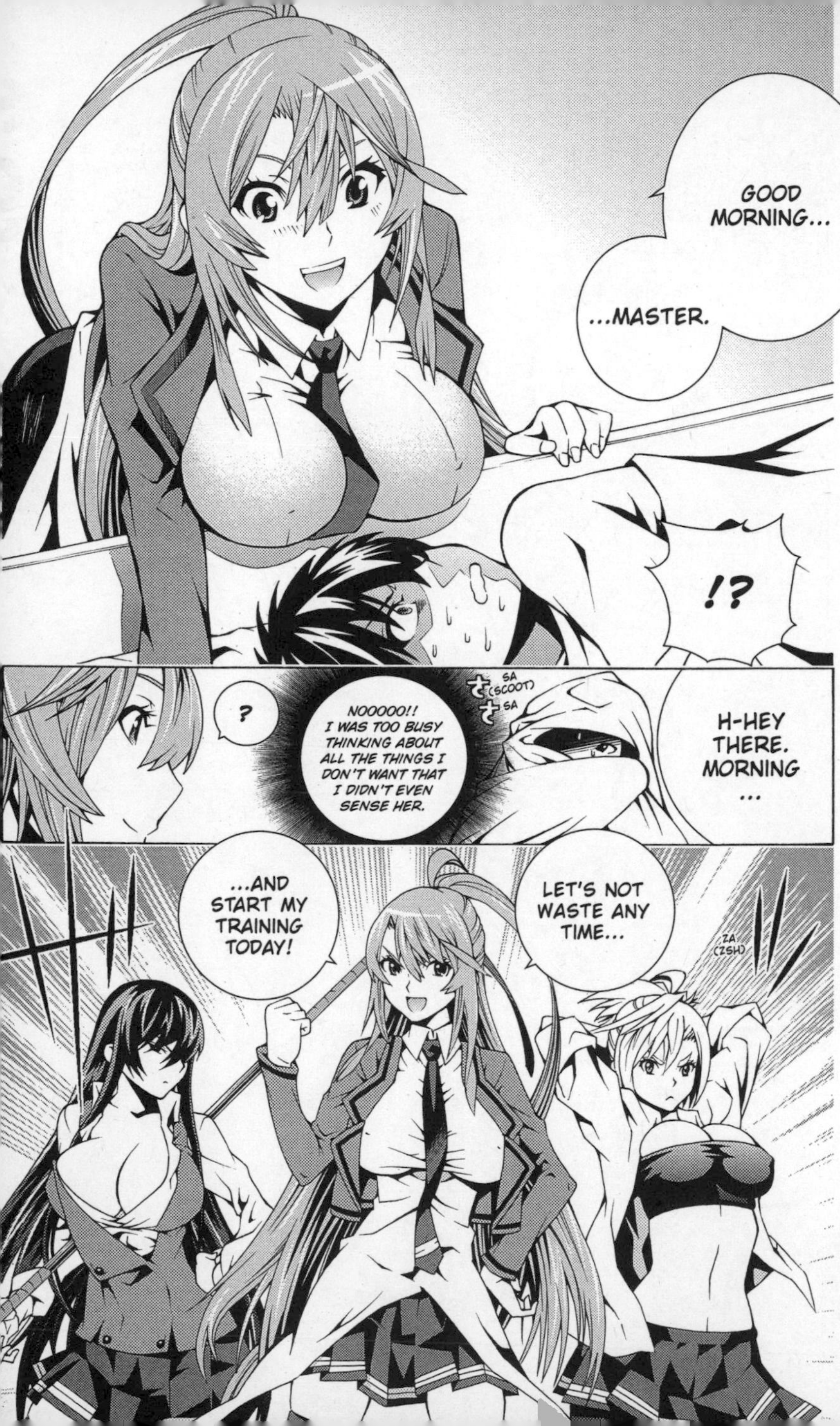
GOOD MORNING...
...MASTER.
!?
H-HEY THERE. MORNING ...
SA (SCOOT) SA
NOOOOO!! I WAS TOO BUSY THINKING ABOUT ALL THE THINGS I DON'T WANT THAT I DIDN'T EVEN SENSE HER.
?
ZA (ZSH)
LET'S NOT WASTE ANY TIME...
...AND START MY TRAINING TODAY!

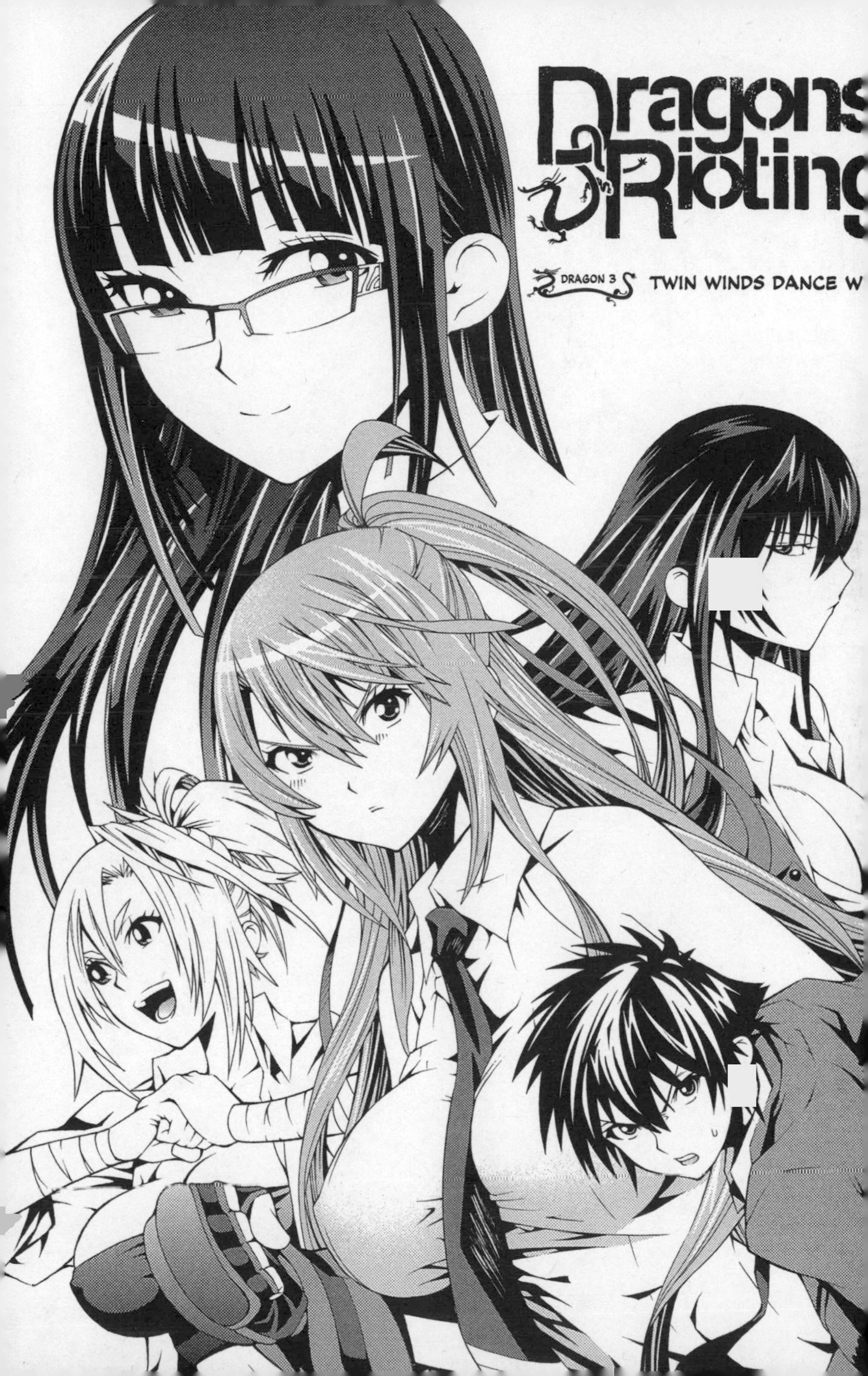
Dragons Rioting
DRAGON 3
TWIN WINDS DANCE W

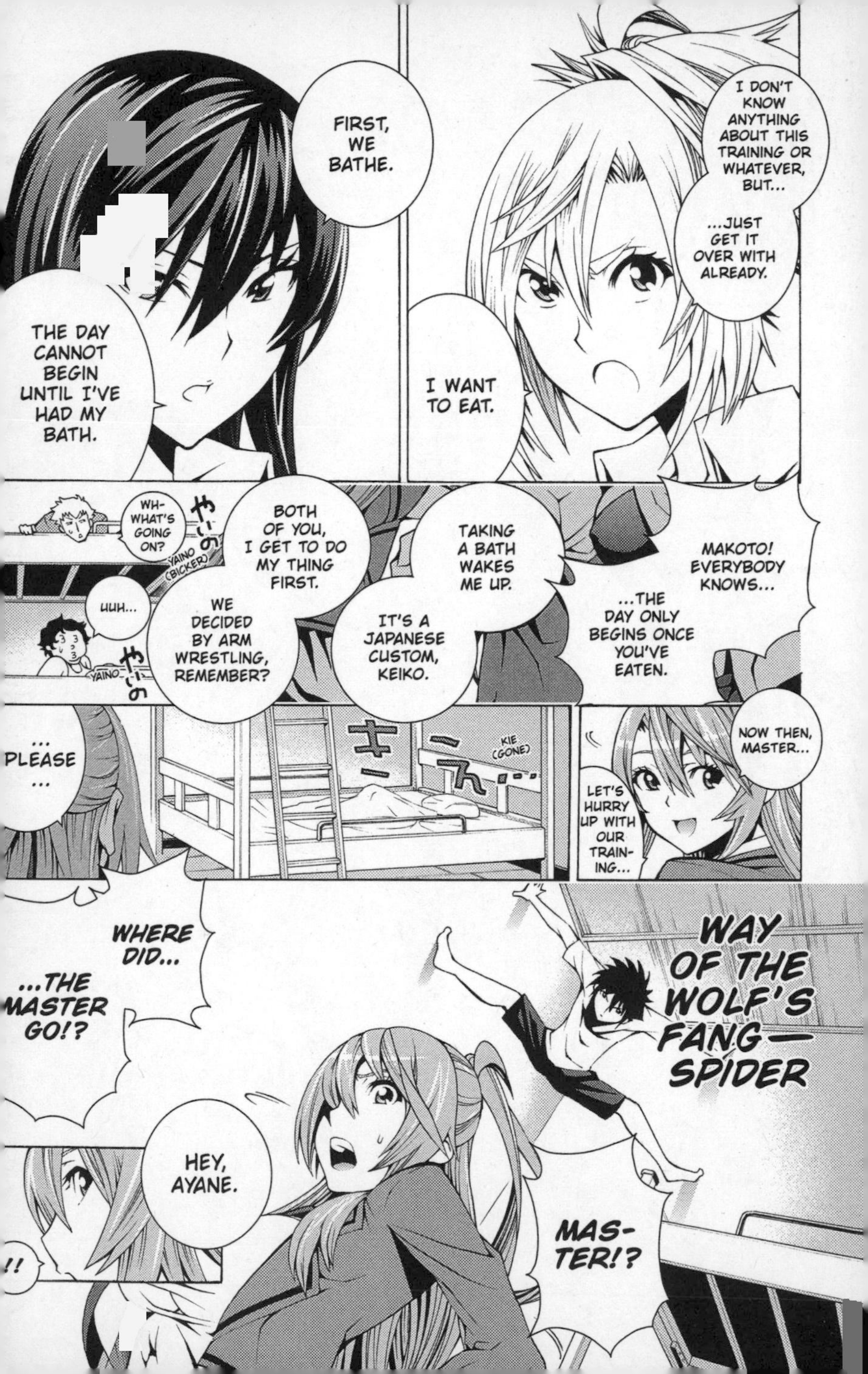
I DON'T KNOW ANYTHING ABOUT THIS TRAINING OR WHATEVER, BUT...
...JUST GET IT OVER WITH ALREADY.
I WANT TO EAT.
FIRST, WE BATHE.
THE DAY CANNOT BEGIN UNTIL I'VE HAD MY BATH.
MAKOTO! EVERYBODY KNOWS...
...THE DAY ONLY BEGINS ONCE YOU'VE EATEN.
TAKING A BATH WAKES ME UP.
IT'S A JAPANESE CUSTOM, KEIKO.
BOTH OF YOU, I GET TO DO MY THING FIRST.
WE DECIDED BY ARM WRESTLING, REMEMBER?
WH-WHAT'S GOING ON?
YAINO (BICKER)
UUH...
YAINO
NOW THEN, MASTER...
LET'S HURRY UP WITH OUR TRAIN-ING...
KIE (GONE)
...PLEASE...
WAY OF THE WOLF'S FANG—SPIDER
MAS-TER!?
WHERE DID...
...THE MASTER GO!?
HEY, AYANE.
!!

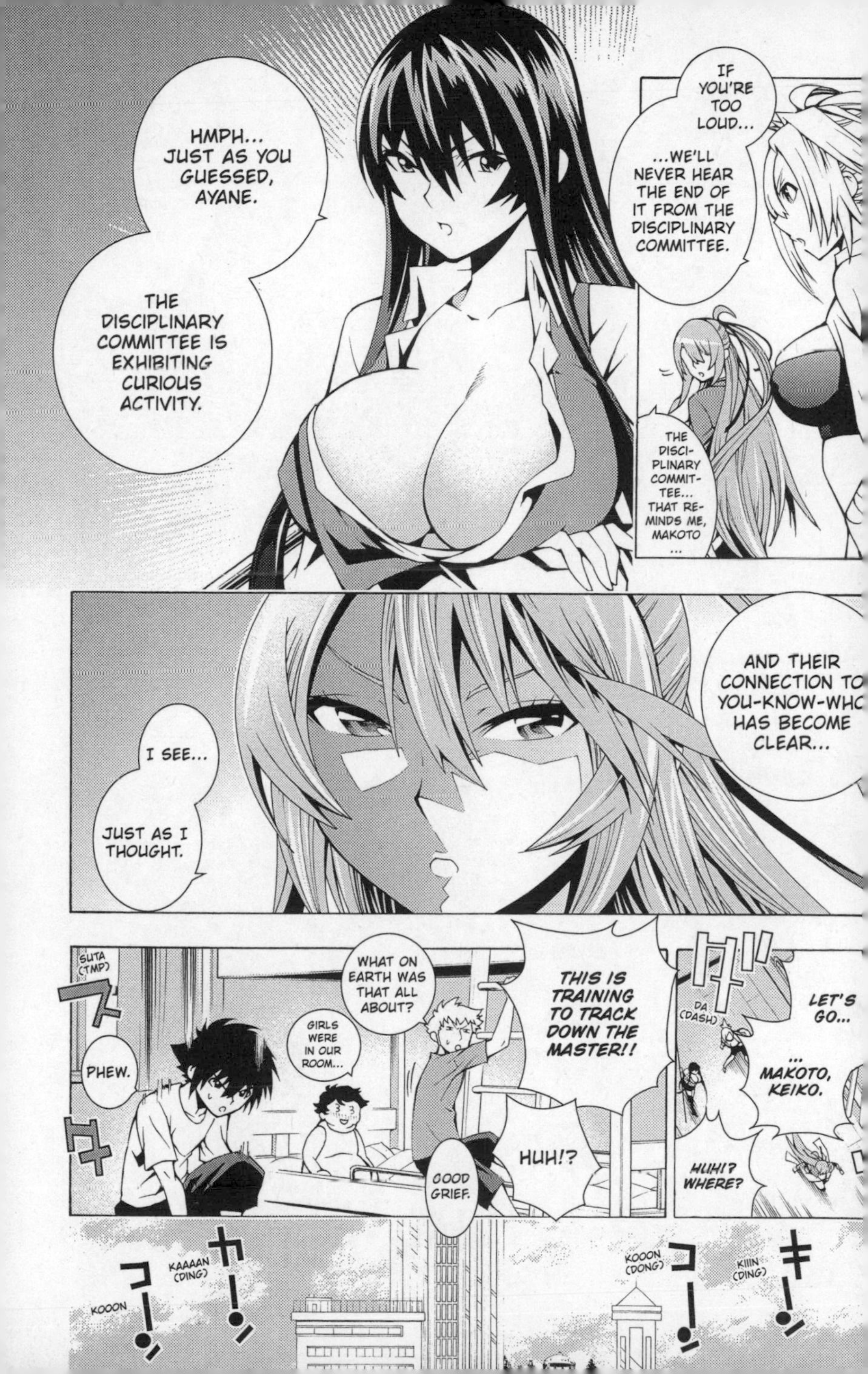
IF YOU'RE TOO LOUD...
...WE'LL NEVER HEAR THE END OF IT FROM THE DISCIPLINARY COMMITTEE.
THE DISCIPLINARY COMMITTEE... THAT REMINDS ME, MAKOTO...
HMPH... JUST AS YOU GUESSED, AYANE.
THE DISCIPLINARY COMMITTEE IS EXHIBITING CURIOUS ACTIVITY.
AND THEIR CONNECTION TO YOU-KNOW-WHO HAS BECOME CLEAR...
I SEE...
JUST AS I THOUGHT.
DA (DASH)
LET'S GO...
... MAKOTO, KEIKO.
HUH!? WHERE?
THIS IS TRAINING TO TRACK DOWN THE MASTER!!
HUH!?
WHAT ON EARTH WAS THAT ALL ABOUT?
GIRLS WERE IN OUR ROOM...
SUTA (TMP)
PHEW.
GOOD GRIEF.
KIIIN (DING)
KOOON (DONG)
KAAAAN (DING)
KOOON

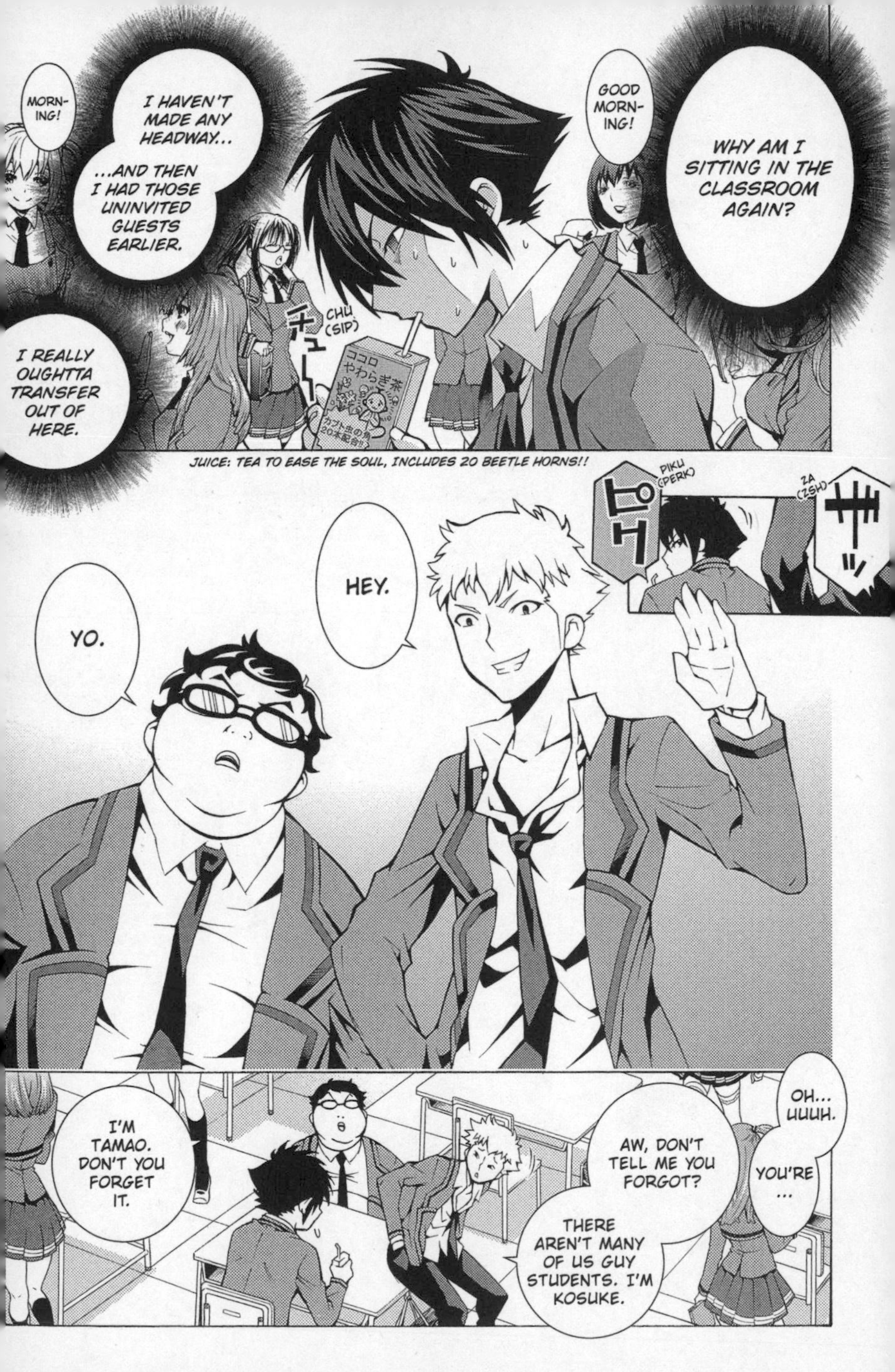
GOOD MORNING!
WHY AM I SITTING IN THE CLASSROOM AGAIN?
チュ～
CHU (SIP)
ココロ やわらぎ茶
カブト虫の角 20本配合!!
MORNING!
I HAVEN'T MADE ANY HEADWAY...
...AND THEN I HAD THOSE UNINVITED GUESTS EARLIER.
I REALLY OUGHTTA TRANSFER OUT OF HERE.
JUICE: TEA TO EASE THE SOUL, INCLUDES 20 BEETLE HORNS!!
ザッ
ZA (ZSH)
ピク
PIKU (PERK)
HEY.
YO.
OH... UUUH.
YOU'RE...
AW, DON'T TELL ME YOU FORGOT?
THERE AREN'T MANY OF US GUY STUDENTS. I'M KOSUKE.
I'M TAMAO. DON'T YOU FORGET IT.

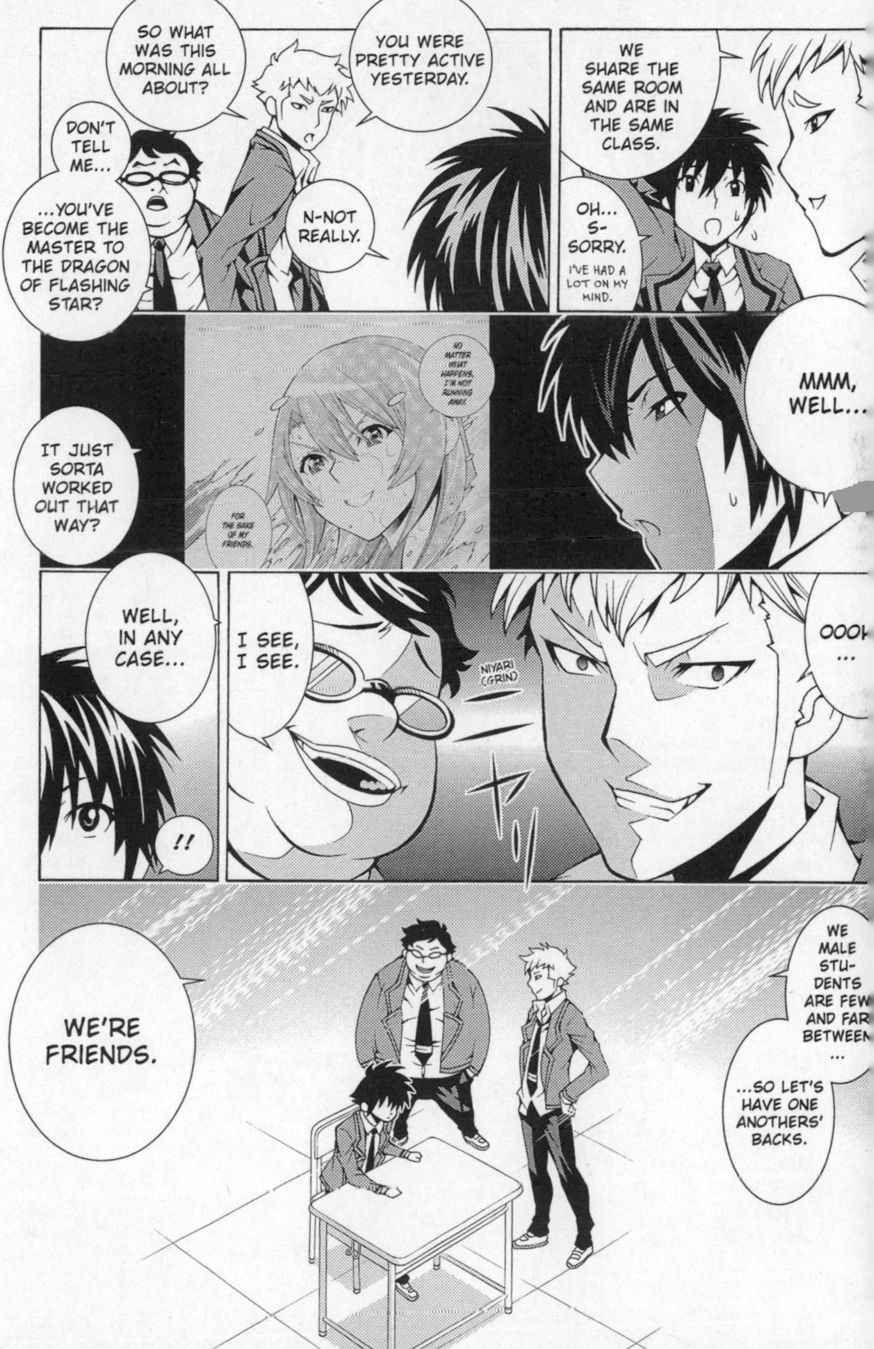
WE SHARE THE SAME ROOM AND ARE IN THE SAME CLASS.
OH... S-SORRY.
I'VE HAD A LOT ON MY MIND.
YOU WERE PRETTY ACTIVE YESTERDAY.
SO WHAT WAS THIS MORNING ALL ABOUT?
N-NOT REALLY.
DON'T TELL ME...
...YOU'VE BECOME THE MASTER TO THE DRAGON OF FLASHING STAR?
MMM, WELL...
NO MATTER WHAT HAPPENS, I'M NOT RUNNING AWAY.
FOR THE SAKE OF MY FRIENDS.
IT JUST SORTA WORKED OUT THAT WAY?
OOO...
NIYARI (GRIN)
I SEE, I SEE.
WELL, IN ANY CASE...
!!
WE MALE STU-DENTS ARE FEW AND FAR BETWEEN...
...SO LET'S HAVE ONE ANOTHERS' BACKS.
WE'RE FRIENDS.

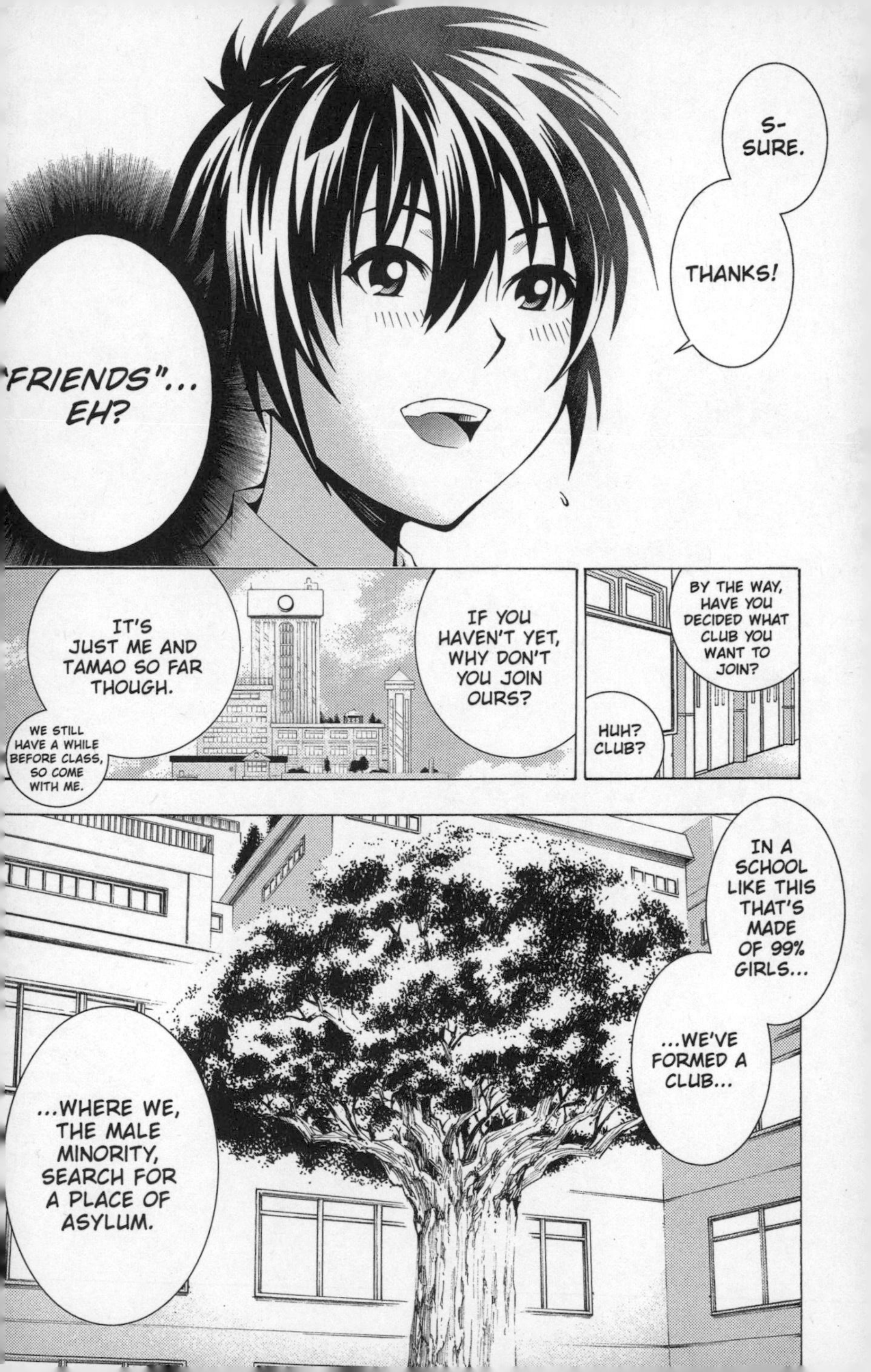
S- SURE.
THANKS!
"FRIENDS"... EH?
BY THE WAY, HAVE YOU DECIDED WHAT CLUB YOU WANT TO JOIN?
HUH? CLUB?
IF YOU HAVEN'T YET, WHY DON'T YOU JOIN OURS?
IT'S JUST ME AND TAMAO SO FAR THOUGH.
WE STILL HAVE A WHILE BEFORE CLASS, SO COME WITH ME.
IN A SCHOOL LIKE THIS THAT'S MADE OF 99% GIRLS...
...WE'VE FORMED A CLUB...
...WHERE WE, THE MALE MINORITY, SEARCH FOR A PLACE OF ASYLUM.

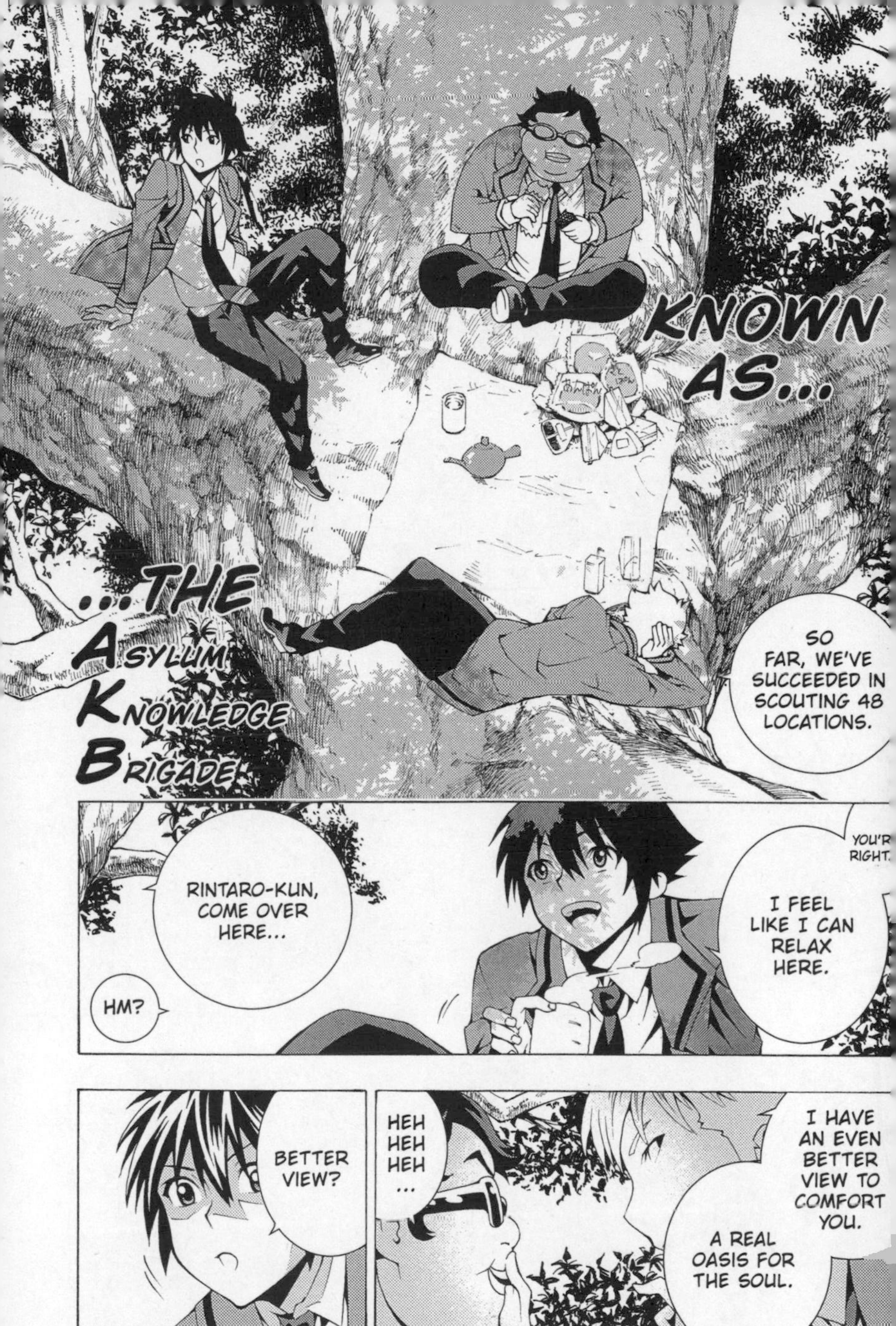
KNOWN AS...
...THE ASYLUM KNOWLEDGE BRIGADE
SO FAR, WE'VE SUCCEEDED IN SCOUTING 48 LOCATIONS.
YOU'RE RIGHT.
I FEEL LIKE I CAN RELAX HERE.
RINTARO-KUN, COME OVER HERE...
HM?
I HAVE AN EVEN BETTER VIEW TO COMFORT YOU.
A REAL OASIS FOR THE SOUL.
HEH HEH HEH ...
BETTER VIEW?

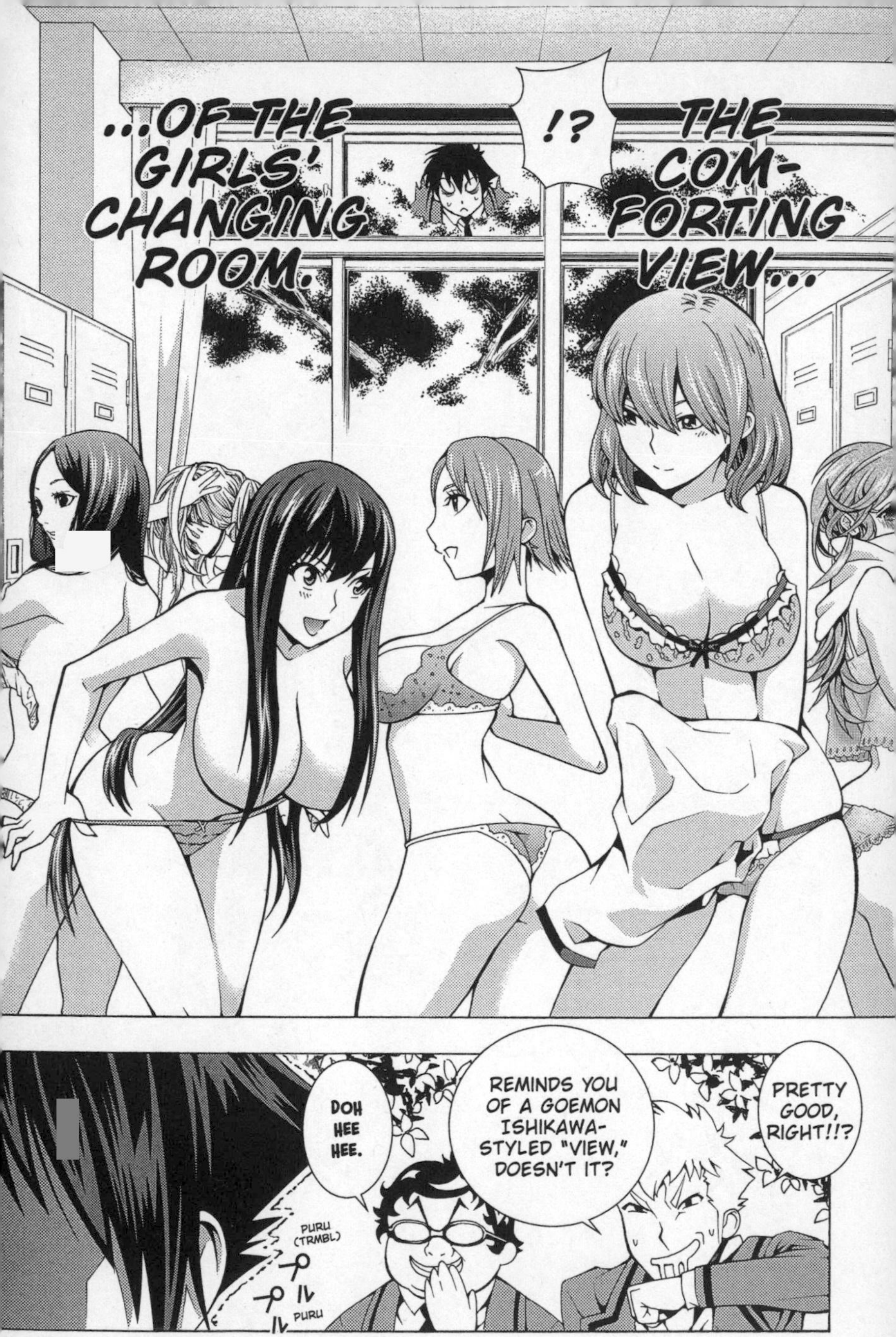
THE COM-FORTING VIEW...
!?
...OF THE GIRLS' CHANGING ROOM.
PRETTY GOOD, RIGHT!!?
REMINDS YOU OF A GOEMON ISHIKAWA-STYLED "VIEW," DOESN'T IT?
DOH HEE HEE.
PURU (TRMBL)
PURU

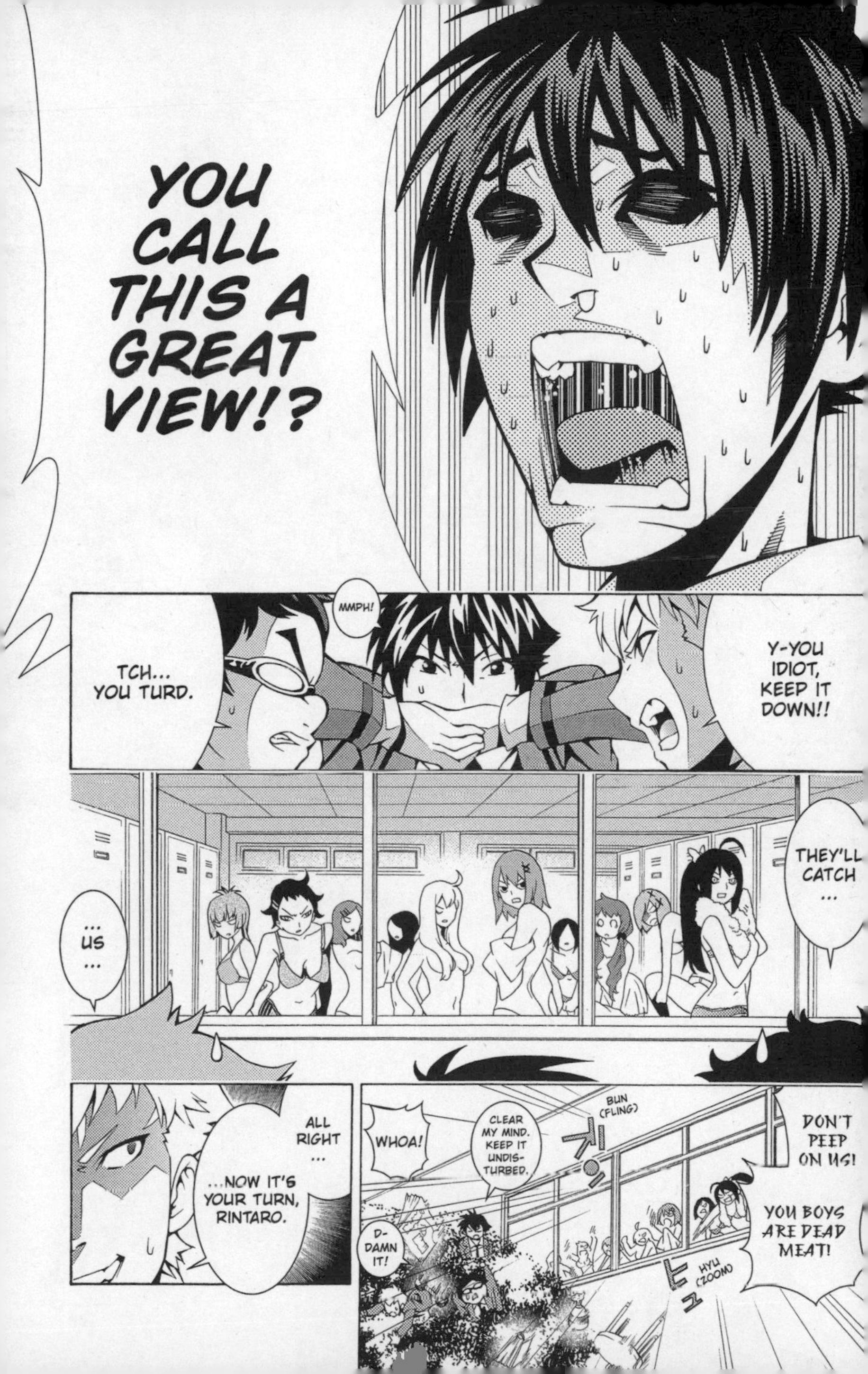
YOU CALL THIS A GREAT VIEW!?
Y-YOU IDIOT, KEEP IT DOWN!!
MMPH!
TCH... YOU TURD.
THEY'LL CATCH ...
... US ...
DON'T PEEP ON US!
BUN (FLING)
CLEAR MY MIND. KEEP IT UNDIS-TURBED.
WHOA!
YOU BOYS ARE DEAD MEAT!
HYU (ZOOM)
D-DAMN IT!
ALL RIGHT ...
...NOW IT'S YOUR TURN, RINTARO.

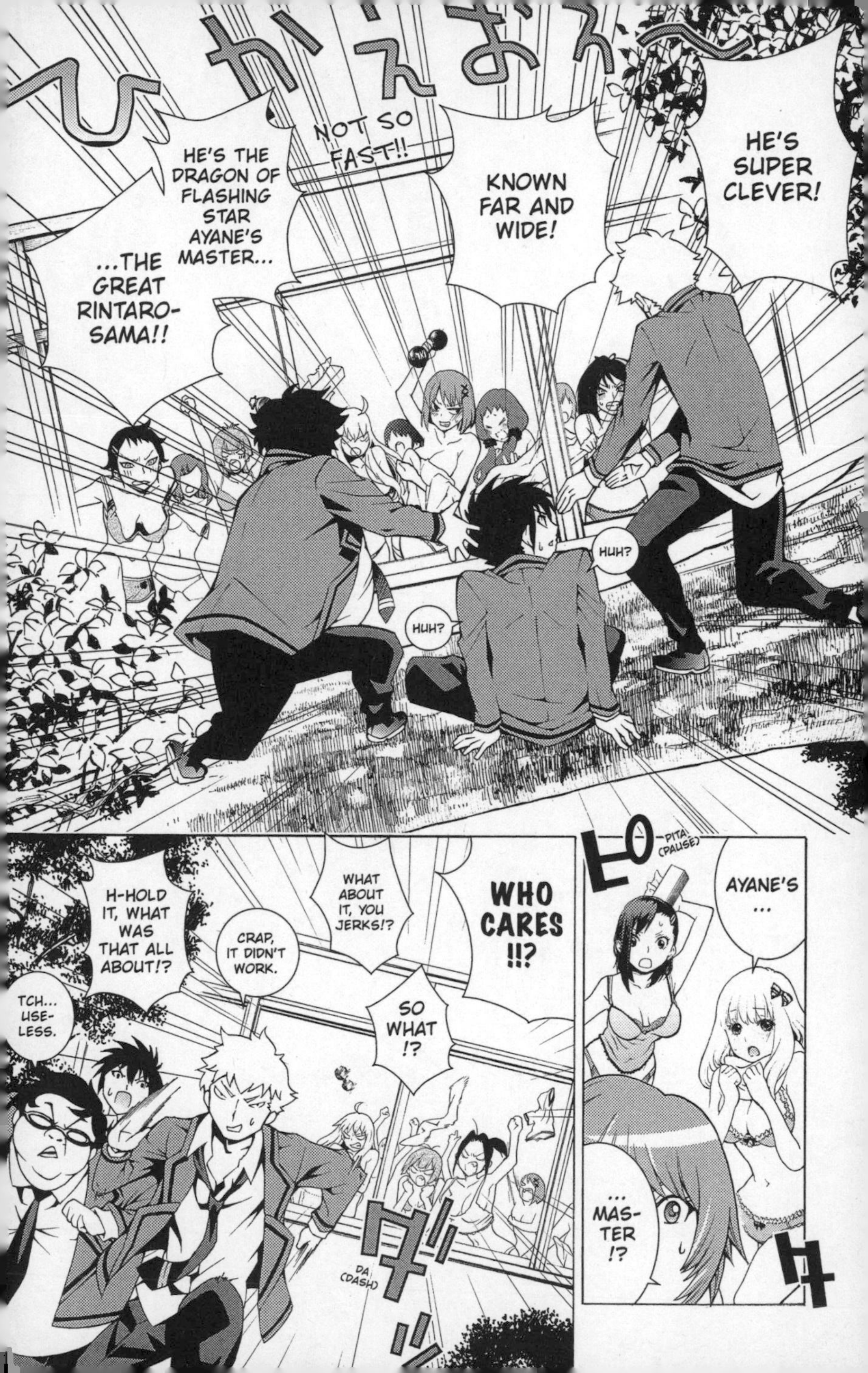
HE'S SUPER CLEVER!
KNOWN FAR AND WIDE!
NOT SO FAST!!
HE'S THE DRAGON OF FLASHING STAR AYANE'S MASTER...
...THE GREAT RINTARO-SAMA!!
HUH?
HUH?
PITA (PAUSE)
AYANE'S ...
... MASTER!?
WHO CARES!!?
WHAT ABOUT IT, YOU JERKS!?
H-HOLD IT, WHAT WAS THAT ALL ABOUT!?
CRAP, IT DIDN'T WORK.
SO WHAT!?
TCH... USELESS.
DA (DASH)

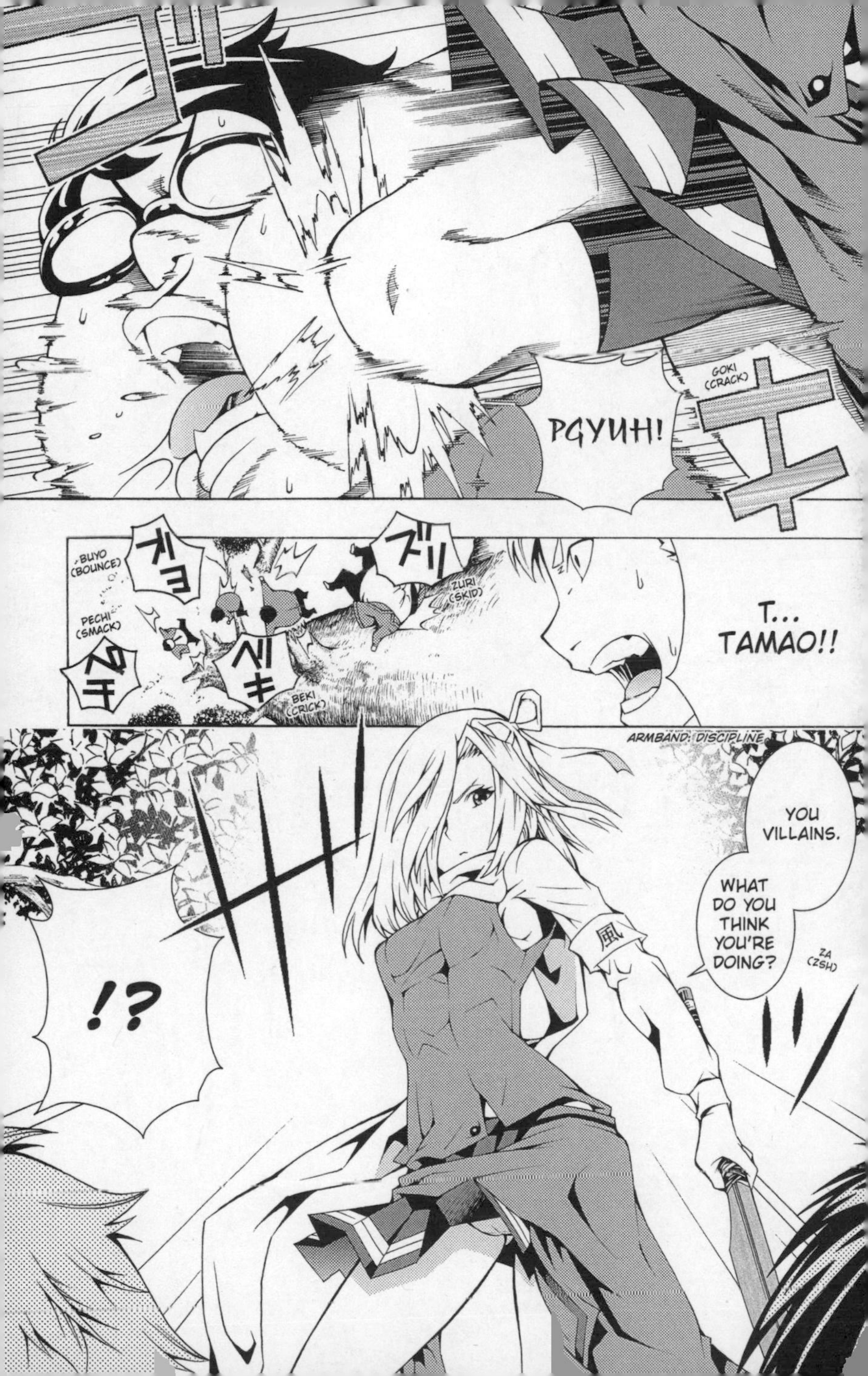
GOKI (CRACK)
PGYUH!
T... TAMAO!!
ZURI (SKID)
BUYO (BOUNCE)
BEKI (CRICK)
PECHI (SMACK)
ARMBAND: DISCIPLINE
YOU VILLAINS.
WHAT DO YOU THINK YOU'RE DOING?
ZA (ZSH)
!?

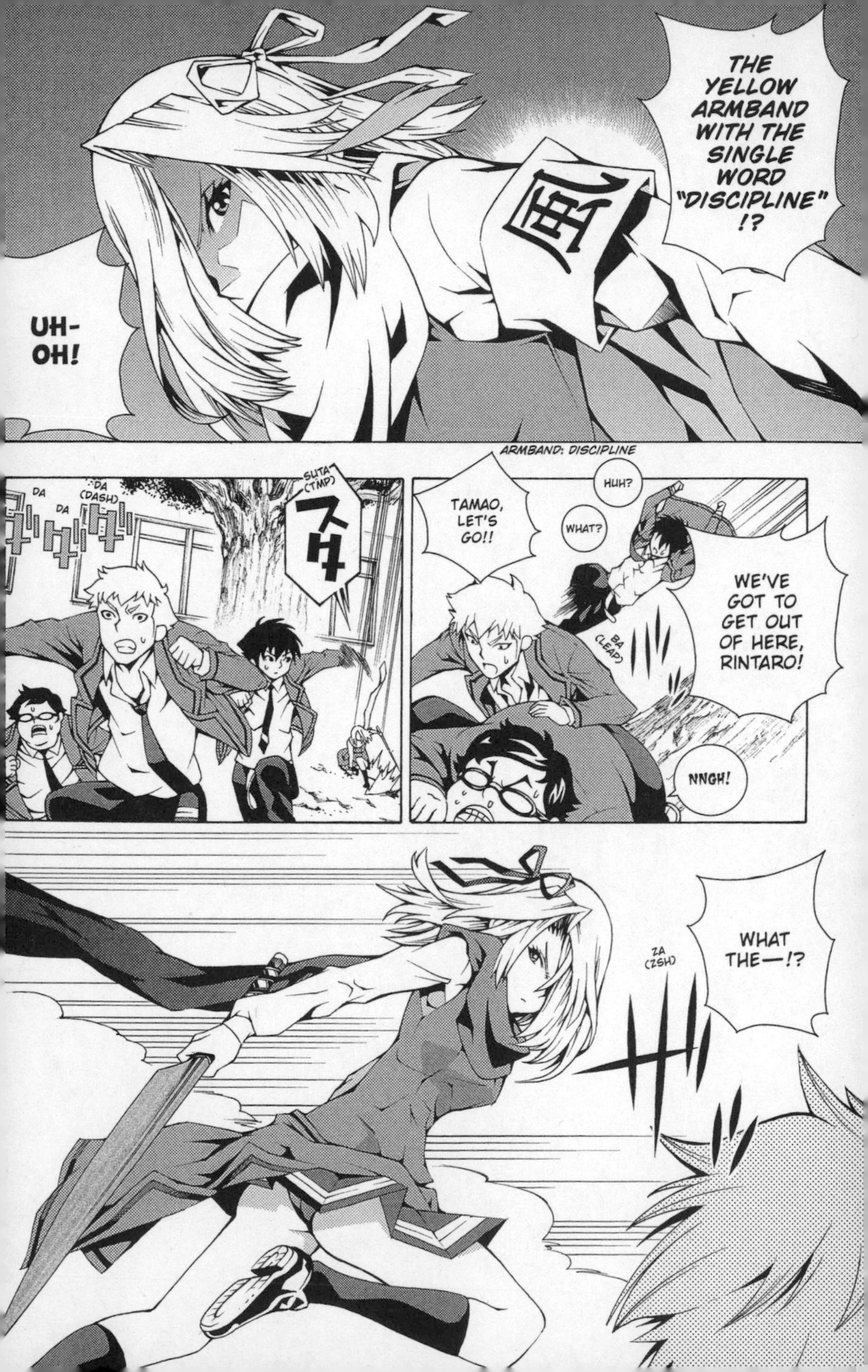
THE YELLOW ARMBAND WITH THE SINGLE WORD "DISCIPLINE" !?
UH-OH!
ARMBAND: DISCIPLINE
HUH?
WHAT?
TAMAO, LET'S GO!!
WE'VE GOT TO GET OUT OF HERE, RINTARO!
BA (LEAP)
NNGH!
SUTA (TMP)
DA DA DA (DASH)
WHAT THE—!?
ZA (ZSH)

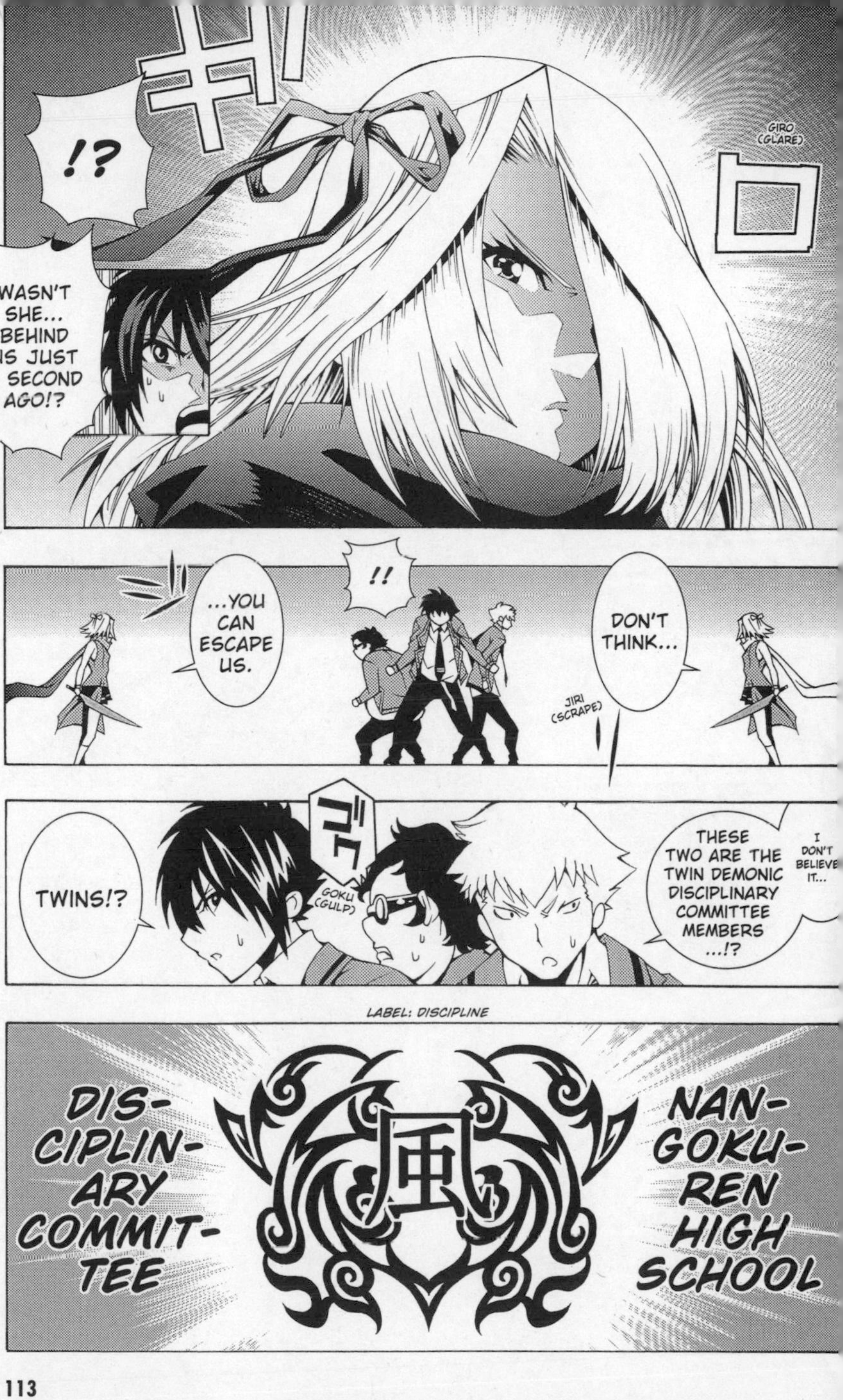
GIRO (GLARE)
!?
WASN'T SHE... BEHIND US JUST A SECOND AGO!?
DON'T THINK...
JIRI (SCRAPE)
!!
...YOU CAN ESCAPE US.
I DON'T BELIEVE IT...
THESE TWO ARE THE TWIN DEMONIC DISCIPLINARY COMMITTEE MEMBERS ...!?
GOKU (GULP)
TWINS!?
LABEL: DISCIPLINE
NAN-GOKU-REN HIGH SCHOOL
DIS-CIPLIN-ARY COMMIT-TEE

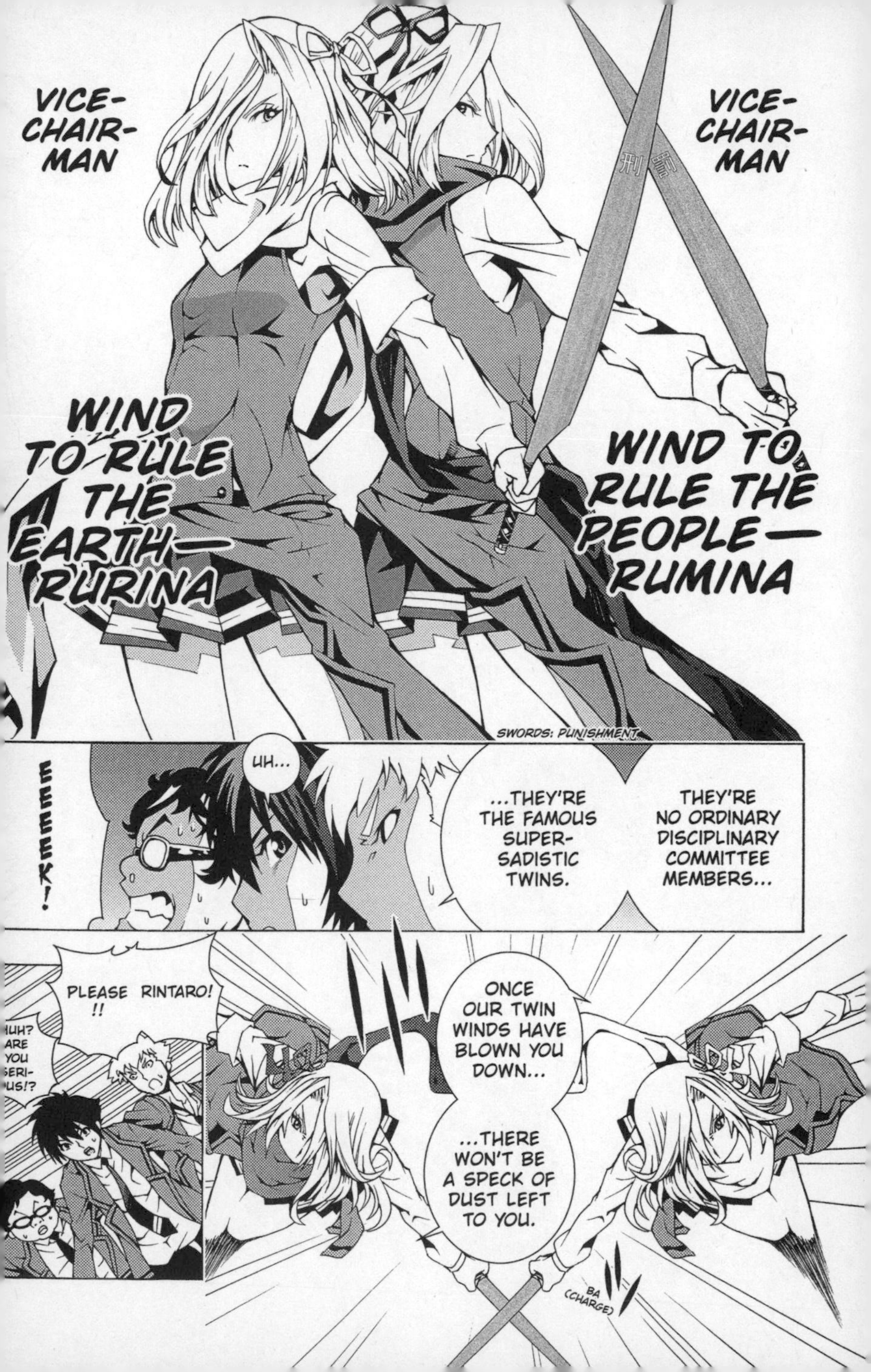
VICE-CHAIRMAN
WIND TO RULE THE PEOPLE—RUMINA
VICE-CHAIRMAN
WIND TO RULE THE EARTH—RURINA
SWORDS: PUNISHMENT
THEY'RE NO ORDINARY DISCIPLINARY COMMITTEE MEMBERS...
...THEY'RE THE FAMOUS SUPER-SADISTIC TWINS.
UH...
EEEEEK!
ONCE OUR TWIN WINDS HAVE BLOWN YOU DOWN...
...THERE WON'T BE A SPECK OF DUST LEFT TO YOU.
BA (CHARGE)
PLEASE RINTARO!!!
HUH? ARE YOU SERIOUS!?

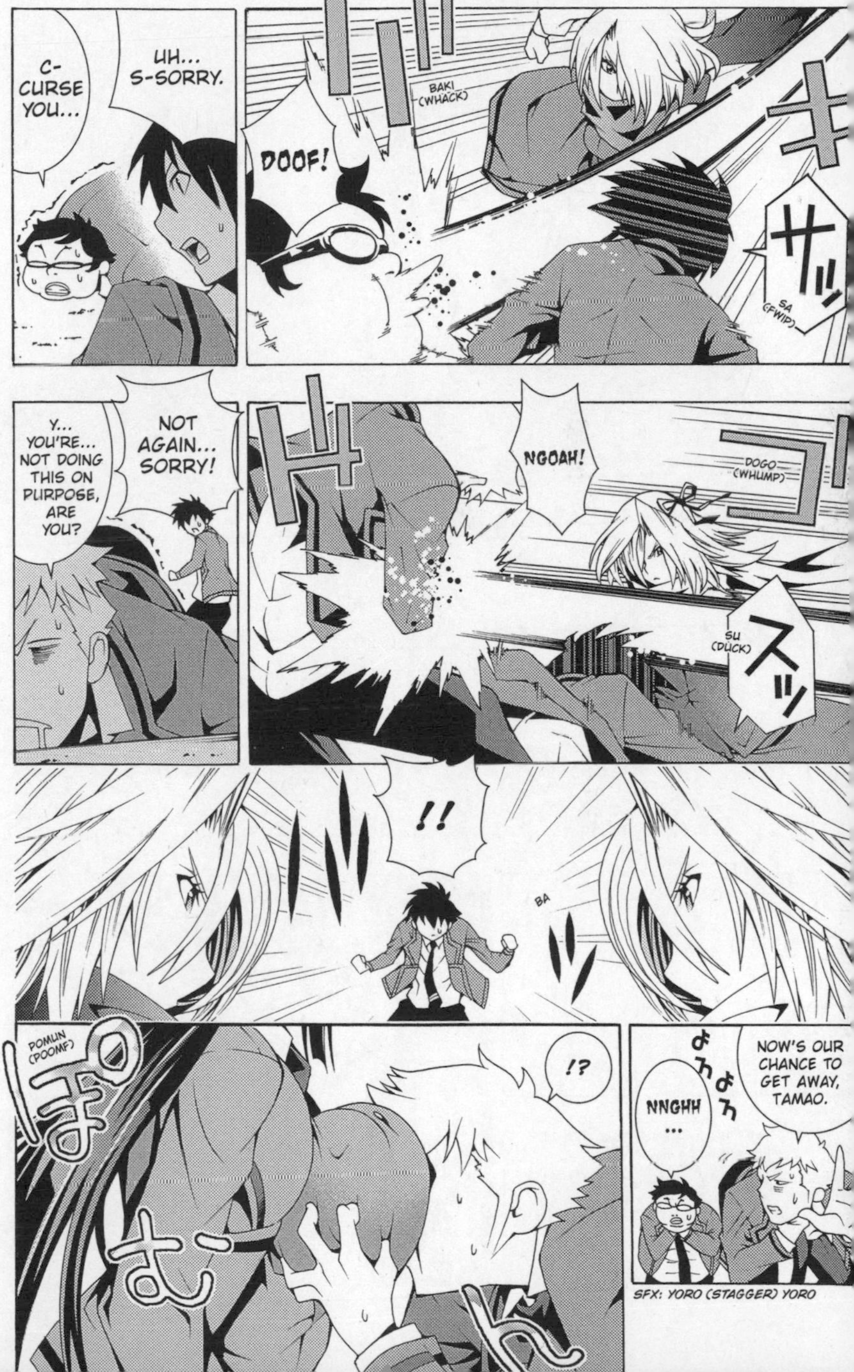
BAKI (WHACK)
SA (FWIP)
DOOF!
UH... S-SORRY.
C-CURSE YOU...
NGOAH!
DOGO (WHUMP)
SU (DUCK)
NOT AGAIN... SORRY!
Y... YOU'RE... NOT DOING THIS ON PURPOSE, ARE YOU?
!!
BA
NOW'S OUR CHANCE TO GET AWAY, TAMAO.
NNGHH...
SFX: YORO (STAGGER) YORO
!?
POMUN (POOMF)

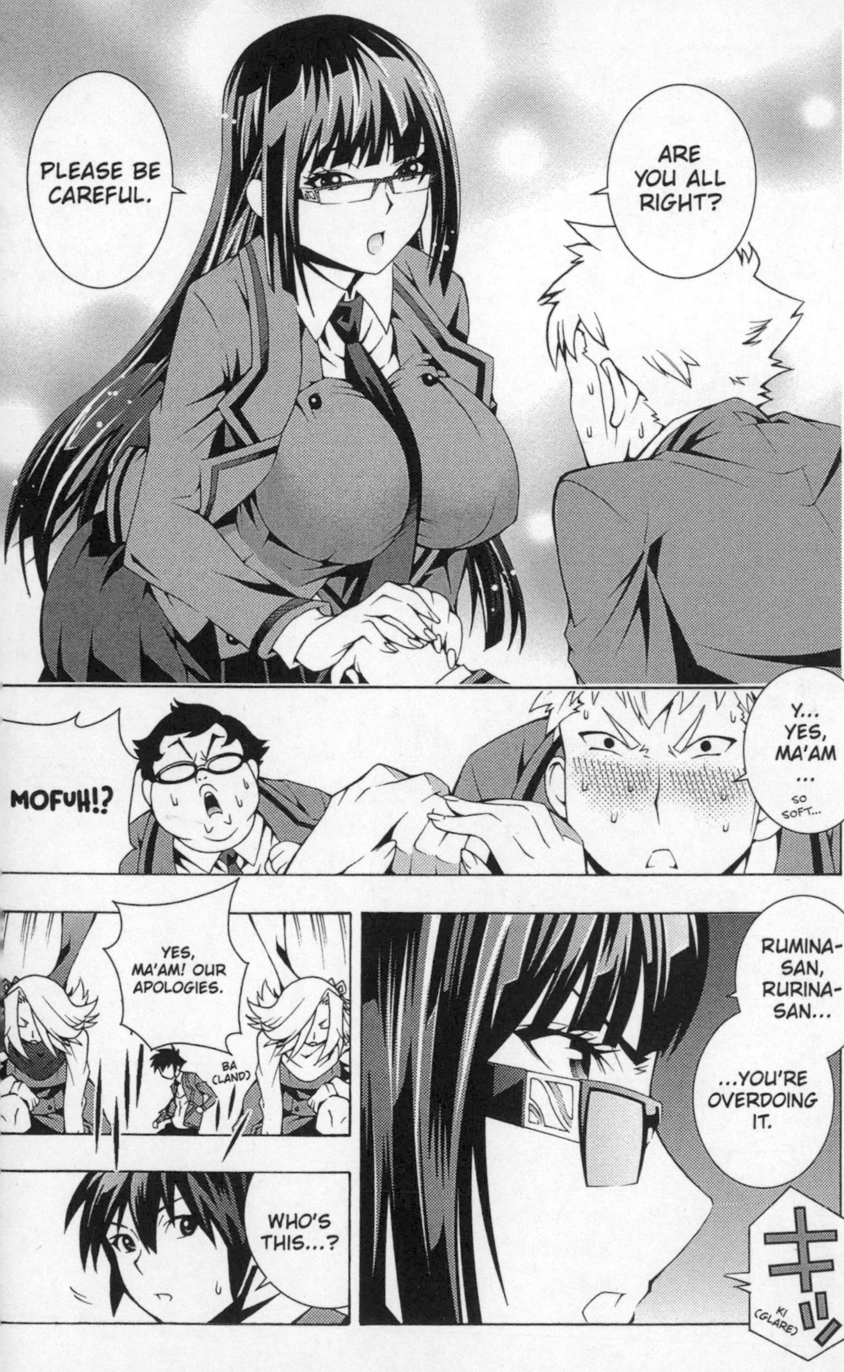
ARE YOU ALL RIGHT?
PLEASE BE CAREFUL.
Y... YES, MA'AM ...
SO SOFT...
MOFUH!?
RUMINA-SAN, RURINA-SAN...
...YOU'RE OVERDOING IT.
KI (GLARE)
YES, MA'AM! OUR APOLOGIES.
BA (LAND)
WHO'S THIS...?

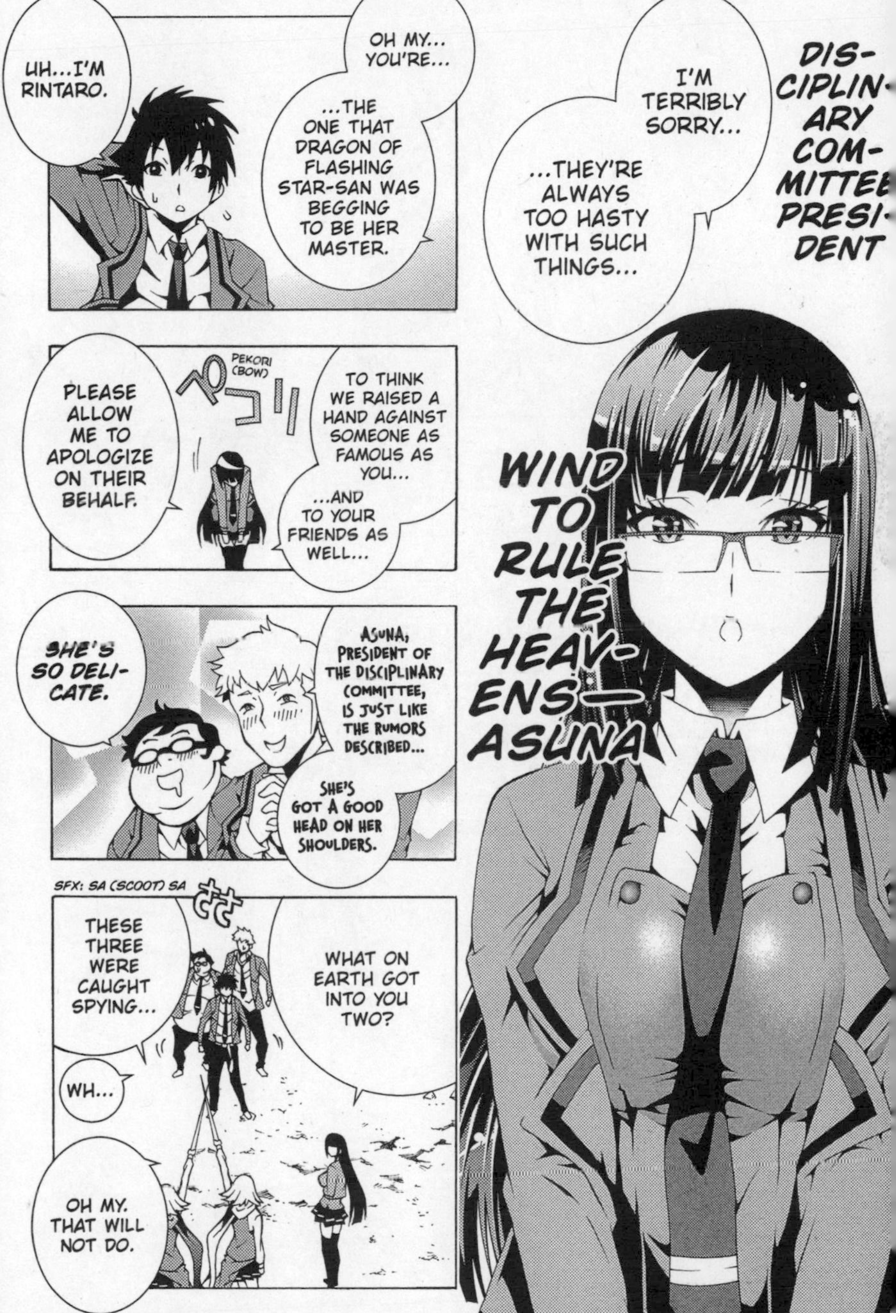
DISCIPLINARY COMMITTEE PRESIDENT
I'M TERRIBLY SORRY...
...THEY'RE ALWAYS TOO HASTY WITH SUCH THINGS...
WIND TO RULE THE HEAVENS—ASUNA
OH MY... YOU'RE...
...THE ONE THAT DRAGON OF FLASHING STAR-SAN WAS BEGGING TO BE HER MASTER.
UH...I'M RINTARO.
TO THINK WE RAISED A HAND AGAINST SOMEONE AS FAMOUS AS YOU...
...AND TO YOUR FRIENDS AS WELL...
PEKORI (BOW)
PLEASE ALLOW ME TO APOLOGIZE ON THEIR BEHALF.
ASUNA, PRESIDENT OF THE DISCIPLINARY COMMITTEE, IS JUST LIKE THE RUMORS DESCRIBED...
SHE'S GOT A GOOD HEAD ON HER SHOULDERS.
SHE'S SO DELICATE.
SFX: SA (SCOOT) SA
WHAT ON EARTH GOT INTO YOU TWO?
THESE THREE WERE CAUGHT SPYING...
WH...
OH MY. THAT WILL NOT DO.

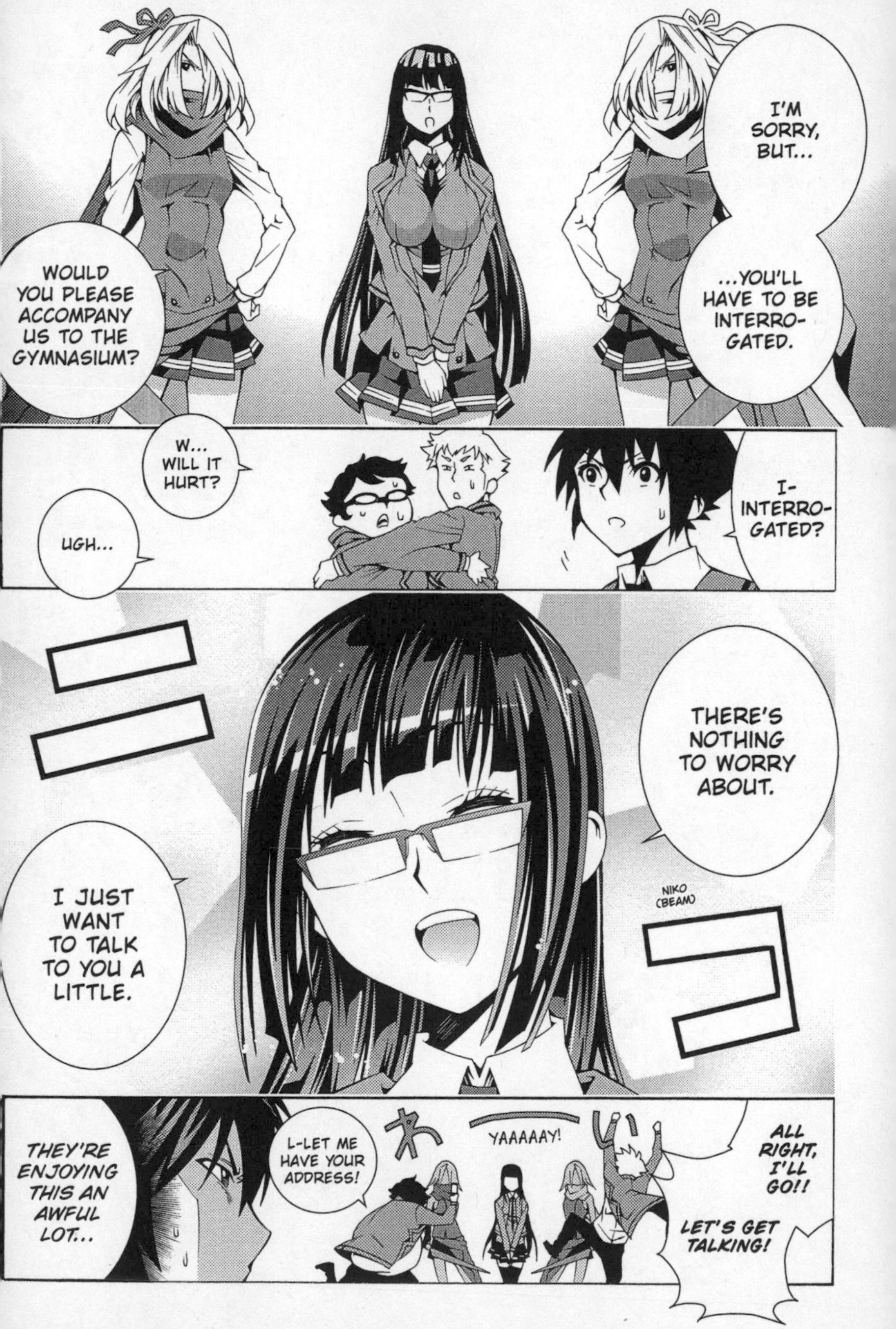
I'M SORRY, BUT...
...YOU'LL HAVE TO BE INTERROGATED.
WOULD YOU PLEASE ACCOMPANY US TO THE GYMNASIUM?
I-INTERROGATED?
W... WILL IT HURT?
UGH...
THERE'S NOTHING TO WORRY ABOUT.
NIKO (BEAM)
I JUST WANT TO TALK TO YOU A LITTLE.
ALL RIGHT, I'LL GO!!
LET'S GET TALKING!
YAAAAAY!
L-LET ME HAVE YOUR ADDRESS!
THEY'RE ENJOYING THIS AN AWFUL LOT...

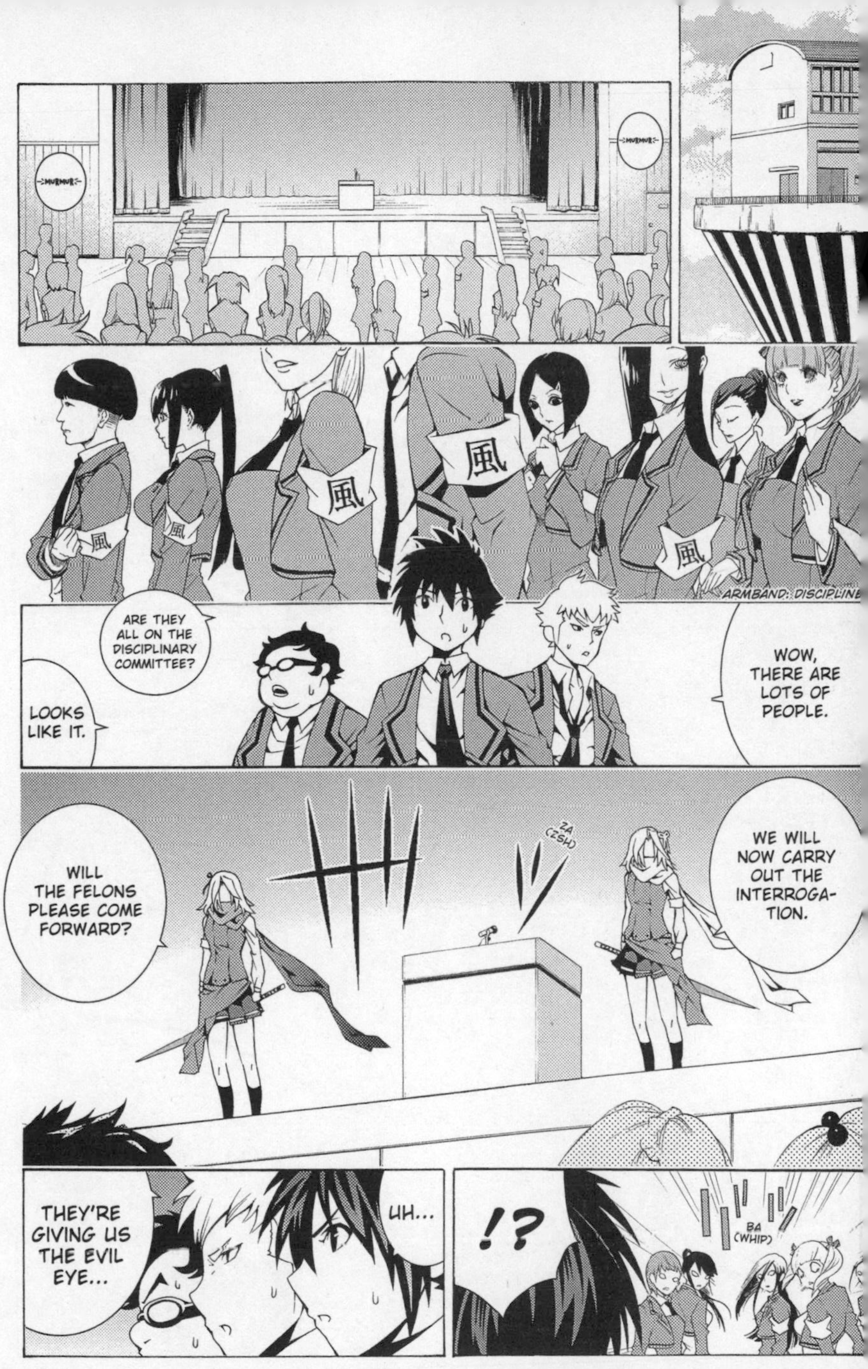
MURMUR
MURMUR
ARMBAND: DISCIPLINE
WOW, THERE ARE LOTS OF PEOPLE.
ARE THEY ALL ON THE DISCIPLINARY COMMITTEE?
LOOKS LIKE IT.
WE WILL NOW CARRY OUT THE INTERROGATION.
ZA (ZSH)
WILL THE FELONS PLEASE COME FORWARD?
!?
BA (WHIP)
UH...
THEY'RE GIVING US THE EVIL EYE...

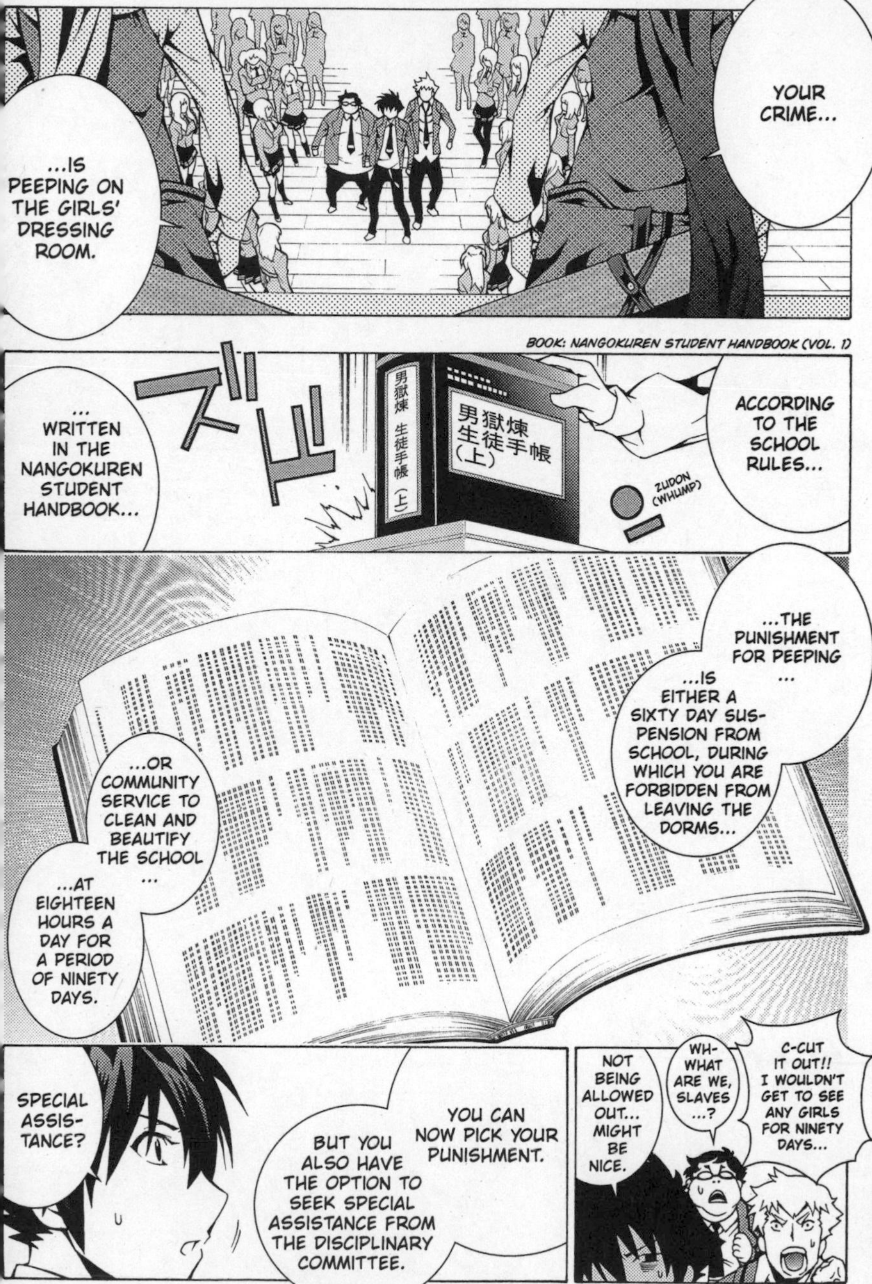
YOUR CRIME...
...IS PEEPING ON THE GIRLS' DRESSING ROOM.
BOOK: NANGOKUREN STUDENT HANDBOOK (VOL. 1)
ACCORDING TO THE SCHOOL RULES...
男獄煉 生徒手帳 (上)
ZUDON (WHUMP)
... WRITTEN IN THE NANGOKUREN STUDENT HANDBOOK...
...THE PUNISHMENT FOR PEEPING ...
...IS EITHER A SIXTY DAY SUSPENSION FROM SCHOOL, DURING WHICH YOU ARE FORBIDDEN FROM LEAVING THE DORMS...
...OR COMMUNITY SERVICE TO CLEAN AND BEAUTIFY THE SCHOOL ...
...AT EIGHTEEN HOURS A DAY FOR A PERIOD OF NINETY DAYS.
C-CUT IT OUT!! I WOULDN'T GET TO SEE ANY GIRLS FOR NINETY DAYS...
WH-WHAT ARE WE, SLAVES ...?
NOT BEING ALLOWED OUT... MIGHT BE NICE.
YOU CAN NOW PICK YOUR PUNISHMENT.
BUT YOU ALSO HAVE THE OPTION TO SEEK SPECIAL ASSISTANCE FROM THE DISCIPLINARY COMMITTEE.
SPECIAL ASSISTANCE?

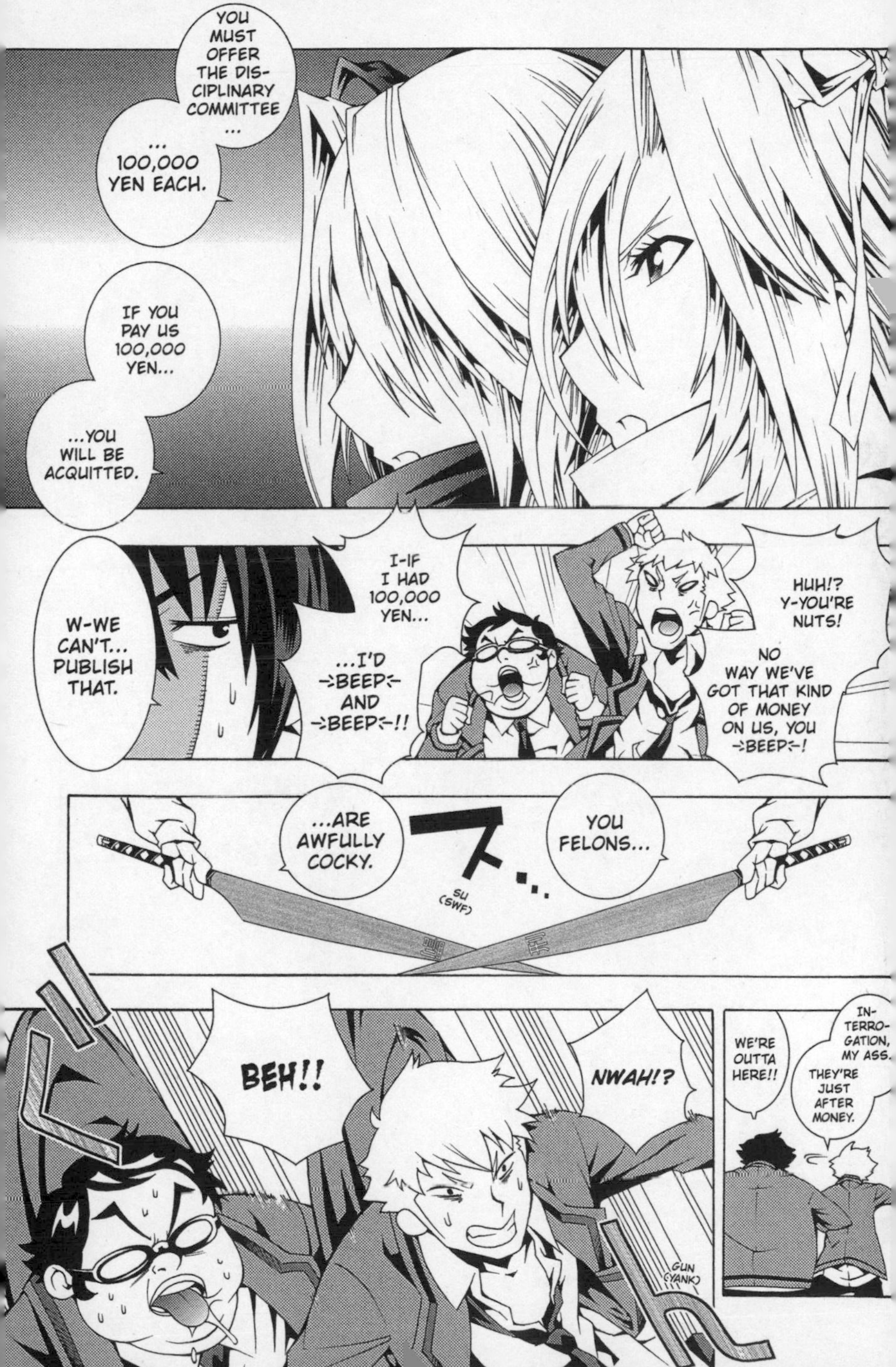
YOU MUST OFFER THE DIS-CIPLINARY COMMITTEE ...
... 100,000 YEN EACH.
IF YOU PAY US 100,000 YEN...
...YOU WILL BE ACQUITTED.
HUH!? Y-YOU'RE NUTS!
NO WAY WE'VE GOT THAT KIND OF MONEY ON US, YOU ->BEEP<-!
I-IF I HAD 100,000 YEN...
...I'D ->BEEP<- AND ->BEEP<-!!
W-WE CAN'T... PUBLISH THAT.
YOU FELONS...
SU (SWF)
...ARE AWFULLY COCKY.
IN-TERRO-GATION, MY ASS.
THEY'RE JUST AFTER MONEY.
WE'RE OUTTA HERE!!
NWAH!?
GUN (YANK)
BEH!!

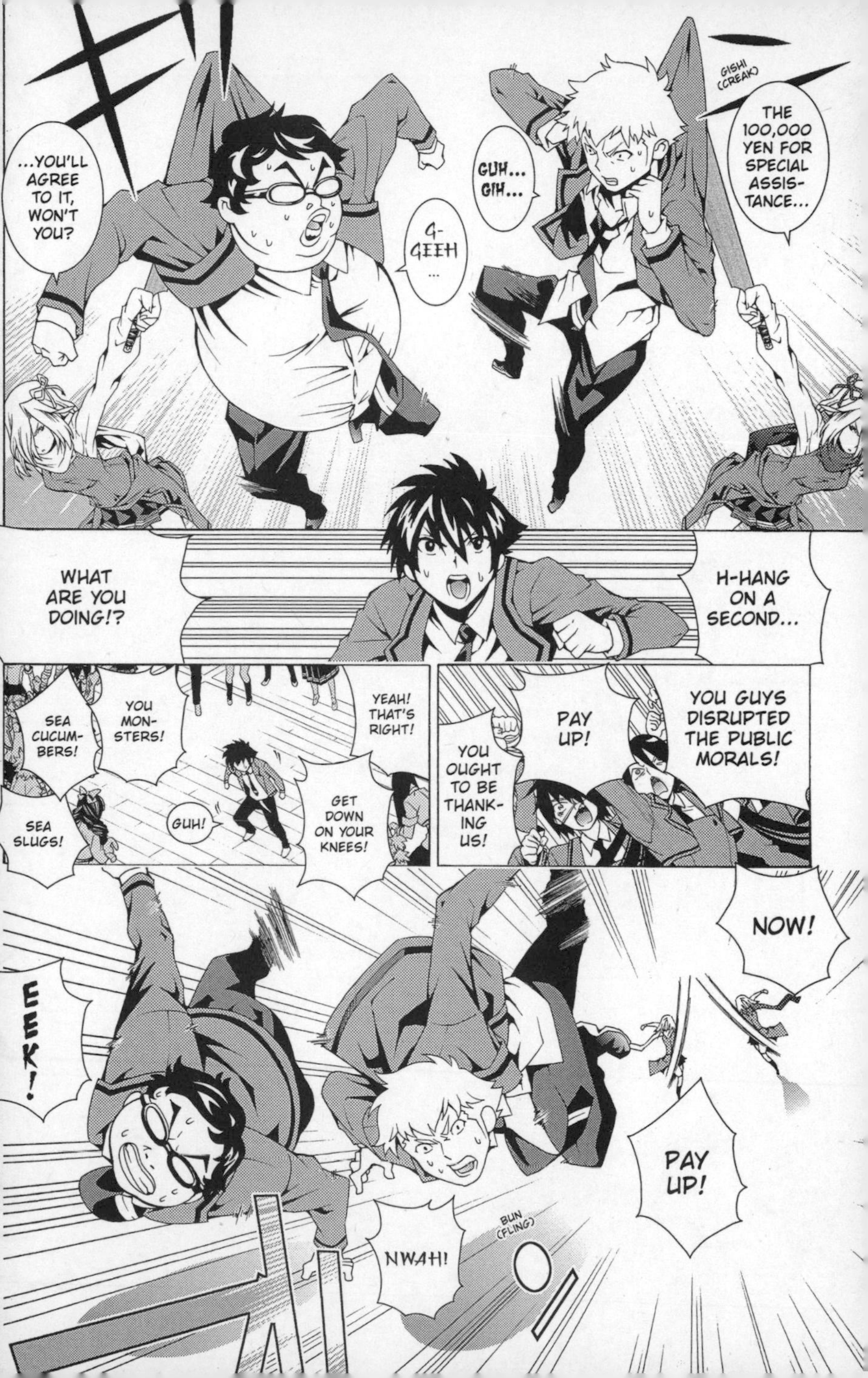
GISHI (CREAK)
THE 100,000 YEN FOR SPECIAL ASSIS-TANCE...
GUH... GIH...
G-GEEH...
...YOU'LL AGREE TO IT, WON'T YOU?
H-HANG ON A SECOND...
WHAT ARE YOU DOING!?
YOU GUYS DISRUPTED THE PUBLIC MORALS!
PAY UP!
YOU OUGHT TO BE THANK-ING US!
YEAH! THAT'S RIGHT!
GET DOWN ON YOUR KNEES!
YOU MON-STERS!
GUH!
SEA CUCUM-BERS!
SEA SLUGS!
NOW!
PAY UP!
BUN (FLING)
NWAH!
EEK!

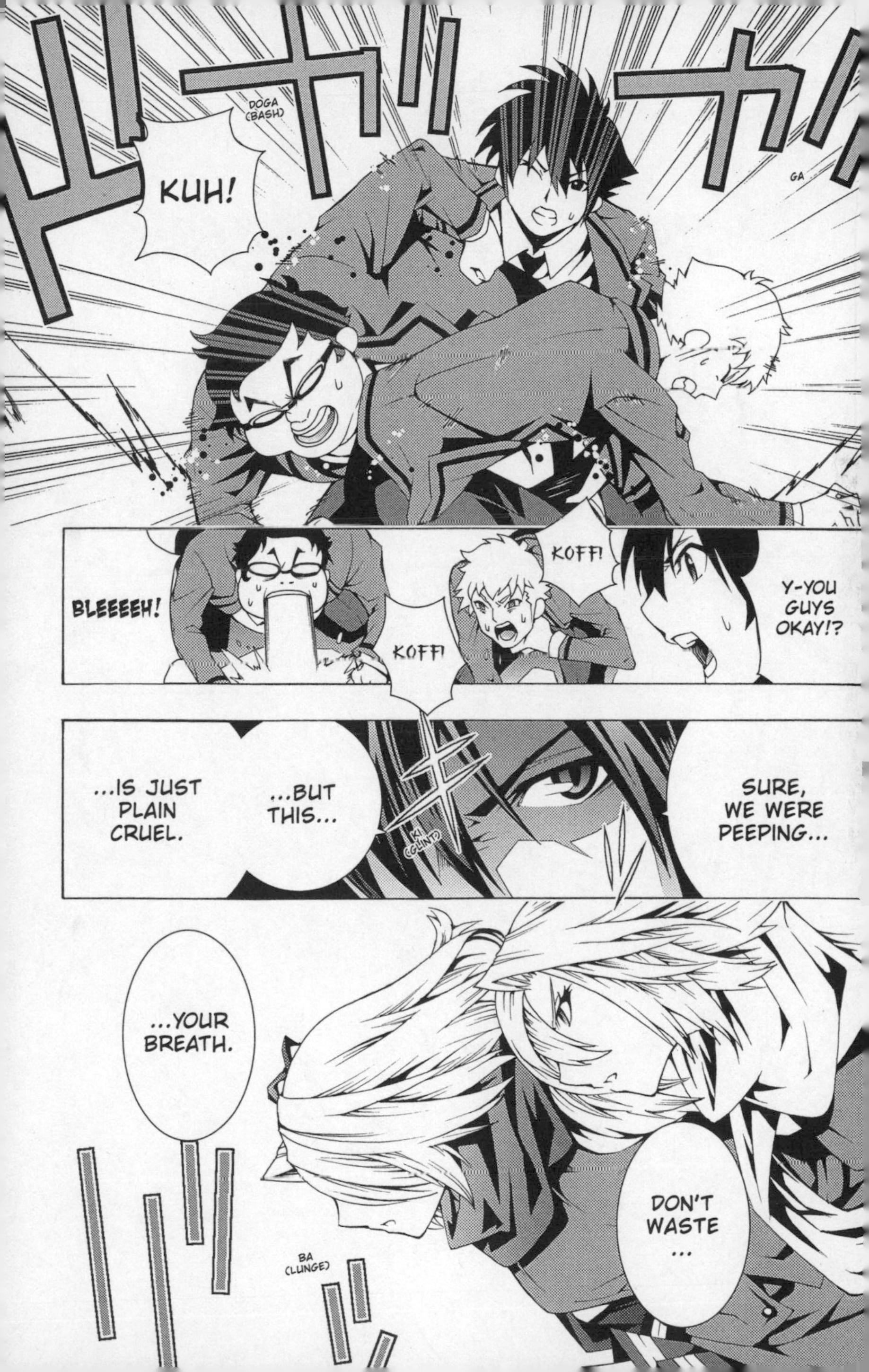
GA
DOGA (BASH)
KUH!
Y-YOU GUYS OKAY!?
KOFF!
KOFF!
BLEEEEH!
SURE, WE WERE PEEPING...
KI (GLINT)
...BUT THIS...
...IS JUST PLAIN CRUEL.
DON'T WASTE ...
...YOUR BREATH.
BA (LUNGE)

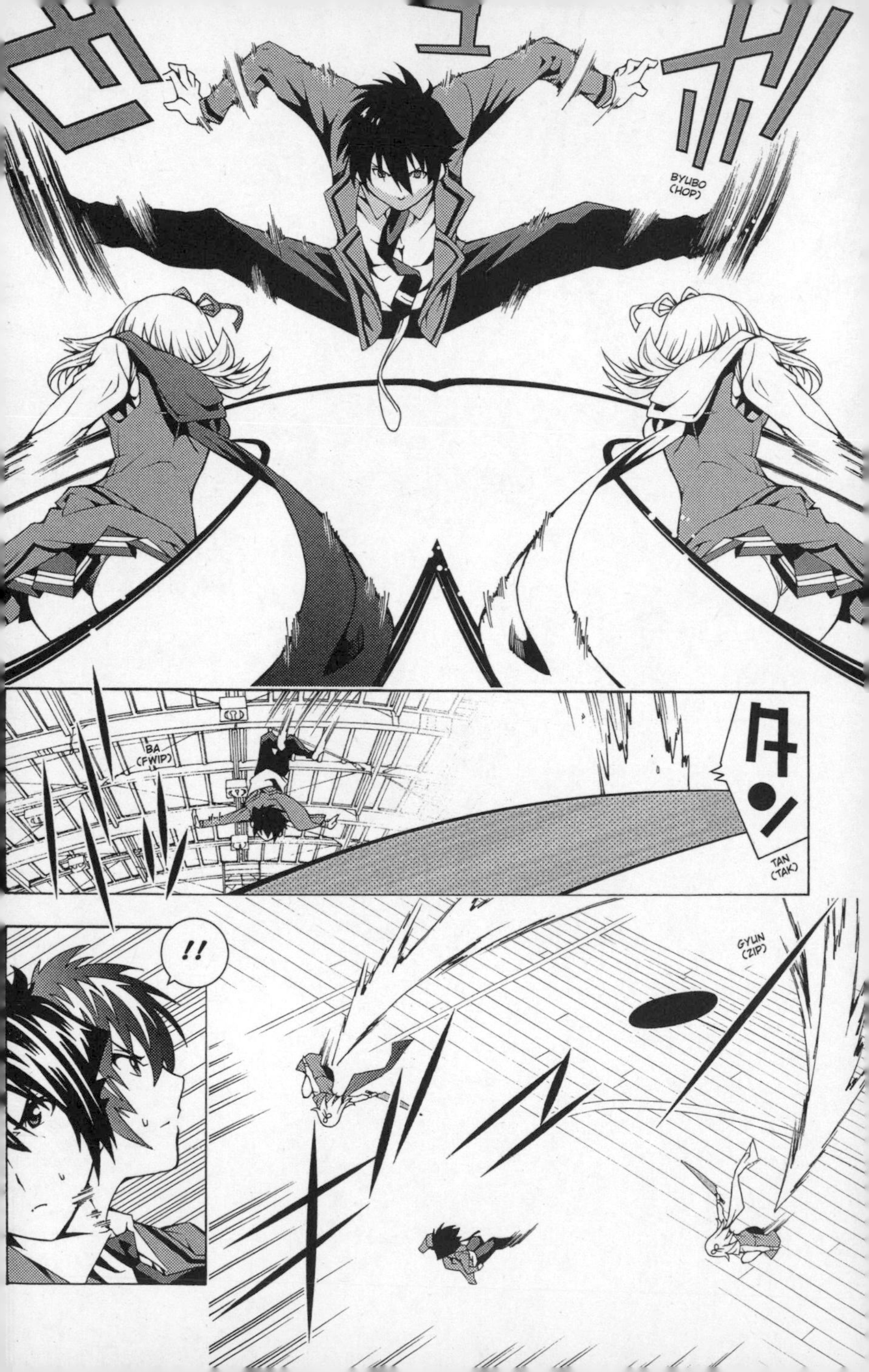
BYUBO
(HOP)
BA
(FWIP)
TAN
(TAK)
!!
GYUN
(ZIP)

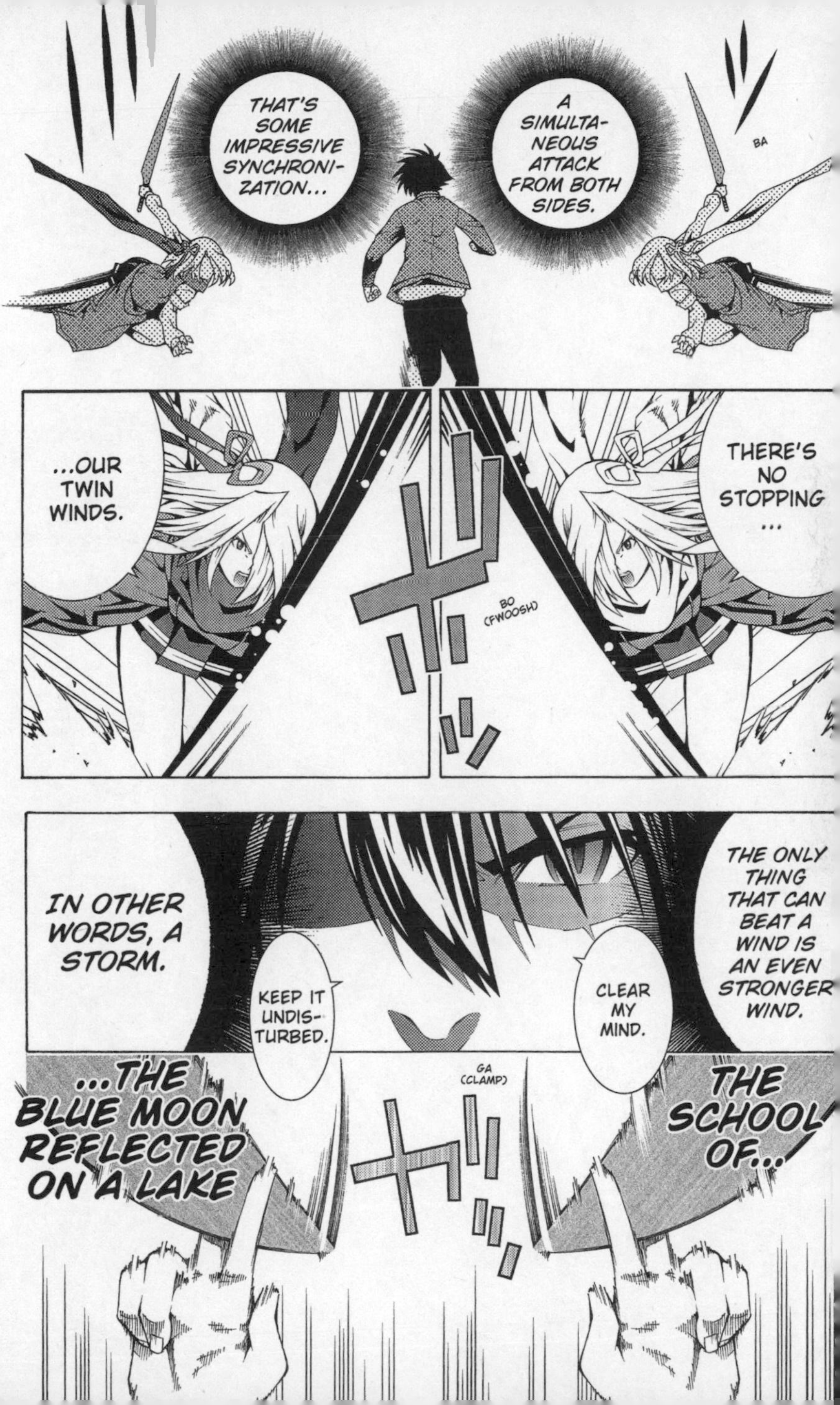
BA
A SIMULTANEOUS ATTACK FROM BOTH SIDES.
THAT'S SOME IMPRESSIVE SYNCHRONIZATION...
THERE'S NO STOPPING...
BO (FWOOSH)
...OUR TWIN WINDS.
THE ONLY THING THAT CAN BEAT A WIND IS AN EVEN STRONGER WIND.
IN OTHER WORDS, A STORM.
CLEAR MY MIND.
KEEP IT UNDISTURBED.
THE SCHOOL OF...
GA (CLAMP)
...THE BLUE MOON REFLECTED ON A LAKE

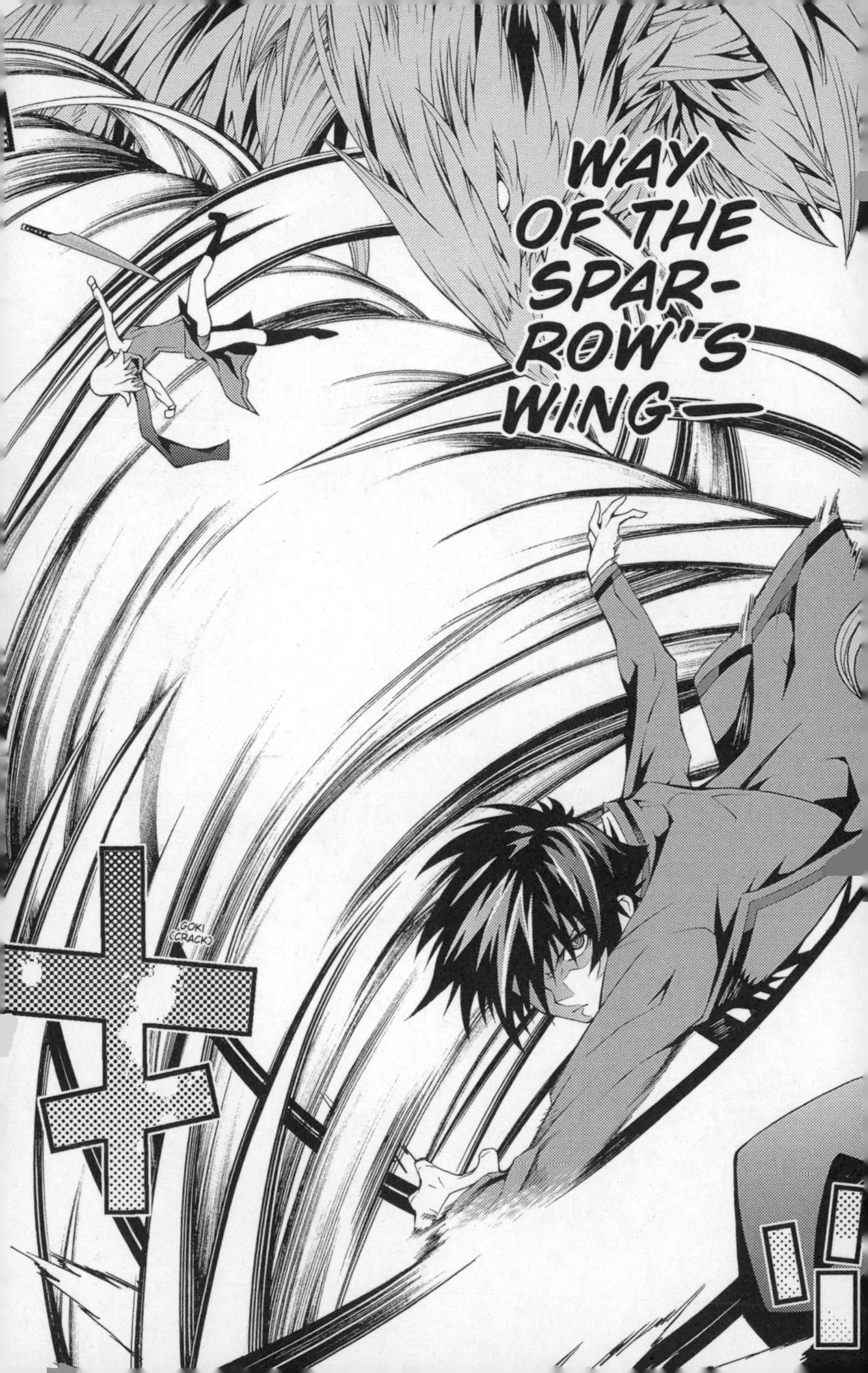
WAY OF THE SPAR-ROW'S WING—
GOKI (CRACK)

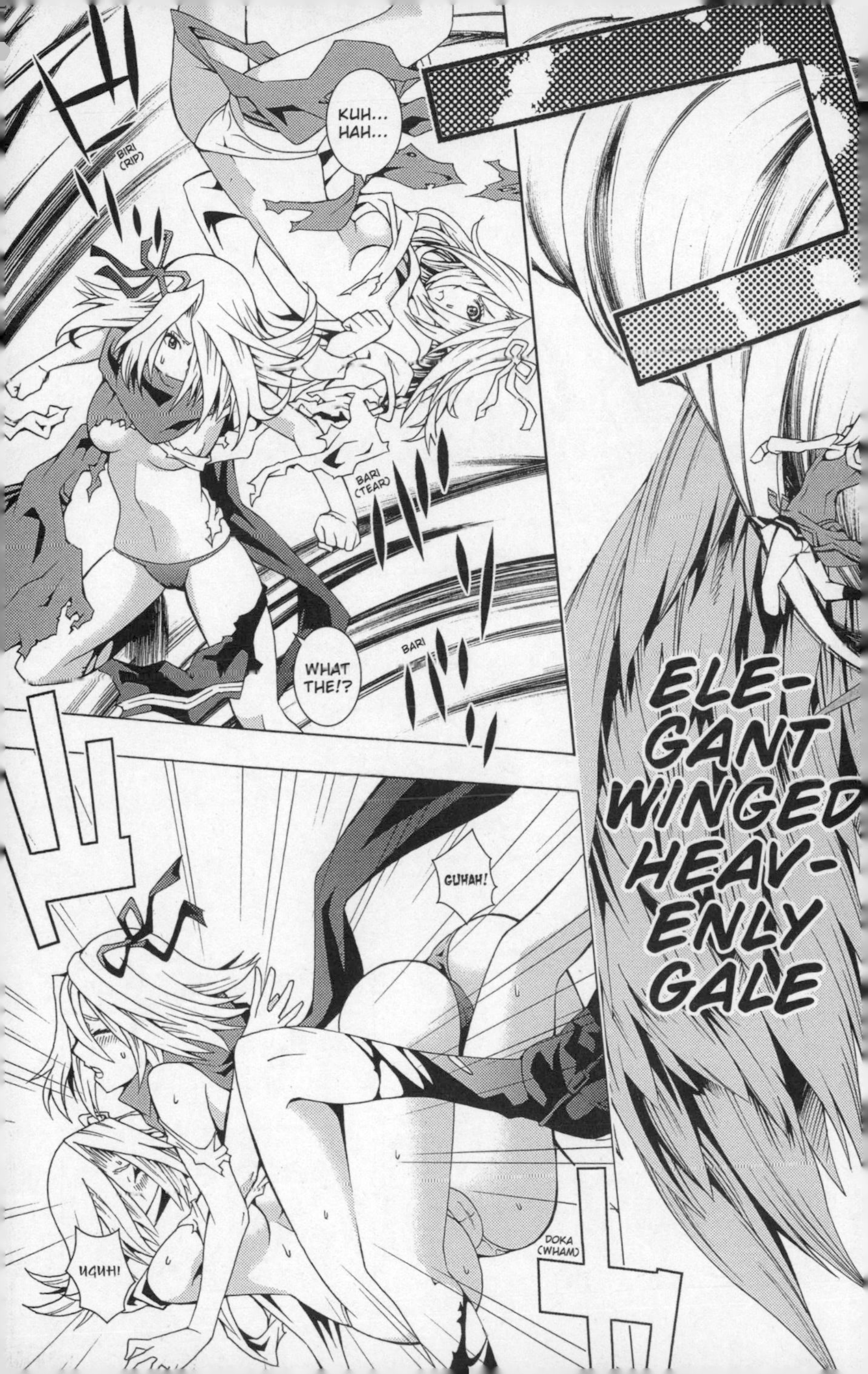
ELE-
GANT
WINGED
HEAV-
ENLY
GALE
KUH... HAH...
BIRI (RIP)
BARI (TEAR)
BARI
WHAT THE!?
GUHAH!
DOKA (WHAM)
UGUH!

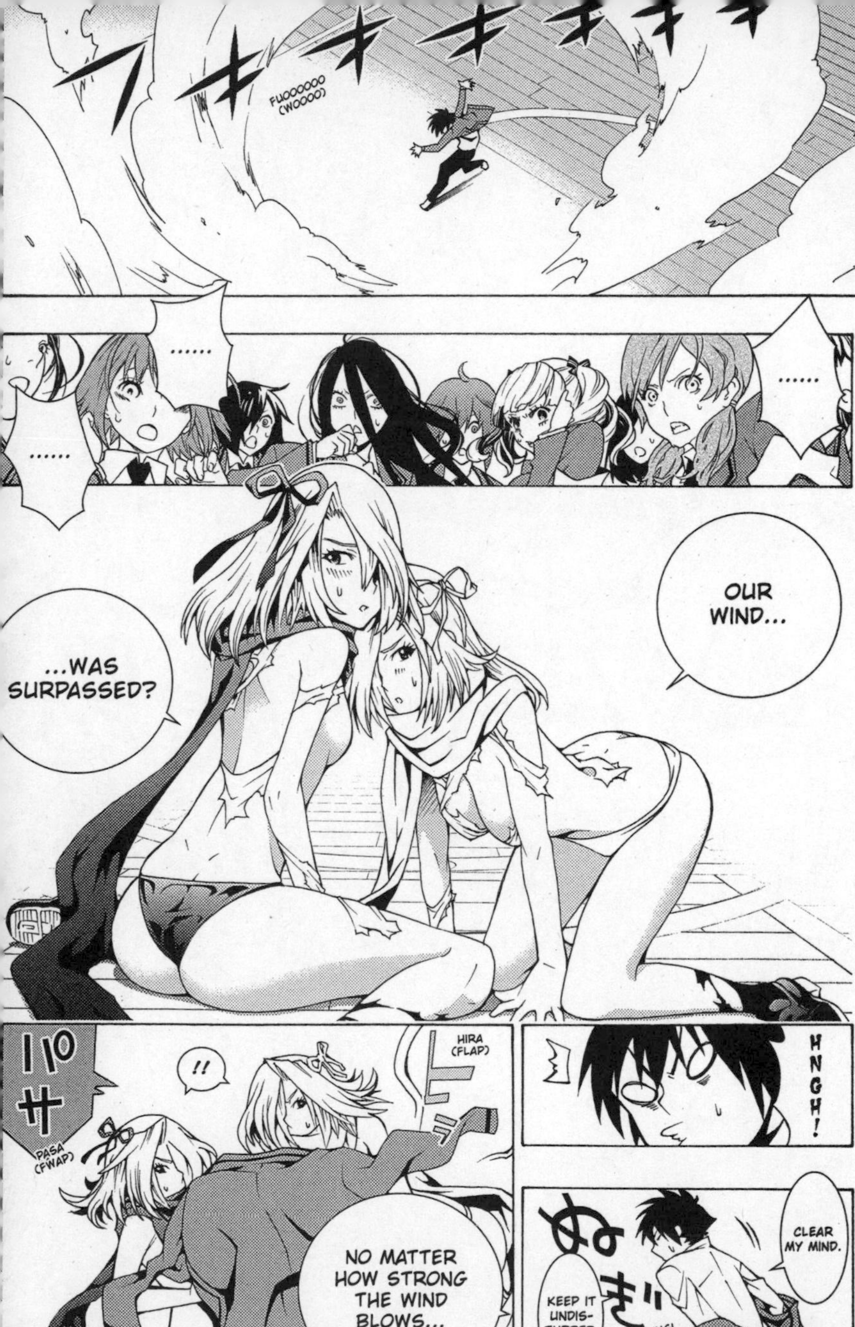
FUOOOOOO (WOOOO)
......
......
......
OUR WIND...
...WAS SURPASSED?
HNGH!
CLEAR MY MIND.
KEEP IT UNDISTURBED.
NUGI (STRIP)
HIRA (FLAP)
!!
PASA (FWAP)
NO MATTER HOW STRONG THE WIND BLOWS...

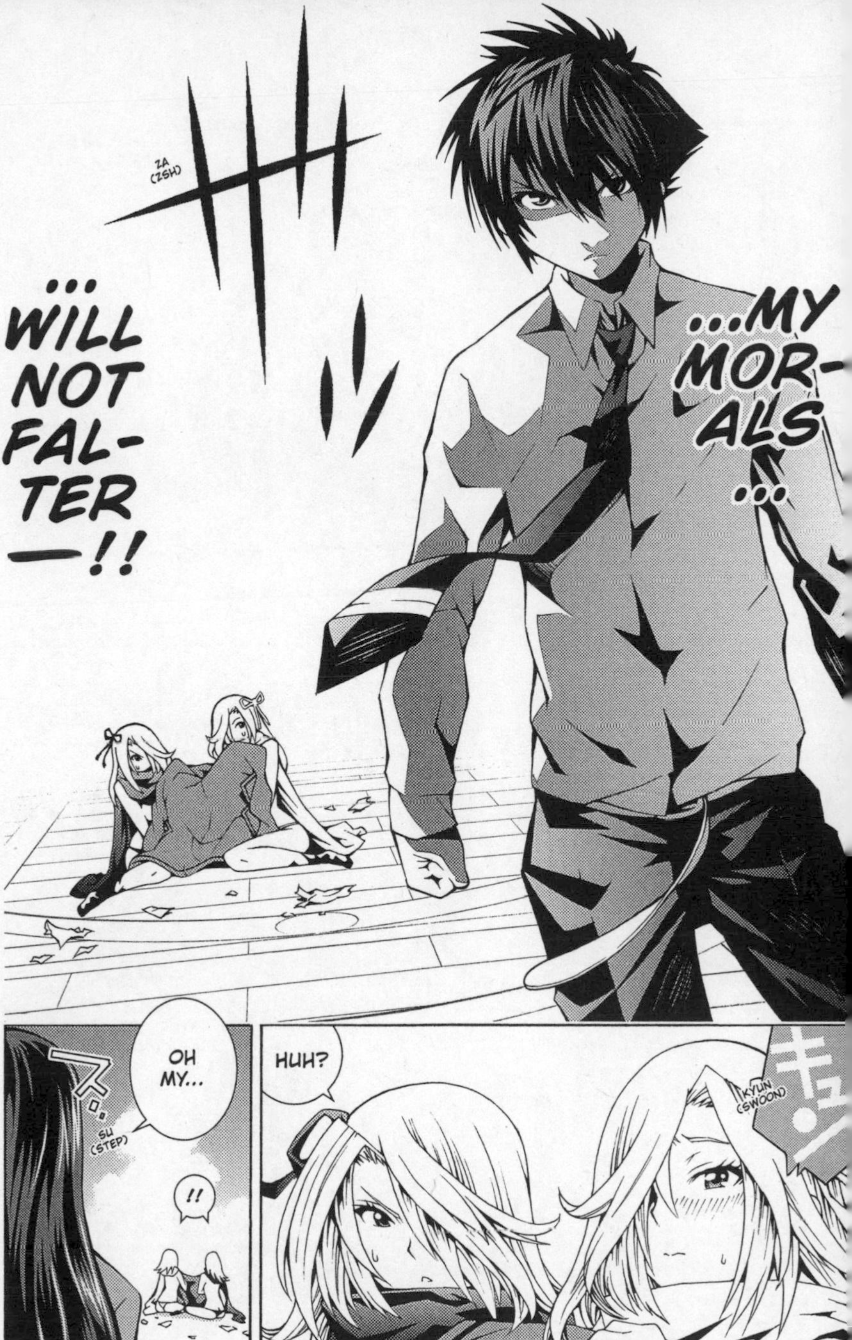
...MY MOR-ALS...
...WILL NOT FAL-TER—!!
ZA (ZSH)
KYUN (SWOON)
HUH?
OH MY...
SU (STEP)
!!

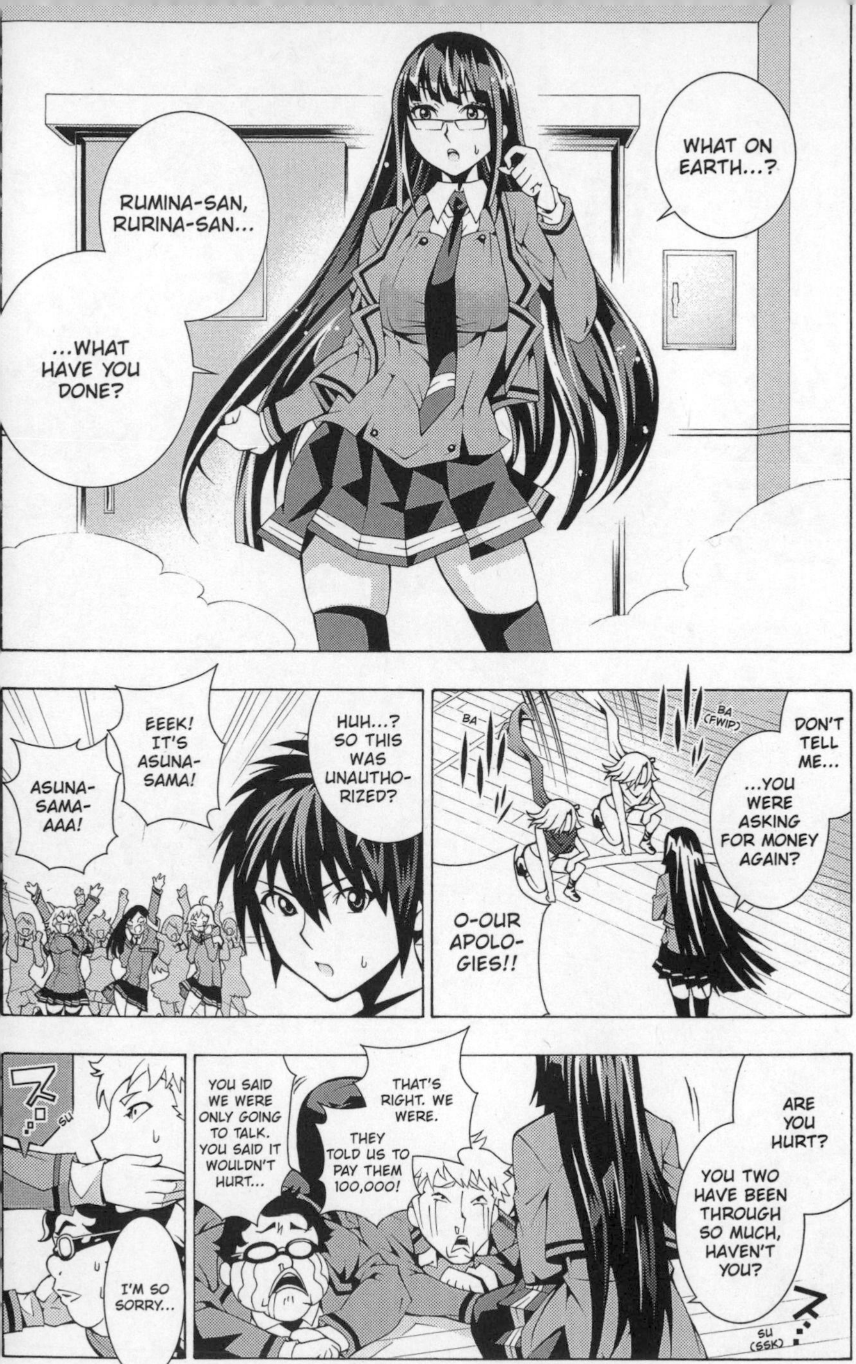
WHAT ON EARTH...?
RUMINA-SAN, RURINA-SAN...
...WHAT HAVE YOU DONE?
BA (FWIP)
BA
DON'T TELL ME...
...YOU WERE ASKING FOR MONEY AGAIN?
O-OUR APOLOGIES!!
HUH...? SO THIS WAS UNAUTHORIZED?
EEEK! IT'S ASUNA-SAMA!
ASUNA-SAMA-AAA!
ARE YOU HURT?
YOU TWO HAVE BEEN THROUGH SO MUCH, HAVEN'T YOU?
SU (SSK)
THAT'S RIGHT. WE WERE.
THEY TOLD US TO PAY THEM 100,000!
YOU SAID WE WERE ONLY GOING TO TALK. YOU SAID IT WOULDN'T HURT...
SU
I'M SO SORRY...

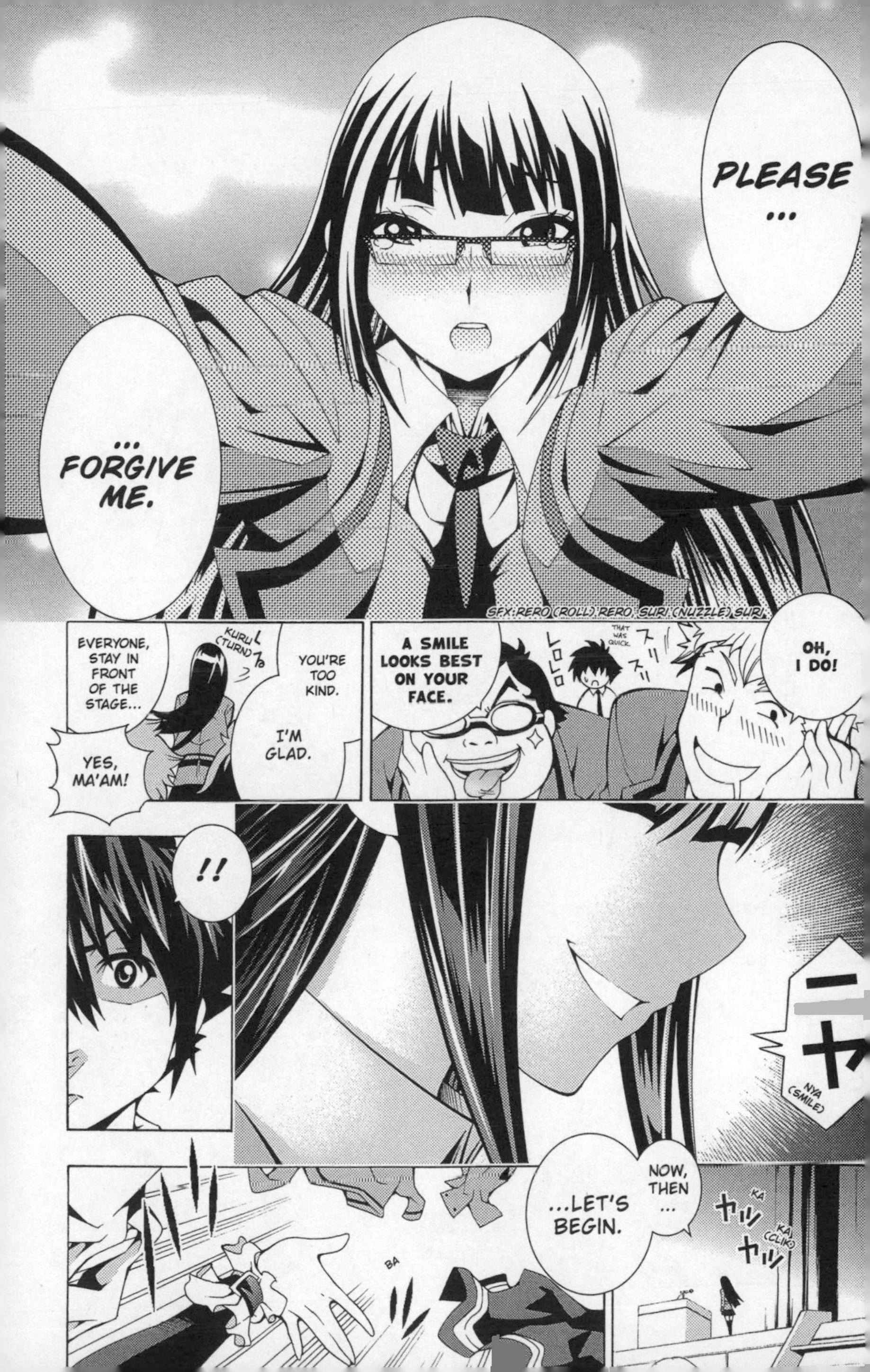
PLEASE ...
... FORGIVE ME.
SFX: RERO (ROLL) RERO, SURI (NUZZLE) SURI
OH, I DO!
THAT WAS QUICK.
A SMILE LOOKS BEST ON YOUR FACE.
YOU'RE TOO KIND.
I'M GLAD.
KURU (TURN)
EVERYONE, STAY IN FRONT OF THE STAGE...
YES, MA'AM!
NYA (SMILE)
!!
NOW, THEN ...
...LET'S BEGIN.
KA
KA (CLIK)
BA

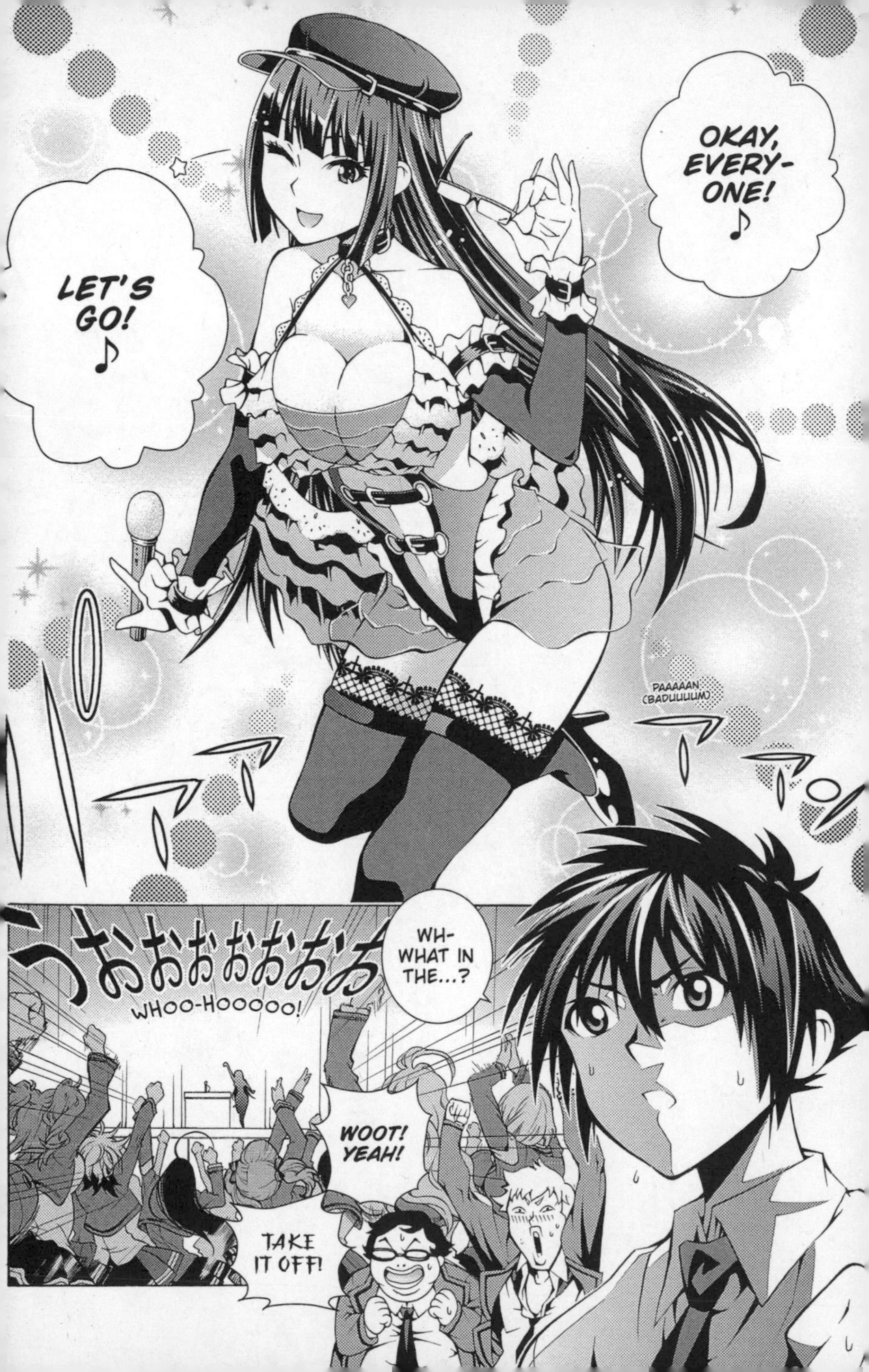
OKAY, EVERY-ONE! ♪
LET'S GO! ♪
PAAAAAN (BADUUUUM)
WH- WHAT IN THE...?
うおおおおおお
WHOO-HOOOOO!
WOOT! YEAH!
TAKE IT OFF!

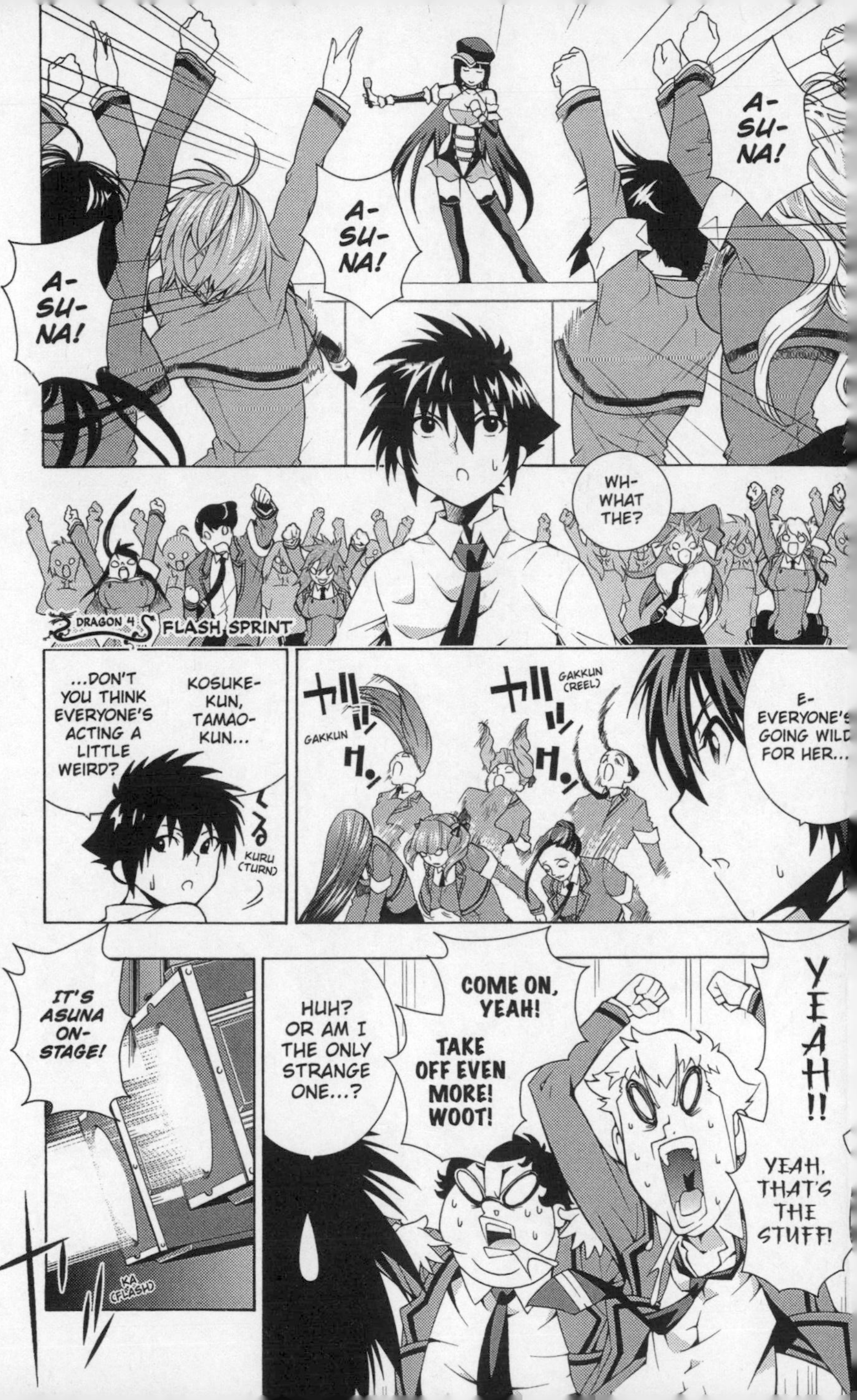
A-SU-NA!
A-SU-NA!
A-SU-NA!
WH-WHAT THE?
DRAGON 4 FLASH SPRINT
E-EVERYONE'S GOING WILD FOR HER...
GAKKUN (REEL)
GAKKUN
KOSUKE-KUN, TAMAO-KUN...
...DON'T YOU THINK EVERYONE'S ACTING A LITTLE WEIRD?
KURU (TURN)
YEAH!!
YEAH, THAT'S THE STUFF!
COME ON, YEAH!
TAKE OFF EVEN MORE! WOOT!
HUH? OR AM I THE ONLY STRANGE ONE...?
IT'S ASUNA ON-STAGE!
KA (FLASH)

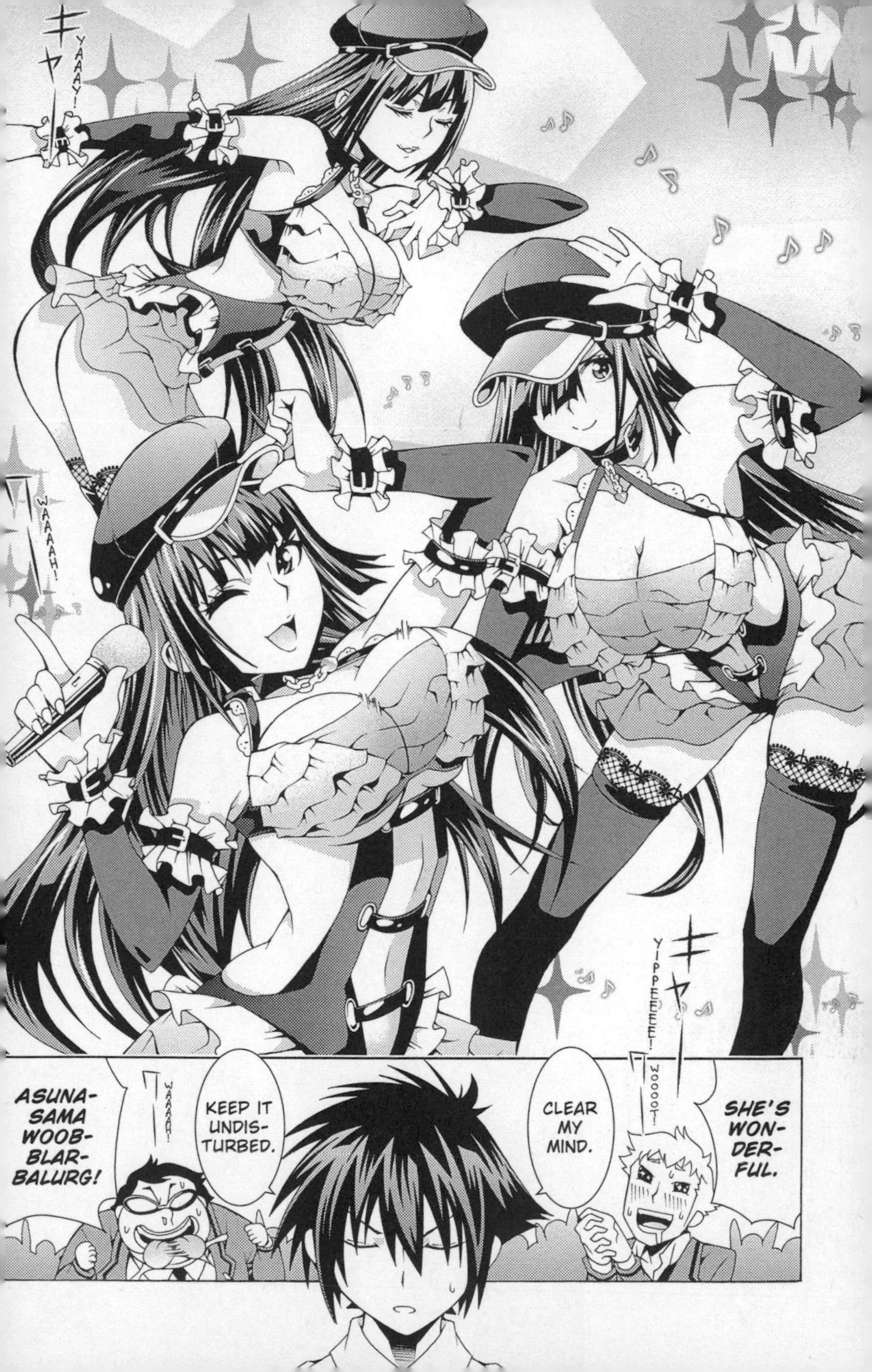
YAAAY!
WAAAAH!
YIPPEEEE!
SHE'S WON-DER-FUL.
WOOOOT!
CLEAR MY MIND.
KEEP IT UNDIS-TURBED.
WAAAH!
ASUNA-SAMA WOOB-BLAR-BALURG!

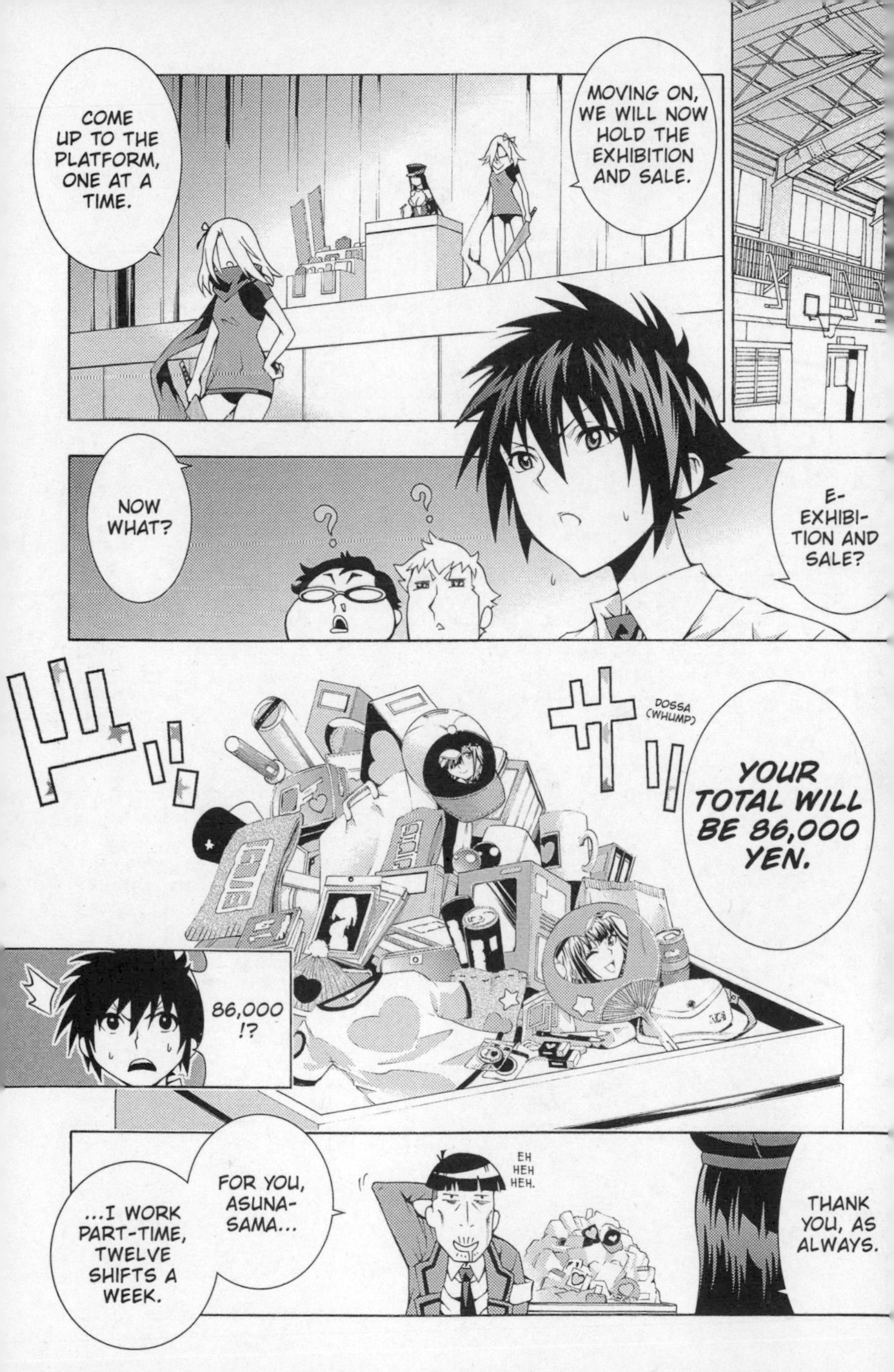
MOVING ON, WE WILL NOW HOLD THE EXHIBITION AND SALE.
COME UP TO THE PLATFORM, ONE AT A TIME.
E-EXHIBITION AND SALE?
NOW WHAT?
YOUR TOTAL WILL BE 86,000 YEN.
DOSSA (WHUMP)
86,000 !?
THANK YOU, AS ALWAYS.
EH HEH HEH.
FOR YOU, ASUNA-SAMA...
...I WORK PART-TIME, TWELVE SHIFTS A WEEK.

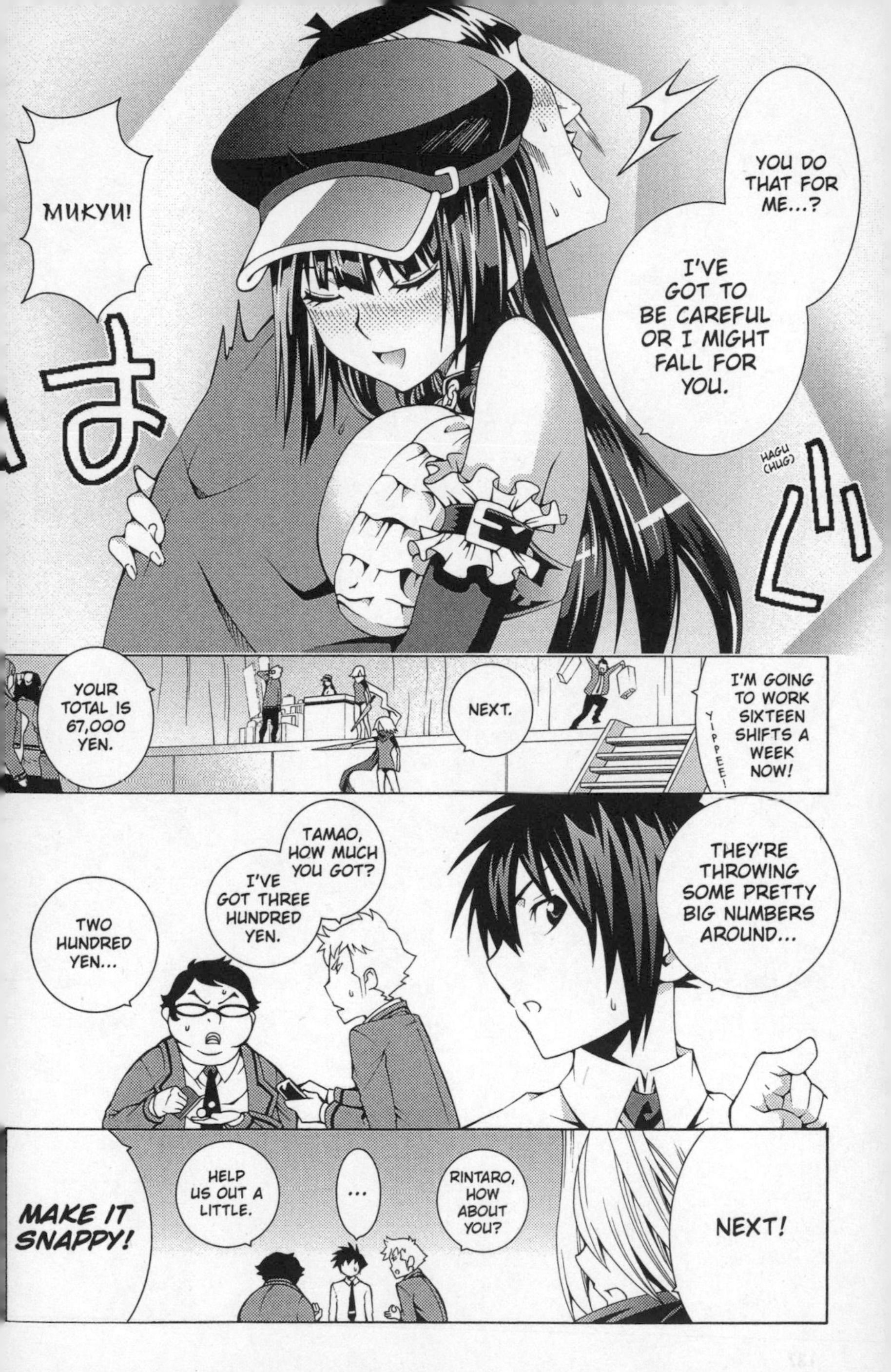
YOU DO THAT FOR ME...?
I'VE GOT TO BE CAREFUL OR I MIGHT FALL FOR YOU.
HAGU (HUG)
MUKYU!
I'M GOING TO WORK SIXTEEN SHIFTS A WEEK NOW!
YIPPEE!
NEXT.
YOUR TOTAL IS 67,000 YEN.
THEY'RE THROWING SOME PRETTY BIG NUMBERS AROUND...
TAMAO, HOW MUCH YOU GOT?
I'VE GOT THREE HUNDRED YEN.
TWO HUNDRED YEN...
NEXT!
RINTARO, HOW ABOUT YOU?
...
HELP US OUT A LITTLE.
MAKE IT SNAPPY!

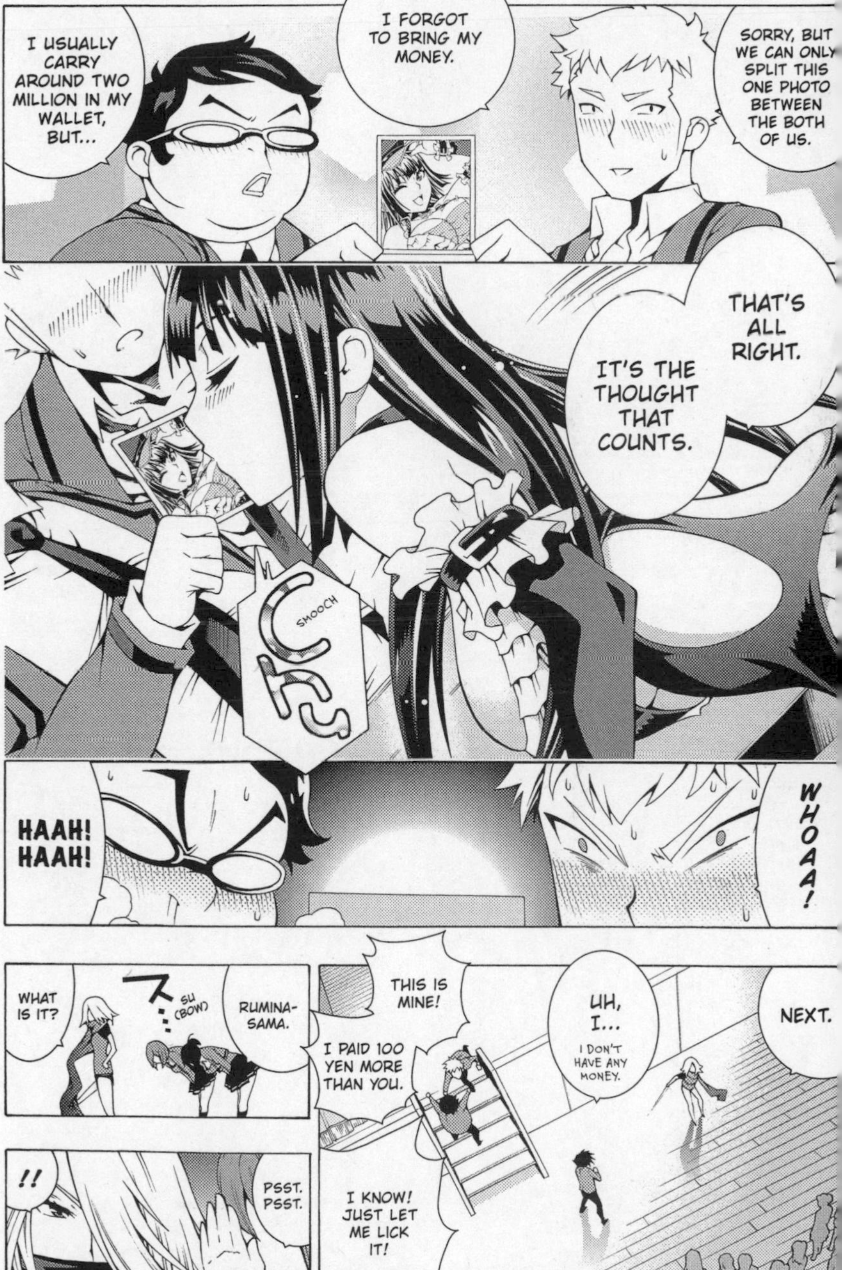
SORRY, BUT WE CAN ONLY SPLIT THIS ONE PHOTO BETWEEN THE BOTH OF US.
I USUALLY CARRY AROUND TWO MILLION IN MY WALLET, BUT...
I FORGOT TO BRING MY MONEY.
THAT'S ALL RIGHT.
IT'S THE THOUGHT THAT COUNTS.
SMOOCH
WHOAAA!
HAAH! HAAH!
NEXT.
UH, I...
I DON'T HAVE ANY MONEY.
THIS IS MINE!
I PAID 100 YEN MORE THAN YOU.
I KNOW! JUST LET ME LICK IT!
RUMINA-SAMA.
SU (BOW)
WHAT IS IT?
PSST. PSST.
!!

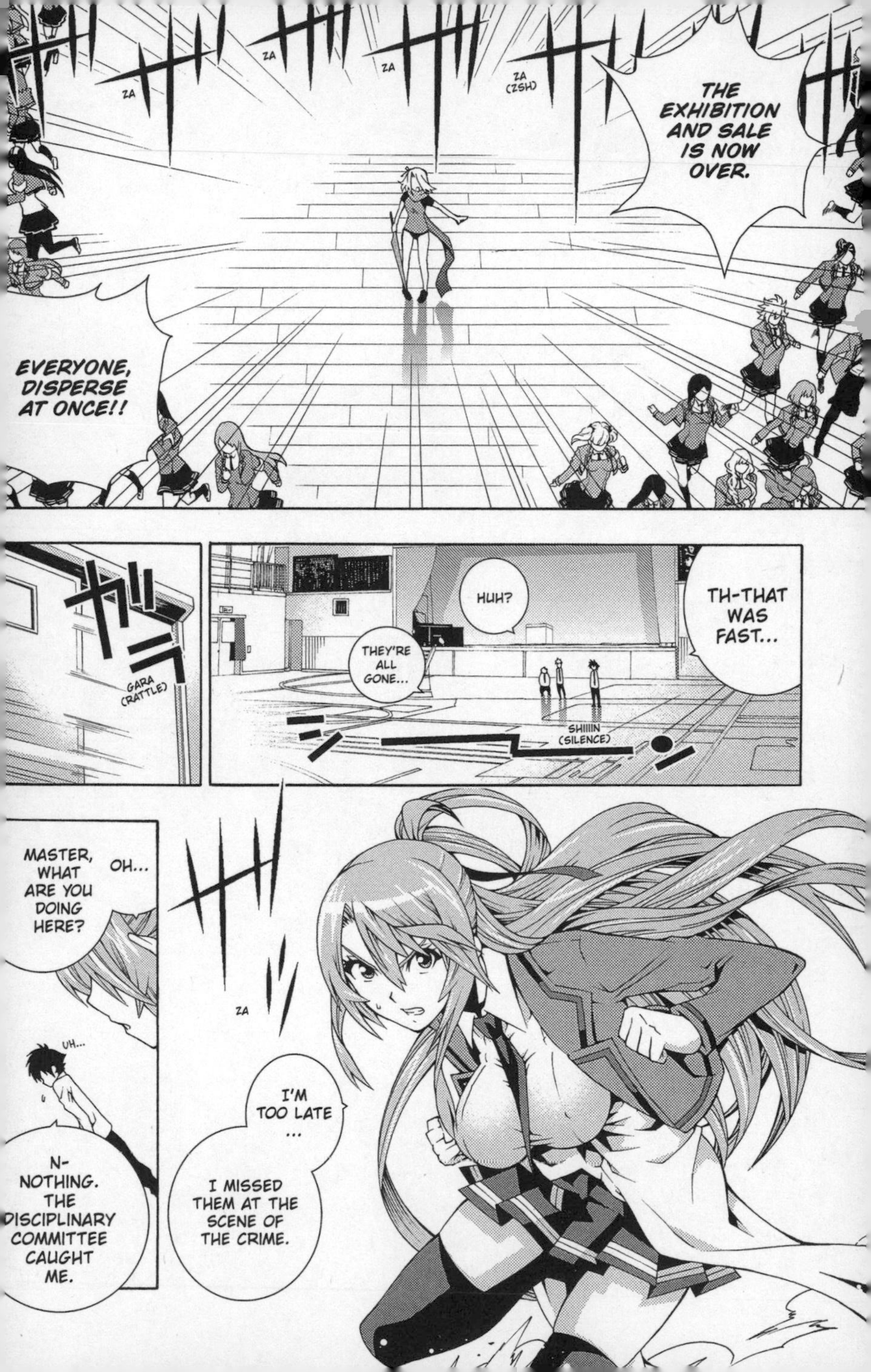
THE EXHIBITION AND SALE IS NOW OVER.
ZA (ZSH)
ZA
ZA
ZA
EVERYONE, DISPERSE AT ONCE!!
TH-THAT WAS FAST...
HUH?
THEY'RE ALL GONE...
SHIIIIN (SILENCE)
GARA (RATTLE)
I'M TOO LATE...
I MISSED THEM AT THE SCENE OF THE CRIME.
ZA
OH...
MASTER, WHAT ARE YOU DOING HERE?
UH...
N-NOTHING. THE DISCIPLINARY COMMITTEE CAUGHT ME.

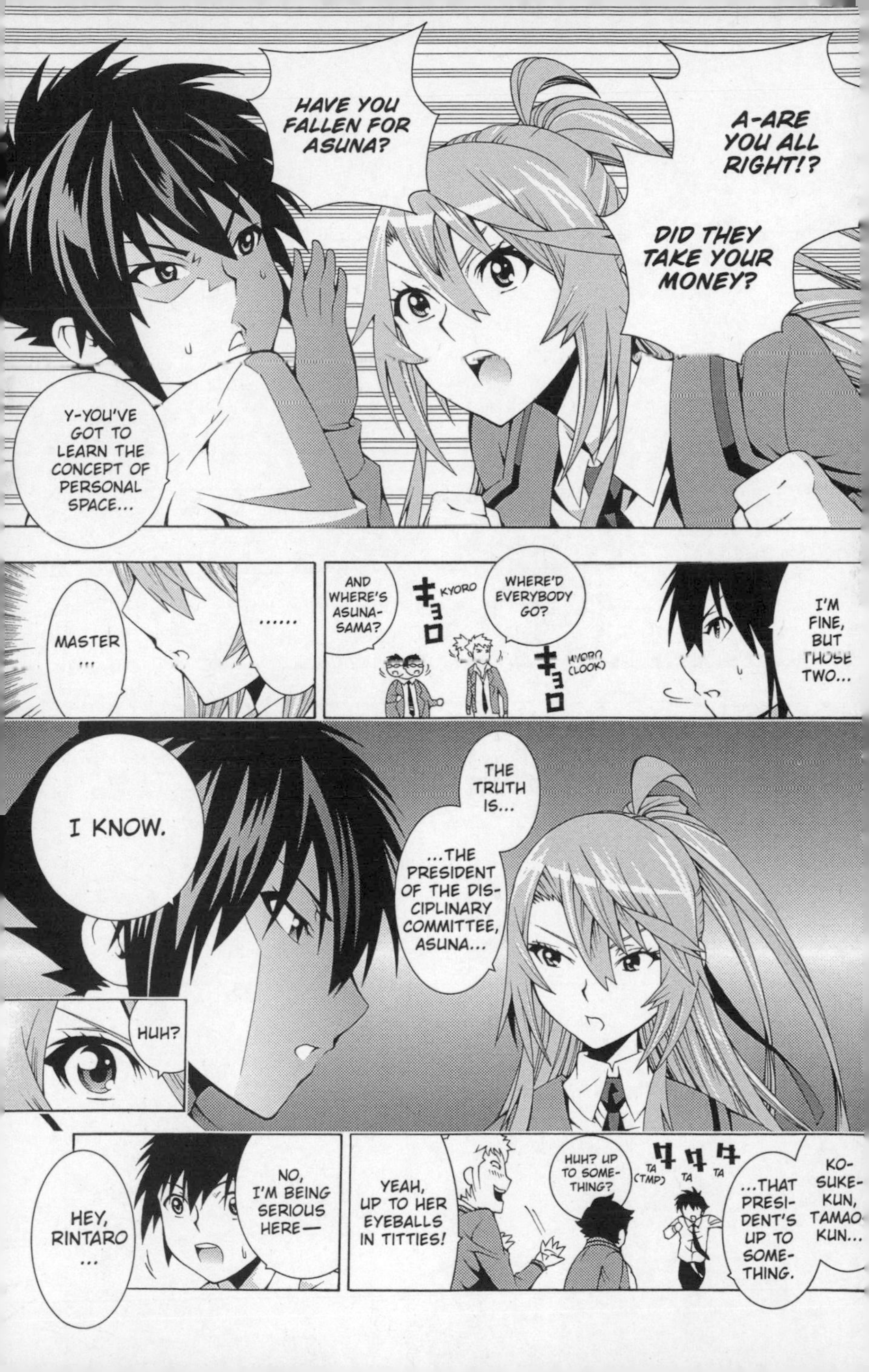
A-ARE YOU ALL RIGHT!?
DID THEY TAKE YOUR MONEY?
HAVE YOU FALLEN FOR ASUNA?
Y-YOU'VE GOT TO LEARN THE CONCEPT OF PERSONAL SPACE...
I'M FINE, BUT THOSE TWO...
KYORO (LOOK)
WHERE'D EVERYBODY GO?
KYORO
AND WHERE'S ASUNA-SAMA?
......
MASTER ...
THE TRUTH IS...
...THE PRESIDENT OF THE DISCIPLINARY COMMITTEE, ASUNA...
I KNOW.
HUH?
KO-SUKE-KUN, TAMAO-KUN...
...THAT PRESIDENT'S UP TO SOMETHING.
TA TA TA (TMP)
HUH? UP TO SOME-THING?
YEAH, UP TO HER EYEBALLS IN TITTIES!
NO, I'M BEING SERIOUS HERE—
HEY, RINTARO ...

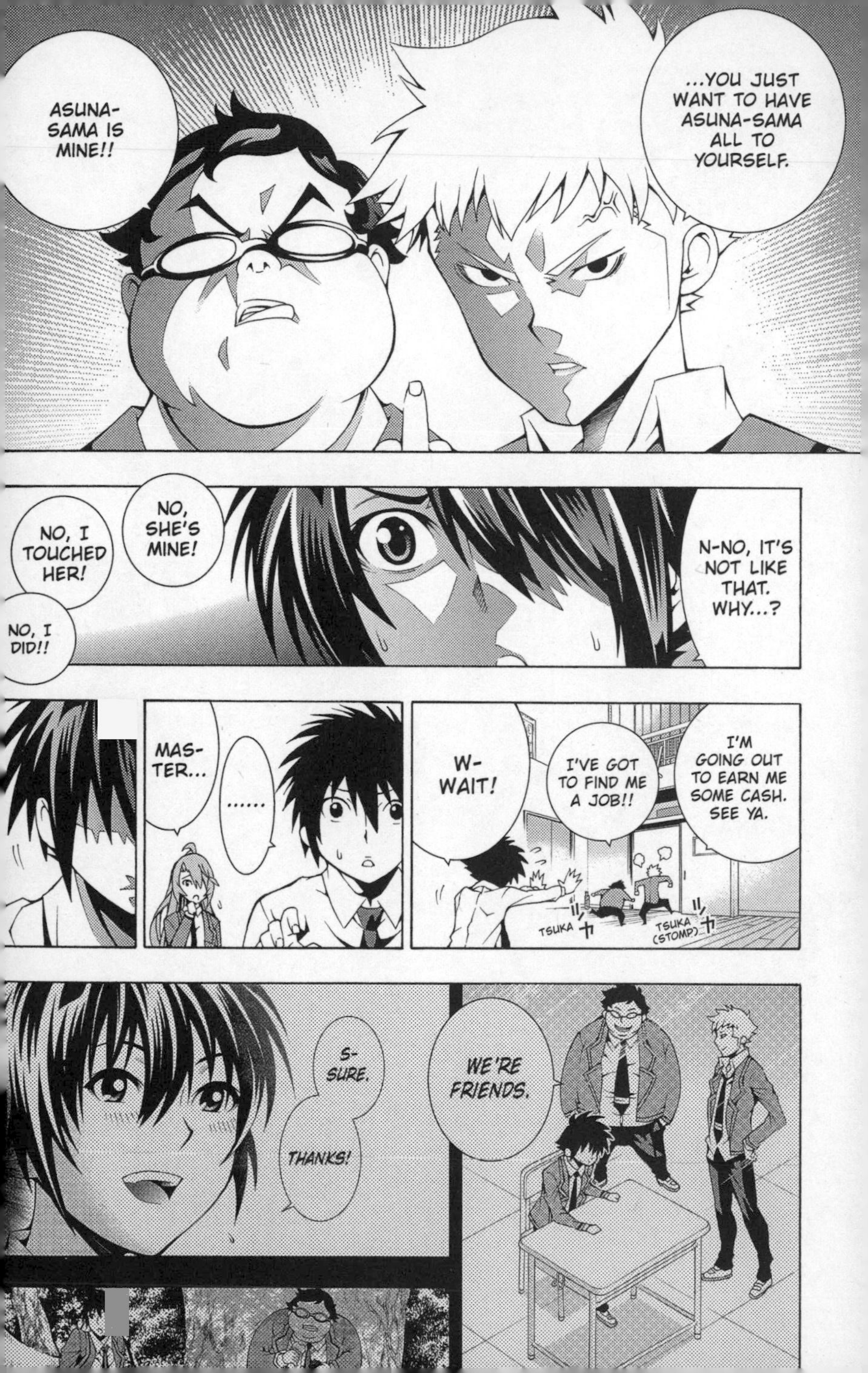
...YOU JUST WANT TO HAVE ASUNA-SAMA ALL TO YOURSELF.
ASUNA-SAMA IS MINE!!
N-NO, IT'S NOT LIKE THAT. WHY...?
NO, SHE'S MINE!
NO, I TOUCHED HER!
NO, I DID!!
I'M GOING OUT TO EARN ME SOME CASH. SEE YA.
I'VE GOT TO FIND ME A JOB!!
W-WAIT!
TSUKA (STOMP)
TSUKA
......
MAS-TER...
WE'RE FRIENDS.
S-SURE.
THANKS!

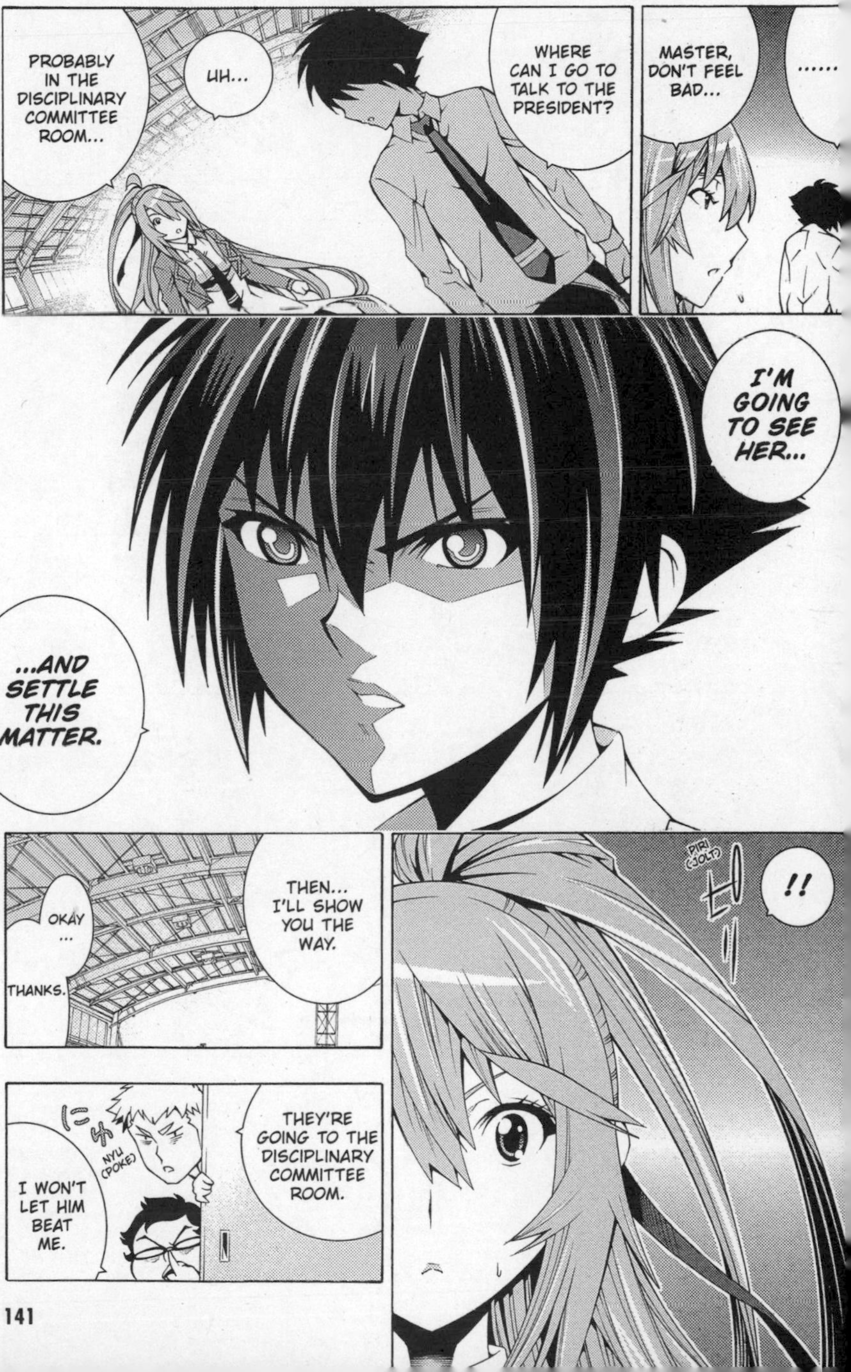
MASTER, DON'T FEEL BAD...
......
WHERE CAN I GO TO TALK TO THE PRESIDENT?
UH...
PROBABLY IN THE DISCIPLINARY COMMITTEE ROOM...
I'M GOING TO SEE HER...
...AND SETTLE THIS MATTER.
!!
PIRI (JOLT)
THEN... I'LL SHOW YOU THE WAY.
OKAY ...
THANKS.
THEY'RE GOING TO THE DISCIPLINARY COMMITTEE ROOM.
にゅ
NYU (POKE)
I WON'T LET HIM BEAT ME.

SIGN: DISCIPLINARY COMMITTEE

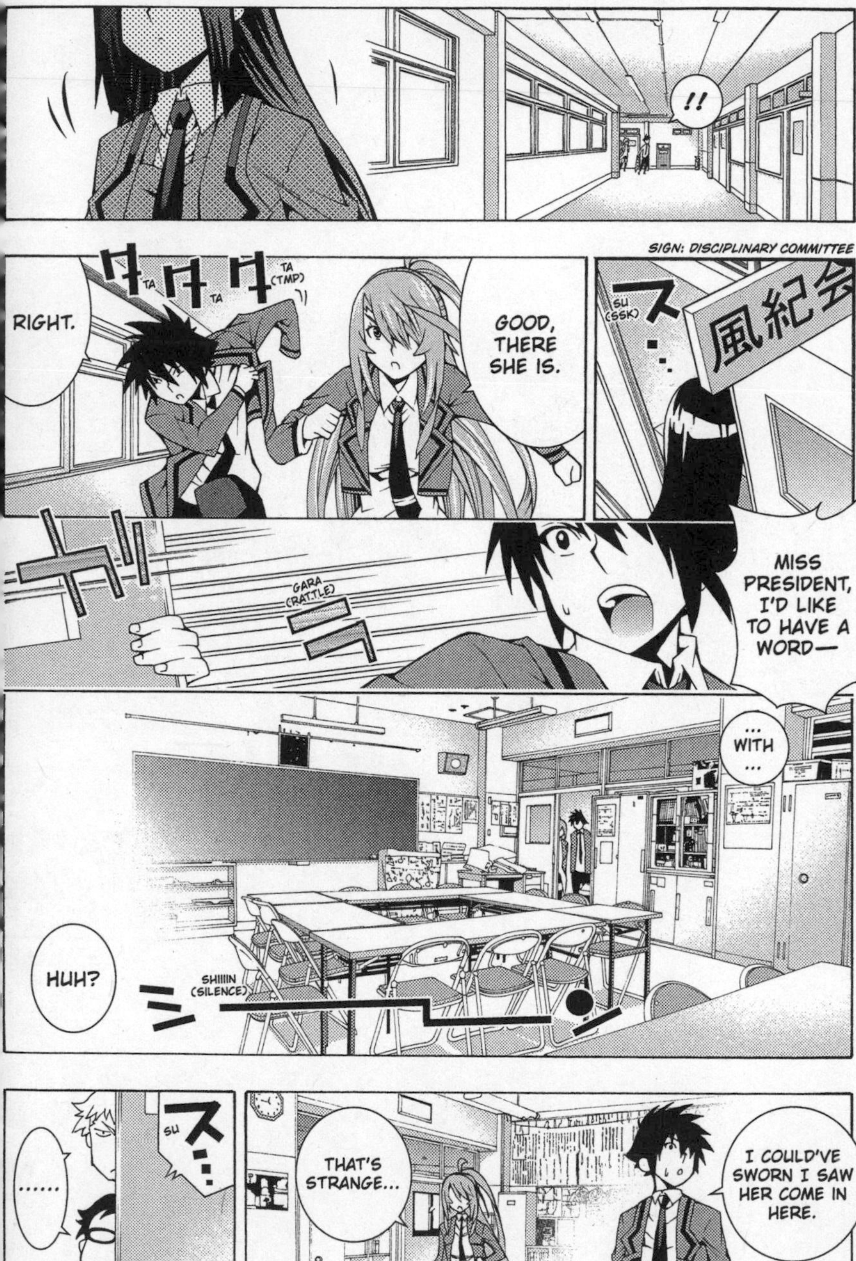

!!
SU (SSK)
風紀会
GOOD, THERE SHE IS.
TA TA TA (TMP)
RIGHT.
MISS PRESIDENT, I'D LIKE TO HAVE A WORD—
GARA (RATTLE)
... WITH ...
SHIIIN (SILENCE)
HUH?
I COULD'VE SWORN I SAW HER COME IN HERE.
THAT'S STRANGE...
SU
....

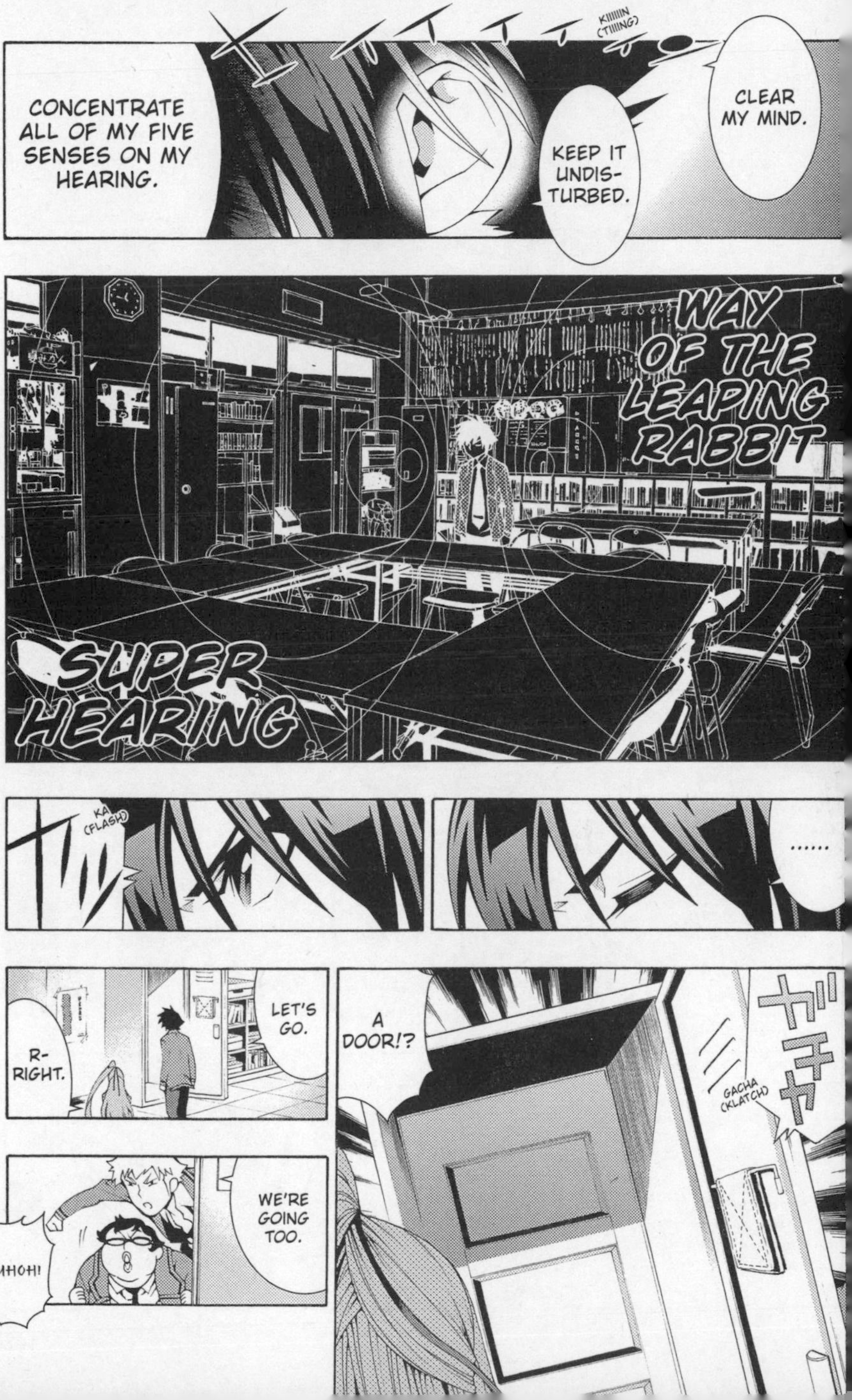
CLEAR MY MIND.
KIIIIIN (TIIIING)
KEEP IT UNDIS-TURBED.
CONCENTRATE ALL OF MY FIVE SENSES ON MY HEARING.
WAY OF THE LEAPING RABBIT —
SUPER HEARING
......
KA (FLASH)
GACHA (KLATCH)
A DOOR!?
LET'S GO.
R-RIGHT.
WE'RE GOING TOO.
MUHOH!

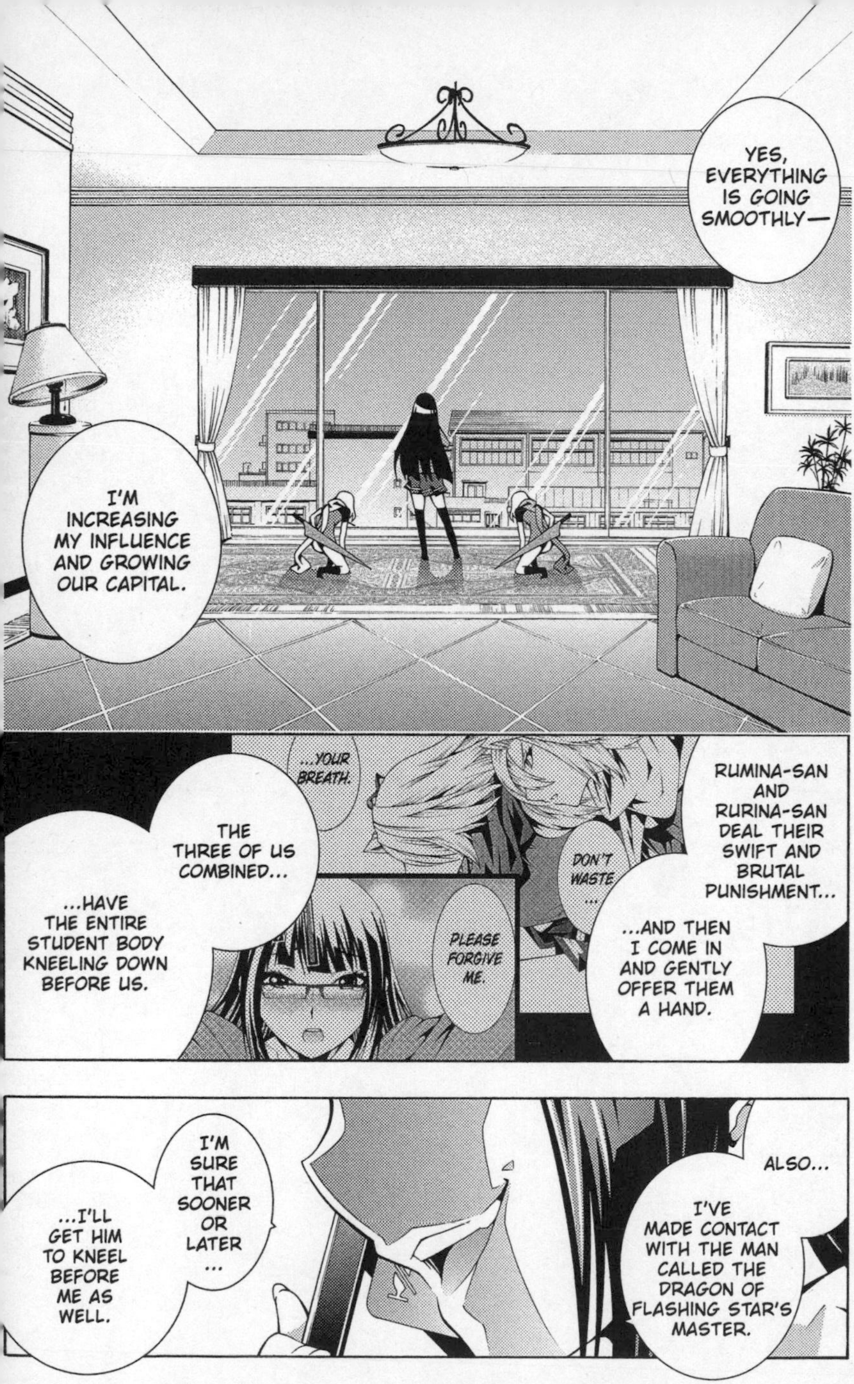
YES, EVERYTHING IS GOING SMOOTHLY—
I'M INCREASING MY INFLUENCE AND GROWING OUR CAPITAL.
RUMINA-SAN AND RURINA-SAN DEAL THEIR SWIFT AND BRUTAL PUNISHMENT...
...AND THEN I COME IN AND GENTLY OFFER THEM A HAND.
DON'T WASTE...
...YOUR BREATH.
PLEASE FORGIVE ME.
THE THREE OF US COMBINED...
...HAVE THE ENTIRE STUDENT BODY KNEELING DOWN BEFORE US.
ALSO...
I'VE MADE CONTACT WITH THE MAN CALLED THE DRAGON OF FLASHING STAR'S MASTER.
I'M SURE THAT SOONER OR LATER...
...I'LL GET HIM TO KNEEL BEFORE ME AS WELL.

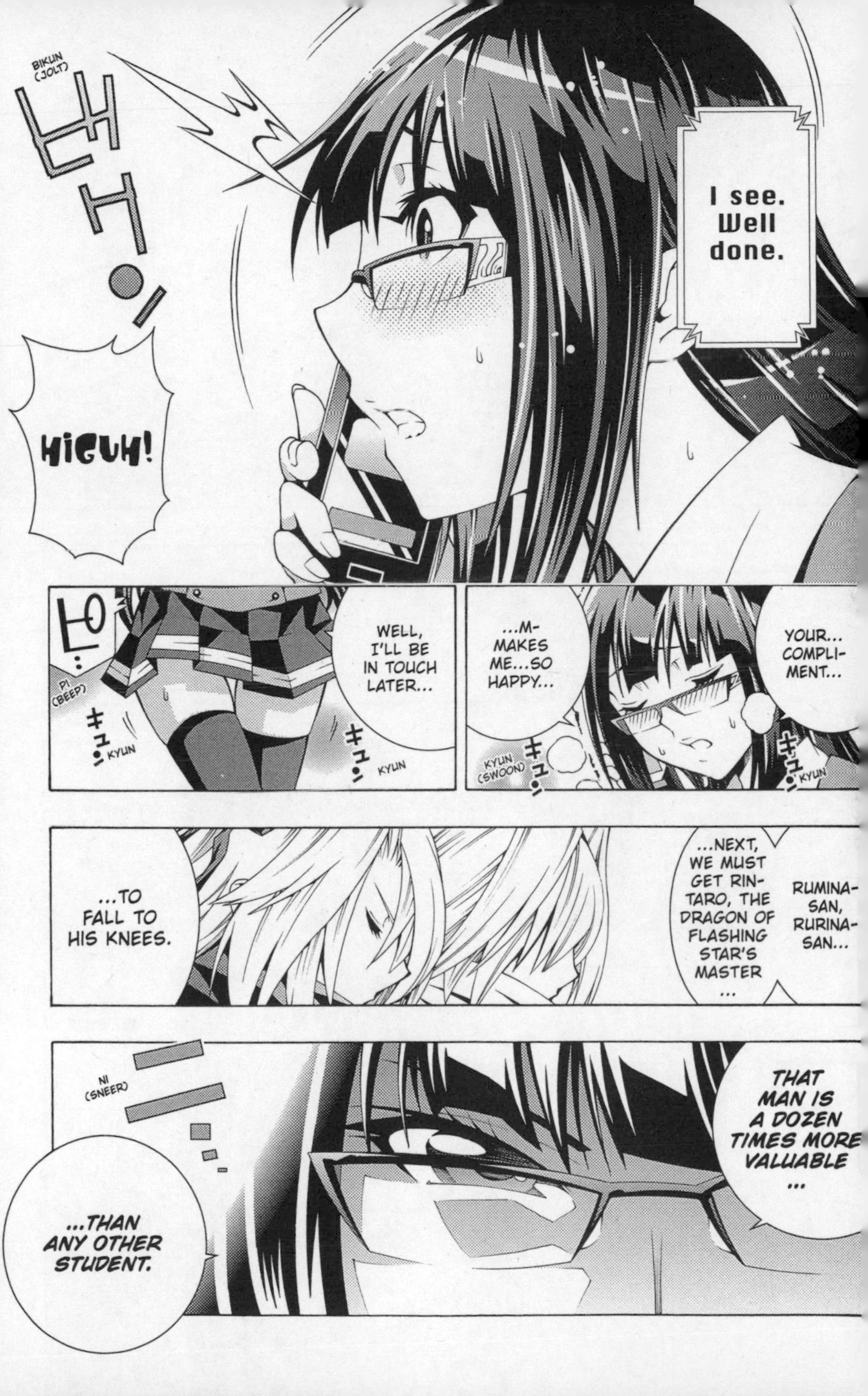
I see. Well done.
BIKUN (JOLT)
HIGUH!
YOUR... COMPLI-MENT...
KYUN
...M-MAKES ME...SO HAPPY...
KYUN (SWOON)
WELL, I'LL BE IN TOUCH LATER...
KYUN
PI (BEEP)
KYUN
RUMINA-SAN, RURINA-SAN...
...NEXT, WE MUST GET RIN-TARO, THE DRAGON OF FLASHING STAR'S MASTER ...
...TO FALL TO HIS KNEES.
THAT MAN IS A DOZEN TIMES MORE VALUABLE ...
NI (SNEER)
...THAN ANY OTHER STUDENT.

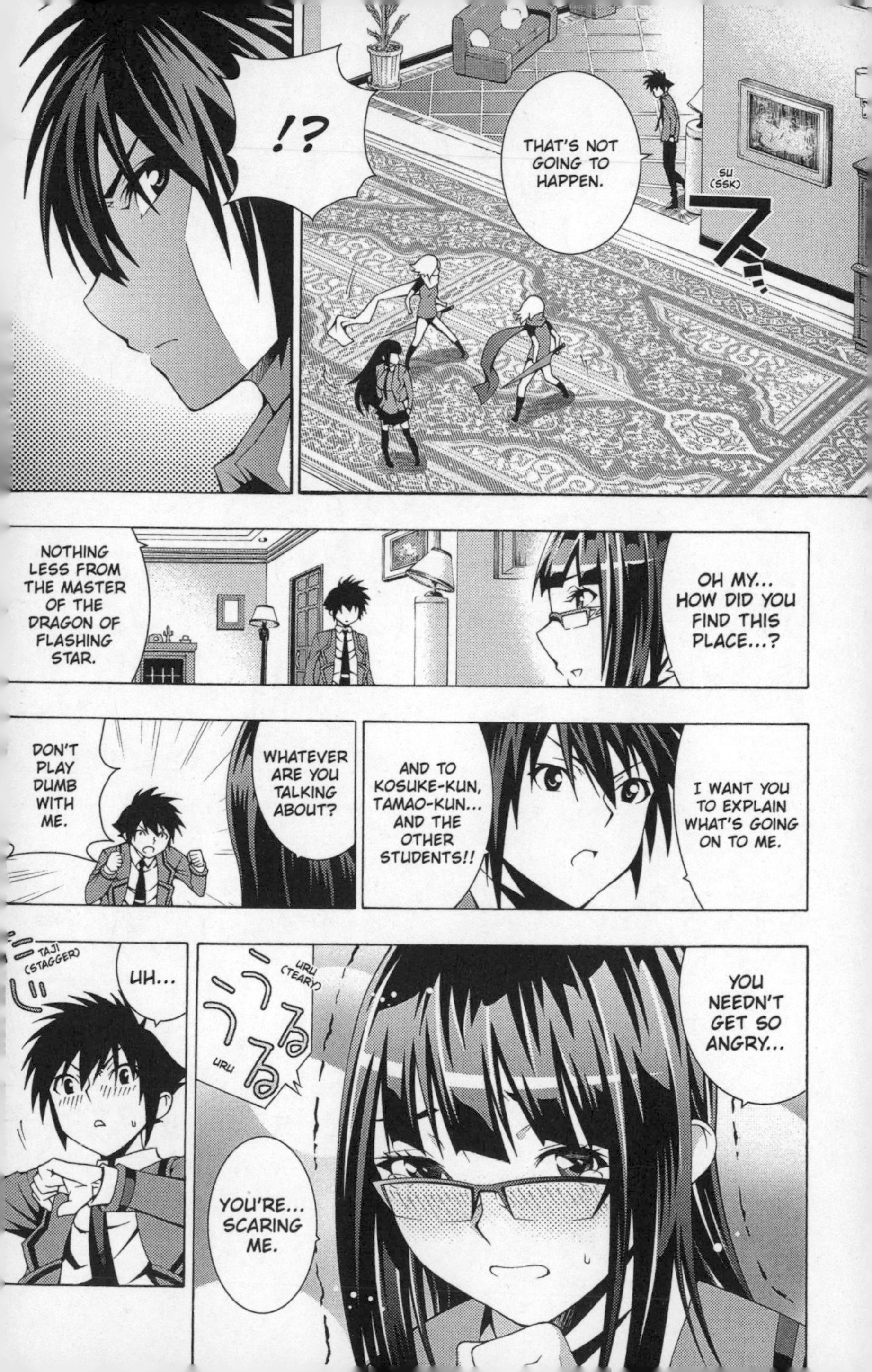
THAT'S NOT GOING TO HAPPEN.
SU (SSK)
!?
OH MY... HOW DID YOU FIND THIS PLACE...?
NOTHING LESS FROM THE MASTER OF THE DRAGON OF FLASHING STAR.
I WANT YOU TO EXPLAIN WHAT'S GOING ON TO ME.
AND TO KOSUKE-KUN, TAMAO-KUN... AND THE OTHER STUDENTS!!
WHATEVER ARE YOU TALKING ABOUT?
DON'T PLAY DUMB WITH ME.
YOU NEEDN'T GET SO ANGRY...
URU (TEARY)
うる
URU
うる
YOU'RE... SCARING ME.
TAJI (STAGGER)
UH...

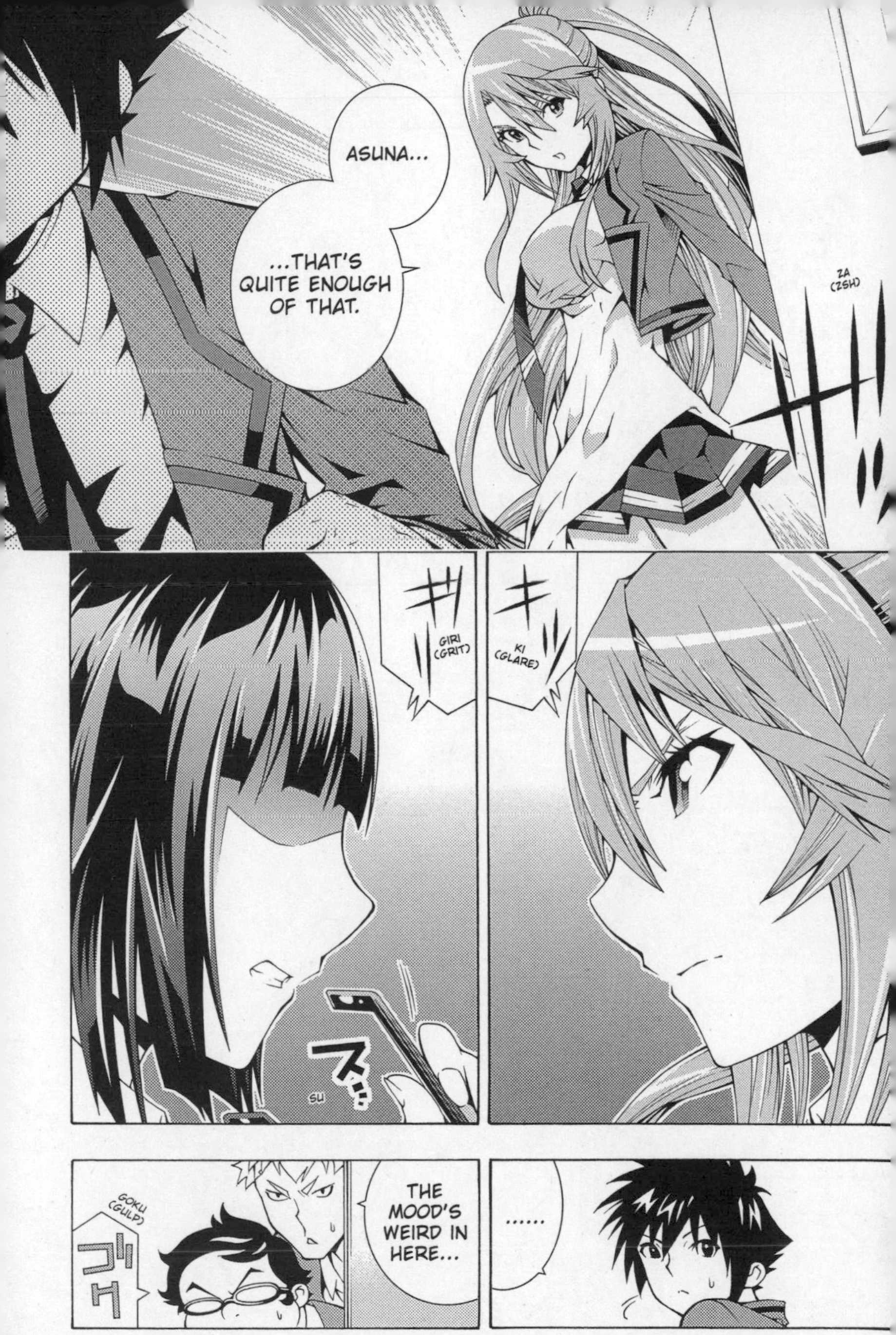
ASUNA...
...THAT'S QUITE ENOUGH OF THAT.
ZA (ZSH)
KI (GLARE)
GIRI (GRIT)
SU
......
THE MOOD'S WEIRD IN HERE...
GOKU (GULP)

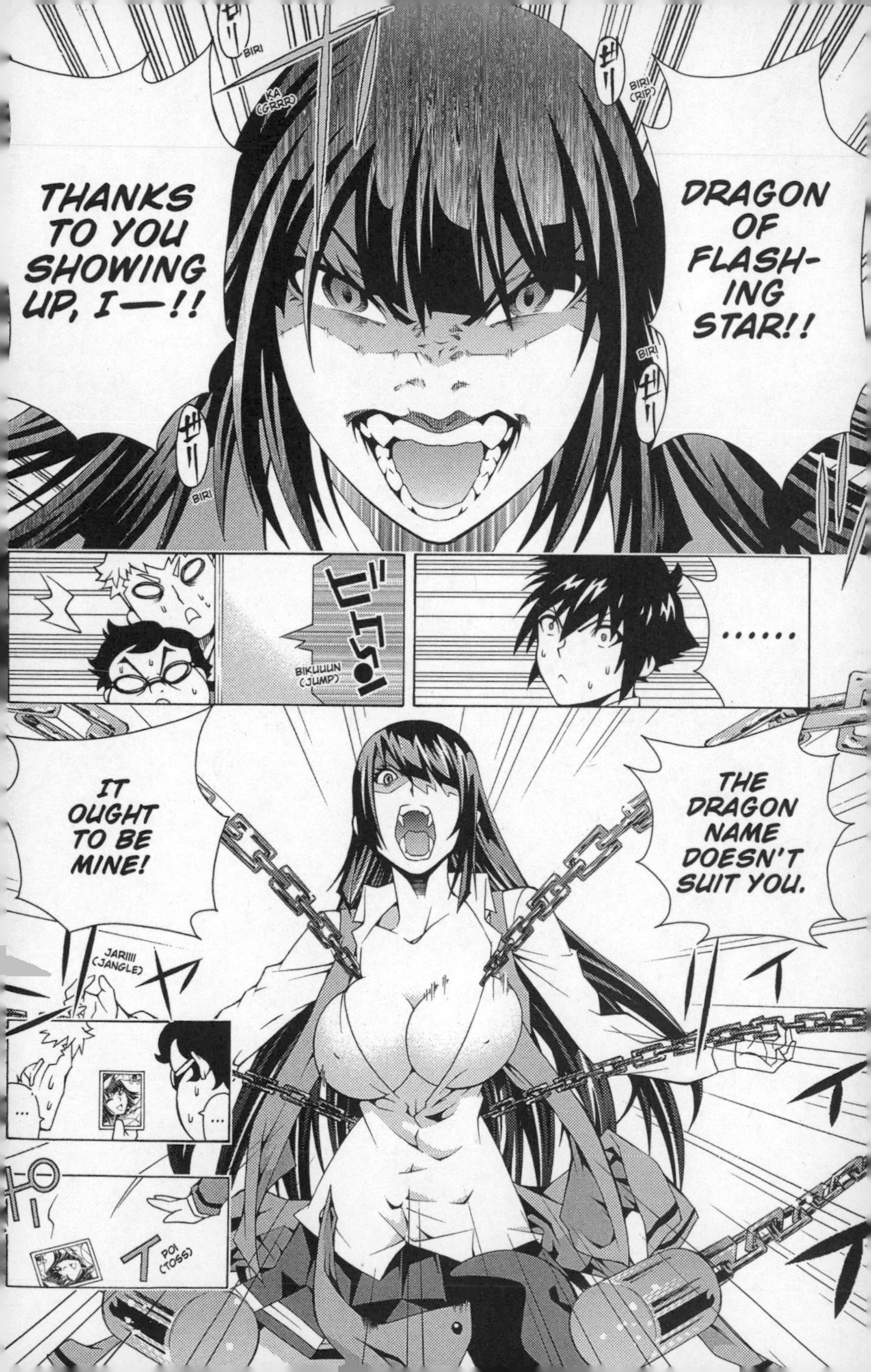
BIRI (RIP)
KA (GRRR)
BIRI
DRAGON OF FLASHING STAR!!
THANKS TO YOU SHOWING UP, I—!!
BIRI
BIRI
......
BIKUUUN (JUMP)
THE DRAGON NAME DOESN'T SUIT YOU.
IT OUGHT TO BE MINE!
JARIIII (JANGLE)
...
...
POI (TOSS)

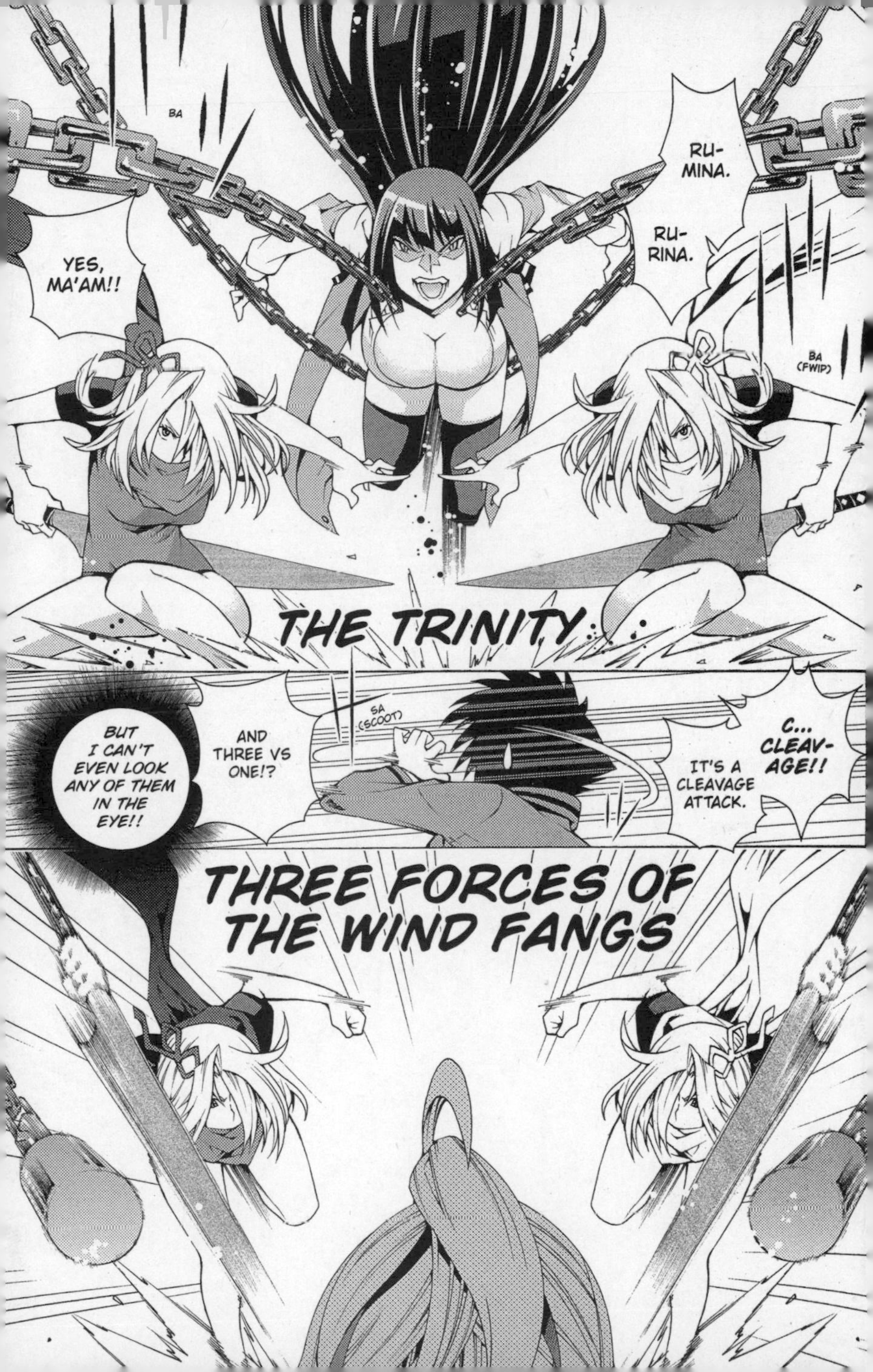
RU-MINA.
RU-RINA.
BA (FWIP)
BA
YES, MA'AM!!
THE TRINITY
C... CLEAV-AGE!!
IT'S A CLEAVAGE ATTACK.
SA (SCOOT)
AND THREE VS ONE!?
BUT I CAN'T EVEN LOOK ANY OF THEM IN THE EYE!!
THREE FORCES OF THE WIND FANGS

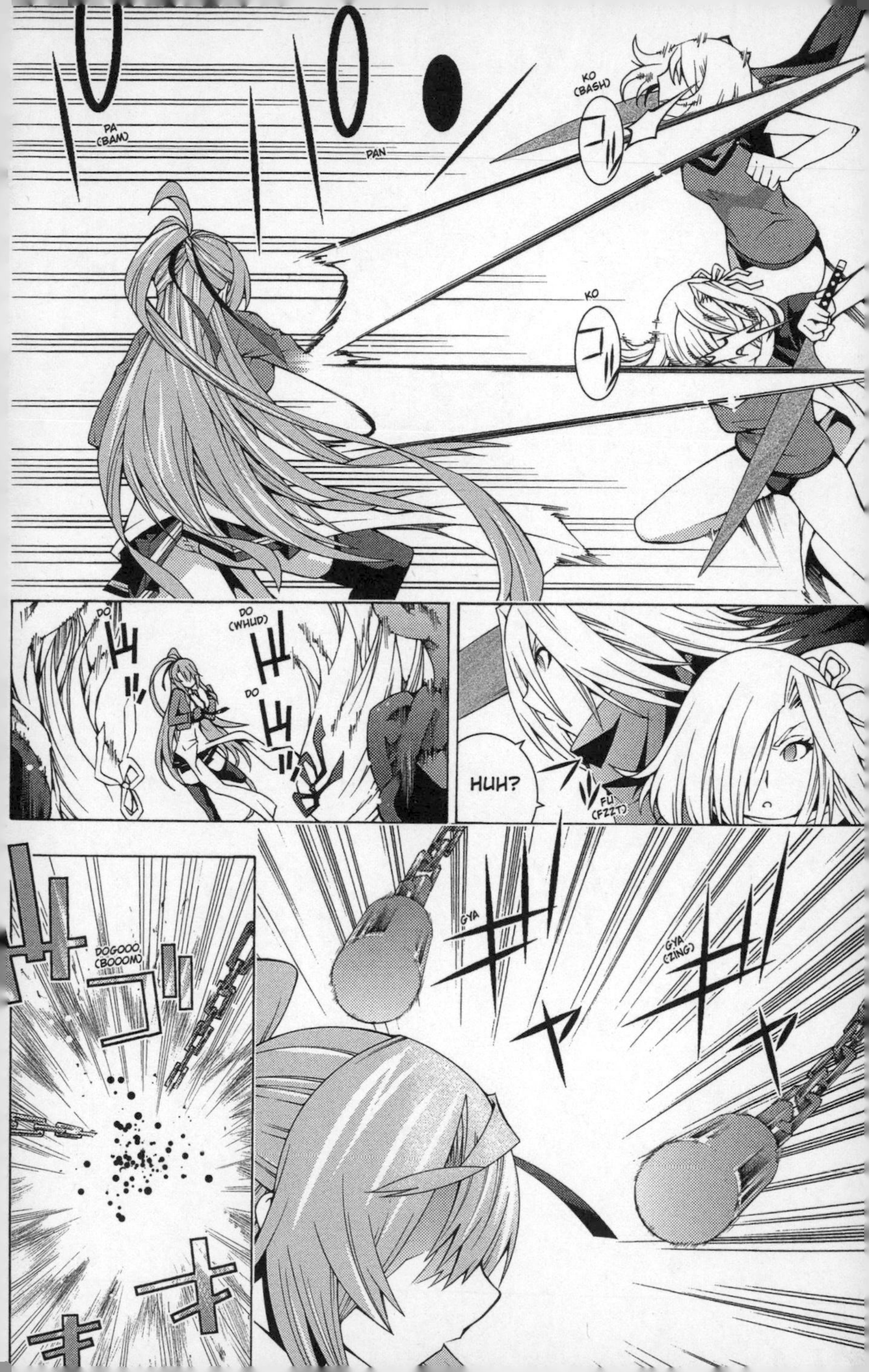
KO (BASH)
PAN
PA (BAM)
KO
HUH?
FU (FZZT)
DO (WHUD)
DO
DO
GYA (ZING)
GYA
DOGOOO (BOOOM)

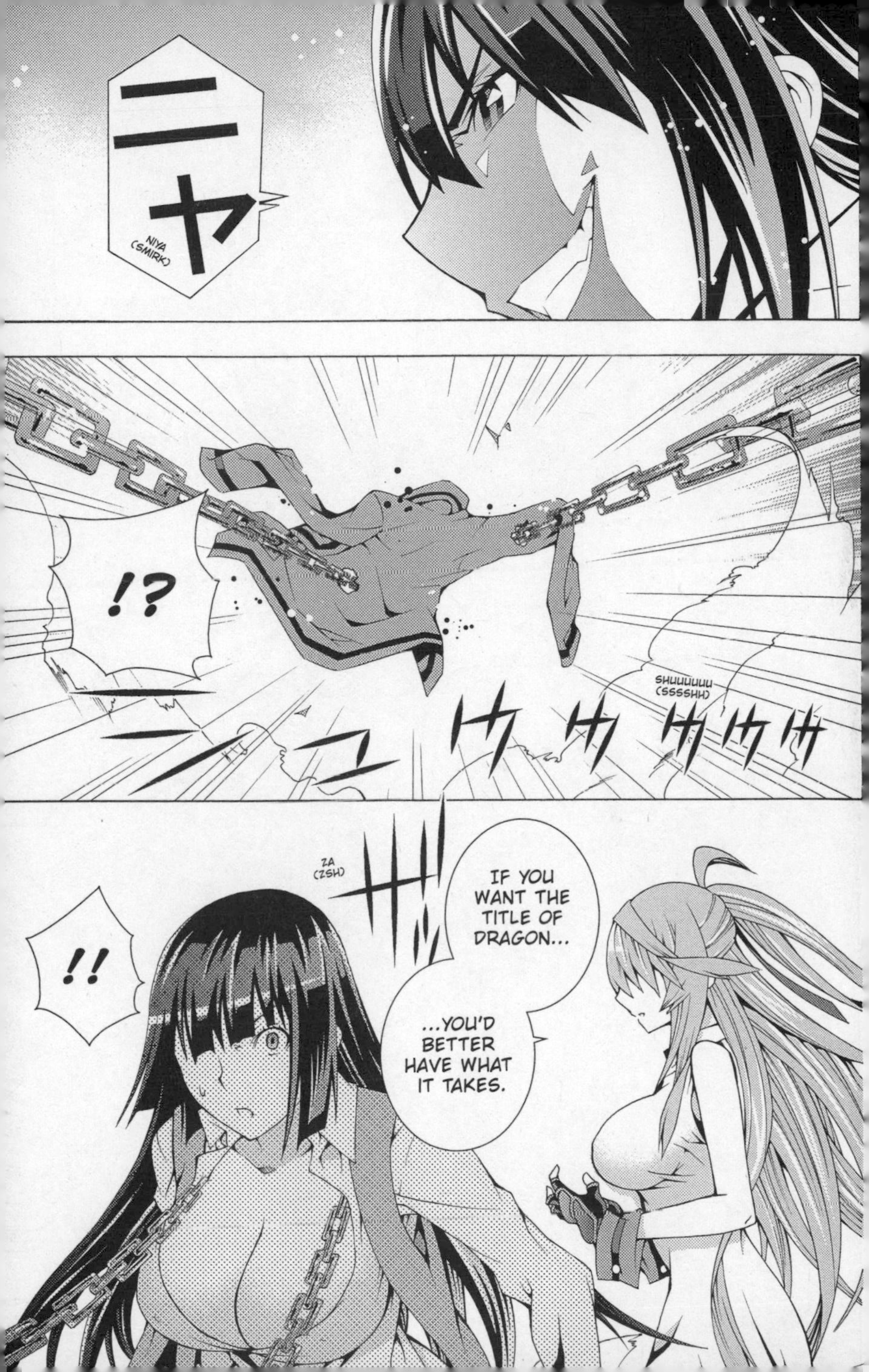
ニヤ
NIYA (SMIRK)
!?
シュウウウウウ
SHUUUUUU (SSSSHH)
ザッ
ZA (ZSH)
IF YOU WANT THE TITLE OF DRAGON...
...YOU'D BETTER HAVE WHAT IT TAKES.
!!

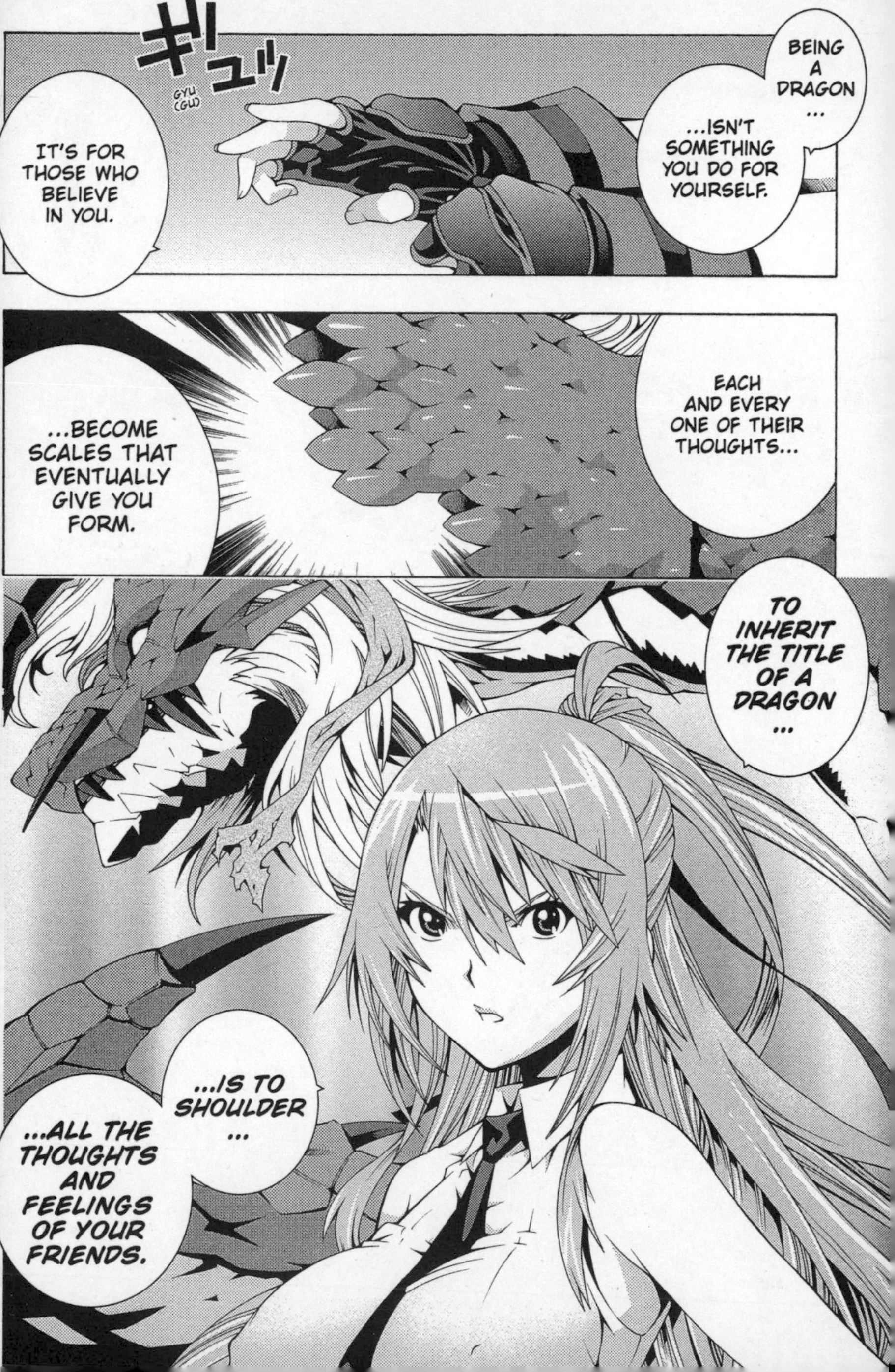
BEING A DRAGON...
...ISN'T SOMETHING YOU DO FOR YOURSELF.
GYU (GU)
IT'S FOR THOSE WHO BELIEVE IN YOU.
EACH AND EVERY ONE OF THEIR THOUGHTS...
...BECOME SCALES THAT EVENTUALLY GIVE YOU FORM.
TO INHERIT THE TITLE OF A DRAGON...
...IS TO SHOULDER...
...ALL THE THOUGHTS AND FEELINGS OF YOUR FRIENDS.

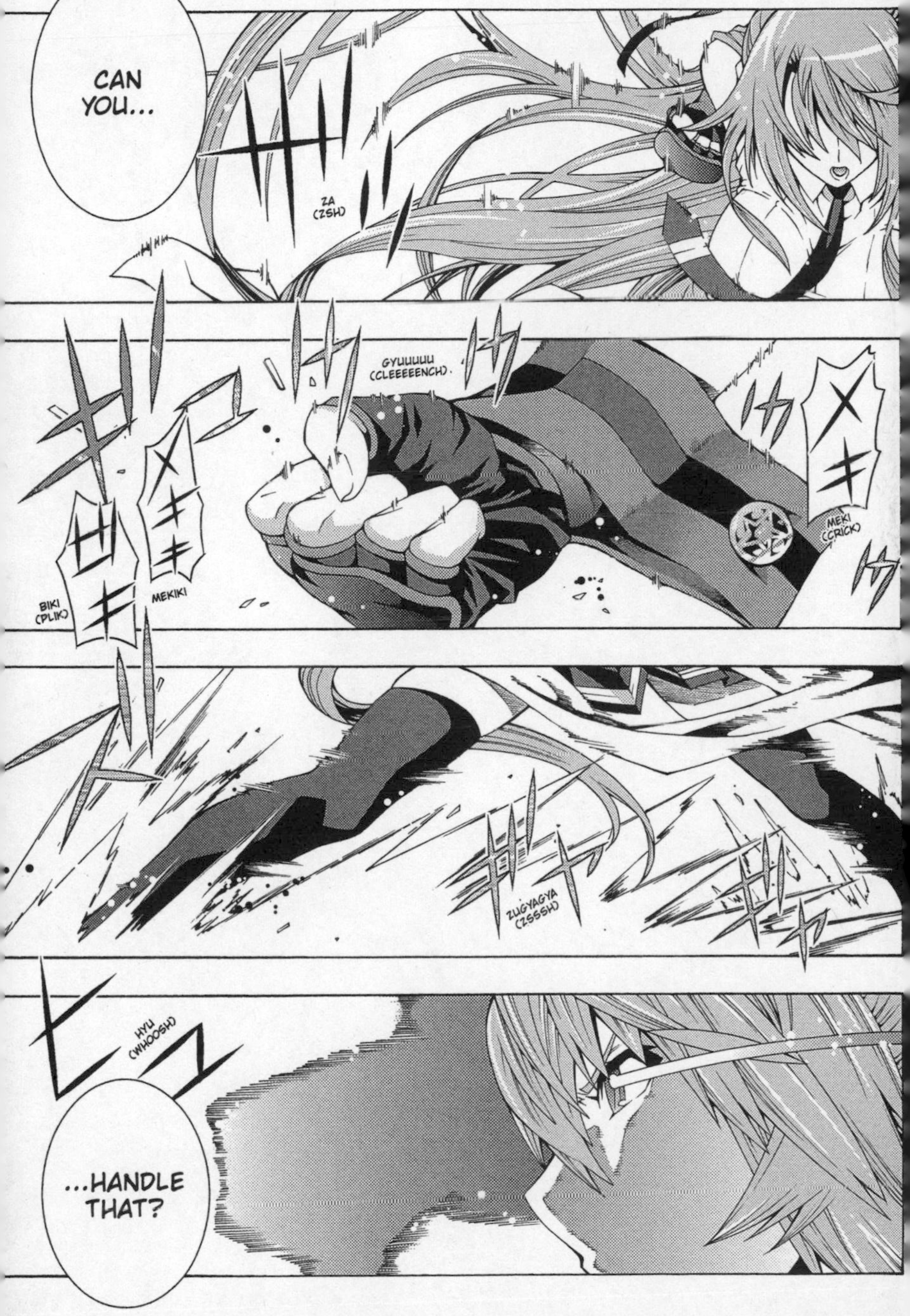
CAN YOU...
ZA (ZSH)
GYUUUUU (CLEEEEENCH)
MEKI (CRICK)
MEKIKI
BIKI (PLIK)
ZUGYAGYA (ZSSSH)
HYU (WHOOSH)
...HANDLE THAT?

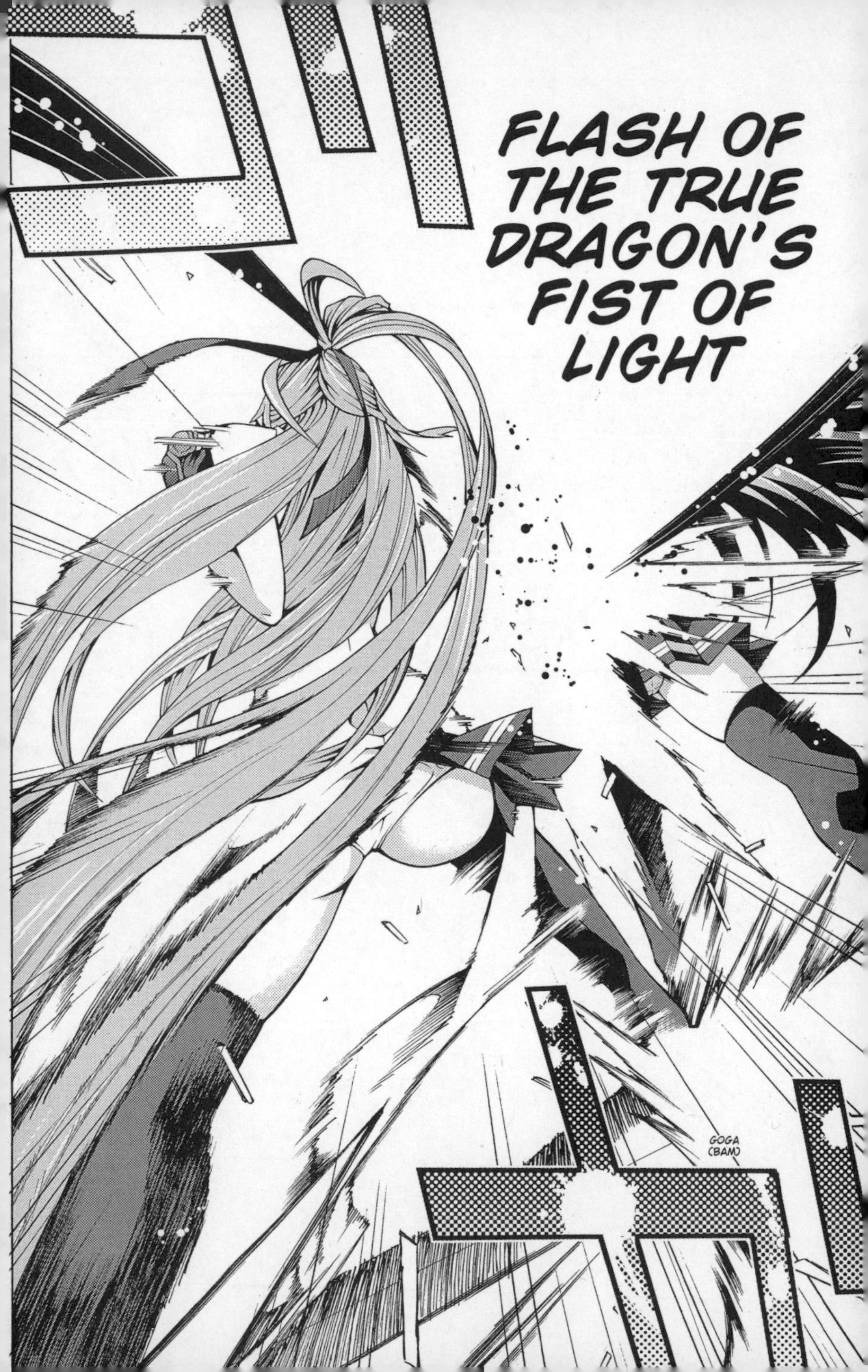
FLASH OF THE TRUE DRAGON'S FIST OF LIGHT
GOGA (BAM)

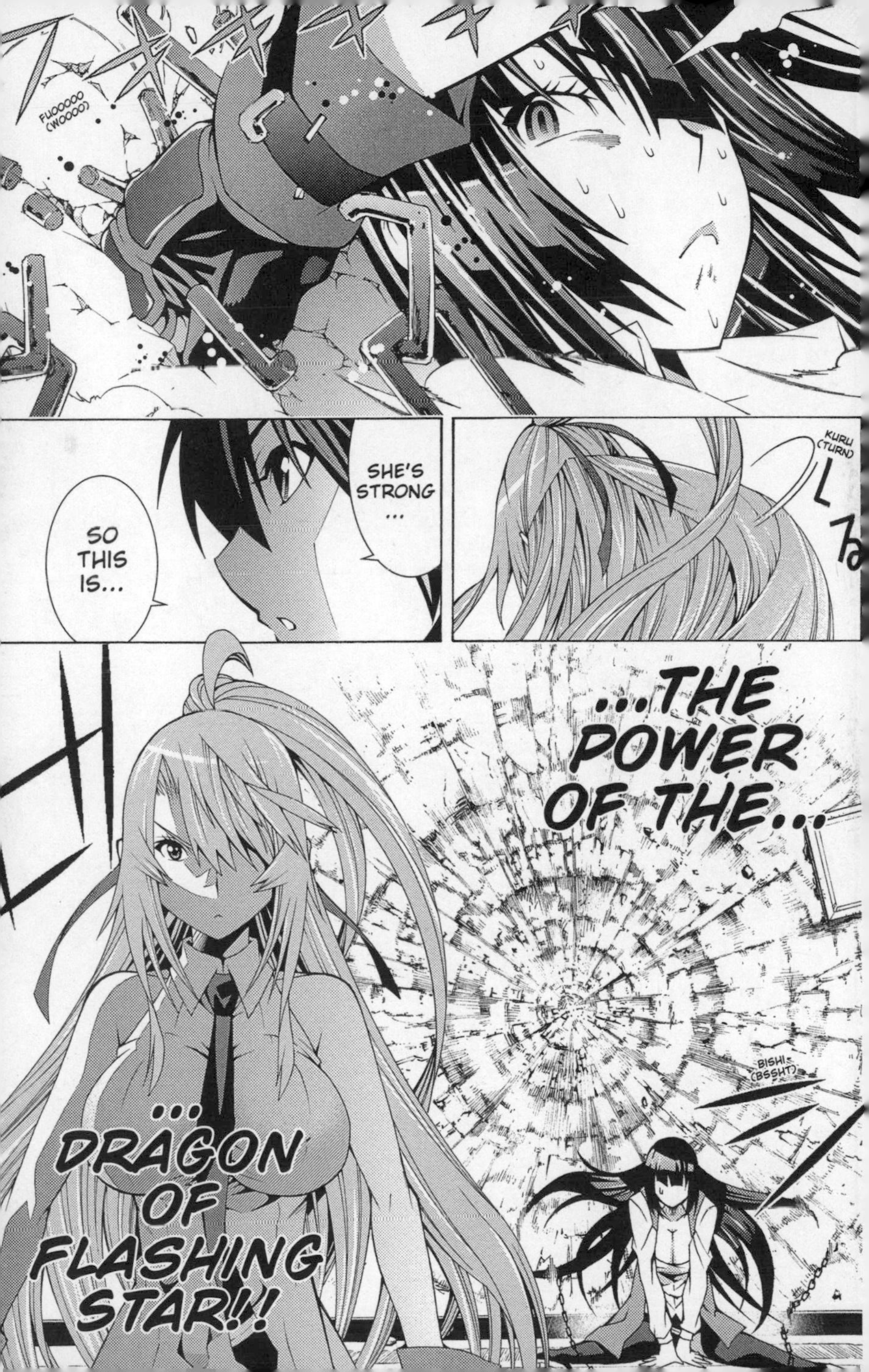
FUOOOOO (WOOOO)
KURU (TURN)
SHE'S STRONG...
SO THIS IS...
...THE POWER OF THE...
BISHI (BSSHT)
...DRAGON OF FLASHING STAR!!!

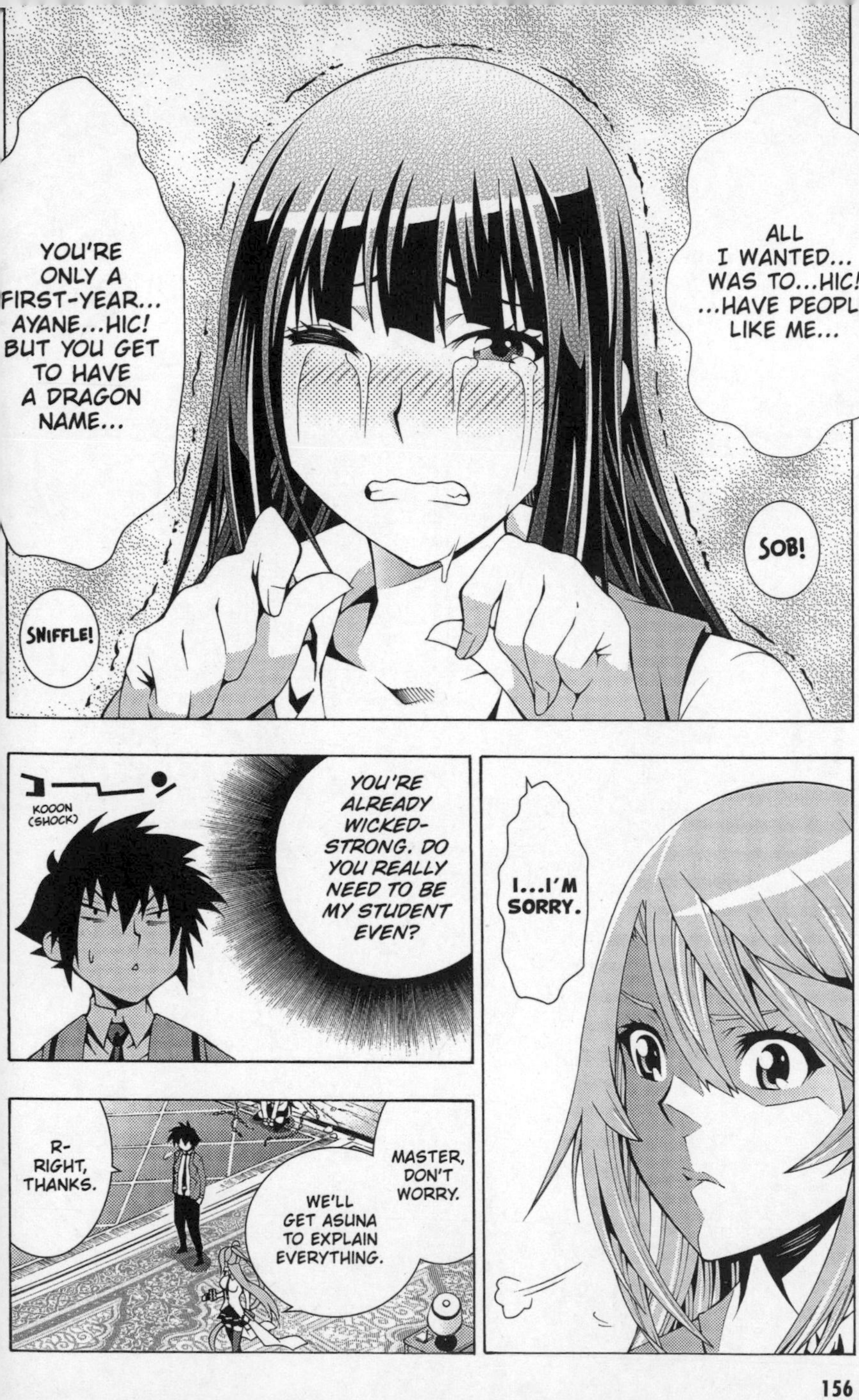
ALL I WANTED... WAS TO...HIC! ...HAVE PEOPLE LIKE ME...
SOB!
YOU'RE ONLY A FIRST-YEAR... AYANE...HIC! BUT YOU GET TO HAVE A DRAGON NAME...
SNIFFLE!
I...I'M SORRY.
YOU'RE ALREADY WICKED-STRONG. DO YOU REALLY NEED TO BE MY STUDENT EVEN?
KOOON (SHOCK)
MASTER, DON'T WORRY.
WE'LL GET ASUNA TO EXPLAIN EVERYTHING.
R-RIGHT, THANKS.

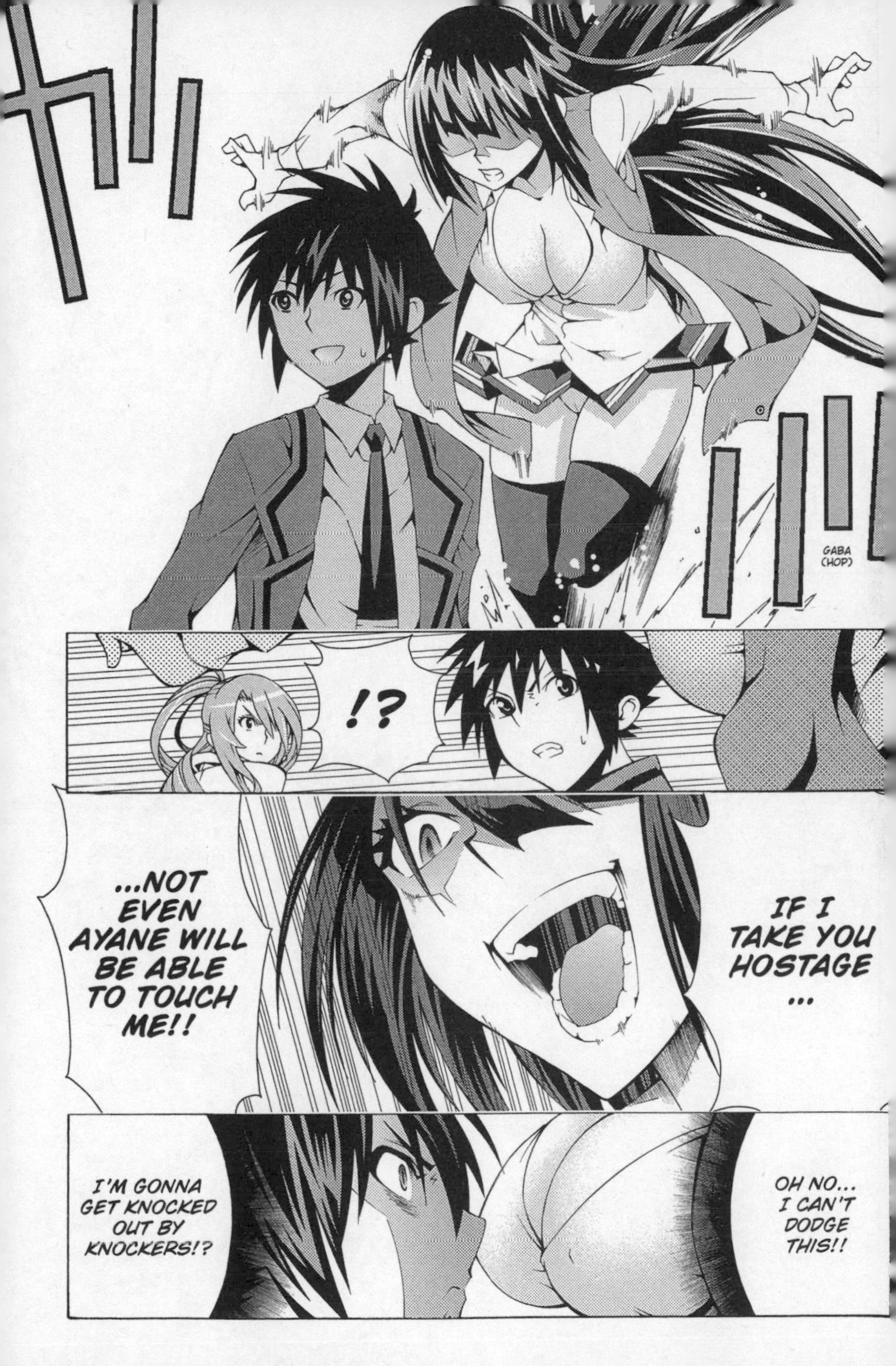
GABA (HOP)
!?
IF I TAKE YOU HOSTAGE ...
...NOT EVEN AYANE WILL BE ABLE TO TOUCH ME!!
OH NO... I CAN'T DODGE THIS!!
I'M GONNA GET KNOCKED OUT BY KNOCKERS!?

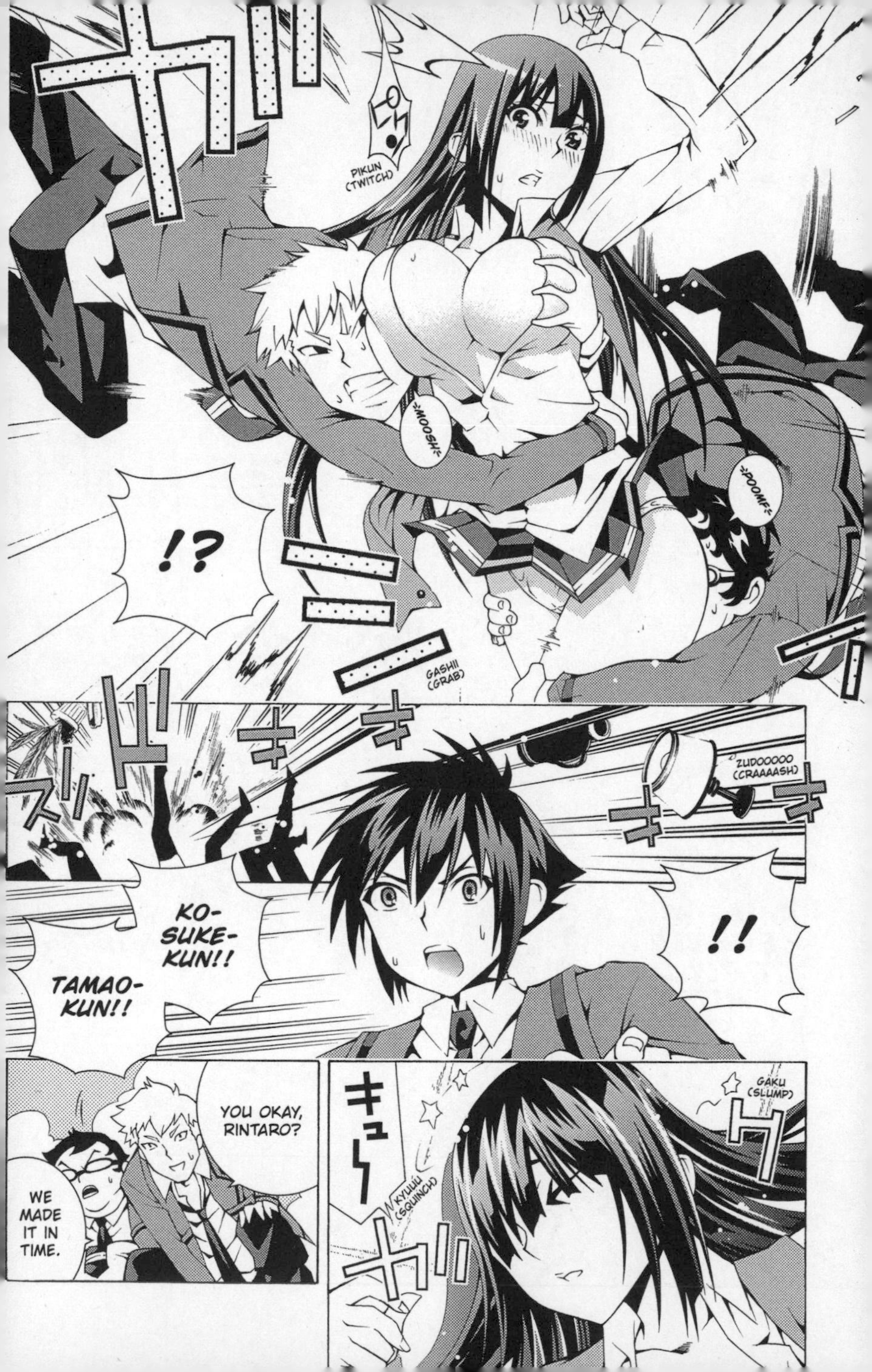
PIKUN (TWITCH)
MOOSH
POOMF
!?
GASHII (GRAB)
ZUDOOOOO (CRAAAASH)
!!
KO-SUKE-KUN!!
TAMAO-KUN!!
GAKU (SLUMP)
KYUUU (SQUINCH)
YOU OKAY, RINTARO?
WE MADE IT IN TIME.

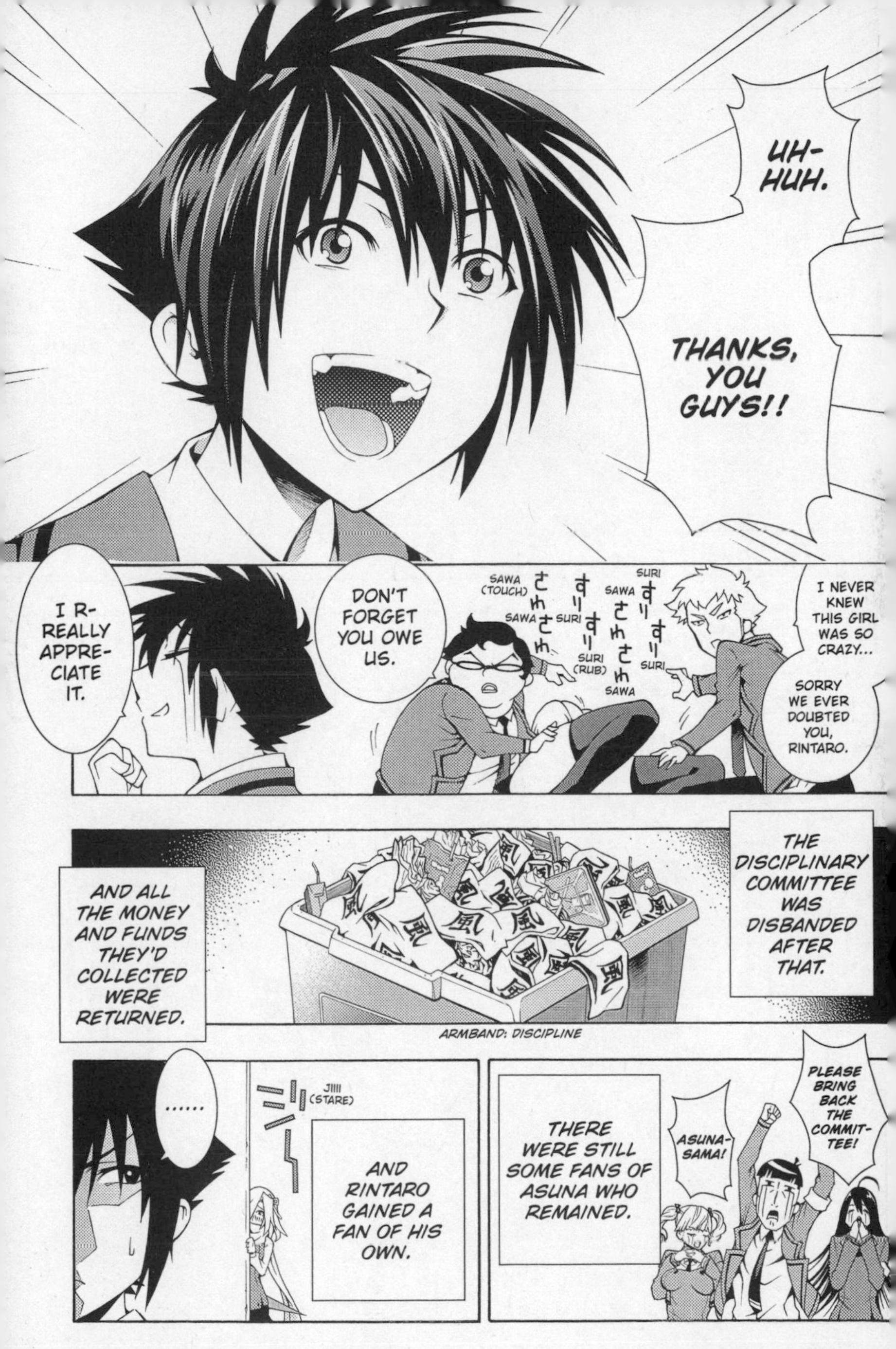
UH-HUH.
THANKS, YOU GUYS!!
I NEVER KNEW THIS GIRL WAS SO CRAZY...
SORRY WE EVER DOUBTED YOU, RINTARO.
SURI すりすり SURI
SAWA さわさわ SAWA
SURI すりすり SURI (RUB)
SAWA (TOUCH) さわさわ SAWA
DON'T FORGET YOU OWE US.
I R-REALLY APPRECIATE IT.
THE DISCIPLINARY COMMITTEE WAS DISBANDED AFTER THAT.
AND ALL THE MONEY AND FUNDS THEY'D COLLECTED WERE RETURNED.
ARMBAND: DISCIPLINE
PLEASE BRING BACK THE COMMITTEE!
ASUNA-SAMA!
THERE WERE STILL SOME FANS OF ASUNA WHO REMAINED.
JIIII (STARE)
AND RINTARO GAINED A FAN OF HIS OWN.
......

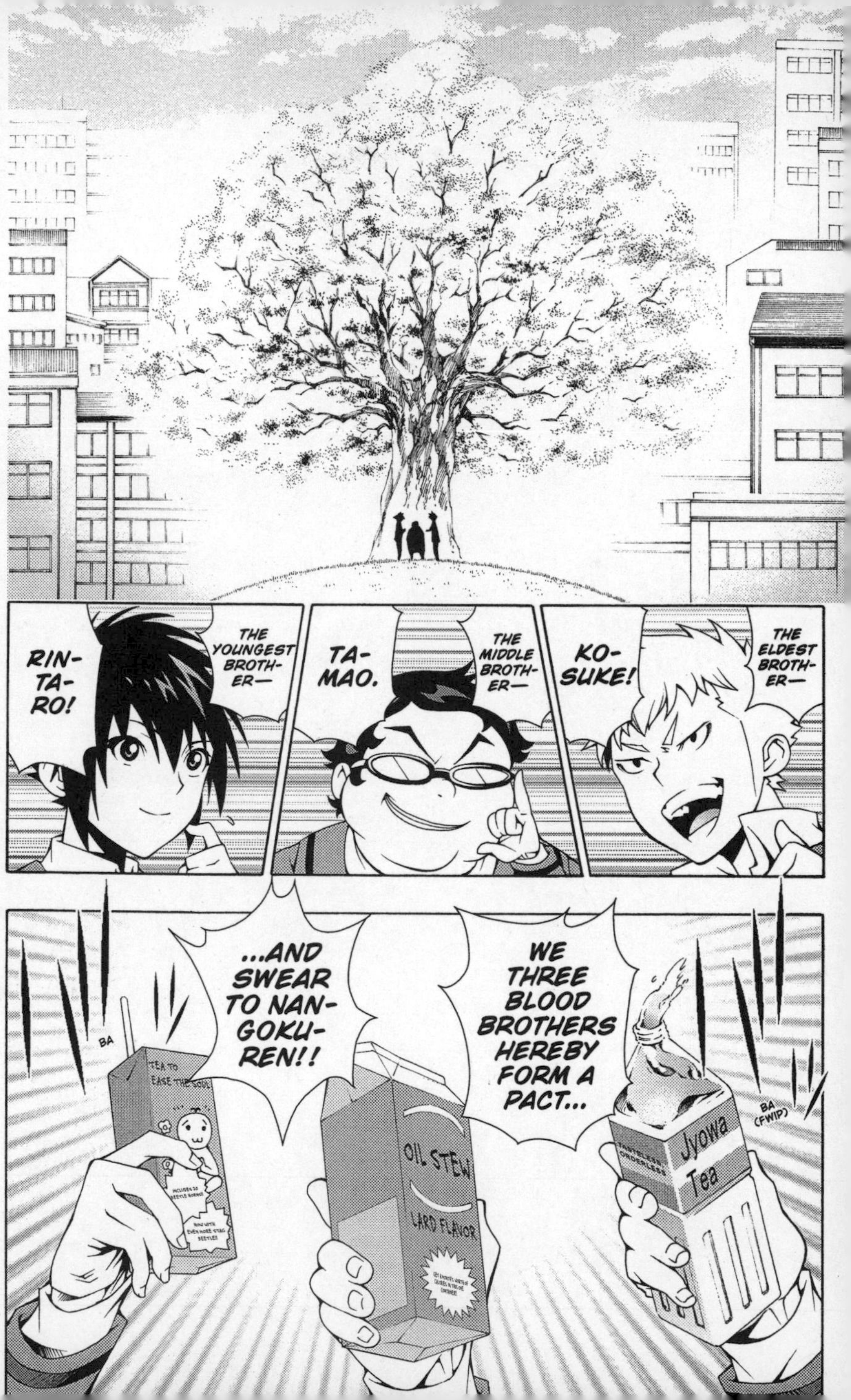
THE ELDEST BROTH-ER—
KO-SUKE!
THE MIDDLE BROTH-ER—
TA-MAO.
THE YOUNGEST BROTH-ER—
RIN-TA-RO!
BA (FWIP)
TASTELESS ODORLESS
Jyowa Tea
WE THREE BLOOD BROTHERS HEREBY FORM A PACT...
...AND SWEAR TO NAN-GOKU-REN!!
OIL STEW
LARD FLAVOR
BA
TEA TO EASE THE SOUL
INCLUDES 20 BEETLE HORNS
NOW WITH EVEN MORE STAG BEETLE!!

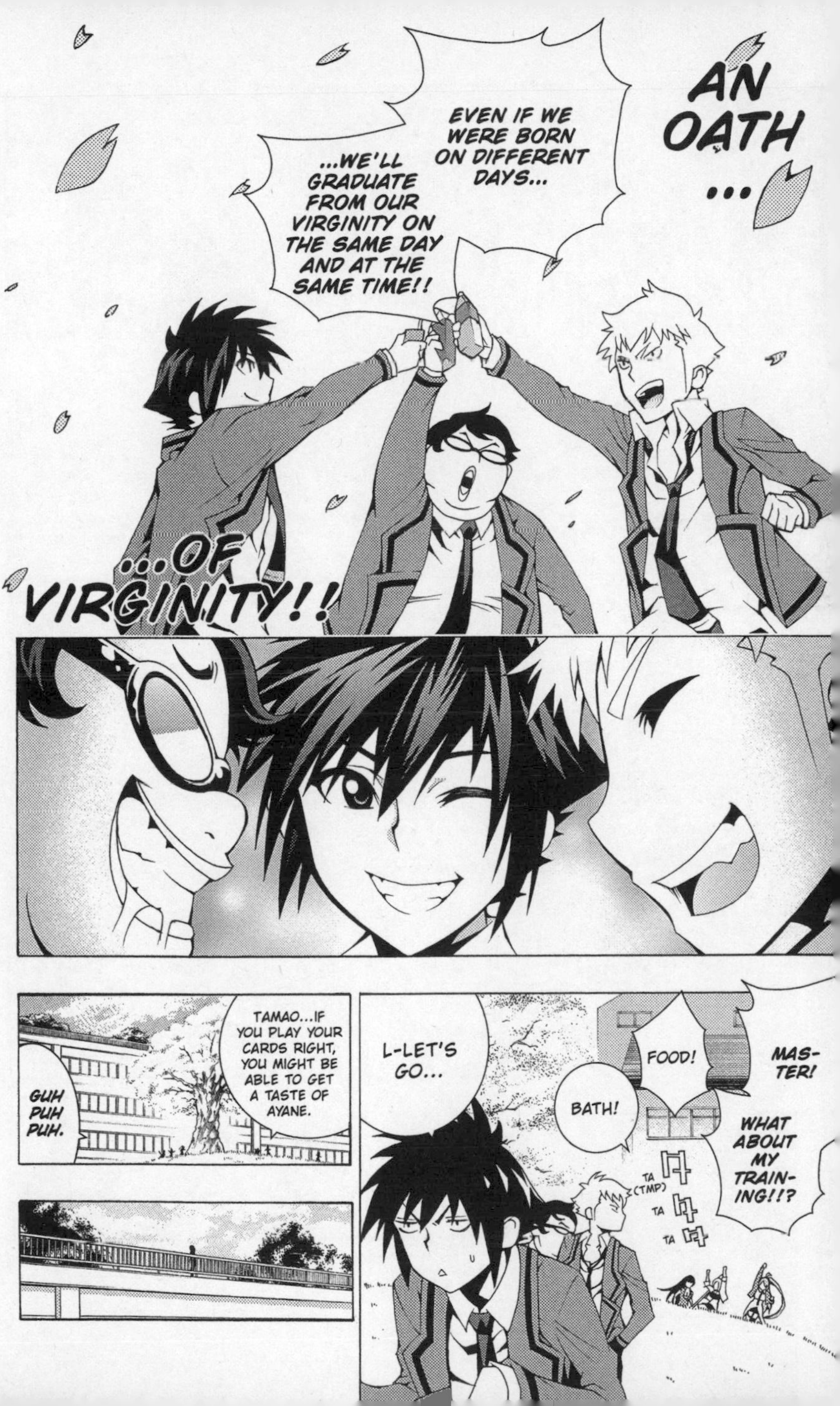
AN OATH ...
EVEN IF WE WERE BORN ON DIFFERENT DAYS...
...WE'LL GRADUATE FROM OUR VIRGINITY ON THE SAME DAY AND AT THE SAME TIME!!
...OF VIRGINITY!!
MAS-TER!
FOOD!
WHAT ABOUT MY TRAIN-ING!!?
BATH!
TA (TMP) TA TA
L-LET'S GO...
TAMAO...IF YOU PLAY YOUR CARDS RIGHT, YOU MIGHT BE ABLE TO GET A TASTE OF AYANE.
GUH PUH PUH.

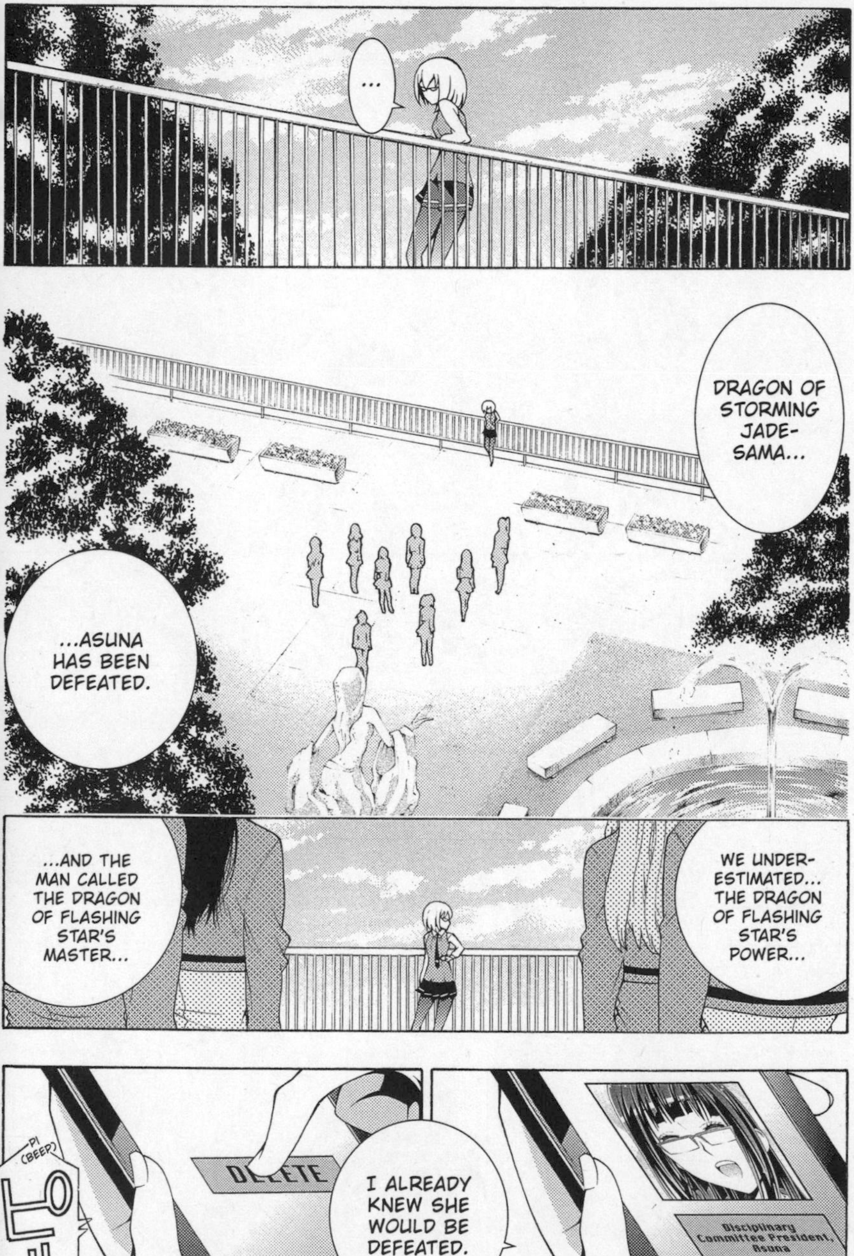
...
DRAGON OF STORMING JADE-SAMA...
...ASUNA HAS BEEN DEFEATED.
WE UNDER-ESTIMATED... THE DRAGON OF FLASHING STAR'S POWER...
...AND THE MAN CALLED THE DRAGON OF FLASHING STAR'S MASTER...
Disciplinary Committee President, Asuna
I ALREADY KNEW SHE WOULD BE DEFEATED.
DELETE
PI (BEEP)

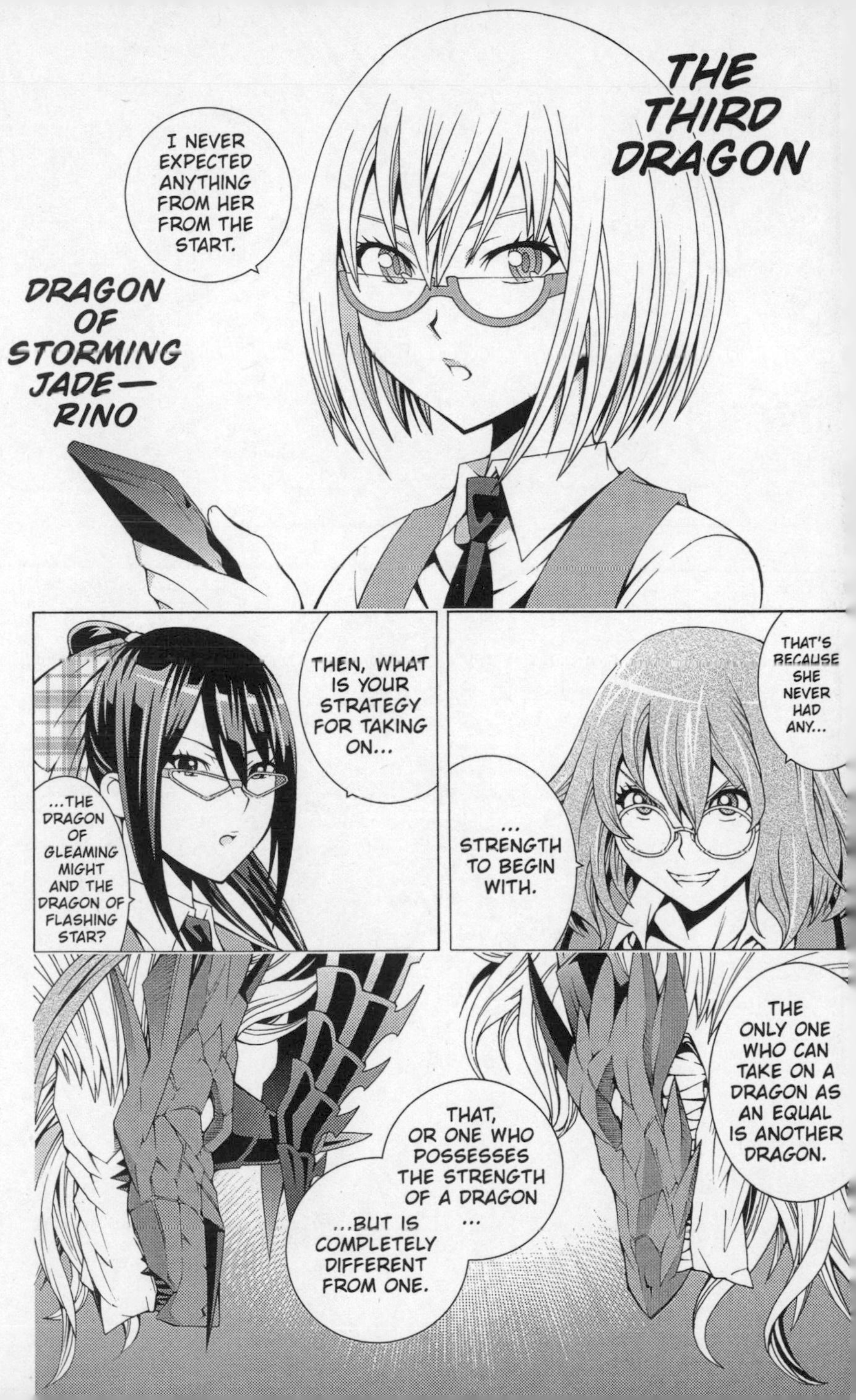
THE THIRD DRAGON
I NEVER EXPECTED ANYTHING FROM HER FROM THE START.
DRAGON OF STORMING JADE—RINO
THAT'S BECAUSE SHE NEVER HAD ANY...
...STRENGTH TO BEGIN WITH.
THEN, WHAT IS YOUR STRATEGY FOR TAKING ON...
...THE DRAGON OF GLEAMING MIGHT AND THE DRAGON OF FLASHING STAR?
THE ONLY ONE WHO CAN TAKE ON A DRAGON AS AN EQUAL IS ANOTHER DRAGON.
THAT, OR ONE WHO POSSESSES THE STRENGTH OF A DRAGON...
...BUT IS COMPLETELY DIFFERENT FROM ONE.

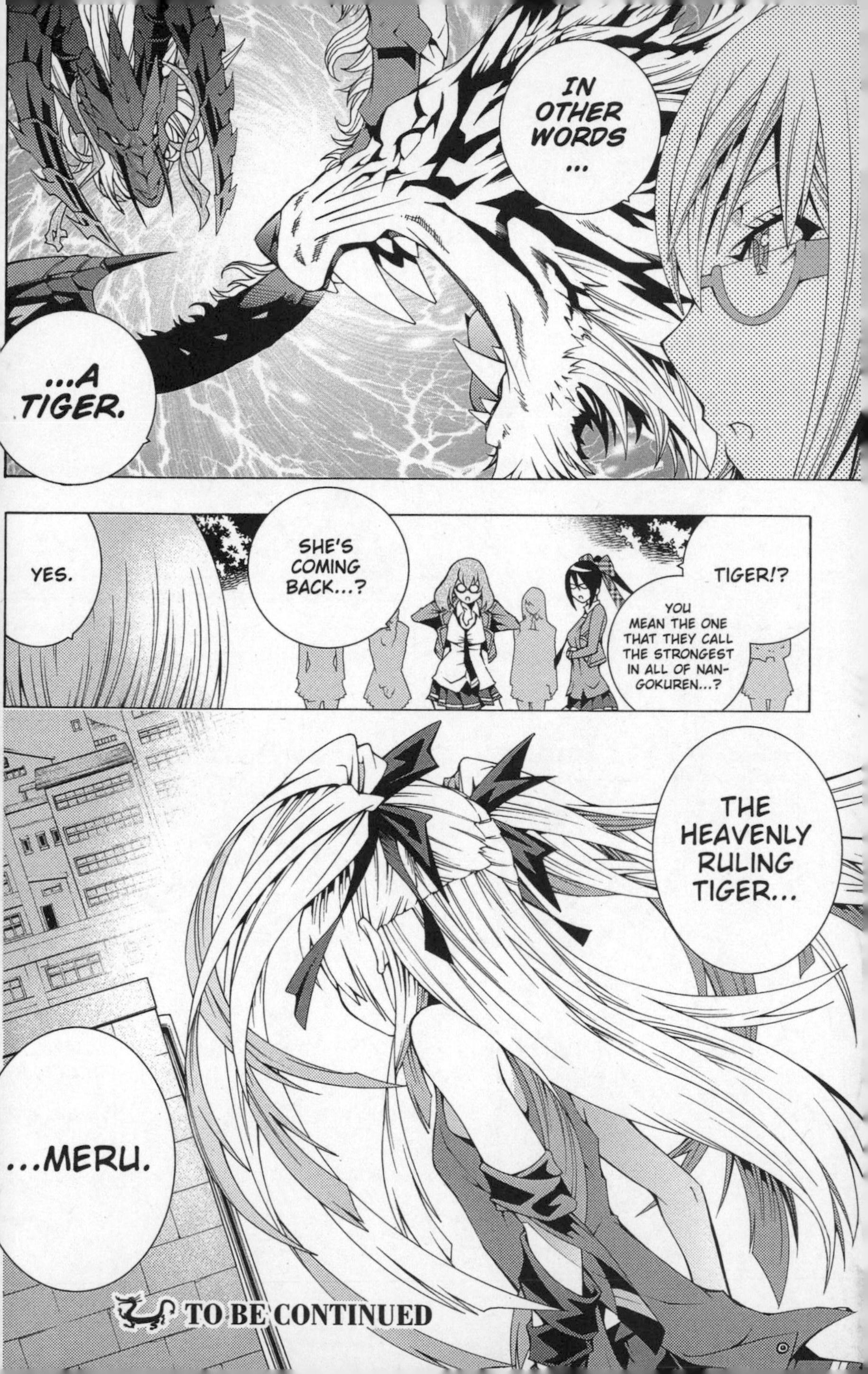
IN OTHER WORDS...
...A TIGER.
TIGER!?
YOU MEAN THE ONE THAT THEY CALL THE STRONGEST IN ALL OF NAN-GOKUREN...?
SHE'S COMING BACK...?
YES.
THE HEAVENLY RULING TIGER...
...MERU.
TO BE CONTINUED

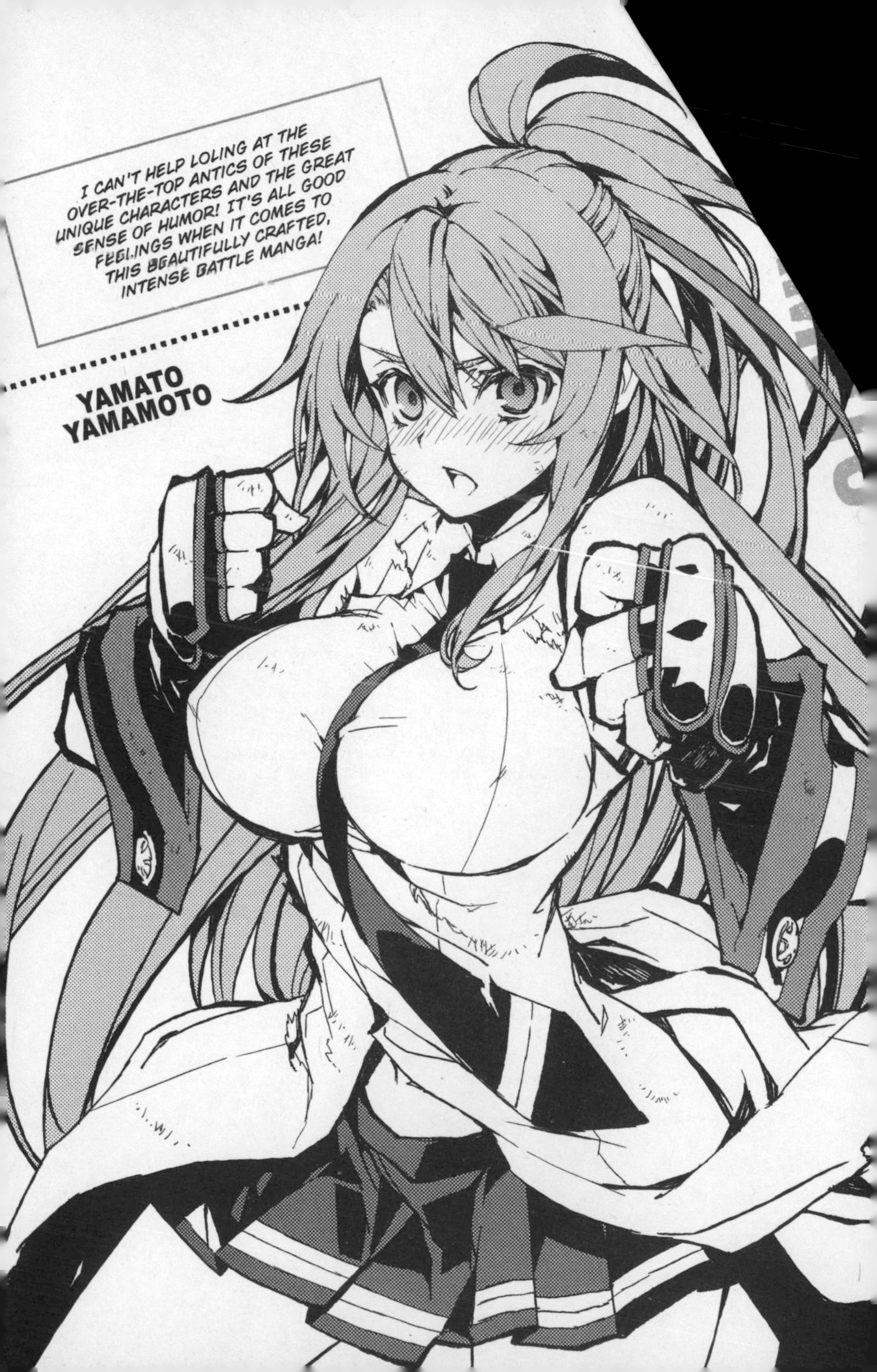
I CAN'T HELP LOLING AT THE OVER-THE-TOP ANTICS OF THESE UNIQUE CHARACTERS AND THE GREAT SENSE OF HUMOR! IT'S ALL GOOD FEELINGS WHEN IT COMES TO THIS BEAUTIFULLY CRAFTED, INTENSE BATTLE MANGA!
YAMATO YAMAMOTO

RIOTING ❶

TSUYOSHI WATANABE

Christine Dashiell

Lettering: Anthony Quintessenza

DRAGONS RIOTING Volume 1
© TSUYOSHI WATANABE 2013
Edited by FUJIMISHOBO
First published in Japan in 2013 by KADOKAWA CORPORATION, Tokyo.
English translation rights arranged with KADOKAWA CORPORATION, Tokyo, through TUTTLE-MORI AGENCY, INC., Tokyo.

Translation © 2015 Hachette Book Group, Inc.

Yen Press
Hachette Book Group
1290 Avenue of the Americas
New York, NY 10104

www.HachetteBookGroup.com
www.YenPress.com

Yen Press is an imprint of Hachette Book Group, Inc. The Yen Press name and logo are trademarks of Hachette Book Group, Inc.

The publisher is not responsible for websites (or their contents) that are not owned by the publisher.

First Yen Press Edition: November 2015

ISBN: 978-0-316-30541-9

10 9 8 7 6 5 4 3 2

BVG

Printed in the United States of America